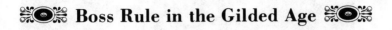

Boss Rule in the Gilded Age

BOSS RULE

in the

GILDED AGE

Matt Quay of Pennsylvania

James A. Kehl

University of Pittsburgh Press

Published by the University of Pittsburgh Press, Pittsburgh, Pa. 15260
Copyright © 1981, University of Pittsburgh Press
All rights reserved
Feffer and Simons, Inc., London
Manufactured in the United States of America

Library of Congress Cataloging in Publication Data

Kehl, James A
  Boss rule in the gilded age.

  Bibliography: p. 281
  Includes index.
  1. Quay, Matthew Stanley, 1833–1904. 2. United States—Politics
and government—1865–1900. 3. Legislators—United States—Biography. 4. United States. Congress. Senate—Biography. I. Title.
E664.Q2K43   328.748′092′4 [B]   80-5254
ISBN 0-8229-3426-4

To
Barbara and Kurt
—respectively—
my inspiration for today
and
my hope for tomorrow

Contents

Contents

Acknowledgments

DURING my early years in the history profession, I enjoyed a colleague who was "trigger-quick" to denounce any conclusion that he suspected to be based merely on inference or conjecture. One learned to expect his cryptic "no documents, no history" which certainly has relevance to this manuscript. Without the documents given to me by Colonel Stanley Quay, Senator Matthew Stanley Quay's grandson, this history of Pennsylvania's most enigmatic boss would have been impossible. I am grateful not only for the colonel's gift, but also for the enlightened attitude that he and his brother Richard have displayed. They realized that their grandfather was one of the most controversial figures in American politics, but did not hesitate to have his career analyzed objectively. When handing over the senator's papers that still remained in the family, Colonel Quay sagely remarked: "Grandfather belongs to history; make of him devil, saint, or what you will." As expected, I found some devil and some saint, but in between were also many clues concerning the functioning of the nation's political process.

In addition to the Quays, I am indebted to W. Scott Moore and W. E. Clyde Todd, both from the senator's hometown of Beaver, who provided their youthful impressions of Boss Matt Quay. Also in the early phase of my study Professor Stanley Hirshson, Queens College, City University of New York, assisted in my overview of the senator's career by sharing a few research notes on the Quay era.

The primary repositories that supplemented these personal contributions were the Library of Congress and the University of Pittsburgh's Archives of Industrial Society. The William L. Clements Library at the University of

Michigan, the Rutherford B. Hayes Memorial Library in Fremont, Ohio, the West Virginia University Library, the Historical Society of Pennsylvania, and the Pennsylvania Historical and Museum Commission in Harrisburg also facilitated my study by making their political collections of the late nineteenth century available.

After my thoughts were assembled and recorded on paper in my almost undecipherable handwriting, they were decoded into a readable transcript with meticulous care by Mrs. Grace Stumpf for whose skill and professionalism I am grateful. The copy that emerged from her typewriter was criticized by Professors H. Wayne Morgan of the University of Oklahoma and Albert V. House of the State University of New York at Binghamton. One crucial chapter also benefited from the critical eye of Professor Samuel J. Astorino of Duquesne University. To their wise substantive counsel, my wife Barbara and Catherine Marshall of the University of Pittsburgh Press added the critical notes that only editors can provide. Undoubtedly the professional work of these five has minimized both substantive and stylistic errors, and with such expert advice the least that I can do is assume responsibility for any deficiencies that remain.

Introduction

O N Saturday morning, May 28, 1904, Agnes Quay opened a telegram from President Theodore Roosevelt imploring, "Pray let me know how he is."[1] With these words, the president was inquiring about the failing health of her husband, U.S. Senator Matthew Stanley Quay, the brilliant and resourceful Republican boss from Pennsylvania. Before the end of the day, the president received his reply. The senator was dead.

With Quay's passing, arguments concerning his power, or supposed power, were rekindled nationwide. All of America had come to know his name, but few spoke of him in neutral tones; he was either revered or despised. An able man, full of surprises, his one aim had been success. He believed in doing the sensational. To some, such actions demonstrated courage; to others, they represented arbitrary defiance. His partisans saw only the velvet glove and his enemies only the mailed fist, but the senator's career was far more complex than either of these evaluations implies.

Supporters hailed him as the Napoleon of the political battlefield whose superb organizational skills were reinforced by a charitable concern for the less fortunate in society—Civil War widows, Indians, Negro boys, congregations of burned-out churches, and the wives of imprisoned criminals. They interpreted his deeds in behalf of such groups as evidence of a genuine humanitarian spirit. His enemies, on the other hand, preferred to reflect on the public relations benefits that accrued from reports of such benevolence. A gift of one hundred dollars to a congregation whose church was destroyed by fire, when reported in fifty to one hundred newspapers, represented inexpensive publicity of the best type. This kind of generosity caused Quay's critics to fear that the nation's newspapers were being duped into providing false impressions of his rather questionable political maneuvers.

His enduring enemies considered him a malevolent political force who had pillaged and plundered his state and nation for several decades with such finesse that the public never fully grasped the impact of his actions. These detractors were grateful to the Grim Reaper; although they had trapped Quay many times, no combination of factions or parties had been able to overcome him. One cynic remarked that alienated Republicans, outraged Democrats, and skeptical reformers all passed the bier just to be certain that the coffin did contain the body of their most persistent foe. In the words of Quay's most acid critic, the *Philadelphia North American,* death "has removed from Pennsylvania a malign influence which for a generation has been the curse and shame of the Commonwealth." It likened Quay to "an evil spirit" that "overhung this state, a mockery to popular government, a blight upon honesty, a sardonic jest in the face of freedom. Barren of uplifting statesmanship, his public history is that of a political boss only. In this function he achieved an unmatched success, a record of sustained victory."[2]

Although Quay suffered many political setbacks, the *North American* was not alone in conceding that his career was "a record of sustained victory." He was a great improviser who could give the impression of success, whether or not it had been achieved. He could implant a thought or arouse an emotion with deft skill. Gifted with remarkable political acumen, he was generally able to convert his enemies' surprises, his subordinates' failures, and his own indiscretions to triumphs, or at least he could nullify their adverse effects. Many of his decisions were defensive—tactical responses to situations that suddenly appeared in his political path, but at times they were erroneously viewed as evidence of the refined strategy of a long-range planner.

Quay was also a scholar who could read Horace and Pliny in the original. With equal facility he could turn from being a student of the past to being the master of the present; "in the calm atmosphere of the classics," he could pause to plot political strategy—which at times included political homicide— and then resume his enjoyment of Augustan literature within the span of an hour.[3] He was also a schemer who could divert state funds to personal and party uses. Through various raids on the state treasury, supplemented by contributions from major industrialists, he filled campaign chests which, in turn, were useful in capturing votes—legitimately, or by purchase. In the process Quay more than any other individual made politics at the state and national levels expensive. Because of the enormity of funds required in subsequent years, many potential candidates for high public office were eliminated; if they could not obtain a party endorsement, and thus party financing, they were forced to withdraw.

This seemed to violate the nation's commitment to equality. The fact that money, directly or indirectly, was determining who could hold office produced a wave of criticism, but the corner was turned. Organization politics was fastened on the nation more permanently than before Quay began his program to recast party structure and election machinery. He learned early that in politics, organization is superior to issues, and that even a mediocre organization can murder a brilliant idea. Frequently he cast himself in the role of idea assassin and demonstrated how it was done. His success converted Quay into a highly successful party boss and prompted him to express one of the more cynical definitions of the American political system: politics, at least in the late nineteenth century, was "the art of taking money from the few and votes from the many under the pretext of protecting the one from the other."[4] During the latter half of his forty-eight-year career (1856–1904), he acted out this thesis on the state and national stages.

Never blinded by the broader and more spectacular opportunities for political manipulation in Washington, Quay was keenly aware of the dynamics of power. In his era national reputations were being forged on the anvil of state politics, and when he entered the U.S. Senate in 1887, he fully appreciated the significance of casting more than a casual backward glance at Pennsylvania. He understood the need to flatter, court, and control the local and intermediate politicians of the legislature and larger municipalities and to retain his authority over the party's state organization—it was his passport to a political tomorrow.

This was also an era in which personalities rather than issues dominated the political stage, and Quay loomed large in the footlights. Intent upon strengthening his power base and gratifying personal ambitions, he quickly became Pennsylvania's Republican bellwether. In the process, he made several significant contributions to the Republican party and the overall political system. Not only did he develop Pennsylvania into the most Republican of states and cajole Philadelphia into becoming the party philanthropist, but he also delivered a Republican-dominated congressional delegation every two years and a set of presidential electors every quadrennium. In short, Quay, more than any other, was responsible for endowing the national Republican party with Pennsylvania's unbroken allegiance from 1877 to 1904.

Shunning prominence through the sponsorship of legislation, this boss from the rural community of Beaver, Pennsylvania, chose to keep in the background. When his position was threatened or he needed a public endorsement, he adopted a personal approach which focused directly on his home-state constituency. He addressed extensive letter-writing campaigns to convention delegates, political candidates, legislators, local officeholders, and other influential groups as the occasion demanded. Long after their intended use, the letters continued to serve the senator; displayed with pride, they were occasionally framed and hung on the sitting-room wall of "many a farmer on the hillsides of Pennsylvania."[5] They became conversation pieces, and as the householder recalled the time that Quay personally wrote to him asking for support, he often enlarged on the facts, and the boss's image profited from each retelling.

Rank-and-file Republicans were not alone in making more of Quay's exploits than the facts warranted; ironically his opponents (Democrats and reformist newspapers) unthinkingly adopted the same practice. Throughout the Harrison administration they represented Quay as the dictator of Republican policy, but the record clearly demonstrated that such an interpretation was ludicrous. Furious with Quay for his "insolent" campaign tactics in 1888, and anti-Republican by nature, these journals sought to destroy the party and the Pennsylvania boss with it. The more successfully they damned the party, the more their disclosures emphasized the power of Quay. Senator Orville H. Platt of Connecticut lamented that "Mr. Quay's position nationally has been unduly magnified by Democratic newspapers, assisted by those who dislike him."[6] Alexander K. McClure and other journalists concurring in Platt's analysis admitted that newspaper accounts gave Quay credit for successes that were as much the result of circumstance as of his own positive acts.

He also had the remarkable good fortune to win repeatedly by the narrowest of margins; these results tended to demoralize his enemies and cause them to strain to devise explanations which cast Quay in the role of culprit. One reporter told of hearing that the Beaver boss was closeted with leading Republicans, plotting the strategy to be played out in a crucial session of the state legislature on the following day. To check out the story, he raced to the senator's hotel and sent up his card. Although it was after midnight, Quay consented to see him. The reporter went up and found him in bed with the inevitable half-read book in his hand, not a single conspirator about.[7] To such rumors and charges, the man of silence said not a word and willingly accepted as much credit for directing the course of events as his opponents cared to give.

From his youth Quay had been a realistic combination of dreamer and planner, capable of converting his ideas into realities. His election to the Senate in 1887 marked the fulfillment of his own prediction, made thirty years before, that "some day he would be registering in a Washington, D.C. hotel as a U.S. senator from a western state, then a territory."[8] Although the boss incorrectly identified the state, he did achieve the goal. Faith in his ability to chart and attain such objectives prompted others to make similar prophecies. In 1878, almost a decade before the boss stepped onto the national political stage, Robert W. Mackey, a one-time colleague in the Cameron machine, had predicted to M. M. Ogden, then a newspaperman with the *Pittsburg Dispatch*, "Quay will be the leader [of Pennsylvania politics] and he will remain leader longer than any man has held political supremacy. . . . Quay is a man who fights best on the defensive. No man nor set of men can defeat Quay when fighting on these lines."[9]

Most of Quay's battles did prove to be defensive. At the state level his skill at defense was reflected in a growing possessiveness, particularly in regard to his political machine. When a lieutenant dared to suggest that he would like to "share the driving," Quay promptly revoked his license; he was politically expelled before he became powerful enough to demand rather than ask.

Quay insisted upon lieutenants who were content to carry out instructions—he alone plotted the strategy and decided the rewards. When the Quay forces received 10,000 shares of Standard Telephone Syndicate Company stock with a par value of $1,000,000 (for undefined services), the boss alone decided into how many equal or unequal parts the stock was to be divided. State Senator William Andrews asked James S. Clarkson how he was to be paid for his efforts in behalf of the company, and in reporting the inquiry to Quay, Clarkson casually admitted that it is "for you to determine how they [the stock certificates] should be divided, if at all."[10]

Of course he recognized the wisdom of concealing such incidents from the public, and his personality, particularly his proclivity for silence, proved to be an able ally in keeping his secrets. To those who did not know him intimately, Quay appeared extremely reticent. Displaying contempt for social chitchat, he talked only to those truly informed on subjects that interested him. Like Martin Van Buren, a wily politician of the previous generation, he discovered early that silence bordering on indifference was more disconcerting to an antagonist than the most rational response: never explain, never retract, and never deny. By the Gilded Age these instructions were refined and revered as the new commandment of bossism: "Never write when you can say it; never say it when you can nod your head."[11] In time this refuge in silence came to be recognized as Quay's social trademark, as well as his solution in many troublesome political situations. His enemies were frequently frustrated because he did not keep controversial issues stirred up with replies to their charges. Even in the face of the most vituperative remarks, he restrained himself. One critic who was also aware of Quay's linguistic proficiency conceded that he knew how "to keep silent in sixteen different languages."[12]

In part, Quay was always able to control his reactions because he never took himself too seriously; he retained his sense of humor even when adversity threatened. After one verbal attack on him, he told his lieutenants that he might reply to the men responsible for the charges: "I'll begin by calling them God-damned liars, but after that I may have to become insulting."[13]

This reputation for silence followed him to the U.S. Senate. Day after day he sat in that chamber listening intently with at least one ear, not so that he might contribute to the debate on the floor but so that he might better understand his colleagues in order to bargain quietly with them at some later impasse. His mind worked like a computer, accepting many diverse bits of information and banking them for use in making future proposals and decisions. Constantly engaged in weighing probability against possibility, he frequently recalled from memory the attitudes and beliefs previously expressed by his colleagues. Because he looked more realistically at the future than most of his contemporaries did, he was not as surprised or perplexed as they by the appearance of hostile or obstructive forces. Never fretting at such misfortunes, he directed all his energy toward playing the political cards that he had been dealt.

Quay's silence was in no way related to a lack of knowledge or self-confidence; although he repeatedly explained this reserve by pointing out that loquacity is the result of vanity and that vain men are generally shallow, he may have been making excuses for his poor speaking ability. Always soft-spoken, he occasionally mumbled and became inaudible when speaking to a group. Even as a boy he had discovered that silence, properly deployed, could substitute for words. One Sunday morning when his father, the minister, was delayed, the congregation became restless and milled about. Matthew quietly ascended the pulpit steps, methodically leafed through the large Bible, and inserted the lesson markers. The congregation became interested and settled back. He had not said a word, but he gained their attention and kept them assembled until his father came.[14]

When he did speak, Quay's utterances were seldom much above a whisper and tended to be more literary than oratorical. Hesitatingly phrased, his extemporaneous speeches reflected his education and reading; his language, classic in its purity and bristling with logic and power, was indicative of a clear and forceful literary style. He was fond of illustrating his points with graphic parallels drawn from the classics. His early experience as a journalist also contributed to terse and incisive writing during his political career. Often impatient with his secretary's phraseology, he took delight in slashing adjectives and superfluous words from his drafts. Disliking such phrases as "with pleasure," "I beg to report," and "in reply I would say that," he admonished his secretary: "We are not beggars," "use the present tense and leave the potential mood alone." He could have been a successful author if he had turned his mind to writing rather than politics.[15]

As these characteristics imply, Quay rarely made speeches. He argued that on most issues politicians were swayed, if at all, at private conferences, in legislative cloakrooms, or over liquid refreshment. His career evolved around deeds rather than words, but when speaking was a prerequisite to action, he spoke a language that was direct and often picturesque.[16] Demonstrating a comprehensive grasp of his subject, he analyzed not only its component parts but also its relationship to other topics.

Quay's potential as a speaker was further compromised by his appearance. Small in stature, medium in frame, unassuming in manner, and facially placid, he exhibited a phlegmatic exterior that masked his capacity for prolonged and arduous labor. During his years in state politics he showed a sartorial indifference suggesting a stereotype of the scholar he was recognized to be. As a national figure, he became extremely scrupulous and fastidious about his appearance, but he did not have the patience to handle the personal details himself. He could win the Congressional Medal of Honor, elect governors, and run the Commonwealth, but he could not tie his own necktie. In the affluent years, he elected not to trim his mustache or shave himself; in both Washington and Beaver the barber came to his home daily. This was one of his few personal extravagances; another was twenty-cent Havana cigars. An inveterate smoker, he literally and figuratively contributed as much as anyone to the smoke-filled-room image of politics.[17]

Quay was not a handsome man. His dark face, with aquiline nose and sharp chin, was expressionless except when warmly aroused in conversation. Beneath the broad, prominent brow was a pair of large, wide-set, almond-shaped eyes that were his most distinguishing facial characteristic. The right eye was usually dull or fishy. The left eyelid drooped, causing him to squint constantly. When possible, he wore a hat to protect it from the light, but it was never so completely shrouded that he could not focus clearly on the political problem of the day.[18]

Quay's health, like his appearance, did not suggest a vigorous leader. With an inherited tendency toward consumption, the malady that struck down his father, mother, and every adult member of his family, he was refused life insurance. As an added complication, he suffered an attack of typhoid fever during the Civil War which weakened him so severely that he never fully regained his health. He ignored the advice of doctors who told him not to assume responsibility for the presidential campaign in 1888 because the strain would endanger his life. But during the first months that followed that grueling ordeal, he himself believed that he had pressed too hard and that his health was irreparably broken. This was incorrect; he was only beginning his physical and his political fight. As the battle became more challenging, he became stronger. In 1892 he sustained his most serious illness when a chest cold developed into pneumonia. Although he was infrequently bedfast for long periods, his precarious health was his constant concern and his political opponents' constant hope.[19]

Quay did take precautions to protect and reinvigorate his health. He sincerely believed that his life would be terminated prematurely if he did not plan extended vacations. At the same time his son Richard was weak and underweight with what nineteenth-century medicine identified as ague. When doctors failed to help him, Quay decided to try the remedy of the Seminoles who, when they became ill, turned southward to the banks of the Indian River on the east coast of Florida, where they remained until the breezes of the Gulf Stream dispelled their ills. In the early 1870s, after several winters in Florida, Richard's health was restored, and Quay had found the climate beneficial to his own health as well. He built a cottage at St. Lucie, three miles north of Fort Pierce on the Indian River, and after almost every election season, spent the remaining months of the winter there. During his terms in the U.S. Senate, he spent so much time at St. Lucie that political enemies referred to him sarcastically as the "third senator from Florida."[20]

Quay's Republican colleagues and lieutenants from Pennsylvania, who were eager to conduct party business during the winter months, began to follow him to his Indian River retreat. Quay therefore arranged for the first railroad to be built into St. Lucie. Visitors then came in private Pullman cars that were parked on a siding and used as hotels while the political affairs of Pennsylvania were being arranged. Patronage was distributed, slates prepared, governors agreed upon, conventions and legislatures organized, and campaign strategies planned—all hundreds of miles from the Keystone State.[21]

Accompanied by his boatman, Ben Sooy, Quay spent most of his vacation fishing in the shark-infested waters of St. Lucie Inlet. Patient and taciturn, he thus adopted a sport compatible with his personality and was determined to excel in it as he did in politics. He once caught thirty-one tarpon in two weeks; the weight and length of each was reported in the newspapers with greater accuracy than many of his political maneuvers.[22] In a two-hour running battle, one of these monsters towed him from the mouth of St. Lucie Inlet, through the tortuous channel to the Indian River, and then one mile down the river before capitulating. On another occasion he was trolling for bluefish when a sawfish took the bait and dashed up the river, pulling the boat against the current for several miles. After he became tired towing his burden, the fish gave a wild sweep with his saw, severed the line, and darted into deep water. Asked why he did not take the initiative to cut the line when he discovered that he was under the power of such a formidable and dangerous creature, Quay remarked: "Well, I rather enjoyed the novelty of the ride. It was exhilarating and interesting, and I was rather sorry when the fish became tired of the little excursion."[23] He might have expressed the same sentiment about many of the individuals and issues that he encountered during his political maneuvers.

Although Quay enjoyed solitude, he almost always manifested a thoughtfulness for the welfare of those around him. He was quietly attentive to his guests—an admirable host who understood people both individually and as groups. In social situations he reflected middle-class conventions. He spoke with an understanding of words that is usually the product of perception and culture; he never spit, he expectorated, not into a spittoon, but into a cuspidor. He made certain that his guest had the most comfortable chair, the most scenic view, and a full glass.[24] Quay at times abstained from alcohol, not out of consideration for his health but his politics. He did not trust his own decision making when there was the possibility that he might drink too much and thus say too much. This led to a peculiar drinking pattern. With absolute self-control during a campaign, he would pour out the liquor for his guests and sit among them with his own glass empty; when the campaign was over, he would go off to drink in private. On those occasions when he did drink in public, he seemed to be intoxicated when actually he had taken very little. His eyes and his speech contributed to this misconception. A few shots of whiskey would cause his eyes to roll aimlessly, and his normal habit of talking to himself while thinking prompted observers to conclude that he was in a semistupor.[25]

Quay's use of alcohol exemplifies the atmosphere of ambiguity that his actions created. In spite of his clarity of thought and his deliberateness in action, his words and deeds seemed almost inevitably to polarize interpretation and understanding. Many cited his boyhood in the home of a Presbyterian clergyman as indisputable evidence of strong moral and religious character. Others argued that this environment merely taught him the necessity of maintaining appearances while deceiving the public. His parents were more objective than either extreme; his mother yearned for some indication that he was a practicing Christian, while his father spoke favorably about his moral habits, but admitted that he was "not professedly pious." He had not been fooled by incidents such as the one that occurred when Matthew was six years old. Returning from one of his missionary travels, the elder Quay brought home a tin sword and a little pocket Bible for his son and daughter. On the assumption that he would select the sword, Matthew was told that, being the older, he could have his preference. Wanting both, he surprised his father by choosing the Bible. Within a few hours his sister had discarded the sword, and his finesse was complete—he had them both. This was a preschool hint of the cleverness he would deploy later in the political arena.[26]

While some observers believed that his superior academic attainments and his study of the law provided a background inevitably suited to statesmanship, others maintained that he prostituted his talents to violate the spirit, if not the letter, of the law. His detractors suspected that his conscience was on a permanent vacation. Even his brief career in journalism was interpreted in dichotomous ways—as a broadening experience and as training in the manipulation of facts pertaining to any crucial issue.[27] Throughout his career Quay's political actions were to provoke interpretations that contained few neutral tones. Although the times, the circumstances, and the general public contributed to this polarization, the basic explanation lies deep within the character of the man.

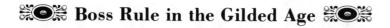 **Boss Rule in the Gilded Age**

From These Roots
1833-1865

DURING a political campaign at the turn of the century, Matt Quay had a desperate need to polish his public image, and he personally attended to the task. In the process he boasted, "There is not a drop of blood in my veins that is not Pennsylvania blood two centuries old."[1] Although there is no logical relationship between the home of his ancestors and his political deportment, this comment at least called attention to a heritage of which he could properly be proud. Quay recalled for his audiences a line of distinguished Scotch-Irish and French Huguenot ancestors who came to Pennsylvania via Canada. He justifiably exhibited pride in forefathers who had shouldered arms in the colonial wars, in the Revolution, and in the War of 1812. The more prominent had also served as provincial assemblymen, ministers, and artisans—ancestors who helped mold a colony into a state.[2]

In addition, his background contained an unsubstantiated legend that one of his Canadian ancestors had married a Delaware or Abnaki maiden. Until chroniclers discovered this report of his Indian roots, they could not fathom his career-long, inordinate concern for all Indians—particularly since Indians had no votes and Quay was considered a *quid pro quo* boss. Although expedient, the inference about the relationship between his background and Indian interests is not conclusive. His sympathetic and supportive attitude toward Indian problems, however, cannot be denied; it is a clear, indisputable record.[3]

A more realistic explanation of this Indian predilection can be found in his home life. Matthew's father, Anderson Beaton Quay, had strong missionary tendencies. He had served as a Presbyterian minister during most of his adult

3

life, although this was not his first career choice. Born in 1802 in Chester County, Pennsylvania, the elder Quay was only a lad at the time of his father's death. After being forced to labor on a farm for several years, he served as an apprentice tailor and became a proficient artisan. Following his marriage to Catherine McCain, he experienced a religious conversion that impelled him to preach the Gospel. Through unflagging initiative and personal sacrifice—he learned Latin grammar "between stitches" as he plied his trade—he was prepared to enter Princeton Theological Seminary in 1827.[4]

Four years later Anderson Quay was installed as pastor of two churches in the Carlisle Presbytery. For the next nine years, Reverend Quay and his wife lived in Dillsburg, where one of the churches was located. There Matthew, their eldest son to survive to adulthood, was born September 30, 1833. Named for General Matthew Stanley, who had raised his orphaned mother, Matthew was one of eight children, of whom only five lived to be adults. Three of these died before reaching thirty: Thetta and Elliot were victims of consumption during the Civil War, and Sarah Stanley, the eldest, died a decade earlier. Only Matthew and Jerome lived to enjoy the fullness of life.[5]

Reverend Quay was particularly interested in the work of the Presbyterian Board of Education and the Board of Foreign Missions, which he described as "the two great chariot wheels of the everlasting Gospel which are being propelled by the great charioteer, the King of Zion, to the ends of the earth." Because of this interest, he was asked to serve as agent for the Board of Education in the district comprising western Pennsylvania, western Virginia, and Ohio. He consented, moved his family to Pittsburgh in 1840, and took up the task of visiting congregations to raise money for educational purposes, primarily the training of ministers.[6]

The assignment proved to be a major disappointment. Travel was arduous that winter; inclement weather, intolerably bad roads, high water, and exposure at night in an open stage made every leg of his journeys dangerous and tedious. Even more depressing were the financial results. The lingering effects of the Panic of 1837 made it extremely difficult for congregations to convert their benevolent instincts into monetary contributions sizeable enough even to sustain their own pastoral needs. So meager were the subscriptions that Reverend Quay frequently delayed drawing his salary and expenses so that the record could show the flow of some funds to the programs of the board.

Disillusioned before the end of a year, he regretted taking his family to the seemingly inhospitable land west of the Alleghenies and developed "a strong and irresistable" desire for a call from the East. That call never came. He did, however, receive a unanimous invitation from the Presbyterian congregation at Beaver, Pennsylvania, to become their pastor. Although not fully satisfied, he accepted the call in 1841 as the best opportunity available at the time. He wrote to Dr. Francis McFarland: "I can only say I am in Beaver, and trying all I can to like it." The congregation appeared anxious to make its new minister comfortable, but money problems continued to harass him. Delays always seemed to prevent his quarterly salary from being paid on time. Almost from the outset he looked for an opportunity to move elsewhere.[7]

In 1843 he became the agent of the Board of Foreign Missions for the Pittsburgh and Wheeling synods and endeavored to solicit funds for the board's work. Meeting with limited success, he resigned within two years and again assumed a pastorate, this time at Indiana, Pennsylvania. Reverend Quay remained there for approximately five years before accepting the final challenge of his career. In 1850 he became the agent of the Pennsylvania Colonization Society, moved his family back to Beaver, and began the difficult and unrealistic task of recruiting Negroes to settle in Liberia. Believing firmly in the potential of this proposed solution to the race problem, he embarked on his mission enthusiastically. Although he identified candidates for resettlement, actual migration always produced complications. As early as 1853 he was discouraged and considered resigning to return to a pastoral charge because a lack of funds impeded efforts to carry out the society's stated purpose.[8] This missionary endeavor, like those for the Boards of Education and Foreign Missions, demonstrated more conviction than accomplishment.

These being formative years for young Matthew, he grew up with hardship, hope, and disappointment as constant companions. Perhaps he drew certain conclusions about individuals and groups, about causes and motivation, about money and power. Obviously he was born to neither wealth nor station. He grew up in a frugal home where the love of God, concern for humanity, and faith in self-reliance were taught, but his political enemies of later years were quick to argue that only rote learning had taken place and that Matthew was devoid of the conscience and spirit that these virtues represent.

Reverend Quay's income was only slightly above the subsistence level, and he was forced to travel much of the time. Yet he did not neglect the education of his children. Both girls, Sarah and Thetta, were sent to academies, and the three boys all had opportunities to attend college. Matthew seemed the most scholarly, and his attainments were certainly the most outstanding. After attending schools in the towns of Beaver and Indiana, he entered Jefferson College[9] where he gained a reputation for scholarship "rarely acquired by one so young." He particularly impressed J. C. Penney of Pittsburgh with whom he studied law a few years after graduation. Penney said he had "never known a young man of his age [17 at graduation] whose mind was so well disciplined and mature."[10]

In the prewar years, Jefferson College was popular among southern families that could afford to send their sons away to school. Quay quickly learned that "southern boys did not have a very high opinion of Yankee dash and vim," but through one incident he corrected that conception, at least as far as he personally was concerned. A Canonsburg farmer who was tired of having his poultry yards raided by the college boys defied them to disturb his turkey flock again. This was construed as a challenge, and that same evening Thomas Griffin, one of Matthew's classmates from the South, devised a plan to pilfer a number of birds. Griffin, armed with a shotgun, stood inside the turkey yard; posted outside, the others came as close as they could to the turkeys' roosting tree. With the crack of Griffin's gun, discharged aimlessly into the flock of sleeping turkeys, they were to scale the fence and retrieve the birds that fell. The gun fired, and four turkeys—three gobblers and a hen—hit the ground. Quay, though the smallest, climbed the fence, grabbed the two largest gobblers, and escaped before any of the others. All were gone before the smoke cleared, and Quay gleefully recalled, "The turkeys were cleaned and half done before the old gent got his socks on." In praising Quay's conduct, Aaron Brandon, another southern classmate, admitted that "the little Yank won us all that night."[11] Although there was no way to recognize it at the time, Quay also demonstrated here a little of the defiance that was to characterize his political conduct in later years.

A principal academic benefit of Quay's college years was the development of his appreciation of good literature, both classical and modern. Of the poets he admired Horace in particular, but also enjoyed Homer, Virgil, Dante, and Shakespeare. Among Americans he preferred Whittier and Longfellow. He became a devotee of biographies dealing with great achievers in all civilizations, and Pericles was his idol. His mind, like his rapidly developing library, ranged over many diverse topics, from the mythology of the Norsemen to American political economy, from heraldry to religious history.[12] This fascination for books persisted throughout his life. In time he came to possess one of the finest working libraries in the nation, divided among his homes in Beaver and Washington, and his Florida retreat at St. Lucie. He was able to achieve this distinction in part because he had a standing order with a leading Philadelphia publishing house to send him all noteworthy books as soon as they came off the press. At one time in his career, when most of his material possessions were sacrificed to satisfy his debts, he refused to surrender any books. He always took a book to bed, and just as often fell asleep with the partially read volume across his chest. Nevertheless, he was familiar with most of the books in his vast collection.

Almost as well versed in literature as politics, Quay spoke freely only on the former. Theodore Roosevelt respected his literary discernment and once thanked him for introducing him to the writings of the Finnish novelist

Topelius. But Quay also loved history and might keep important political leaders waiting in an anteroom while he discussed the age of Pericles with a kindred spirit. At times in his career, it seemed that he merely interrupted his scholarly pursuits to handle pressing political tasks. During one such interruption he was called upon to endorse a job applicant; he simply scrawled the words attributed originally to William Kemble, "He understands addition, division, and silence," and settled back to read Horace in the original.[13]

In Search of a Livelihood

After graduation in 1850, Quay accepted Thomas Griffin's invitation to his family's Mississippi plantation. With diplomas in hand, both young men realized that their heads were crammed with Latin and Greek, along with mathematics, logic, rhetoric, and general history, but they had no practical skills with which to earn a living. They considered and rejected the possibilities of law, teaching, and medicine. Then Tom's father suggested that they become traveling lecturers. They liked the idea, but realized that they needed a "gimmick" such as a stereopticon, with scientific slides, to illustrate their lectures. They ordered one and spent much of the time before its arrival fishing and hunting. Quay also indulged in a little self-pity. Comparing his lot with that of the slaves on the Griffin plantation, he lamented, "They have no care, they are fed, clothed, drs. bills paid, nursed when sick, and I am thinking how I shall make a living." Overhearing the comment and wanting to lift Quay out of the doldrums, Tom laughingly suggested, "Squad [his nickname for Quay], bring the blacking brush and I can black you up."[14] Such self-indulgence had no place in his later life, but by that time his power to make things happen, instead of waiting for fate, encouraged a positive outlook.

Normally Quay did not express his personal feelings; even in these early years, his silence was evident. It so impressed Tom's younger sister that fifty-five years later her most vivid recollection of him was that he "was quiet and had at times a sad expression, and I used to think he was homesick, and would hang around him, bringing him fruit and flowers to cheer him up." Her brother reaffirmed this impression, saying that Quay was "very reserved in manner" and apparently a bore until he took an interest in a specific topic.[15]

The Griffin family attempted to include Quay in the daily plantation routine. On one occasion they took him into the gin house to see how the cotton was processed. In the lint room, where the cotton was pressed into bales, lint lighter than snow constantly floated in the air and settled in a fine fleece over anyone present. When Tom and Matt emerged, their clothes covered with a thin dusting, Matt immediately attempted to brush the lint off. Tom said, "Hold on, I will clean you off in a second," but Quay was not prepared for what followed. Tom lighted a match, touched it to his friend's clothing, and in an instant Quay was a flash of fire from head to toe. The fire extinguished itself almost at once, but Quay, like anyone else unfamiliar with this phenomenon, was horrified. Tom cavorted in laughter, but when a spark unexpectedly caught the lint on his own suit, Quay's expression changed to a broad smile.[16]

The stereopticon finally came. Tom and Matthew settled down to the serious business of writing commentary to accompany their slides. Well rehearsed, they joined the lecture circuit through the rural communities of Mississippi and neighboring states. During their first presentation an irreparable malfunction of the lantern ended the tour and doomed their careers almost before they were launched. Since Quay had a feeble voice and never spoke well in public, this technical deficiency merely hastened the inevitable.

Electing now to emphasize their talents for writing rather than speaking, the young men turned to journalism. In this role they could exploit Matt's gift for political analysis, a talent demonstrated in community discussions during his visit to the Griffin plantation. They established a newspaper in Shreveport, Louisiana, but for unknown reasons quickly sold what appeared to be a promising enterprise in favor of touring Texas. Finding no situation in these meanderings that either beckoned their talents or challenged their imaginations, they headed their buggy back toward Louisiana, made their way to the mouth of the Red River, and decided to return to their respective homes.[17]

Tom went directly to the family plantation. In a last desperate effort to find suitable employment in the South, Matt continued on to New Orleans. The commercial capital of the South was also a disappointment. Forced to roll bales of cotton on the levee after his funds ran out, he ultimately wrote to the Griffins for transportation money back to Beaver. It was provided, but further contact with them was suspended until after the Civil War when Quay not only repaid the loan in full, but also helped the Griffins recover from the Northern invasion.[18]

During the southern tour and his journey home, Quay obviously reconsidered the possibilities of studying law or teaching school. Willing to make the sacrifice in time required to prepare for the legal profession, he decided to read law with the firm of Penney and Sterrett in Pittsburgh. Beginning October 3, 1851, he spent the next thirteen months in this pursuit. Still not firmly convinced that this was the appropriate career for him, he interrupted his studies for a second trip to the South. On this occasion he headed directly for Texas with the specific purpose of teaching school. In the winter and spring 1852-1853, he searched unsuccessfully for a community that needed and could support a teacher permanently. He did find a few students in Colorado and Montgomery counties, but the sparse numbers precluded his staying.[19]

The major compensation that he derived from his efforts was an excessive amount of leisure time which he spent hunting. Irked by his son's tardiness in corresponding, Reverend Quay sent a hasty reply to one of the infrequent letters: "I would suggest that you shoot less and write more. Though I should think unless your school increases numerically you will have ample time for both."[20]

A favorable trend did not develop. Again penniless, Matt returned to Pittsburgh and resumed the study of law. In October 1854 he was admitted to the bar in Beaver County. In the same year he married Agnes Barclay of Beaver, two years his senior. The combination of marriage and admission to the bar gave him an identification with Beaver that lasted throughout the remainder of his life.

The following year Andrew Gregg Curtin, then secretary of the Commonwealth, and Alexander K. McClure, superintendent of public printing, jointly recommended to Governor James Pollock that Matt be appointed to complete an unexpired term as prothonotary in his home county. Neither could personally speak in behalf of Matt's qualifications. In fact, McClure had never even met him, and Curtin's contacts with him had been limited. Both were motivated by their respect for Reverend Quay, whom they had come to know during his early ministry in the Cumberland Valley. They knew only that he had an intelligent and promising son, and they wanted to honor the father. Knowing that Pollock was partial to Presbyterian clergy, they easily induced him to sign the appropriate proclamation on April 24, 1856. Later that year and again in 1859, Beaver County elected Matt to regular three-year terms as prothonotary. This inauspicious beginning marked the outset of his career in local politics. He had no presence, no voice, and was never imperative, but gradually he converted these liabilities to assets, which, in turn, produced one of the most potent forces in the state's history and one of the most feared in the nation.[21]

In Defense of the Union

In April 1861, during Quay's second full term as prothonotary, Confederate shells fell on Fort Sumter to launch the nation into four years of civil war. Reaction to this bombardment was like a bucket of ice water tossed in the face of a sleeper; almost every American awakened to the full reality of the times. The career of a budding politician like Matt Quay was directly threatened. Consciously or unconsciously he was called upon to make an important decision. When in months or years the civil strife would end, he must inevitably account for his wartime activity. Those alert to political realities knew that they must decide whether their civilian positions held enough prestige to a nation at war to warrant retention or whether they should seek reputations on the battlefield in order to ensure a political future in the postwar years.

With the experience of the Mexican War only fourteen years in the past, many recognized that the most certain way to project themselves into the political future was to enlist in the defense of their states. Quay was one of these. Leaving nothing to chance, he committed himself to the service of his state in a combination of military and civilian roles for the entire period of the sectional war and distinguished himself in all assignments.

Amid the confusion that marked the hasty development of an army, Quay was commissioned twice in the month of May 1861. Being among the first from Beaver County to volunteer for military service, he was appointed a first lieutenant of the Curtin Rifles in the 19th Division of the Pennsylvania Uniformed Militia on May 22, but he did not see combat in this capacity. The new Republican governor, Andrew Curtin, whose election campaign in Beaver County had been managed by Quay, delayed his departure for the front. The overwhelming response of the voters had attracted the new governor's attention to Quay's outstanding administrative ability. He appointed Quay to the rank of lieutenant colonel, effective May 15, and assigned him to Harrisburg as the assistant commissary general of Pennsylvania, an action that preceded the endorsement of his commission to the Curtin Rifles by a week.[22]

Within a short time the functions of the Commissary Department were transferred to Washington, but Quay held the post long enough to demonstrate his efficiency. His apparently boundless energy, capacity for organization, and concern for the most minute details brought praise from both state and national military authorities. The governor recognized these talents and retained Quay in Harrisburg as his private secretary. It was a signal honor for the former Beaver prothonotary to be invited to serve as secretary to a distinguished and popular political leader like Governor Curtin, and he clearly recognized the ramifications presented by the opportunity.[23] Since Quay was relatively unknown in political circles beyond the borders of Beaver County, this appointment marked an advancement in state politics.

Through the war years Curtin's devotion to the Union cause never wavered. He exhibited a steadfast loyalty to President Lincoln and a moving enthusiasm for the efforts of Pennsylvania troops serving the nation. Conspicuous among the wartime governors for his "heroic humanity," he was the first to inaugurate a system for ministering to troops in the field. In the name of the state, commissions were organized to visit every battlefront, camp, and hospital, and seek out Pennsylvania troops in need of help.[24] After every battle involving Pennsylvania troops, Curtin himself supplemented the efforts of his commissioners if his schedule permitted. He was frequently among the first camp and hospital visitors. Every Pennsylvania soldier was made to feel that the governor was his personal ombudsman. As a result his military mail multiplied. Hundreds of letters poured into Harrisburg daily, each appealing to him for redress of grievances, real or imagined. In response, the governor decreed that every soldier's letter addressed to him would be answered no matter how trivial or unreasonable the request.[25]

Responsibility for this correspondence was delegated to Matt Quay, who executed the assignment flawlessly. His keen perception of human nature and practical understanding of the problems disturbing the men in uniform simplified the task, while buoying troop morale and polishing the governor's image. According to Alexander K. McClure, a close political ally of the governor, Quay dictated and sent thousands of letters in Curtin's name to soldiers in the field without Curtin's seeing either the original or the reply. The governor's signature was written so perfectly by Quay "that Curtin himself could not have disputed it."[26]

Temporarily Quay remained unknown to the soldiers who received the letters from Harrisburg. He witnessed the rise of Governor Curtin's political star in the military firmament and received satisfaction from hearing the state's chief executive acclaimed "the Soldiers' Friend," but undoubtedly he realized that these achievements could have future significance for him. As a result he was a tireless worker, day and night if necessary, in fulfilling assignments entrusted to him by the governor.[27]

Quay succeeded admirably, in part because he attempted to understand thoroughly every aspect of the administration's policy. Not only did the governor and the members of his cabinet agree that he completely achieved this goal, but they also recognized that he possessed a rare talent for "meeting sudden and severe emergencies," of which there was no shortage. He was doubly acceptable as the governor's alter ego because he made no apparent effort to advance himself. When the federal government delegated the selection of regimental and company commanders to the individual state governors, Curtin confidently called upon Quay to issue the hundreds of military commissions as he approved them. This was done with the same precision that marked the signing of the correspondence to soldiers in the field.[28]

Almost from the moment the tocsin of war sounded, a national reaction against the Republican party began to take form. In Pennsylvania, Curtin faced possible loss of control in the state house of representatives. The Democratic triumph in the 1861 elections threatened to slow the processes of government and handicap Curtin's conduct of Pennsylvania's war effort. Personally popular with members of both political parties, Quay succeeded in becoming a working bridge between the governor and a legislature that was, at least partially, unfriendly. Largely through his efforts, an alliance between the Republicans and War Democrats evolved, thereby arresting the threat to Curtin's political strength.[29]

After more than a year of successful administrative manipulations in Harrisburg, Quay restated his desire for a field command. Although there is no evidence of dissatisfaction or disillusionment with his desk assignment, he believed that he had fulfilled his obligation to Governor Curtin and now desired to carry out his original intention. His younger brother, Elliot, who had answered President Lincoln's first call (April 15, 1861) for troops and had been wounded in the battle at Winchester, took a dim view of front-line service: "My opinion is that $1500.00 per annum and a snug little corner in Andy Curtin's office is much better than being marched and countermarched through the country as a soldier—alternately running from and after the Confeds."[30] Matt ignored this advice. While rendering valuable service in Harrisburg, he undoubtedly observed that headlines were lavished on men at the front and not on those who were constructing the war machine and tuning its interrelated parts until they functioned smoothly. Although reluctant to release him, Governor Curtin finally consented, and on August 20, 1862, commissioned Quay a colonel with command of the 134th Regiment of Pennsylvania Volunteers. "I prefer volunteering for nine months as an officer to carrying a musket as a drafted man and the result is I am now Colonel of the 134 Regiment," he explained to his wife. "I did not desire anything higher than major or lieutenant colonel, but the highest office in the regiment has been thrust upon me."[31]

The assignment of the 134th to a division in McClellan's Army of the Potomac seemed to indicate that Quay would at last get to the front. Yet when his regiment received its first orders to march, there was a further delay because Quay's private horse had been stolen. He immediately directed his orderly, J. R. Swan, to conduct an all-out search of the camp grounds, including the government stockade. Unable to locate the missing steed, Swan decided to substitute one from the horse and mule corral of General Humphreys, the division commander. He gave the guard a receipt stating that the horse would be returned when the division headquarters needed it more than Quay did. Without asking any questions, Quay mounted and joined the march. An observant quartermaster noted the brand "U.S." on Quay's horse and reported it to General Humphreys, who relieved the colonel of his sword pending courtmartial for possessing stolen property. The orderly promptly explained what he had done. This implicated the guard who, along with the orderly, was arrested and brought before Humphreys for a hearing. When the guard produced the receipt indicating that he had consented to the removal of the horse from the stockade, the charges against all three were dismissed. The thoughtfulness of the orderly in providing the receipt saved Quay from the humiliation of a courtmartial.[32]

When Humphreys's division was ordered to reinforce McClellan's army, which had recently engaged Lee at Antietam, the prospects for battle were favorable, and the prophets of a short war were optimistic. In describing the tense scene for his wife, Quay reported: "We reached the battlefield the morning after the battle after a night march of twenty miles; found the armies lying facing each other with the enemy in sight and were immediately marched to the front and placed in support of a battery." To the surprise of all, the order to attack never came. The armies of Lee and McClellan faced each other all day with muted muskets. Quay went to sleep that night confident that on the next day he would take part in the greatest battle of the war. But in the darkness the Confederates slipped away, recrossing the Potomac into Virginia, and McClellan was content to let them go.[33]

Shortly thereafter Quay contracted typhoid fever and was hospitalized in a weakened condition. Since he had never been robust and could not easily withstand such a shock to his system, a surgeon advised him bluntly to go home to recuperate or face death. On this advice he forwarded a letter of resignation that was officially accepted on December 7, 1862, but its endorsement did not reach him for several days.[34]

In the meantime the Army of the Potomac, to which Quay's regiment was still assigned, became increasingly embarrassed with each passing week because of its failure to make serious contact with the enemy. This frustration, to which the civilian North was keenly sensitive, prompted President Lincoln to change commanders. McClellan was replaced by General Ambrose Burnside, who proposed a quick attack on Fredericksburg. Located midway between Washington and Richmond on the south bank of the Rappahannock River, Fredericksburg commanded the most direct route to the seat of the Confederate government. The vanguard of Burnside's troops arrived at the river bank opposite Fredericksburg on November 17, but logistical difficulties postponed their crossing. On December 11, under an early morning fog, the federal forces began laying pontoon bridges and effected a landing within two days. They arrived only to discover the Confederates firmly entrenched behind natural barriers, prepared for a major defense of the area.

During Union preparations for an assault on the Confederate position, Quay received notification that his resignation had been accepted. He was promptly and honorably discharged on the basis of the "surgeon's certificate of disability." The troops had just been paid, and since he was leaving for his western Pennsylvania home, a number of men from the regiment asked him to deliver money to their families. He agreed to provide this personalized mail service and prepared to depart, a haversack bulging with approximately eight thousand dollars from the payroll slung over his shoulder.[35]

At this precise moment, the 134th was alerted to participate in the Fredericksburg confrontation. Quay, though relieved of his command, refused to depart because, like many others, he believed that this would be one of the crucial engagements of the war. He reasoned that the payroll entrusted to him would be relatively safe in battle because "every man will know that I have this money; then my bones won't be left on the field." Cautioned that he was better qualified for a hospital bed than for a charge across the open wintry plain at Fredericksburg, Quay responded promptly and decisively: "I cannot afford to go home in the face of battle. I have promised the 134th to stand by them in this fight and I intend doing it." He continued his pledge forcefully, almost biblically: "I will go as far as you go. It may seem foolish, but I would rather die and be called a fool than live and be called a coward."[36]

Quay requested reinstatement to his old command, but since his resignation had been accepted, this was denied. Asserting that no responsible soldier would leave with the smoke of battle in the air, he declared that he would accompany his regiment "either carrying a musket, or as an officer." He urged General Erastus B. Tyler, who was commanding the brigade that included the 134th Regiment of Pennsylvania Volunteers, to accept him as a member of his staff. The general was sympathetic and agreed that, with the approval of the surgeon, he could serve as a volunteer aide-de-camp. Approval was reluctantly granted. With this final obstacle removed, Quay prepared to join the bloody, fruitless charge against Marye's Heights, the primary Confederate stronghold.[37]

The topography at Fredericksburg gave a definite advantage to the defense. The Confederates occupied all the high ground (Marye's Heights, Willis Hill, Lee's Hill, and Prospect Hill), dominating the plain over which the Union forces had to advance. A road, lined on both sides with stone retaining walls, ran along the base of Marye's Heights and gave the Confederate troops an additional advantage. Since the roadbed was below the level of the inclined plain, it provided their infantrymen with a fortified entrenchment from which they could command the open field sloping down toward the river and the Union lines. The only protection for a Union advance was a slight depression in the slope about one hundred fifty yards from the stone wall on the nearer side of the road. Since the wall was constructed in such a way that only its very top was visible above the surface of the slope, the commanders of the first Union assault, launched before noon on December 13, did not suspect the existence of Confederate defenders at the base of the Heights; they feared only the artillery at the crest.[38]

This sunken road gave the defenders an impregnable position, but General

Burnside hurled wave after wave against the concealed Confederate riflemen in an utterly hopeless effort to reach the stone-wall bastion. The sixth and final assault was led by Generals Humphreys and Tyler, whose troops faced the most formidable obstacles. An earlier wave had been pinned down in the one depression in the terrain, and the final charge had to advance through these prostrate soldiers. Because they had sustained heavy losses, they tried to dissuade the men of Humphreys and Tyler from advancing. "They called to our men not to go forward, and some attempted to prevent by force their doing so," Humphreys recorded in his final report on the battle.[39]

This unorthodox behavior spread confusion through the attacking force, disrupting the line of advance. But the command staffs rallied the troops to continue toward their objective. At this moment, inspiring his men "to the very muzzle of the enemy's musketry," Quay cried out, "March over them; tramp them down!" With bullets whistling and cracking on all sides and the carnage of impending defeat evident everywhere, Quay encouraged the unseasoned Pennsylvania volunteers to remain on the offensive. As they advanced closer to the wall than any preceding assault, he shouted, "Damn it, boys, what are you dodging for! If I can sit on my horse, and the bullets go over my head they certainly can't hit you." Although he did not receive a scratch, his appraisal was less than accurate; almost half the men engaged in this final assault were killed or wounded.[40] Fearful that the road could be taken by sheer numbers, General James Longstreet had reenforced the Confederate position before this last futile Union attack so that he had men, three or four deep, firing in rotation. This massing of defenders produced a density of fire unsurpassed "by any defense force during the entire war." In the semidarkness that marked this last desperate thrust, the stone wall radiated like a sheet of flame, but the gallantry of these Pennsylvania volunteers carried them to within twenty-five or thirty yards of the wall before succumbing to superior Confederate strength.[41]

Thus ended the Fredericksburg fiasco. Despite the damaged reputation of the commanding Union general, individual acts of bravery and sound judgment were widely acclaimed. Colonel Quay was among those cited immediately and long after for daring leadership, particularly during the final charge against Marye's Heights. In his brigade report General Tyler praised Quay profusely and reaffirmed his feelings in statements to Governor Curtin.[42] Surviving rank-and-file members of the 134th were living witnesses of Quay's distinguished service, and some later recorded their impressions. They recalled that when he had urged them forward during the final assault, he not only refused to dismount and protect himself as did many of the other officers, but he also rode to the front "where bullets fell as thick as hail." Never losing sight of his "boys" in that memorable charge, he was the dynamo that moved them close to the stone wall.[43] His unforgettable display of self-discipline, composure, and bravery remained so vivid in their minds that through their initiative and that of General Tyler, Quay was awarded the Congressional Medal of Honor in the summer of 1888 while in the midst of another campaign—one waged on the political battlefield.[44]

The guns at Fredericksburg were barely silent when Quay left for his home in Beaver. But before he could fully regain his strength, Governor Curtin urged him to undertake the management of Pennsylvania's military agency in Washington. The agency had become disorganized and now required the hand of one not only familiar with governmental affairs, but also compassionate in the performance of demanding duties. In the interest of all Pennsylvania servicemen, the governor appealed to Quay to unravel the administrative tangle. Disregarding the ill effects that a premature return to vigorous activity might have on his health, he consented.

Throughout the war, but particularly at this time, Curtin's relationship with the war department was strained. For the governor personally, difficulties began the moment that President Lincoln appointed Simon Cameron—Curtin's principal Republican rival in Pennsylvania politics—as secretary of that department. Tension mounted as conflicting strategies pertaining to the administration of the war emerged. One man endorsed national centralization of both the military and political phases while the other adopted a states' rights position in which governors were the principal wielders of administrative power. With Cameron in sympathy with the centralization theme (and anxious for any advantage over Curtin), the war department became more and more of a focus for the problems of Pennsylvania particularly and the states generally. The governor knew that an astute military agent was needed to prevent this potentially explosive issue from affecting the men in uniform adversely. Quay stepped into the controversy and had to work with Simon Cameron for the first time.

Early in the war the federal government had revealed its commitment to centralization by assuming primary responsibility for the army. When the governors recognized that they were being reduced to glorified recruiters, they assumed the role of protectors of their fighting men against unreasonable and inappropriate demands of the central government. In this way they attempted to salvage the remnants of power and prestige. Secretaries in the offices of the various governors at first performed such functions. But as President Lincoln continued to minimize the military control exercised in the states, access to personnel records, particularly those in the war department, became increasingly important to state representatives designated to handle soldiers' requests and complaints. This required liaison in Washington, and many governors appointed their own deputies, known as military state agents, to work in the nation's capital. The agent was instructed to review each letter promptly and extend to the soldier every favor consistent with military regulations. In a state as large as Pennsylvania, this office was a vital public relations instrument for the governor and an anchor for the morale of the troops.[45]

The Curtin-Cameron rivalry produced frequent irritations over troop procurement during the early stages of the war and complicated the assignment of the agent from Pennsylvania. Remembering Quay's ability to encourage cooperation among diverse political groups, the governor concluded that he was well qualified for the post. Replacing J. Henry Puleston, he assumed duties similar in many ways to those he had left behind in Harrisburg when he accepted command of the 134th Regiment.

Quay revamped Pennsylvania's military state agency as Governor Curtin intended, but he was not happy in the new assignment. The war had kindled his desire for a political career, and he regarded the nation's capital as remote from the seat of action. With the election for governor of Pennsylvania being held in the fall of 1863 and that for president of the United States a year later, Quay yearned to be back in Harrisburg. After repeated requests to the governor to be relieved, he obtained a transfer to the state capital where he agreed to serve as military secretary. In this role he still directed much of the flow of correspondence to Pennsylvania's troops, and in time his duties were combined with those of master of transportation and telegraphing. Although this added to Quay's responsibilities, the fusion was designed primarily to provide a basis for increasing his salary.[46]

Spending most of the last two years of the war in Harrisburg, Quay entered actively into state politics. More instructive for his political future, however, was the opportunity for political observation. During 1861 and 1862 the Republican tide ebbed, and conditions continued to look bleak in 1863 when Governor Curtin's health was shattered by the strain of the war. He announced that he would not be a candidate for reelection, but the public refused to accept that decision. The Republican state convention nominated him on the first ballot, and he accepted the call.

Although assailed at home during the campaign, Curtin was strongly supported by the soldiers, whether their party affiliation was basically Democratic or Republican. General Tyler, for example, indicated that he had 358 Pennsylvania soldiers in camp, and "there is but one man from Penna. here that is not very desirous to aid in the Govs re-election." The most common political comment from a Pennsylvania soldier in the field to his family at home was an enthusiastic endorsement of Curtin's conduct of the war effort. In Democratic households the vote for Curtin was strongly influenced by such reports. When Curtin was reelected by a large majority,

Quay had graphic proof of the impact of a unified soldier vote on election returns.[47]

With the failure of General Grant's early assault on Richmond and the overall uncertainty surrounding the military operation, prospects for Lincoln's reelection the following year seemed equally discouraging. This was particularly true in Pennsylvania, but again the soldier vote was decisive. The common belief among political analysts was that confidence in the president's ability to prosecute the war had to be renewed. In a key state like Pennsylvania, this meant that he must attract a majority of the civilian vote, not merely a majority of the combined home and field ballots. Alexander McClure advised Lincoln that the home vote could be secured with certainty only if 10,000 Pennsylvania soldiers were furloughed to vote at home. The president respected this advice and acted accordingly. Anxious not to weaken Grant's tactical position, he requested that Generals Meade and Sheridan each send 5,000 soldiers to their Pennsylvania homes just prior to election day. Both complied, and troops poured into the state. Lincoln carried the home vote by a majority of 5,712, and the soldiers voting in the field swelled his state margin to an impressive 20,000.[48]

Again Quay observed the impact of the soldier ballots and profited from it. He himself became a successful candidate for the state house of representatives in 1864, thus concluding an instructive wartime career by becoming an elected official. Through the fortunes of war, he established many friendships, extended many courtesies, became recognized as a confidant of Governor Curtin, and above all, like Curtin, established himself as a "friend of the soldiers." The last was a distinction that he not only cherished, but also exploited to advantage in future political skirmishes.

A Lieutenant in Cameron's Army
1865-1867

I N 1854, only days after Matt Quay reached his twenty-first birthday, the Republican party of Pennsylvania presented its first slate of candidates to the voters. Identifying with the pious hopes and lofty ambitions espoused by the new party, he became a charter Republican and retained an active party membership for half a century.[1] Since the Republican party was a nebulous entity in its first years, adherents saw no necessity for enunciating a specific political credo. Aside from administration Democrats and slavery partisans, the broad umbrella of the new party provided refuge for individuals of almost every political faith. Only gradually were party goals refined, organization perfected, and top leadership identified.

During his years as prothonotary (1856–1861), Quay found no need to advocate or defend any particular faction or set of principles. As the party became more highly structured, however, individuals had to clarify their positions on various issues and leaders. Quay managed to delay his first such organizational confrontation until after the Civil War, but even then it was almost disastrous. Amid extremely controversial circumstances, he was forced to take a position that threatened his whole political future. Near failure in this first test dramatically illustrated to Quay how easily the political thread holding the public to a leader can become frayed.

Curtin Falls

Civil War problems and issues were dominant factors in determining alignments within the Republican party of Pennsylvania. Although numerous

19

regional groups demanded respect from time to time, the basic power struggle was between former Whigs, headed by Governor Andrew Curtin, and a faction of former Democrats, led by Simon Cameron, Lincoln's first secretary of war. Although Quay was recognized as the governor's chief administrator for military affairs, there was a minimum of factionalism attached to the conduct of his office. Both camps acknowledged that the prosecution of the war had the highest priority and that the governor, regardless of political affiliation, had to surround himself with the most competent men available.

Quay fell within this category, but with his election to the state house of representatives in 1864, his quasi immunity was, in effect, lost. To those interested in the spoils of office, this shift from staff to legislative position meant that he was carving a niche for himself in the party's councils, and his loyalties became a vital concern to both groups. Their demands to ascertain his preferences sometimes received erratic responses; although his sympathies and beliefs were with Curtin, he occasionally found it politic to act otherwise. In 1866 Quay was strongly opposed to the party's gubernatorial nomination of John W. Geary, a Cameron choice. He favored open revolt because he thought the party could not survive the authoritarian rule that Geary's election would bring, but other Republicans who also opposed Geary were even more opposed to Quay's suggestion of a candidate fight. Fearing that a party split would spell victory for the Democrats in the state and thus aid President Andrew Johnson's hated reconstruction policy, they swallowed their political philosophy with less trauma than Quay could. The next year his dissatisfaction assumed an even more varied course. Seeing Simon Cameron about to maneuver past all opposition and win a seat in the U.S. Senate, Quay contemplated entering the race against him. Buoyed by oil tycoon George K. Anderson's offer of substantial financial support, he flirted with this option for several days, but concluded that possible failure and the premature exposure of his interest in the Senate seat constituted an unwarranted risk. He retreated to the other extreme and moved the unanimous nomination of Cameron.[2]

Since terms in the Pennsylvania house of representatives were for one year only, Quay had to be reelected in 1865 for the 1866 session. He accomplished this easily and was rewarded with the chairmanship of the Committee on Ways and Means. In this capacity he reported the general appropriations bill earlier than it had been reported for many years and moved it rapidly to final passage. Seldom participating in debate, rising only to make brief explanations when appropriate, he directed his aspect of the legislative process with skill and aplomb. The stamp of political leadership was clear for all to see.[3]

By the time he was elected to his third consecutive session of the legislature (1867), Quay was acknowledged as the house leader of the Curtin forces.

Since this was the largest single cohesive faction, political custom dictated that he seek the speakership, the traditional mantle of factional superiority. Unfortunately for Quay the selection of speaker became irrevocably tangled with the election of a U.S. senator, as well as with lesser state offices and various committee memberships.

The contest began in the summer of 1866, months before the election of the representatives who would ultimately consider these appointments. In his preliminary survey, Quay introduced the personal letter, a political technique that he deployed frequently thereafter to solicit opinion and gain commitments from local candidates and officials. He wrote to almost every Republican candidate for a house seat, requesting candid comments concerning the speakership. The responses demonstrated how unorganized the state's Republican party was; regionalism bordering on countyism was the common denominator of political wisdom. Quay learned that he had two principal rivals for the speakership, D. B. McCreary and John P. Glass, and that the final choice would not rest on the political merits of the individual contenders. The would-be representatives reported that they were, or expected to be, under pressure from local leaders to barter their votes on the speakership for the endorsement of a specific candidate for the U.S. Senate. In this latter competition there were also three avowed contenders— Cameron, Curtin, and Galusha Grow—but since they were not paired with particular speakership hopefuls, the campaign became many-sided. The house candidates' varied replies to Quay's inquiry suggested an almost limitless number of combinations. Many expressed their own committee preferences and hinted that their speakership votes depended on assurances of those appointments. In later years, after Quay established his mastery over the party machinery, few local candidates had the audacity to inquire about the spoils they could expect; they were grateful for the privilege of cooperating. On this occasion, however, Quay did not overplay his hand; in spite of the stakes and the temptation, he did not make promises that might not be redeemable.[4]

After the October elections had determined the composition of the state house of representatives, the Cameron forces recognized the need to intensify their senatorial campaign. The returns indicated that a definite majority was sympathetic to Curtin. The governor's friends were confident that Quay would become the speaker and Curtin the senator. Judging from the limited evidence of activity on behalf of Curtin and from a statement by McCreary, one of the three principal speakership candidates, they were overconfident. Privately Quay did not share their certainty of victory, and when McCreary attempted to persuade Quay to withdraw from the speakership race and support him, it became apparent that there was reason to be wary.

Encouraged by Curtin's statements that Quay did not covet the speakership and that his candidacy was not essential to Curtin's victory, McCreary as well as the governor falsely concluded that Quay's support could be transferred to the former. Quay realized, however, that even if he withdrew, a majority of his supporters would not shift their loyalties to McCreary. Their votes would go instead to John Glass of Allegheny County, the third contestant, who was quietly being supported by Cameron. What seemed both certain and logical to McCreary and Curtin was only pliable putty to the Cameron managers.[5]

To Curtin's rivals for the Senate seat, Cameron in particular, the challenge was clear; only a coalition could stop the governor. And the first task facing any such combination would have to be the defeat of Quay, whose election as speaker was absolutely assured in the minds of the Curtin followers. No one understood more clearly than Cameron what victory for a man as able and skillful as Quay actually meant. With the speaker's power to appoint committees and assert a general control over legislation, he could deter representatives elected on a Curtin platform from bolting to the Cameron camp. If Quay were permitted to exercise such discipline, he would surely strike the final blow to Cameron's ambition to recapture the Senate seat he had occupied for two partial terms before the Civil War.

Since Curtin was the frontrunner among the senatorial candidates, with Cameron the serious challenger, other contenders realized that a standoff between the two was a distinct possibility. This encouraged each of them to assert his claim as vigorously as possible in hopes of becoming the compromise choice. With support throughout the northern tier of counties, Galusha Grow stepped up his quest. Thaddeus Stevens saw his chance for a long-coveted Senate seat. John W. Forney of Philadelphia and J. Kennedy Morehead of Pittsburgh also announced their candidacies. Their actions further depleted the Curtin ranks because most of their legislative supporters were drawn from those who would have favored the governor in a Cameron-Curtin showdown. The most decisive blow to Curtin, however, was struck by Stevens. The Lancaster delegation was committed to Quay for the house speakership as long as Stevens was not in the Senate race, but once "Old Thad" exerted pressure, the representatives did his bidding.[6]

Each of these four secondary contenders understood that, if the legislature became deadlocked between Curtin and Cameron, he had an opportunity to become the dark-horse senator; the stakes were right, and they were all willing to play. This was vital to Cameron's scheme since he could not reach an agreement with Quay directly. The two had met and tried to find a basis for negotiation, but failure strained relations even more. As one of Quay's backers wrote: "How I should have liked to overhear the fracas between you and Cameron. Lord, it must have been a rich scene!" With the impasse obvious by December 1866, Cameron had no alternative except to maneuver these other Senate aspirants into the act. His own subordinates were "bolstered up with the idea that the old man has made arrangements to knock into pie the slate, speaker, and state treasurer." They reportedly ran about "rubbing their hands and appearing in great glee over something that is going to happen which will astonish the natives." All Curtin's rivals and their endorsers knew that stopping him was essential, and denying Quay the speakership was a necessary first step. With a little maneuvering by Cameron, the combination of anti-Curtin forces united behind Glass and elected him. Without realizing the consequences of their action, they enabled Cameron to harvest all the fruits of victory for himself, because Glass was secretly "his man."[7] With his control over committee assignments in the house, Glass quickly captured the necessary number of Grow, Stevens, Morehead, and Forney representatives.

An anticlimactic rematch between the Curtin and Cameron forces on the senatorial appointment itself was scheduled a few days later. With Glass now openly a Cameron subordinate, the corner had been turned even before the Republican caucus met to debate the issue. To assure that the trend would not be reversed, J. Donald Cameron, Simon's son, made his first appearance on the political scene as the manager of his father's campaign. Although a clear majority of Republicans had committed themselves to support Simon in the caucus, he judiciously took the steps necessary to stave off a possible revolt on the part of the Curtin faction. If those who had remained loyal to the governor joined with the Democrats behind a compromise candidate of their own, the elder Cameron could still be defeated. Donald conferred with Quay, ticked off the specific votes he could command, offered amnesty to Curtin followers, and appealed to Quay to move the unanimous nomination of his father after the party caucus gave him a majority. Quay consulted Curtin, who declared that he had no intention of leading any resistance movement against the consensus of Republican legislators. Armed with the knowledge that the governor had given up the fight, Quay resumed his discussions with the younger Cameron, accepted the olive branch, and after the party caucus formally declared its preference for Cameron, moved that the action be unanimously endorsed.[8]

Victory in this nominating caucus marked the beginning of Cameron's domination of Pennsylvania politics and the sharp decline in Curtin's power. Rank-and-file Republicans at first resented the wartime governor's defeat by what they feared was a Cameron cabal. They preferred to have Curtin represent them in Washington and expressed their displeasure at the party's state convention in 1868 by nominating John Forney, not Cameron, as chairman of the delegation to the national convention and instructing the group to support Curtin as a vice-presidential nominee. Partly because this demonstration made its point, President Grant appointed Curtin as minister to Russia the following year. Even this was to Cameron's advantage because Curtin's absence from Pennsylvania for almost four years precluded any revival of power, especially since Grant deferred to Cameron on practically all federal appointments in the Commonwealth. Any effort on Quay's part to champion Curtin during his Russian sojourn would have been a hopeless gesture with only negative results for himself.[9]

Quay nevertheless was accused of selling out to the Camerons, not merely for personal political advantage, but also for a financial consideration. That he gained politically cannot be denied, but the latter charge seems to be unfounded. His action was widely denounced as political treason, and in almost every subsequent battle within the party, Quay was again condemned publicly. The most severe critics denounced his alleged duplicity in frustrating popular will. Those who were more charitable considered the failure to carry the caucus for Curtin as his only crime. Throughout Quay remained stoically silent, knowing that the least he had done for himself by endorsing Cameron in the caucus was to preserve his own political future. He anticipated public reaction so accurately that he did not attempt to capitalize on this personal gain immediately. When the 1867 session of the legislature ended, he astutely appeared to remove himself from the political scene until the air could clear.[10]

Adaptive Politics and the Environment

This alliance of Cameron and Curtin forces, with Matt Quay symbolic of the latter, brought Pennsylvania Republicanism a unity and dominance that it had not known before. In the years before the Civil War, the Commonwealth had responded less decisively to sectional issues than other large and wealthy states in the Northeast, such as New York and Massachusetts. In 1856 when the Republican party presented its first presidential ticket and announced its opposition to the extension of slavery into the territories, both these states gave their endorsement. In Pennsylvania the trend was also Republican, but the majority still favored Democratic electors. Like all northern states, Pennsylvania was not unsympathetic to the antislave cause, merely hesitant to accept change—a follower rather than a leader, at least on this issue.[11]

By passing a resolution endorsing the Wilmot Proviso, the state legislature had tried to set the tone for more positive responses. The lower house gave a unanimous endorsement, and the state senate voted twenty-four to three to encourage implementation of Wilmot's principle, but the rank-and-file voter was not inspired to such affirmative action. The first modest indication of popular success for Republicanism in Pennsylvania did not come until 1858, when a loosely organized group of Republicans, Whigs, Know Nothings, and Anti-Nebraska Democrats wrested control of the lower house of the legislature from the Democratic party. Even as late as 1864 Pennsylvania failed to stand assertively for Union, demonstrating a reluctance to reelect Lincoln. If the president had not furloughed 10,000 soldiers to vote at home, the Democrats would have carried the "civilian" vote.

This irresolute attitude lingered into the era of Reconstruction. When the states were individually called upon to consider the Thirteenth Amendment, granting freedom to Negroes, Massachusetts and Pennsylvania again stood in contrast. Both houses of the Bay State's legislature voted unanimously for ratification while the Keystone State, not so strongly committed, mustered only slightly more than a 60 percent endorsement. Although both states were securely in the Republican column in the generation following the Civil War, their attitudes differed widely. Adhering to an ideological Republicanism, the Massachusetts constituency supported idea-oriented leaders such as Charles Sumner, George Frisbie Hoar, and even Henry Cabot Lodge—men who could never have dominated the Pennsylvania scene where change and innovation were resisted until either necessity or the likelihood of a favorable result was clearly established.[12] Only opportunistic, power-conscious leaders such as Simon and J. Donald Cameron, Matt Quay, Samuel J. Randall, and Christopher L. Magee, who concentrated their talents on achieving direct, tangible results, could relate to "the Pennsylvania mind," which Henry Adams described as "admirably strong and useful if one wanted only to run on the same lines." Adams concluded that, "as minds go, [it] was not complex; it reasoned little and never talked, but in practical matters it was the steadiest of all American types; perhaps the most efficient, certainly the safest."[13]

Later in his senatorial career, in the course of defending the patriotism of Pennsylvania protectionists, Quay acknowledged the conservatism identified by Adams, but denied that it was related to a deficient public spirit. He cited the patriotism of business interests in the eastern counties, particularly Philadelphia, that had enjoyed extensive commercial ties with the prewar South. When the war came, "there was no portion of Pennsylvania and no portion of any other state which sent proportionately more troops to the army than Eastern Pennsylvania" although it was dominated by conservative business leaders.[14]

This conservatism was deeply rooted in ethnic rivalries among the state's Quakers, Germans, and Scotch-Irish. Through years of crises these groups found resolution in compromise and irresolution, an approach that later permitted big business and a powerful Republican organization to respect each other and live in harmony.[15]

In the generation following the Civil War, the whole nation confronted the challenge of a rapidly spreading industrialism. When the corporation supplanted the partnership as a more viable means of concentrating great sums of money for a single enterprise, larger businesses became common. Accompanying this shift was the concentration of population in urban areas, caused by the accelerating tempo of immigration and by the movement of individuals from rural communities where their quest for the American dream had been unfulfilled. Changes of such cataclysmic proportions produced severe strains on the nation's social institutions. Social problems developed much more rapidly than solutions, creating an atmosphere of instability and uncertainty.

The challenge was particularly crucial in Pennsylvania, the most highly industrialized of the states. Before the Civil War the state's businessmen and other "social elites," particularly in Philadelphia, played a major role in government on a part-time basis, both as officeholders and as party leaders, but the advent of the corporation upset that relationship. The burgeoning business world offered a seemingly limitless vista for material gain to those who focused their energies on the mass production of essential goods required by an increasingly complex society.[16] Such opportunities did not go unnoticed by most young men from middle-class families. No longer willing to divide their time and talents between government and business, most opted for the latter. Ironically, business discovered that it was losing control of government precisely when its need for the services of government was expanding dramatically.[17]

For those who filled the political void after many middle-class leaders withdrew, the retreat of business from government provided new leverage. As government and business evolved into more distinct entities with separate personnel, dependence on each other became inevitable. Political survival depended upon an ability to recast party organization and management so that it could compete with the growing power of business and industry. In specific terms this meant that in the late 1860s and 1870s, Pennsylvania's party leaders had to gird themselves to compete with some of the nation's most powerful economic forces. Foremost among them was the Pennsylvania Railroad (PRR), a company whose power could be assessed not only in terms of real estate and rolling stock, but also in terms of 150,000 employees who, under pressure, might represent 150,000 controllable votes.

In contrast, the governor of Pennsylvania presided directly over five hundred employees whose votes he could command with less certainty. The city of Philadelphia had between twelve and fifteen thousand municipal workers who did not respond to any single political voice. The power differential becomes even clearer when one considers that the PRR had approximately two hundred officials who exercised more power than the state's governor. Furthermore, in an era of increasing emphasis on material rewards, a $10,000 annual salary for the governor suggested a position inferior to that of the PRR president who received five times that amount.[18]

There were probably twenty other powerful companies in the Commonwealth, all somewhat smaller than the PRR. Their presence, particularly when they sought a common objective, made it perfectly clear to political leaders who hoped to survive in competition with them that they would need a power base rivaling that of industry. To the observant this signified that only through the full-time efforts of professional politicians, who would adapt industry's more effective organization techniques to the political scene, could government and the parties retain control over society's destiny.

By experience the Camerons were well equipped for this kind of challenge. From his canal projects, railroad enterprises, and banking facilities, Simon had not only amassed a fortune, he had mastered the art of administration. Donald had also gained valuable experience in his father's business ventures, becoming a bank president, as well as vice-president and later president of the Northern Central Railway Company of Pennsylvania, while simultaneously dabbling in mining and manufacturing.[19] Although the same age as the younger Cameron, Quay was less business oriented, but his boldness and keen analytical abilities in both politics and business made him a fierce competitor. He was an "even tempered, level headed man," constantly alert to changes in the political environment which he permitted to condition his attitudes and alter his actions. He was much more flexible mentally than Donald Cameron, who "never permits himself to be moved one inch."[20] In time he was able to supplement, even surpass, the Cameron adaptations to politics.

Thus a common ingredient brought to the Pennsylvania political scene by the Camerons and Quay was an awareness of business practices that would help to remodel and revitalize the political structure. Like their successful counterparts in other states, they confidently undertook the necessary restructuring. They realized that their political organization had to be dramatically enlarged in order to keep pace with the rapidly increasing size of businesses. Hastily moving toward that end, party leaders everywhere increased the size of their political armies more rapidly than at any other period of our history. Retaining control in the face of such expansion was a major problem; while industry created the trust and holding company to provide control under such conditions, politicians devised and revised the party machine.[21] By the last two decades of the century, Tom Platt's New York Republican organization embraced more than ten thousand regulars, maintained by an annual expenditure of nearly $20 million.[22] The Pennsylvania machine, dominated by Quay during most of these same decades, was proclaimed "the most perfect and complete" of all such state organizations. This is not a distinction that was acquired at modest expense. According to an account by John Wanamaker, who seemed delighted with an opportunity to expose Quay's party manipulations, Pennsylvania's Republican payroll contained some twenty thousand individuals who profited from the party's largess at an estimated yearly rate of $24 million. Although only two-thirds as large as the state budget, that of the Republican party nevertheless assumed the character of big business, and party expenditures at the time compared favorably with the budgets of several railroads (Reading, Lehigh, and B&O), but was not as large as that of the Pennsylvania.[23]

This growth enabled the Republican party to meet the state's corporations on more or less equal terms. Although these political and economic forces were both highly competitive, neither was intent upon destroying or absorbing the other. They acknowledged their interdependence and regarded coexistence as the most beneficial route to survival. Business leaders accepted the Republican party as the most efficient means of preserving their interests in the economy; protective tariffs, stable currency, favorable rights-of-way, and lenient incorporation laws depended upon sympathetic state or congressional action.[24] But the price for these benefits was high. Realizing that party payrollers and successful campaigns were increasingly expensive, industry grudgingly accepted the fact that it would have to assume a major responsibility for replenishing party coffers.

To obtain this much-needed support, the Republican party succumbed at times to industry pressure, but its power was also deployed on occasion to restrain business. In Pennsylvania the Republican party was the only entity capable of mustering such influence. Thus business could not dictate political decisions, nor did it go to the other extreme and defend any particular course adopted by the party. There were times when business leaders quietly reveled in the fact that a party chieftain who had "leaned" too heavily on them was being badgered by the press or the courts or by reformers or the public in general. They did not quarrel openly with any course being pursued by the machine because that would have weakened the machine's effectiveness, an effectiveness they depended upon for the promotion of their own interests in the economy.

In the process of being returned to the Senate in 1867, Simon Cameron effectively applied business methods to Pennsylvania's politicoeconomic relationships for the first time. His technique not only made him master of the state's political scene, but successfully launched a dynasty that ruled for more than fifty years. Many lesser politicos and the general public accepted the result with reluctance, but Cameron boldly demonstrated that he had taken charge. Politicians hostile to him were systematically and severely punished both in the legislature and in congressional districts. Within a short time it was difficult in many districts for any Republican opposed to the Camerons to be nominated.[25]

This power continued to spread and was so intensified under Quay that the *Atlantic Monthly* lamented that he even enjoyed an effective control over the Democratic party. Although this statement was designed to shock the American public, it nevertheless contained important realities of political life. As the *Atlantic* observed, Quay had attracted enough local Democratic leaders onto his payroll to sway many of that party's decisions.[26]

On those occasions between the Civil War and the turn of the century when the Democratic party captured the presidency (Grover Cleveland, twice) and the governorship of Pennsylvania (Robert Pattison, twice), its members naturally found their way into state and federal offices. Not so naturally Quay retained them in significant numbers—in exchange for promises to guide *their* party in *his* interest.[27] Even Democrats protected by civil service were not exempt from such propositions; they had less faith in the civil service system than in the power of the Republican machine. As early as 1876 federal officeholders were being routinely assessed for party contributions. Within six years the Republican organization in Pennsylvania was making similar requests, and state employees of either party could not escape the feeling of intimidation when they received copies of a form letter that read: "Two percent of your salary is ____. Please remit promptly. At the close of the campaign we shall place a list of those who have not paid in the hands of the head of the department you are in."[28]

Such Cameron-Quay tactics marked Pennsylvania as an exception to the national pattern which, in the thirty years between Cameron's return to the Senate and the inauguration of the McKinley administration, was characterized by a Democratic-Republican equilibrium.[29] Nationwide the two parties were so evenly matched that the Republicans edged the Democrats by capturing a mere 50.1 percent of the seats in the House of Representatives held by the two parties. Viewed from another perspective, the Democrats appeared to have an equally slight advantage in this era of delicate balance. They organized eight of the fifteen congresses (the fortieth through the fifty-fourth), but on only one occasion (1893-1895) did they dominate the presidency, the Senate, and the House of Representatives simultaneously. Republican statistics were somewhat more impressive. The Republicans controlled all three during five congresses, including the first four in this period. But after the Forty-third Congress (1873-1875), they too were limited to one sweep—the Fifty-first Congress (1889-1891) when Matt Quay was the Republican national chairman.

While Republicans outside the Keystone State were winning 46.6 percent of the House contests, within the Commonwealth they were seating 66.9 percent of their House candidates. Thus the Pennsylvania victory rate was almost 50 percent better than the party's national average. This convergence of the major parties nationally encouraged third parties to aspire to control the balance. As a result they elected seventy-six congressmen during these thirty years, but in Pennsylvania where the principal parties were not so evenly matched, third parties rarely threatened. The state sent Republican-dominated delegations to fourteen of these fifteen congresses, the exception being 1875-1877. Only on two occasions, 1882 and 1890, when factionalism disrupted the state's Republicans, were the Democrats able to carry a gubernatorial contest. In 1882 the combined Republican and third party vote against Robert Pattison, the successful Democratic challenger, was greater by more than 32,000; on the second occasion, when Pattison again provided the opposition, his margin was a mere 222 votes.

Thus the efforts of the Camerons and Quay transformed Pennsylvania politics. No longer a hesitant convert to Republicanism, the state abandoned the role of follower and became a leader—the most consistent, outspoken advocate of the party's principles among the large states during the last third of the nineteenth century. Full-time devotion to party affairs, augmented by applicable business techniques, produced a dominance that submerged Democrats, held business in reasonable check, and won the allegiance of most voters.

A Profile Low in Politics,
High in Visibility
1867-1877

AFTER 1867 politicians who remained hostile to Cameron were severely chastened. In most districts throughout the Keystone State, a Republican aspirant had the choice of joining the Cameron organization or going into political retirement. Young, ambitious, and bitten by the political bug in 1867, Quay yearned for a future in politics. His role in the senatorial nomination had opened the door to friendly relations with the Camerons who respected his skill, but he realized that unfortunate overtones accompanied his move. Not wanting to be classed as a traitor to Curtin, he moved so cautiously that his transition to the Cameron camp took five years (1867–1872) to complete.

Because of his identification with the Cameron-Curtin controversy, Quay, as a candidate for any significant office, was temporarily a Republican liability, capable only of keeping the factional pot boiling. He could contribute neither to the cohesiveness of the party nor to his own political advancement. He understood the signs and withdrew from the limelight to found and edit a weekly newspaper in his hometown.

Power of the Fourth Estate

Known as the *Beaver Radical*, Quay's weekly first appeared on December 11, 1868, and he continued as editor and publisher for four years. It was an instant success. The name itself struck a responsive note with the rural readers. The term *radical* suggested that the editor intended to go to the root or heart of crucial issues, that his political plow would dig beneath the surface of the problems that troubled the state and nation. This the readers came to expect, and this they received. Circulation grew rapidly, and by 1872 the *Radical* claimed to be the most widely distributed weekly in western Pennsylvania.[1]

In the first issue Quay declared that the *Radical* was Republican in politics, devoted to the interests of no individual or faction, and intended as an instrument to keep pace with the progressive spirit of young Republicanism. He portrayed Grant as "the last hope of this distracted country and confiding in his wisdom and patriotism, I shall yield an unhesitating support to his administration." In his effort to make the *Radical* a quality paper and at the same time an organ useful to his friends, Quay initiated a series of special articles by outstanding Republicans. The first guest columnist, A. K. Mc-Clure, was followed by John Forney. In order to emphasize that the *Radical* was not published "in the interest of Gen. Cameron's opponents," Quay invited Wayne MacVeagh, an active politician and Cameron's son-in-law, to write an article "upon what you please & as you please."[2]

Quay was still considered part of an active "Curtin ring," or at least his political enemies so portrayed him for their own political advantage. One such critic was the *Argus*, an established and competitive Beaver journal that was still battling the Curtin faction as the most "corrupt and remorseless corporation ever organized in this State." Quay was described as "continually on the wing, looking after its interests, seeking control of every County Convention, every District Conference, organizing the legislature before even chosen, and striving to monopolize every position from U.S. Senator down to the most insignificant delegateship."[3]

This account is undoubtedly an accurate description of Quay's conduct, but its purpose was not as open and direct as his critics believed. He did retain a loyalty to Curtin both publicly and privately, even when such action complicated his own political life. Since Pennsylvania was the only Middle Atlantic state to cast its electoral ballots for Ulysses S. Grant in 1868, Quay concluded in a forthright editorial that it should be rewarded with a cabinet post. Without embarrassment or hesitation, he proposed that the honor go to Curtin, whose tireless and patriotic efforts had guided the state through the ordeal of civil war. Declaring that in the public mind Curtin "has no rival in Pennsylvania," he discounted as rumor the suggestion that Donald Cameron was a candidate for secretary of the treasury. While depicting Cameron as eminently qualified, he was certain that the younger Cameron's personal and political relations with the wartime governor were so "intimate and kindly" that he would not permit his name to be inserted into competition with "such a distinguished gentleman as Curtin."[4]

All believers in the Curtin ring eagerly clutched this editorial to their breasts trusting that they had the full truth. On the other hand, those who believed that Quay was a devil in the Cameron ring read other passages from his editorial scriptures. They were suspicious of his denunciation of Cameron's old nemesis, the Pennsylvania Railroad, as "the great monopoly of our State." (Cameron was the owner of a rival railroad; the PRR wielded political power independently of him.) And his endorsement of the protective tariff was interpreted as soothing music for the ears of Cameron's industrial allies. The *Radical*'s lack of enthusiasm for the report submitted by Grant's civil service investigators was also construed as an endearment to Cameron and a vote for machine politics. The editor admitted that he could discern no injustice in collecting voluntary contributions from officeholders for political purposes. His rhetorical question, "If office holders should not pay the necessary expenses of political campaigns, who ought to pay them?" contained its own answer. In addition, it was certainly an analysis acceptable to Cameron, without whose endorsement Quay could not have been appointed secretary to the Republican State Central Committee during the years of his editorship.[5]

The editorial columns were the *Radical*'s most distinctive feature. The editor was an incisive writer whose words, often reprinted, influenced political sentiment throughout the state. He strongly opposed President Johnson, whose last annual message he regarded as the firing of treason's final gun. At the same time he satirized the Tenure of Office Act, designed to curb Johnson's power, as a "political outrage . . . unprecedented, revolutionary, and in defiance of the plainest provisions of our Constitution."[6]

In equally vigorous language he condemned his own party for evading the issue of voting rights for Negroes. When conferring his unqualified approval on the Fifteenth Amendment, assuring universal suffrage, he chided Republican colleagues in the northern states for their inconsistent approach to the issue. On the one hand, they recognized that impartial suffrage was a logical result of the war by making it a *sine qua non* for the readmission of rebel states to the Union and by requiring compliance in the District of Columbia and the territories, as well as in the constitutions of all new states. On the other hand, northern leadership, whether Republican or Democratic, did not seek equality within their own borders. In the name of justice he called upon his party to act:

> The Republicans of this State must give no uncertain sound upon this vital question. The next Republican platform should place the party in Pennsylvania unqualifiedly in the advanced line of progress, and demand that our State shall no longer be faithless to justice and the noblest fruition of Freedom. Weak men may hesitate and the groveling

and ambitious may tremble as is ever the case when the world is to advance; but Right points the way so clearly that no man can mistake its demand and none but the cowardly or treacherous will fail to obey it.[7]

Forty-four years before its enactment, Quay was in the forefront pressing for another constitutional revision almost as significant as the Fifteenth Amendment. The process by which state legislatures elected U.S. senators had degenerated to the point that money, patronage, and the promise of office commanded more respect than a candidate's qualifications. Quay argued that bribery and corruption would be minimized if senators were answerable to the people through direct election. Observing that a wealthy individual without ability could easily procure a senatorial appointment, he bemoaned the fact that a poor and honest man of great ability would find the same task exceedingly difficult. He pointed out that government suffered when millions were squandered annually by the votes of senators who were committed to certain railroads, contracts, and subsidies by agreements made at the time of their elections. He also noted the unfortunate effects on ambitious men of modest means who were forced to witness others being applauded, courted, lionized, and even sustained by their party through election after election with only passing attention to the corruption that contributed to their rise to power. Enticed down the same road, the aggressive but poor looked upon such practices as both ethical and legitimate since they were "necessary."[8]

Written in the language of a reformer, Quay's analysis may have been a personal lament. Since the period of his editorship represents a career crossroads, he may have been assessing his own limited resources and prospects—perhaps in contrast to those of the Camerons. As his subsequent career shows, he found it necessary to turn his back on reform and follow, even perfect, the election techniques that in 1869 he characterized as detrimental to the American system of government. As Quay's practical career in politics unfolded, he lost faith in the reform principle that he espoused in the pages of the *Radical*. Ironically, his own machine control of politics in subsequent years provided one of the most shameful examples of how the system might be corrupted. This practical demonstration helped immeasurably to convince the nation of the need to institute the direct election of senators, a change that was achieved in 1913 by constitutional amendment. Although he at times struck a reform pose for political purposes, his basic convictions were otherwise. Emotionally Quay identified with reformers, but through bitter experience he discovered that too often reform was an altar "where knaves minister and fools kneel."[9]

As an editor Quay worked assiduously to expand the influence of the *Radical.* He designed its columns to provide himself with an acceptable and forceful political image. During that period he excelled as an analyst, but championed only two issues of a practical political nature. One was local, with statewide consequences; the other was state-oriented, with national implications. Both advanced his political objectives. On the local scene Quay saw that his political hegemony in Beaver County was being mildly threatened by William W. Irwin, a New Brighton neighbor whose appointment as commissary general of Pennsylvania he had arranged during the Civil War. Months before the speakership contest of 1867, Irwin had tried to dissuade Quay from seeking the post because of his own ambition to be elected state treasurer that year. Irwin knew that, since both offices enjoyed statewide powers, the presence of two candidates from one rural county threatened to doom both. Neither stepped aside for the other, and neither succeeded, but the incident convinced Quay that he would have to free himself of such handicaps in the future.

Before Quay was prepared for that conflict, Irwin succeeded in having the legislature elect him state treasurer in 1868, and he fully expected to be reelected the following year. Apparently Irwin's designs on a political career did not upset Quay, but he was disturbed because the state treasurer did not recognize the need to take "political orders." Before the 1869 election, according to rumor, Irwin had refused a Quay request to deposit state funds in certain Cameron banks. This show of independence forced Quay to come to the defense of the Cameron interests and sparked his determination to unseat Irwin, but he concealed his feelings until the eleventh hour, when he produced a comparatively unknown challenger. Quay managed a campaign against Irwin with such finesse that the name of Robert W. Mackey was not discussed publicly as a candidate until the legislature was due to meet. Enough votes had been quietly solicited that the caucus unceremoniously shunted Irwin aside and brought to the forefront a man who for a decade would be as prominent as Quay in steering the Cameron machine.

At the age of thirty-one, Mackey, a cashier at the Allegheny Bank in Pittsburgh, was the youngest treasurer ever elected in Pennsylvania. Quay praised him as "a capable and faithful steward" of the state's revenues and without any evidence of bitterness acknowledged the conclusion of Irwin's term by noting that the retiree had demonstrated an eminent fitness for office.[10]

Cursed with a consumptive cough, stooped shoulders, and a shuffling gait, Mackey was the picture of ill health. Like Quay, his physical appearance did not suggest a man of vigor, but the two were political equals in both imaginative planning and bold execution. Little known beyond the limits of Pittsburgh at the time of his election, Mackey was in office less than a year when he established himself as an able Cameron lieutenant. In fact, Mackey,

whom Quay endorsed for reelection to an 1870–1871 term, became the
political bridge for Quay's passage from the Curtin to the Cameron camp.
Irwin's 1870 campaign tactics inadvertently assisted in this realignment.
With inducements from Thomas A. Scott and the Pennsylvania Railroad,
Irwin managed to unite the Democrats with fifteen anti-Cameron Republicans
and thereby defeat Mackey, Quay, and the Republican caucus.[11]

Stunned by this political reversal and forced to explain it in the columns of
the *Radical,* Quay temporarily lost his composure. He drastically revised
his estimate of Irwin's fitness for office without reference to any previous
evaluation. Characterized as a man perplexed by such basics as the King's
English and simple arithmetic, Irwin was condemned for incompetency
during his previous term which "made him the shame and laughing stock of
his own subordinates." The Republicans who bolted the caucus and joined the
combination were assailed with even greater vehemence. Denounced as
"fifteen bastards" who had the reasons for their dastardly deed folded in their
pockets, they were charged with threatening the "integrity, unity, and
ascendancy" of their party.[12] Mackey, on the other hand, was inclined to be
less vaporish and accepted Irwin's victory more gracefully. Trying to divert
Quay's energies from this one issue, he wrote to chide him for dwelling on it:
"What the devil is the matter with you? Has the late election upset you or
have you concluded to stay in Beaver the balance of your life? . . . I would
like to see you. Send me word when you will be up."[13] Now the most active and
effective of Cameron's subordinates, Mackey was as anxious as Quay to have
Irwin removed from the scene. But, though his own return to the state
treasurer's office was at stake, he had a more detached perspective than Quay,
whose local, as well as state, ambitions were temporarily thwarted by Irwin.

With all the weapons of Cameron's political arsenal available to them, Quay
and Mackey proceeded directly to their goal. Mackey was again elected
treasurer, a position he retained from 1871 to 1875, and with Irwin displaced,
Quay emerged as a Cameron ally and as a state power who did not have to cast
a backward glance to the political maneuvering in Beaver County.

Coalitions such as the combination of Democrats and disenchanted
Republicans that had permitted Irwin to unseat Mackey in 1870 were a
continuing source of danger to Quay. The Republican party had so completely
humbled the Democrats in the Keystone State that the task of maintaining
party discipline was a major challenge. Quay saw that the opposition was as
badly disorganized as the Whigs after the election of Franklin Pierce in 1852.
Without the pressure of a strong rival to keep factionalism submerged, the
Republican party's strength was also its greatest potential weakness. He
foresaw no immediate escape. Hope for Democratic resurgence was dim

because, in his opinion, his generation would neither forget nor forgive the Democratic party for its record during the Civil War.[14]

This assessment of public opinion, at least for the immediate future, was shared by leading Democratic analysts. The *St. Louis Republican* and the *New York World*, respected party organs, frankly confessed that no man nominated by the Democratic party or on a Democratic platform had the remotest chance to defeat Grant in 1872. They urged that in selecting presidential and vice-presidential candidates, the party consider only nonadministration Republicans; in so doing they advocated a concept that reached fruition in the Liberal Republican movement and provided the Republicans with at least a token challenge at the national level.

At the state level, the opposition in Pennsylvania continued under the Democratic banner. For the gubernatorial election in 1872, the Republicans nominated John F. Hartranft, a war hero of the Cameron camp, who had been serving as the state's auditor general. The tone of the campaign was set early. Under the heading "General Hartranft's Campaign Speeches," the *Radical* merely listed the general's twenty-three military engagements, ranging from the first battle at Bull Run to the final siege at Richmond. Since Grant was better known to the people of Pennsylvania than Hartranft, those concerned primarily with the president's reelection worried about the prospects of Hartranft's defeat in the state's October election; this would undoubtedly handicap Grant's bid for a second term the following month. Conversely, Grant's opponents realized that the road to his defeat in Pennsylvania turned on a concerted effort against Hartranft, a more acceptable political target than Grant.

When Grant was first elected in 1868, almost all Republicans were optimistic, but the character of his appointments and the nature of his legislative program alienated certain individuals and groups over the succeeding four years. The lack of precise information on the number and distribution of the disenchanted caused Quay to be apprehensive. The president's reliance on Stalwarts like Cameron, who pressed for a vindictive policy toward the South, was a major source of the state's ambivalence. Quay launched a vigorous campaign for Hartranft, stressing that his defeat would imperil Grant's chances. He equated one vote for Hartranft in October with two votes for Grant in November; an October vote for Charles R. Buckalew, the Democratic candidate for governor, carried the force of two votes against Grant in November. With his ranks shattered by elections held in other states prior to October, Horace Greeley, Grant's presidential opponent, found little comfort in surveying his prospects for the future. Quay intended that Pennsylvania should keep the Greeley forces from getting the proverbial camel's nose in the election tent. He editorialized toward that end and was not disappointed in the result: Hartranft and Grant both won impressive victories. Promptly rewarded for his efforts, Quay was named secretary of the Commonwealth. He gave up the *Radical* and moved back into the mainstream of Republican politics.[15]

First View of the National Arena

As secretary of the Commonwealth and a manager in Cameron's political empire over the next four years, Quay was a logical choice for delegate to the 1876 Republican National Convention in Cincinnati. His selection by the Pennsylvania state convention gave him his first opportunity to mingle with the giants of the political field. According to one analyst, the "talent assembled in that hall has never been surpassed in the annals of American politics."[16] George W. Curtis, Richard H. Dana, James Russell Lowell, John Sherman, Robert G. Ingersoll, James A. Garfield, John A. Logan, Zachariah Chandler, Frederick Douglass, and Benjamin F. Wade all took their seats at the party's highest council. Some had already rendered significant service, while others were destined to make major contributions in the future. But the lesser-known Quay remained in the political limelight longer than any of them. He attended six of the next seven conventions and asserted an influence on national conventions collectively that represented one of his more prominent legacies to political history.

As the convention date approached, popular sentiment among Republicans nationwide unmistakably favored James G. Blaine for the presidency. Taking his cue from the more conservative element, Grant registered his disapproval. Roscoe Conkling and Oliver P. Morton were rumored as possible Stalwart candidates, but that faction as a whole was more intent on stopping Blaine than in advancing any particular individual. Just a few weeks before the convention opened, the Stalwarts intensified their campaign to besmirch Blaine's reputation. By introducing the Mulligan letters, which allegedly identified him with improper manipulations involving the Little Rock and Fort Smith Railroad Company, they hoped to win public sympathy or at least to prevent a backlash of indignation at their planned derailment of Blaine's presidential express. This was not a new tactic, but a supplement to an earlier effort to involve him in the Credit Mobilier scandals.[17]

By the time the convention assembled, the seeds of party disunity that Quay had seen germinate six years before had grown into a sturdy plant. The party was divided into two hostile factions: the Stalwarts, controlled by such Senate leaders as Simon Cameron, Logan, Morton, and Conkling; and the Half-Breeds, headed by Blaine, Sherman, Garfield, and Hoar. Since President Grant aligned himself with the Stalwarts, the Half-Breeds, as the nonadministration element of the party, found themselves starved for patronage while confronted with seceders of their own, the Independents. The Half-Breed core was party oriented and disciplined enough to limit its fighting to intraparty skirmishes, while the Independents, behind such leaders as Carl Schurz, E. L. Godkin, Henry Ward Beecher, and George W. Curtis, were issue oriented and indifferent to whether their programs triumphed under Republican, Democratic, or hybrid banners.[18]

As in the nation at large, Blaine was the popular choice in Pennsylvania, but here too the Stalwarts were at work to override public sentiment. In May 1876 President Grant appointed J. Donald Cameron as secretary of war to fill a vacancy in his cabinet. With this bonus in hand, the Camerons, Mackey, and Quay launched the Pennsylvania phase of the larger scheme to frustrate Blaine's nomination.

Although the state's Republican convention was decidedly in favor of Blaine, it was maneuvered to pass two resolutions that seemed both politically dutiful and innocent. The first instructed the delegation to Cincinnati to cast its votes on the first ballot for a favorite-son candidate, Governor Hartranft, who, in the minds of all, had no chance of gaining the nomination. The second required the delegation to vote solidly for Hartranft on all subsequent ballots as long as his total convention vote kept increasing. This second resolution ultimately prevented Blaine from being the party's nominee because the Cameron manipulators arranged with the Morton manipulators of Indiana to have a few of the latter's votes transferred to Hartranft on each succeeding ballot in order to keep him in the competition.[19]

Donald Cameron personally headed the Pennsylvania delegation to Cincinnati and helped direct the attack against Blaine, who had seven formally endorsed rivals for the nomination. By the sixth ballot Blaine had made notable gains, and although short of a majority, he seemed likely to procure one unless all his opponents could unite on one "stopper." At this point Cameron and Conkling, whose delegations dominated the convention, arranged a delay in the proceedings, sacrificed their ambition to nominate a Stalwart, and persuaded all Blaine's rivals to release their delegates to Rutherford B. Hayes, the governor of Ohio. All complied, and the Hartranft candidacy achieved its basic purpose. Blaine was defeated and Hayes incidentally nominated. In spite of his contempt for Hayes, Conkling was willing to advance him in order to suppress Blaine. The Stalwarts preferred taking their chances with the Ohio governor to surrendering the nomination to the leader of the Half-Breeds.[20]

Immediately upon learning that Hayes had been nominated, Hartranft congratulated him, pledging both his personal support and that of his state in what he predicted would be a bitter campaign. Shortly thereafter he wrote again, presenting what was intended as a letter of introduction for Matthew S. Quay, who had become chairman of the Republican State Committee in Pennsylvania. The governor described Quay as "one of our ablest and most faithful leaders" in whom the nominee could place his confidence. Such a trust never developed, however. Their relationship was one of mutual distrust. In a preliminary note on the same day, Quay wrote that he had no personal ambitions from the campaign except its success. Maintaining that prominent members of the party were anxious for the two to discuss campaign strategy, he utilized what leverage he had for a face-to-face discussion. Although the meeting was held, they established no meaningful rapport. Hayes remained too suspicious of Quay's Stalwart friends.[21]

In his capacity as chairman of the state committee, Quay again resorted to his reliable letter-writing technique. Showing himself to be a master of detail, he addressed a charge to the Republican leaders in every one of the state's voting districts and pointed out that with 3,300 election precincts in the Commonwealth, the loss of a few votes in each by defective registration could imperil statewide success. He implored these grass-roots leaders "to give to the task the few hours necessary to perfect your list." He outlined the ramifications of the loss of Pennsylvania to the Republican party: "the re-establishment in power in the Nation of a party dominated by the rebel element of the South, where supremacy will bring in its train free trade, Southern claims, a debased currency, repudiation of our national obligations and the recognition of the heresy of States Rights which occasioned the Rebellion." Then in conclusion he admonished them: "Our billions of treasure will have been spent in vain and our soldier dead will have died as the fool dieth" if vigilance at the polls was not maintained.[22]

Because of such attention to detail, Hayes carried Pennsylvania, but by less than ten thousand votes. The national result was not even that decisive. Disputed returns in South Carolina, Florida, Louisiana, and Oregon kept the outcome in doubt for months. The Pennsylvania Stalwarts of Donald Cameron, Mackey, and Quay were active in two states where the Republican claim on the disputed electoral votes was weakest—Florida and Louisiana. The promptness with which Cameron, as secretary of war, ordered federal troops to the aid of Republicans in those states enabled them to make the most forceful case possible in behalf of their claim. With the power to throw out votes that they considered spurious, canvassing boards in both states reviewed incidents of suspected fraud and intimidation. Both parties sent observers to witness the proceedings. Quay was among twenty-five Republicans invited by President Grant to go to Louisiana, and Mackey was among those sent to Florida where, according to legend, he acted forthrightly in Hayes's behalf.[23]

A few years earlier Mackey had bought the *Pittsburgh Commercial* from C. D. Brigham who then retired to Florida and became politically influential. On the train south, chance seated Mackey near two Democratic representatives traveling to Florida on a mission similar to his. Behind a sickly appearance that suggested he was going south for his health, Mackey was not recognized. He overheard the two Democrats discussing in detail their plans to rescue Florida's electoral vote for their party. When the train stopped en route, Mackey sent a telegram to Brigham outlining their plan, and before they arrived at the state capital, roadblocks had been strategically placed. Because of such frustrations the Democrats were unable to mount an effective case for their candidate.[24]

Soon after an electoral commission concluded that Hayes had been elected, Quay, Mackey, and other Stalwarts began to wonder if the result was worth the effort. Two of their arch enemies, Carl Schurz and William M. Evarts, were rewarded with cabinet posts, and Hayes made it clear that he intended to appoint a new secretary of war instead of retaining Donald Cameron, who had held the office less than a year. Pennsylvania's Republican leaders found it difficult to conceal the fact that they regarded him as an obtuse ingrate. In an angry moment Quay wrote Hayes a caustic note pointing out that he had failed to understand and appreciate what he had been told and advising him to consult state organizations in the future. Realizing that he had dressed down the president, Quay recanted and sent a follow-up letter the next day. "I write to apologize for a very impertinent and silly letter. . . . If it reaches your eye, please consider it as unwritten except so far as it was expressive of my regard for yourself and sincere desire for the success of your administration."[25]

Hayes's ingratitude irked Simon Cameron in particular. When contrasted with his influence in the Grant years, his failure to induce the president to appoint his son to the cabinet was a political humiliation. On a Saturday afternoon in March 1877, he returned from Washington to Harrisburg determined to demonstrate his power for the benefit of the president. After consultation with Governor Hartranft, Quay, and Mackey, his scheme was ready for launching. On Sunday morning Republican members of the legislature who had not gone home for the weekend were systematically sought out and brought to Donald Cameron's residence. They were informed confidentially that the elder Cameron had resigned his Senate seat and were asked to endorse Donald as his successor. Each was asked to pledge his support on the spot, and in most instances the commitment was made. On the following day Cameron subordinates met every train and ushered returning Republican legislators into similar sessions where their pledges were requested. When the legislature convened that Monday evening, Governor Hartranft sent messages to both houses announcing the resignation of Simon

Cameron and requesting the houses to meet in joint session to elect a successor. The legislature dutifully elected Donald that same evening, thereby demonstrating to Hayes that he might be able to reject a cabinet member, but was powerless to prevent the election of a U.S. Senator.[26]

With this display of political strength, the elder Cameron dramatically passed the mantle of power to his son. He could retire with confidence; his son was buttressed by two subordinates of proved ability. Mackey and Quay knew how to anticipate, how to overcome. They could rise to almost any occasion, and this manipulation even helped perfect their technique. At least for Quay it was a practical demonstration which he relied on later in his own career. By isolating legislators at Cameron's residence and procuring their individual endorsements prior to a formal meeting of the legislature, the managers could gain commitments that might not have been forthcoming in a public session. Divide and Conquer was indeed a maxim not to be forgotten by those who expected to play the game of practical politics successfully.

From Lieutenant to General
1877-1884

BECAUSE of the circumstances surrounding Hayes's election, a cloud of uncertainty hung over the administration, but it was comparatively unnoticed by Republican leaders who detected other more ominous signs in the political sky. With the economy still feeling the crippling effects of the Panic of 1873, prosperity was at best a mist beyond the horizon.

Disturbances erupted across Pennsylvania in 1877, the most disastrous year of the depression for that state. Mob violence took charge of Pittsburgh's railroad strike, which was quelled only by state and federal troops after the loss of sixteen lives and millions of dollars in property damage. Rioting spread to Reading, Scranton, and Wilkes-Barre and threatened to infect other areas. Unrest was prevalent throughout the Commonwealth, and in the local election returns of 1877 the voters appeared to attribute much of the responsibility to the Republican party. Soundly defeated but not demoralized, the party leadership displayed a remarkable resilience. It regrouped, supplied its organization with the necessary resources, and sallied into the 1878 campaign. The party's stakes were extremely high. Completing the unexpired term of his father, Donald Cameron expected to be returned to the U. S. Senate, but renewal depended upon the composition of the new legislature. Since a governor was also to be elected, the makeup of the legislature would be determined, in part, by the campaign strength of the party's gubernatorial nominee. With the key offices so intertwined, the Republicans had to rebound from their 1877 election losses if they hoped to win them all.

Cooperation within the party and division without permitted Pennsylvania Republicans to make such a recovery. With the Camerons centrally located in

Harrisburg, Mackey in Pittsburgh, and Quay a few miles away in Beaver, the geographical distribution of the party's high command left Philadelphia and the eastern counties uncovered. On the assumption that victory required complete statewide cooperation, the Cameron brain trust decided that Mackey should manage affairs in the west and Quay should move to Philadelphia to direct the eastern part of the organization. Quay needed financial help to make this move. Prodded by the Republican leadership, a subservient legislature re-created the office of recorder of Philadelphia with an annual income of $30,000 to $40,000 from salary and fees. Governor Hartranft signed the measure that gave him, with approval of the senate, responsibility for appointing the recorder. Almost before his signature was dry, he nominated Matthew S. Quay for the lucrative post, and the senate promptly confirmed the appointment.

Public reaction was not so sympathetic and understanding of the party's needs; the people of Philadelphia particularly were indignant. Although the law did not require that the recorder be a resident of Philadelphia at the time he was commissioned, the appointment of a politician from a western county for obviously political reasons shocked the civic pride of the eastern metropolis and aroused the ire of most Democrats and reform-minded Republicans. Quay quickly discovered that this maneuver to tighten central control over the various county organizations did as much to weaken the party as his active labors in the east could do to strengthen it. Acknowledging the mistake, he accepted abuse for a year and then resigned to return to Harrisburg, again as secretary of the Commonwealth.[1]

Although this ploy to develop a cohesive Republican team before the election was abortive, Quay's second efforts were more successful. For the crucial 1878 campaign, the Cameron leaders were unwilling to entrust the chairmanship of the Republican State Committee to anyone outside their own select group: Quay was chosen for the position. He understood that the rivalry between Stalwarts and Half-Breeds was a danger to the Republicans, and he accepted the challenge to unite the party. Publicly branded a Stalwart because of his actions at the 1876 national convention, Quay knew that he had to involve popular and eloquent Half-Breeds in the campaign. He requested assistance from the Republican Congressional Committee. "We are in great need of the services of Mr. Garfield and Mr. Blaine in the State," he confided to the committee's chairman, Eugene Hale. "Cannot you possibly arrange to give us these gentlemen for a few meetings during the campaign? The sooner the better."[2] Quay also corresponded directly with Garfield, the Ohio congressman, who accepted several speaking engagements in Pennsylvania during the campaign. After one such tour Garfield told Senator Cameron that he would return to the state if he were needed. When this word was passed on to Quay, he immediately replied: "We would be glad to have you as soon as you can come—to remain with us until [the] first of November."[3]

With this kind of cooperation and interdependence, the breach between Stalwarts and Half-Breeds, outwardly at least, seemed to be healing. Not convinced that unity alone was sufficient to carry the election, Quay and Mackey both believed that it was imperative to keep the opposition from coalescing. Fortunately for these two managers a third party, the Greenbackers, had entered the contest, and from the popular acceptance of their platform Quay sensed that they might hold the balance of power between the two major parties. To prevent any fusion of Greenbackers and Democrats he and Mackey worked quietly with the new third party and conveyed a general sympathy for its economic objectives. In return they wanted the Greenback gubernatorial nominee, Samuel E. Mason, to promise not to merge his party with the Democrats against the Republicans.[4]

Mason and the other Greenback leaders accepted the Quay-Mackey argument; neither the prestige of their party nor the integrity of their platform, Mason said, could be materially advanced by cooperating in either a Republican or a Democratic victory. In spite of pressure to do otherwise, Greenbackers fought successfully to retain the party's independence throughout the campaign, and by this action the Republicans were returned to power. Although the GOP received working majorities in both branches of the legislature, Henry M. Hoyt, the party's candidate for governor, had a plurality of only 22,253. The 81,758 Greenback ballots not only underscored a growing popular dissatisfaction with both major parties, but also marked Hoyt as a minority governor.

Elated with the result, Simon Cameron, the inventor of the political machine that carried the election, proclaimed: "All honor to Quay for his glorious victory." It was indeed a triumph for both strategists—Quay and Mackey—but the insecurity of Hoyt was nonetheless a blow to Republican prestige. A second setback occurred only weeks later when Mackey died, January 1, 1879. Over the preceding years Donald Cameron had gradually withdrawn into the background. A poor speaker, he shunned the popularity of the platform, as well as the regimen of correspondence and local meetings so necessary to a smoothly functioning political machine. He preferred the accolades of the party's influential members in caucus and in committee "to any amount of huzzaing in the streets." Now with Mackey's death Quay was the only visible ruler of the Cameron empire, and he ruled from the office of the secretary of the Commonwealth to which he was reappointed by Governor Hoyt in January 1879.[5]

An Old Soldier Who Never Fadeth

Although Quay was the chief administrator of the party in Pennsylvania, he was not so secure in his position that he was willing to challenge Donald Cameron, decreed by his father to be the chairman of the Pennsylvania Republican "board of directors." As they looked toward the presidential election in 1880, both Quay and the younger Cameron were disgusted with Hayes and distrustful of Blaine, but their private views of possible solutions to the party's dilemma differed widely. Cameron intended to return the nation to the "good old days" of Grant, when Stalwart leaders managed state affairs and federal patronage came to them without administrative interference. Grant was still available, and Cameron was determined to nominate him for a third term. Without evidencing any concern for Quay's feelings, he promised Conkling and Logan, the Stalwart leaders of New York and Illinois, that Pennsylvania would send a delegation to the national convention in 1880 committed to Grant and bound by the unit rule.[6]

Quay represented a different political generation. Cameron wanted to recapture the past while Quay focused on the future. Hoping to cement relations with the Half-Breeds and build on the foundation he had painstakingly laid in 1878, he also realized that the possible nomination and election of Grant could not inspire the young Republicans of Pennsylvania. The former president was the political creature of those who had first elected him a decade before. The more youthful leadership of the party could expect no recognition or satisfaction "except what they might receive at the hands of Cameron." Although Quay regarded Cameron as a personal friend and did not complain about his own treatment within the Cameron organization, others relatively new to the political scene could not expect similar opportunities. Acceptance of a Cameron choice, particularly one interpreted as a step backward, forced Quay to exhibit a dependence that was not flattering to a young, aggressive politician. In addition, he could not readily be enthusiastic about a nomination that was not "what I wanted for myself."[7]

In the weeks before the state convention, Quay was not firmly committed to any candidate. He leaned toward John Sherman, an Ohio Half-Breed, but his was not a name that touched popular imagination like that of Grant, who he believed would be elected if nominated. When Quay went to confer with Cameron about the state convention, F. C. Hooton implored him: "Quay, for God's sake induce Cameron to give up the Grant instructions." He replied: "I will do it if I can," but, unable to sway the senator, he moved at once to prevent a rift from developing. He submerged his personal convictions and endorsed the choice that Cameron had openly espoused. Bowing to this "popular sentiment" that Stalwarts had whipped up, Quay "went with them," but "was not of them." He may have resigned his direct affiliation with the Stalwarts, but he remained a most valuable associate and took the lead in moving the Grant bandwagon forward.[8]

The first indication in states other than Pennsylvania that Cameron had formidable support for Grant's nomination came in mid-December 1879 when the Republican National Committee was called upon to elect a chairman. Conkling and Logan endorsed Cameron for the post, and the Half-Breeds were powerless to find a worthy challenger. To Quay this was evidence enough. He recommended that Pennsylvania hold its state convention early in order to choke off factional debate and officially resolve the issue as soon as possible. Cameron saw the merits of this proposal. Advance word quietly went out to Stalwart leaders in the various counties to send Grant delegates to the state convention. The Republican State Committee convened on December 30, docilely accepted a Quay-sponsored resolution setting an early convention date, and formally scheduled it for February 4, 1880, a mere five weeks hence.[9]

This behind-the-scenes maneuvering for Grant was a well-guarded secret. The Half-Breeds had almost no knowledge of the systematic planning that preceded the formal call for the February convention. They dismissed rumors of Grant's candidacy as a puff of political smoke. Regarding his name as a temporary rallying point that would vanish as soon as the Stalwart managers reached a consensus concerning the most acceptable challenger to Blaine, the Half-Breeds concluded that the former president would fade from the scene well in advance of the national convention in Chicago on June 2.

This was a misinterpretation of the signs. Grant was fronting for no one; he was the Stalwarts' bona fide choice. Blaine's supporters in Centre County misconstrued the facts so badly that they compromised the five to one superiority that Blaine held over all other Republicans in their district by unanimously selecting General James A. Beaver, a Grant supporter, as a delegate to the GOP convention. A four-time casualty of Civil War fighting, and an amputee, Beaver was already being groomed in certain parts of the state as a nominee for governor in 1882. His endorsers were guided by two regional objectives; not only did his selection as delegate give the district's gubernatorial hopeful a political visibility before Republican leaders throughout the Commonwealth, but it also meant that Centre County was represented by a man with a distinguished military record and a spotless character. Focusing on these local objectives and overlooking the seriousness of the Grant candidacy, the Centre County Republicans were not perturbed by Beaver's presidential pronouncement. "I am for General Grant," Beaver insisted. "If I am chosen, I will not go back on my old commander, as long as he is a candidate before the Convention." Beaver's second choice was Blaine. Centre County Republicans were convinced that Beaver would be forced to retreat to this secondary position because the name of Grant would inevitably be withdrawn. As the convention drama unfolded, however, Beaver was never freed from his primary commitment. Ironically, he was elected chairman of the Pennsylvania delegation, and his steadfast support of Grant ultimately assisted in the defeat of Blaine while greatly enhancing his own public image.[10]

Throughout January 1880 the Blaine followers complained bitterly because the state convention was being held earlier than ever before. They bemoaned their inability to identify and campaign for convention representatives committed to Blaine within the time allotted. Cameron rejected all pleas to reschedule the convention and thereby assured Stalwart domination. With its delegates almost unanimously committed to Grant, Pennsylvania became the first state to declare a presidential preference. New York quickly endorsed this action, and with the two largest blocs of votes in the national convention corralled, a third-term nomination for the Union general seemed inevitable.[11]

When the national convention opened in Chicago, Donald Cameron stepped to the podium to preside. General Beaver swung from his crutches to the aisle seat of honor for his state. The Pennsylvania delegation was controlled, however, from the second seat, where Matt Quay was speaking for Cameron. When Conkling and Logan positioned themselves prominently within their state delegations, the stage was set for a Stalwart drama that never completely unfolded. To Cameron the plot was simple enough: "We have three hundred to start with, and we will stick until we win." By this he implied that his faction expected to capture the additional seventy-eight votes necessary for a majority, but his analysis was only two parts correct. The drama collapsed on the third. Although the Stalwarts had packed the convention with 300 delegates and although these delegates, in turn, were uncompromising in their support of Grant's candidacy, this reactionary effort failed because of an inability to expand their delegate strength.[12]

The Stalwarts, properly prepared to take on Blaine, were upstaged by a politically unknown Philadelphia banker, Wharton Barker, who was determined that the nomination should go to Garfield. An Independent with no credentials as a political strategist, Barker had visited Garfield in February 1880 and attempted to convince him to become an active candidate. Realizing that he could procure the nomination only through a convention deadlock, Garfield not only refused to throw his political hat into the ring, but was also unwilling to maneuver to achieve such an impasse. Barker ignored this reaction and proceeded as though he were sponsoring a willing candidate. His spirit was not dampened even when Garfield agreed to nominate John

Sherman for the presidency. Convinced that he could do more for Garfield than Garfield could do for himself, Barker simply wanted to be free to plot. In a sense Garfield's open declaration to support Sherman contributed to Barker's strategy because it indicated that the Half-Breeds were not united behind Blaine and that there was a bloc not committed to either Blaine or the Stalwarts. On the other hand, with Garfield managing Sherman's bid for the nomination, any attempt by Barker to have Garfield nominated from the floor would of necessity have prompted the Ohio congressman to forbid the use of his name. In order to circumvent this certainty and also place Garfield's name before the convention, Barker persuaded a lone Pennsylvania delegate to vote for Garfield in the early balloting. In time he also persuaded James McManes of Philadelphia to show his independence of the Cameron organization by having the delegates whom he personally controlled defy both the Grant instructions and the unit rule.[13]

Ballot after ballot the Republicans voted on without either Grant or Blaine demonstrating much progress toward a majority. Finally the Blaine bloc began to weaken. On the thirty-fourth ballot delegate sentiment drifted cautiously from Blaine to Garfield, gathered momentum on the next, and crested on the thirty-sixth, which gave Garfield the nomination. Such a realignment was necessary to break the stalemate, because the Stalwarts had held firm. They ended where they entered, with approximately three hundred votes, a display of steadfast loyalty unprecedented in the annals of American party conventions. The intensity of their common struggle engendered an intimacy that prompted the group to retain its identity long after the battle on the convention floor. Those voting for Grant on the final ballot became known as the "Immortal 306"; they developed an embryonic organization of their own and held annual dinners. In 1893, Thomas Platt, reflecting on that heroic struggle, identified Quay and Logan as the group's most distinguished leaders. Justifying the Stalwarts' stand, he pointed out that "the result of thirteen years of demoralization, mingled with defeat, has confirmed the wisdom of our choice."[14]

Outwardly the Stalwarts seemed to accept Garfield. Conkling, Logan, and Beaver all spoke in behalf of a motion to make the nomination unanimous, but their unity sentiments had a hollow ring. General Beaver, in his endorsement speech, recalled for the delegates that his state had the distinction of first bringing Garfield's name before the convention, but in the interest of his own position wisely skirted the circumstances under which it had been done. He assured the nation at large that Pennsylvania was heartily in accord with the nomination and predicted that his state's majority for Garfield would be the greatest given a presidential nominee in many years. To observers of the political scene, this was a shallow boast without any basis in fact. Although repeatedly Republican, the Keystone State had not registered particularly large majorities for presidential candidates. The margin of victory had steadily declined with each election after 1860 with the exception of 1872 when the Democratic party offered only token resistance.[15]

Personally disheartened by their failure to nominate Grant and publicly chided for their achievement in sidetracking the more popular Blaine, these Stalwart leaders could generate little enthusiasm for the election campaign. On the final convention ballot, Pennsylvania Republicans had been badly split, casting thirty-seven votes for Grant and twenty-one for Garfield. With Cameron, Quay, and Beaver all numbered among the Immortal 306, they could not expect to be in the inner circle of the next national administration, even if Garfield was elected in November. Confronted with such prospects, the Republican state organization had difficulty in mounting a vigorous campaign focused on the head of the ticket, but Garfield picked up 51 percent of the state's popular vote. In the contests for the state senate, the state house of representatives, and the U.S. Congress, the Republicans were more decisively triumphant. Garfield was carried to his narrow victory in Pennsylvania on the coattails of relatively obscure local politicians.

From Limelight to Twilight

As one of the more transparent displays of the local character of American politics, this presidential contest left Keystone Republicans sharply divided. The Stalwarts had obviously failed, but the extent of their setback was not apparent until the disclosure that Blaine would head the Department of State. He had campaigned vigorously for Garfield and fully expected to become the president-elect's chief adviser on all important issues, both foreign and domestic. The Stalwarts viewed Blaine as much a victor as if he had won the election and moved into the White House. In anticipation of further affronts from the Garfield administration, the Pennsylvania Stalwarts recognized the necessity to regroup and expected to manipulate the state legislature toward this end, but the Half-Breeds were unwilling to rest with their partial success. They wanted at least the same sense of victory within the state that had been achieved at the national level, where they had forced the acceptance of a respected compromise candidate.

The first postelection contest came in the 1881 session of the legislature, where the priority assignment was the election of a U.S. senator. The Stalwarts planted themselves firmly behind Henry W. Oliver of Pittsburgh. But the Half-Breeds commanded enough votes to prevent a majority and stubbornly refused to permit Cameron's Stalwart machine to name his colleague. A marathon struggle covering seven weeks and thirty-five ballots ensued. Not perceiving that the Half-Breed force was immovable, Donald Cameron vowed on January 27 that there would be no compromise. Shortly thereafter his Stalwarts, desperate to adhere to his dictum, switched their allegiance from Oliver to General Beaver, but to Cameron's embarrassment the Half-Breeds remained adamantly opposed. In their determination to show rank-and-file members of the party, as well as the general public, that the Stalwarts had lost their power to appoint a senator, the Half-Breeds continued their uninterrupted endorsement of Galusha Grow. The Democrats, on the other hand, smugly looked on as these factions clawed at each other, and dutifully voted for William Wallace for senator every time the Republicans wanted to try again to break the deadlock.

During the protracted debate Quay wrote several letters to the president-elect in an effort to enlist his good offices in settling the issue and thereby prevent the factions from pulling the state's Republican party completely apart. He hoped to placate one faction with the Senate seat and the other with a cabinet position, but Garfield, either preoccupied or skeptical, refused to be drawn into the controversy. Trying to convince Garfield of the necessity to act, Quay wrote: "As you are doubtless aware, the condition of political affairs in Pennsylvania is not gratifying to any who have at heart the success of the Republican party and the welfare of the incoming administration." More specifically, Quay proposed that Galusha Grow be appointed to the cabinet. This solution would have dealt the Senate seat to the Stalwarts who could then claim victory in the battle that had raged for weeks in the legislature and in the partisan press. Garfield's failure to respond to Quay's plea for intervention forced the Stalwarts to admit another defeat. Without any compensating recognition in return, they submitted on February 22 to the senatorial appointment of a confirmed Half-Breed, Congressman John I. Mitchell of Tioga County.[16]

Simultaneously New York Stalwarts were experiencing similar political indignities. Garfield stabbed at the heart of Conkling's empire by proposing one of Blaine's men to be collector of customs in New York City. Having aided materially in swinging the states of New York and Indiana to Garfield in the November election, "Lord Roscoe" felt that he had earned the right to retain control of domestic appointments in New York. He interpreted the president's action as base ingratitude. When the Democrats offered to make enough votes available to the administration to assure confirmation of the appointment in the Senate, Conkling and his colleague, Thomas Platt, in an unprecedented act of defiance against the president, resigned from the Senate. They fully expected the New York legislature to rise in righteous indignation, reelect both to the Senate, and thereby demonstrate the power of Platt and Conkling, in contrast to that of the president, in the largest Republican state.[17]

Before the legislature could react, the Conkling scheme was doomed by two bullets from the gun of Charles Guiteau, hitting President Garfield in the back as he strolled across the Union Station plaza in Washington on July 2, 1881. A disappointed office seeker, Guiteau shouted: "I am a Stalwart, and Arthur is President now." Capitalizing on this remark, certain Half-Breed leaders referred to their Republican rivals in the years immediately following this mortal attack on the president as "Guiteau Stalwarts."[18]

The incident prompted two responses from the American public: a clamor for reform which culminated in the Pendleton Civil Service Act of 1883 and a discrediting of leaders such as Conkling and Platt who were prominently involved in the patronage controversy at the time of the tragedy. Public reaction to the assassination not only precluded the reelection of the state's senators—Conkling forever and Platt for sixteen years—but also disrupted the state's Republican organization. Nationally the party's factions were again transposed. The four-year lease on the White House that the Half-Breeds had won in 1880 was reduced to less than seven months by the assassin's fatal shots. Arthur, a Stalwart, was president, and Blaine resigned from the State Department before the new chief executive had an opportunity to fire him. To Pennsylvania the changeover meant that once again the president of the United States responded to Cameron commands. In a fruitless effort to prevent renewal of the practice permitting the Cameron machine to dominate politics in the Keystone State, Senator Mitchell appealed to the president to withhold the appointments requested by Cameron in the interest of party harmony. Loyal to his Stalwart colleague, Arthur replied that he had been a practical politician for twenty-five years and neither understood nor appreciated "abstract politics."[19]

The gravity of the intraparty strife that continued to plague the Republicans became more discernible in 1882. With more significant offices at stake than in the previous year, their disunity was dramatically exposed to public view. In all the large states of the North and West called upon to elect governors that year (New York, Pennsylvania, Massachusetts, Connecticut, Michigan, and California), the Democrats prevailed. In Ohio, Indiana, and Illinois, where there were no gubernatorial elections, the Democrats recorded significant gains. Fundamentally this trend reflected a reaction to machine domination by the Republican party; more specifically, injuries suffered in the machine's collision with the Half-Breeds during the 1880 campaign remained not only unhealed but aggravated.[20]

Pennsylvania Republicans were not exempt from any of the symptoms afflicting the party nationally. For two years General Beaver, linked with the Immortal 306, was rumored as a likely gubernatorial nominee. Painfully aware of his background and sensitive to the political drift, many of the Half-

Breeds, or Independents, as they preferred to be known, found him suspect. In early 1882 when Donald Cameron announced his support of Beaver for governor, he provided the Independents with a definable target, and they concentrated their attack on him even before the state convention. Cameron's action made Quay apprehensive, and he tried to silence the Half-Breeds by declaring his preference for Galusha Grow. Considering it unwise to have a nominee identified so early and "paraded in the newspapers as the candidate of any leading politician or any clique of politicians," he was skeptical of a Beaver victory in the general election as early as April 1882. At the same time he realized that the Beaver bandwagon had gathered so much momentum among rank-and-file Republicans that it would be difficult to derail without public embarrassment. He estimated that only "a violent exertion of boss power" could displace Beaver, but fully recognized that the Stalwarts were already unpopular because of heavy-handed tactics.[21]

Quay was more of an opportunist than Cameron. Not wishing to reveal his choice for any office until he had received all available data pertaining to the candidate's qualifications for victory, Quay preferred to delay official endorsements as long as possible. He therefore indicated a preference for Grow, a perennial choice among Republicans of the northern tier and the previous year's Half-Breed candidate for the Senate. In all probability Quay was not seriously committed to Grow, but would have endorsed him fully if he believed he could win. Cameron could not make this kind of pragmatic decision. Grow was definitely not a member of the Cameron machine, and the senator could view him only as an enemy, perhaps more despicable than a Democrat because he had the temerity to use the Republican highway without a Cameron license.

Grounded in the premise that change should originate at the top, Cameron was a true oligarch. His uncompromising insistence on complete loyalty by all party candidates placed him in an untenable position. Quay, on the other hand, had no such commitment to any organizational theory. He was more strategist than disciplinarian. Determined to win by adapting to prevailing circumstances, he was considered to be closer to the people. He understood that for a party's continued vitality its leadership must identify and respond to ground swells among the rank-and-file. This conviction was derived not from pure democratic principles, but from a clear political understanding of the nature of power. Identifying the insurgence of the Half-Breeds as such a movement, Quay quietly ignored Cameron's preference and dangled the olive branch, in the form of Grow's nomination, before the Independents, whose partial cooperation was essential to a Republican gubernatorial victory. Quay knew that in a political machine, as in a mechanical one, friction was the enemy of power. His plan always was to eliminate rather than combat the enemies in his path, and frequently he did so by accepting them into the full fellowship of his camp. Although such converts could deceive or betray him later, he believed that it was part of the game of politics to take that chance. Unable to convince Cameron that the magnanimous tactics of absorption and assimilation really succeed and should at least be considered every time new enemies appear, Quay lost the argument in 1882.[22]

In the interest of binding up party wounds, Quay also took the initiative to arrange a conference of five Independents and a similar number from the Cameron-Quay machine at the Continental Hotel in Philadelphia on May 1, 1882. In the quest for "practical results," this group achieved only a limited understanding. The Stalwarts agreed to concessions in party rules and regulations, but evaded the more controversial issue of candidates for the forthcoming election. Since the delegates to the May 10 state convention had already been selected and were largely of the Cameron stripe, the slate was a foregone conclusion. With Beaver at the head, it would inevitably have a distinct Stalwart cast, and there would be no visible gains for the Independents.

Miffed that he had not been one of the Independent conferees appointed by Senator Mitchell and angered that the conferees had been trapped into accepting such minor concessions, Frank Willing Leach, who had worked full-time for many months for the Independent cause, called a statewide Independent convention to challenge the Stalwarts openly. The idea of such a convention had been under discussion since January. When the Independents gathered on May 24, it was clear that the five who had conferred with the Stalwarts did not accurately reflect the mood of their estimated fifty thousand constituents. As a body, they repudiated the harmony effort as merely an agreement in which Cameron's "power over the good things of this world would be acquiesced in by the rebellious spirits." Mitchell threw out the Half-Breed challenge: "We must fight or sit idly by and see Guiteau Stalwart notions realized." He had been encouraged by a conversation with Blaine whose "whole heart is with the movement" and whose convictions in behalf of the Pennsylvania uprising were so strong that he promised to "take the stump were it necessary and helpful."[23]

Under the leadership of Mitchell, Leach, and Barker, the convention nominated state senator John Stewart for the governorship. Realizing that a Civil War background enhanced a candidate's image and that Beaver was a disabled veteran, Leach guided the Independents in selecting a slate designed to checkmate the Stalwarts' appeal to military heroes. The four statewide candidates—governor, lieutenant governor, secretary of internal affairs, and congressman-at-large—were all veterans, two of whom had lost legs in the war. Leach pointed out that the Independents could go the Stalwarts one better or one less, depending on one's perspective, because their candidates together had one leg fewer; Leach bizarrely remarked that 1882 was literally a "stumping" tour for three of the candidates.[24]

The goal of the Independents was clear. They wanted to be Republicans with pride, not members of a party "owned" by the Camerons. Subscribing to the theory that the situation had to get worse before it could get better, they nominated candidates to compete with those selected by the Cameron-dominated convention in order to divert enough regular Republican votes to permit a Democratic victory and bury boss rule before the end of the year. The first phase of their plan worked perfectly; Robert E. Pattison was elected the first Democratic governor since the Civil War. But boss rule was not dead, only contained until it could be remodeled.[25]

Quay had expected the Independents' solidarity to crack in the course of the campaign. Personally scanning the political horizon for any indication of an Independent lapse, he also alerted Beaver to this contingency and assured him that, if such a weakness were detected, "the machine [was] armed and ready" to roll; but none became obvious. Instead, a breakdown within the ranks of the regular Republicans further curtailed the prospects of victory. In the final month of the campaign, Governor Hoyt, elected primarily because of Quay's skillful management, unexpectedly endorsed the Independent nominee. To register his displeasure and recoup what he could for the regular Republicans, Quay immediately resigned his position as secretary of the Commonwealth. But the advantage of both time and tide was with the Independents. In addition to Pattison, the Democrats elected the lieutenant governor (Chauncey F. Black), a supreme court judge, the secretary of internal affairs, the congressman-at-large, and a majority of the representatives in the lower house of the legislature.[26]

Out of office, disgusted with his Republican colleagues, and uncertain of his political future, Quay temporarily withdrew from the political limelight. In need of rest, relaxation, and a new political perspective, he spent most of the year following the election fishing in Atlantic City and Florida. When he returned to Harrisburg, he refused to be drawn into the political battle, declaring that he was better versed on alligators than on the state's Republican party. Although no one believed him, newspaper reporters and politicians discovered that it required a major "fishing" expedition just to learn that Quay had no comment. In the absence of fact, rumor took over. Quay reportedly had abandoned politics and returned to the field of journalism. One account had him editing a Philadelphia paper and another placed him at the head of the *Harrisburg Telegraph*. But anyone who understood the man knew that the lure of politics was too compelling for him to be resigned to an editor's desk.[27]

In 1883 Quay skirmished only briefly in the political arena. Endorsing an Independent for state treasurer before a Cameron nominee was selected, he was soundly defeated, perhaps so soundly that the incident must not be evaluated merely in terms of the votes cast. Obviously not interested in playing a major role in Republican affairs that year, he may actually have been indifferent to the treasury candidate, desiring only to win the confidence of the Independent masses. Quay made a special effort to identify with the Independents in Philadelphia. A reform group headed by the Committee of One Hundred had drafted a new city charter, known as the Bullitt Bill, designed to combat the heavy hand of political bosses on the governmental affairs of the city. Quay startled Independents everywhere by turning up in Harrisburg to marshal support for the reform charter.[28] Although the legislature did not find time to consider this measure before the session adjourned, Quay had an opportunity to declare again his conciliatory spirit. After the state elections, he praised the Independents and acknowledged their assistance in the Republican victory, which he interpreted as their attempt to show resentment for the Democratic administration that they had helped to create in 1882. Declaring that the Independents were back in the Republican fold, he admitted in one of his rare newspaper interviews that they would remain only as long as the party deserved their support. He again had special words of praise for the Philadelphia Independents: "An Independent Republican organization that can whirl around 20,000 votes in a table of election returns, and especially one that is not a mere sudden tide of politics, but deals in practical municipal reform, is an admonition to the Republican Party that wise backers will respect."[29]

During this politically inactive year, Quay moved his family back to Beaver. Since he had lived there prior to being named recorder for the city of Philadelphia in 1878, there was no political significance attached to this decision, but for those who knew Quay, there should have been. The following year he shocked the local citizenry by announcing that he was a candidate for Congress from the three-county district of Beaver, Washington, and Lawrence. His potential rivals charged that at best he would be a nonresident congressman, but he promised otherwise: "I am a resident and a voter of the borough of Beaver and have made my last move this side of the cemetery."[30]

After winning Republican endorsement for the congressional seat, Quay suffered defeat in the general election. That was his only political involvement in 1884 except for a brief excursion to the party's state convention, where his participation seemed at the time to be confused and out of political character. Instead of the machine lieutenant maneuvering to mount a ground swell or to prevent one, he cast himself in the role of a sincere "loner" vitally interested in discovering popular sentiment regarding the most qualified presidential nominee.[31]

Having assessed the wreckage of the Cameron machine, he was already weighing the advantages of repair versus replacement. His keen sense of political awareness had also taught him that the time for a public declaration had not yet arrived. Even if his plans and convictions had crystallized, this was the time to follow, not to lead. The mood of rank-and-file Republicans was such that they alone should determine the destiny of their party at this crossroads. Quay understood. He was content to show interest rather than commitment. At one point he declared that it was appropriate for the Pennsylvania delegation to endorse Blaine (as it ultimately did). But he was not about to lead the convention to such a decision. At the same time he declared a personal preference for Arthur, hastening to add that such a statement should not be interpreted to mean that he necessarily favored his nomination. To the extent that he registered any preference once the convention formally assembled, it was in behalf of the incumbent. He spoke favorably about him to fellow delegates, but not enthusiastically enough to want to attend the national convention. This was the only convention that he missed between 1872 and his death in 1904; his decision not to be identified with the national convention and campaign was a political calculation. On the judicious assumptions that the prospects for a Republican victory were doubtful under any circumstances and that the nomination of Blaine, which he could afford neither to oppose nor endorse, was almost inevitable, he deferred to the less astute.

Time proved both assumptions correct. Blaine was nominated, and the Republicans were defeated by Grover Cleveland and the Democrats in November. With this final blow the rivalry between Stalwarts and Half-Breeds crumpled into nothingness; both were out of power. The twelve-year controversy over Blaine's fitness for the presidency ended in defeat for both pro and con factions. The assassination of Garfield and the midterm reverses in 1882 finally forced the Stalwarts to submit to the Half-Breeds' choice. Platt accurately summed up the Stalwart capitulation when he seconded Blaine's nomination: "Believing as I do, that his turn has come . . . [and] believing as I do, that the Republican people of the Republican states that must give the Republican majorities want him," the New York Stalwart delivered his faction's blessing.[32] Blaine's nomination nevertheless was a Pyrrhic victory because the voting public rejected him in November. After three successive presidential campaigns of turmoil, the factions had at last succeeded in destroying each other.

Reflecting on this outcome, Quay lamented that the lofty motives that had drawn the North into the Civil War had now been shunted aside or at least severely compromised. In an address prepared for a Pittsburgh audience, he placed this first presidential victory for the Democrats since Buchanan in a decidedly sectional perspective: "The sod is thick on the graves of the Union and Confederate dead. Their widows and orphans have put aside the veil of mourning. A Democratic President sits in the seat of Lincoln elected by the votes of the States recently in rebellion. There are Confederate soldiers in the cabinet—there are no Union soldiers there. Confederate officers sit in both branches of Congress and represent us at foreign courts. What was not accomplished by the bullet has been accomplished . . . by the ballot."[33]

The Unofficial Government
1884-1895

ON these ruins the Republicans had to rebuild, and Quay had prepared himself to be the design engineer. Schooled in the fundamentals of the political arts and capable of in-depth analysis of political variables, he contributed more than any other individual to the new model of the political machine that emerged in the late eighties and remained politically fashionable for more than a generation. Relatively isolated from the Republican debacle in 1884 and less of a political villain in his home state than Cameron, Quay was in a strategic position to take command, and he seized the opportunity.

As both Camerons had learned from their business ventures, an organization functions most efficiently under centralized leadership. Convinced of Quay's political savoir faire, and comforted by the knowledge that he did not possess the financial independence to stray far from their principles, they accepted without challenge his move to assume domination of Pennsylvania's Republican party. In time Quay developed his own source of funds, but the Cameron trust was well placed. He never prevented them from sharing fully in the spoils that his innovative techniques produced. This cooperative spirit may have been fostered by gratitude, but, given Quay's instincts for good politics, any other course would have been unthinkable. To brush the Camerons aside would have disrupted the party, and there was no need for that. There were enough spoils for all.

Boss Rule in Transition

In a preliminary review of the crisis, Quay assessed the characteristics—particularly the weaknesses—of the obviously obsolete machine that

Cameron and the other Senate bosses had operated since the Civil War. He concluded that a power base in the central government was too vulnerable for effective boss rule. The system under which such senatorial oligarchs as Cameron, Conkling, Zachariah Chandler, Oliver P. Morton, and John A. Logan labored was founded on patronage wrung from Grant almost at will. Having come to the presidency as a military conqueror with few political ideas and nothing that could pass as a political philosophy, Grant relied so heavily on those trained in political warfare that he surrendered the function of his office almost unconditionally to their demands. Because he had a simplistic view of government, he conceded all policymaking responsibilities to the Congress and looked upon the presidency as a purely administrative office.[1]

On many occasions these bosses merely advised the president of their needs, suggested how they might be met, and promptly received satisfaction. Only so long as the president responded to such petitions did the state and regional machines run smoothly; dependence upon presidential cooperation was paramount. No one appreciated this better than Simon Cameron, who for years had been an overachiever in the school of federal patronage. Assessors, internal revenue collectors, marshals, attorneys, and numerous lesser officials owed their positions to his personal dictates. In the time of Grant, there was not one anti-Cameron appointee from Pennsylvania at the federal level. Even the president's appointment of Curtin as minister to Russia was a positive stroke for Cameron: the president sent the senator's long-time antagonist into four years of political exile without further alienating the many Curtin loyalists across the state.[2]

In the hands of Grant's successors, however, this kind of party machine sputtered and by the mid-eighties stalled with a frequency that was alarming to the bosses. When Hayes took office, four cabinet positions went to opponents of the spoilsmen. William M. Evarts as secretary of state and Carl Schurz as secretary of the interior were both avowed enemies, while Charles Devens and David M. Key were considered less obstreperous foes. Key, in fact, was a Democrat, and all four had endorsed Liberal Republicans in 1872. In addition, Hayes had replaced a number of Grant appointees, who in reality were boss appointees, at the various patronage levels in order to develop a Republican party loyal to himself.[3]

When an independent Republican such as Hayes, or a Half-Breed such as Garfield, or a political opponent such as Cleveland was in the White House, this boss system might function, but Quay understood just how precarious the system was. Upset even by the reluctance of such a Stalwart Republican as President Chester Arthur to dole out adequate patronage to Pennsylvania, he once grumbled: "Arthur has a great many apples in his basket. If he is not careful, some of them will rot on his hands."[4]

Only months were required to prove the accuracy of his prediction. Pennsylvania Stalwarts made it clear that their health could not be sustained on the number and size of "apples" that Arthur wished to dispense. The president and the Cameron machine were caught in a political stand-off. On the one hand, Arthur, who desired the 1884 presidential nomination, could not afford to antagonize the Blaine element of the party by appearing too charitable to the Cameron machine; on the other, the Pennsylvania Stalwarts could not gamble on endorsing Arthur without his full commitment to their needs because of Blaine's popularity in the Keystone State.

This impasse caused the Pennsylvania leaders to change their strategy radically from that of 1880. They "planned no desperate coup" for 1884 such as that foolishly undertaken in behalf of Grant four years earlier. Instead they realized that reliance on federal patronage had permitted national elections to disrupt their state organization, and that such a practice could no longer be tolerated. As 1884 approached, Blaine, not Arthur, was clearly the popular choice in Pennsylvania; neither Quay nor Cameron considered it expedient to pit "the Cameron interest against the Blaine sentiment." That would disturb the uneasy peace achieved with the state's reformers after the 1882 debacle. The machine was still in the process of regaining control and dared not ignore public pressure.[5]

With the 1884 state convention decidedly pro-Blaine, Quay moved decisively to prevent a Blaine nomination from splitting the party again. He arranged, without contest, to surrender the office of temporary chairman to the Blaine forces, and in return, enough Blaine advocates sponsored a Cameron lieutenant, Thomas V. Cooper, for reelection to the state committee chairmanship to ensure his victory. This compromise preserved control of the state's political machinery in Cameron hands. Quay was willing to acquiesce in the nomination of Blaine and accept defeat at the national level in order to retain state control. This tactic had long been a key to good political strategy; it kept the state boss strong so that the Stalwarts might contend again another day on both the state and national scenes. Unable to alter the Blaine trend and unwilling to be identified with it, Cameron and Quay were conspicuously absent from the 1884 national convention and the inevitable nomination of their archenemy.[6]

In addition to a sympathetic president, a nationally based "boss-dom" needed congressional support. Although the Stalwart bosses themselves dominated the standing committees of the Senate and could stymie almost any piece of proposed legislation, this control was at best a negative asset; generally the cooperation of the House was required to achieve positive action. In the years between 1868 and 1884, the House was more often anti- than pro-Stalwart in composition. Any attempt to revise the tariff, set conditions for the sale of public land, or grant subsidies to private enterprise required more political muscle than the Senate bosses collectively could muster. The Pendleton Civil Service Act of 1883 also signaled further change; the availability of spoils at the national level was systematically being reduced. Where the trend would taper off was not certain, but to the practical mind of Matt Quay a system of boss rule dependent upon tap roots in Washington had lost the security and power that it once possessed.[7]

Quay's reaction to this political drift was not to repair the Cameron machine, but to design a new model that shifted the locus of power from Washington to the individual states. In his blueprint, federal patronage became subordinate to the power sources in the states that had been the focal units of party power prior to the era of the Stalwart bosses. Quay sought to return political emphasis to its normal channel. In the process he revised the functions of his party organization and made it more responsive to the demands of an expanding and increasingly industrial economy. In Pennsylvania, Quay personally became the connecting link between the "interests" and legislative approval of their growing demands. Both businessmen and social service agencies welcomed a leader who could end the chronic discord that disrupted the flow of legislation and appropriations in which they were vitally interested. They looked with satisfaction on the appearance of a central source to which they could turn to receive a desired franchise, amend a limiting charter, push an added appropriation, initiate a preferential bill, or energize a recalcitrant committee chairman. Quay planned to be such a political broker because he knew that control of such services represented a firm foundation on which to build his empire.[8]

Corporate interests, as well as a burgeoning number of utility and traction companies, viewed a state boss as the most direct route to legislation and protection. The reputable and disreputable alike had to have their grist ground at the state mill, and miller Quay, in turn, had to have a myriad of groups dependent upon his services so that he could put together the combinations necessary to force acceptance of the requests of all, or nearly all, his clients. Thus appropriations to hospitals, school districts, penal institutions, charitable societies, and asylums became an integral part of the system, along with the needs of railroads, iron and steel, oil, and other corporate interests. By controlling the appropriation committees of the state house and senate, Quay influenced the flow of funds to public institutions. Their allocations were regarded as allowances granted by a watchful parent who would withhold part, or all, of an institution's share if the legislators and others primarily interested in it did not play the logrolling game according to his rules.[9] Lawmakers working in behalf of a particular institution or program quickly discovered that legislative enactment did not depend upon either the quality of the program or the availability of funds. Quay injected himself between proposals and their approval by the legislature, and from that vantage point he exacted a price—the commitment of the interested legislators to other issues important to him—before clearing their measure for passage. Businessmen, however, paid in dollars for Quay's services. They were actually relieved that there was an efficient and effective broker to receive their money, distribute it judiciously, and assure the desired results. In previous years there had been no such middleman, and the railroad interests had disbursed funds to legislators through their own agents only to be embarrassed by both legislative failure and public disclosure.

Quay's pivotal position in the overall legislative structure rested squarely on his ability to deliver. Business support presumed that he possessed the ability to guide to enactment the legislation for which he accepted private and corporate funds. Actual success depended on control of crucial committees and that, in turn, could result only from the proper makeup of the legislature. In previous years that body had not always purred at the command of Cameron and his lieutenants because they lacked adequate control over essential parts of the political machinery. To relieve that uncertainty required a major monetary infusion, relatively independent of the business interests, that would permit Quay to buy political support from party members just as the corporate interests had bought his good offices. In short, Quay's political empire was built on a mastery over those directly and indirectly concerned with legislation and a seemingly limitless supply of money.

Quay's indefatigable and methodical attention to detail both in record-keeping and in personal surveillance brought individual legislators, both Republicans and others, under close scrutiny. Not content to judge them on their Harrisburg voting records alone, he instructed his subordinates to study the political conduct of legislators in their local communities. From information derived through these two sources, the Quay leaders divided the opposition into two categories: those who were forceful and incorruptible and those who were nonentities. The first group was vigorously opposed in all subsequent elections, and the others were treated with indifference, entitled only to a brief character evaluation filed in Quay's private records. This analysis became the basis not only for consigning campaign funds, but also for determining in advance legislative opposition that would have to be overcome or neutralized.[10]

More insidious than these evaluations of individual politicians were the card files known as "Quay's coffins." As factually accurate as his trusted investigators could make them, these files contained records of all favors granted and all services rendered to each individual, as well as any indiscretions of a political or personal nature that would embarrass the subject. The fundamental purpose of these closely guarded secrets was "to clinch the requests which the wily old leader had in mind" from time to time. Successful results appeared in various forms: silence from vociferous reformers, endorsement from recalcitrant legislators, financial commitment from skeptical businessmen, acquiescence from traditional opponents. When the legislature convened or a convention assembled, Quay generally reserved a two-room hotel suite with connecting bath. Some visitors came of their own volition and others by invitation, but in either event he was prepared. The file drawers were set up in the bathroom in the care of a trusted clerk. Before going into either room to greet a guest, Quay stopped to consult the card file and refresh his memory. The visitor usually left committed to the Quay candidate or the Quay legislation.[11]

These card files, however, did not always possess the potent evidence essential to make a convert. Monetary bait might be needed. When added to the expense of maintaining lieutenants in all the towns and many of the hamlets of the Commonwealth, the need for a steady flow of funds became compelling. With this incentive Quay unveiled the political potential of the state treasury. Lax statutory regulations governing the handling of state funds simplified his task and even provided a choice of avenues through which funds could be siphoned from the treasury into the party coffers. Since state receipts were the responsibility of the state treasurer, who deposited them in private banks of his own choosing, he wielded both political and economic power. Because there was no regulation pertaining to interest on the consigned funds, banks were not asked to pay any, but they were more than willing to make other types of remuneration for the privilege of receiving state deposits. They eagerly competed for the opportunity: on a later occasion, when Quay himself was state treasurer, he received a letter from former Governor Hartranft asking him to appease a banker who complained that his consignment of state funds was limited to $15,000 while his two local competitors received $40,000 to $50,000 of interest-free money. Thus the state treasurer was often the key to a bank's success, and bankers made every effort to win his favor and that of his political allies.[12]

The office of state treasurer had been a storm center of suspicion and scandal since the Civil War. Quay had a general appreciation of the political value of the office when he first battled to unseat W. W. Irwin in favor of Robert Mackey. Since men of modest means who had assumed the office departed a few years later as wealthy individuals, the banks either rewarded them in some manner or they privately invested state funds and retained the profits.

How early Quay personally profited from the manipulation of state funds is not clear, but by 1880 he was involved in a major treasury scandal. J. Blake Walters, the cashier of the treasury, deposited worthless securities with several "pet" banks and retained the state money for a stock speculation with Quay and others. Since Walters and the state treasurer gave assurances that the funds would not be called for by the state until the worthless securities were exchanged for dollars, the banks considered this a minor concession to their benefactors. Unfortunately for all participants, the speculation failed miserably. The group's indebtedness exceeded its assets by more than a quarter million dollars; but this was a minor consequence when compared with a simultaneous political disruption. Samuel Butler, the anti-boss candidate, was elected state treasurer in 1880. He insisted upon an examination of all state accounts before assuming office, uncovered the worthless securities and unsecured notes in the favored banks, and demanded immediate restitution.[13]

Quay was at the brink of financial disaster and political despair. This was the most serious economic crisis of his career. Although he claimed to be unaware that Walters had dipped into the treasury, he accepted total responsibility for the restoration of all of the funds in question. After selling much of his private and personal property, he was still $100,000 short. Senator Donald Cameron came to his rescue and was repaid in full on May 19, 1886.[14]

The public accepted Quay's plea that Walters had acted without his knowledge, and his willingness to endure personal hardship in order to return the money won their sympathy—on which he capitalized at once. To Quay, an incurable gambler, politics was an exciting game in which the glittering stakes were won by the bold, the cool-headed, and the unscrupulous. In 1885, to prove the point, he suddenly announced his candidacy for state treasurer. This rash declaration was motivated, in part, by the fear that Cameron was freezing him out of his political domain. The general inference was that Christopher L. Magee of Pittsburgh was being groomed as his replacement to handle state politics for the Camerons. This was particularly noticeable in 1884 when Cameron, like Quay, elected to ignore the presidential campaign. On the eve of the Republican National Convention, Cameron departed for Europe, leaving a clue that could be interpreted variously. As a member of the national committee, he entrusted his proxy to Magee, not Quay. Although the latter had already decided not to attend the convention, he feared the interpretation that might be placed on Magee's designation and resolved to abandon the role of Cameron lieutenant and attempt to become a statewide leader in his own right. On the morning after the announcement that he would run for state treasurer, Frank Leach called on him to ask if the candidacy had any special significance. Quay, who was still in bed, pounded his elbow into the pillow, propped his head on his forearm, and blurted out: "It means a fight for self-protection and self-preservation."[15]

Quay wanted to be named U.S. Senator in January 1887 in order to gain a status equal to Cameron's, but before he could expect a favorable nod from the legislature, he had to master the Republican state organization. The most conclusive evidence of this power was direct control of the treasury purse strings, but with the scars of 1882 still visible in certain areas, such a lunge for power raised the possibility of another Independent revolt. Quay understood this, but also realized that only heroic action could save him from political oblivion. He tested the political climate by visiting or writing many Independent leaders to ascertain their personal reactions to his candidacy. One of his most outspoken critics was Wharton Barker, who viewed Quay's bid for this crucial office as "a reconstruction of the Cameron machine" and a renewal of a direct attack on the philosophy of the Independents. Surprisingly, this was a minority opinion among the Independents. Like the general public, these leaders were satisfied with Quay's restoration of the treasury funds and agreed either to endorse him openly or quietly acquiesce in his candidacy. Although some eyebrows were raised, he was nominated and elected without serious challenge. But Barker was partially correct— expecting to remain in command, the Camerons rejoiced in the victory. After the nomination, Simon Cameron, the grand old Stalwart himself, predicted the general election outcome and told Quay, "You earned it . . . by your unselfish services to the Republican Party and the country in the last 25 years."[16]

With this election success the little colonial Treasury Building that stood at the north end of Capitol Hill in Harrisburg assumed new significance. It became the citadel of Quay's power, sharing responsibility for the action that took place under the big dome. While governors and legislators directed the affairs of Pennsylvania on one side of the street, Quay manipulated the affairs of governors and legislators on the other. The power of the treasury often elected the officials who came to Harrisburg and just as often dispatched them to their homes when they ceased to fulfill the purposes that Quay and his Harrisburg ring had designed for them. The treasury made and unmade men; by juggling the state's millions, it could arrange personal successes or frame personal tragedies. A remorseful Blake Walters, for example, distraught over his implication with Quay in the 1880 scandal, was the first—but not the last—suicide victim of treasury manipulations. The political and personal fruits were so tempting that many, unsuspectingly or otherwise, were brought under the spell of the treasury. Quay's position, more than that of any other, depended on this control, and he was once quoted as saying: "I don't mind losing a governorship or a legislature now and then, but I always need the state treasuryship."[17]

There were various formulas by which the state funds farmed out to the banks were converted to political capital. For banks engaged in small-scale operations, the most common was the payment of a "substitute-interest" to the state treasurer or to Quay or to both. Quay was apparently drawing on such funds when he replied to a request by A. L. Conger of Ohio in 1889. Admitting that he had no party funds to allocate to Conger's state and no available source to tap, he generously concluded that "if you are hard up for actual cash, you may draw on me for a thousand dollars at sight at the Beaver Deposit Bank. . . . This is my personal contribution to the cause of Governor Foraker."[18]

One option, more lucrative and more selective than the others, required banks to lend money without interest or without security or without either to designated politicians for investment purposes. Any bank enrolled in this particular plan was expected to advance approximately 50 percent of the state's deposits under one of these conditions, and in exchange it was free to invest the other 50 percent for its own profit. The bank was, however, confronted with one major hazard; its liability extended to the total state deposit because the politicians had no collateral. If their speculative venture failed, the bank was legally responsible for the loss. Quay personally subscribed to this plan under its most favorable conditions—no interest and no security. To minimize the risk of detection, most of his investment capital was procured through one source, the People's Bank of Philadelphia, an indispensable agent of his machine. Organized by politicians for politicians, this bank received more state funds on deposit than any other in the Commonwealth. The state's balance ranged from $300,000 to more than $1 million, reserved for the political speculators while school districts, hospitals, and state charities languished because of unpaid appropriations. According to estimates from Quay's enemies, an average of $5,000,000 per year in state funds was deposited in selected banks throughout Pennsylvania, with a conservative yield of $150,000 annually to the Quay machine.[19]

With this political mint at his disposal, Quay was the new proprietor of Pennsylvania. No longer a subordinate figure with a precarious future, he became a dominant force in party leadership and a central, though quiet, figure on the public stage. Master of his own political destiny, he was content to manage the state treasury personally only until he could procure a seat for himself in the U.S. Senate and turn over the care of the treasury to trusted lieutenants.

Before Quay could focus directly on the legislature's next senatorial appointment, in January 1887, he had to run the gauntlet of the gubernatorial and other state elections in 1886. Although not a candidate, he was definitely on trial; he was expected to lead the party to victory. Since this was the first election for governor after the Independents' uprising in 1882, which resulted in the election of a Democrat, a leader had to be able to reestablish Republican solidarity and carry the election in order to expect a senatorial reward from the legislature. As part of his daring move to capture the state treasury in 1885, Quay had secretly committed himself to the gubernatorial candidacy of General Beaver, who possessed both Stalwart and Independent antecedents. Not because of his qualifications or character but because of his selection by the Cameron machine, the Independents had opposed Beaver's nomination only four years earlier. Quay's foresight proved to have the accuracy of hindsight. Circumstances changed rapidly. Quay was able to shake off much of the Cameron image, and the voters responded with a strong ratification in the state treasury election. Both Beaver and Quay became wholly acceptable to the Independent element.[20]

Apparently having failed to comprehend Cameron's mistake in 1882, Beaver and a segment of his supporters were anxious to make his gubernatorial intentions public almost as soon as the 1885 election results were known, but Quay advised him otherwise:

> On no account do anything of this kind. Your policy is to stand aside and allow the procession to pass until the Convention is safely in hand—and then only to interfere in case a mistake is imminent.
>
> I may seem a little officious in my proffers of advice, but when I tell you that I am gravely alarmed about results next year [1886], and that I am personally interested as much, if not more, than yourself, I am certain you will pardon my anxiety. The next campaign will not be a walk among the roses, not by a _____ sight.[21]

With this explanation Quay inserted himself into the nomination and election campaigns. Suspecting that prohibition could become a platform issue, he scheduled a rump meeting of party leaders to agree tentatively on a platform before the state convention convened in order to prevent this sensitive issue from becoming divisive. Since the issue had arisen in this body in 1884, he was alert to the need for a ready solution because he could not dismiss it as he had done on that occasion. "I disposed of it by reference to a committee upon resolutions which had been discharged, [but know that] we can scarcely meet it that way this time." Aware of the danger in being identified with either side of the issue, he wrapped himself in the democratic cloak that he reserved for such occasions, declared his support for a popular referendum, and proclaimed: "Let the people speak in the manner provided by the Constitution."[22]

Quay moved into the election campaign not particularly confident of Beaver's discretion. With a friendly legislature and the possibility of a Senate seat for himself in the balance, he felt compelled to take charge. He counseled Beaver when to speak, when not to speak, and what subjects were appropriate for discussion. At one point the candidate was instructed to talk to a picnic of the Amalgamated Iron and Steel Association, and Quay expressed the hope that Beaver could appreciate the organization's "strength and intelligence." Beaver was informed, "There is no politics in the organization—you will be expected to talk *tariff* only unless I write you otherwise." In the first draft of the note he omitted "be expected to," but apparently decided to use less direct language. On another occasion a reporter appealed to Quay for a letter of introduction to the Republican nominee. Fearful of what Beaver might say in an informal interview, Quay scribbled a short note that he handed to the journalist in an unsealed envelope. Thinking that he had scooped his colleagues but curious to learn what Quay had written, the reporter opened the envelope and read: "Dear Beaver, Don't talk. M. S. Quay."[23]

Because of Quay's crafty management during the campaign, Beaver was elected, along with a Republican legislature. Harmony prevailed, and Quay was applauded. His name was immediately identified with the senatorial appointment to be made in January, and he did nothing to dispel the rumors. Although he fully expected such a reward, the party's Independent faction had other plans; both Galusha Grow and Wharton Barker coveted the appointment. Neither had a chance to carry the legislature, but the candidacy of both sealed the fate of both. Barker in particular had expected the endorsement because during the campaign Quay had promised to support him if the local leaders in Philadelphia concurred. Believing that he had such an endorsement, Barker urged Quay to make a public announcement that he was not a candidate for the U.S. Senate under the threat of Independent reprisals: "I am sure you do not forget that the peace between the Republican factions was on the basis of loyal adherence to political agreements," Barker reminded him, before warning that "there can be no party action when the leaders do not keep faith with each other. Of course, you do not want to be the first to break faith."[24]

Quay knew what Barker did not: the Philadelphia bosses, suspicious of the latter's motives, would not support him if the alternative was politically palatable. The Republican caucus overwhelmingly supported Quay, the legislature agreed, and he stepped onto the national stage. In surveying freshman senators elected to that Fiftieth Congress, *Harper's Weekly* accurately predicted that this was not just another senator from Pennsylvania: "He is a man whose influence on national party politics may become marked, as he has an aptitude for managment joined with much experience of its practical methods."[25]

In the Galaxy of the Bosses

Harper's not only assessed Quay's qualities accurately, but also understood that management techniques and practical skills were imperatives for political success by the mid-1880s. With the expansion of the public service concept of government following the Civil War, the battle for control of jobs became more factious. During the Grant years patronage was recognized as the great senatorial emolument, but when his less cooperative successors presided over job disbursement, conditions changed drastically. State patronage once again became the cornerstone for both state and national power, and the political stakes became more lucrative than ever before.[26]

The efforts of nationally oriented leaders such as Matt Quay and Tom Platt of New York to exercise greater influence within their states did not go uncontested. But the challenge, primarily from urban areas that were changing dramatically in both size and character, was less severe in Pennsylvania than elsewhere in the Northeast. During the last four decades of the nineteenth century, all the other heavily populated states of that section—New York, New Jersey, Massachusetts, and Connecticut—were more urban than Pennsylvania.[27] Over these same years the populations of Boston and New York (including Brooklyn) expanded 124 and 157 percent, respectively, while Philadelphia recorded only a 92 percent rise. Moreover, every census from 1870 through 1900 demonstrated that the percentage of foreign-born inhabitants in Boston and New York was appreciably higher than in Philadelphia. The percentage of "foreign-borns" in both Boston and New York between the 1870 census and that of 1900 increased about 125 percent while in Philadelphia the increase was less than half that rapid (61 percent). As a result, Pennsylvania's deeply rooted traditions and her political structure were not shocked as severely either by urban growth in general or by the influx of immigrants as were those of the other large states in this area.[28]

Nevertheless, there was growth and change everywhere, and cities naturally turned to state governments to satisfy their socioeconomic needs, demanding as forcefully as they could that their requests be fulfilled. More liberal charters, additional revenues, tax redistribution (away from the corner saloon, for example, and toward the countryside), and assistance with utility and transportation projects were a few of the more urgent requests. In their efforts to achieve these goals, city leaders coveted the same state patronage as the holders of national office who were relying primarily on legislators from the countryside to maintain their positions.[29] Throughout the final three decades of the century, cities remained at a disadvantage in this competition. Although major urban centers increased rapidly in population, the states remained predominantly rural. In 1870, for example, Boston represented only

17 percent of its state's population, Philadelphia 19, and New York 30 percent. State legislatures were stirred more with anger over the emerging urban-rural dichotomy than with sympathy for the uniqueness of the mounting city problems. They developed rather negative pictures of urban growth and with some success ignored the developments in their midst. As defenders of a more traditional America, rural legislators felt justified in this complacency. There was no incentive to enact special legislation for the troubled cities whose "insolent" leaders viewed rural residents as "hayseeds."[30]

The high incidence of crime, the mushrooming of urban ghettos, vast armies of landless industrial workers, a burgeoning labor union movement through which grievances could be channeled, poverty more conspicuous than at any previous time in the American experience, and threats of violence to promote change—all combined to suggest to many legislators that a new, unruly element, unworthy of special consideration, inhabited America's major cities. Such conclusions played into the hands of Quay, Platt, and their counterparts in other states, because they were attempting to manipulate the legislatures for their own purposes.

Growth of urban centers, as well as of the many business organizations within them, had prompted a change in the leadership of both. Before the Civil War neither was complex. Local politics, even in the cities, required only the part-time attention of many officials. This had permitted the middle class, particularly the business elite, to serve both government and the economy, but the growing complexity in postwar years called for a separation of duties and a greater professionalization of talent. Not all executive skill gravitated to the more lucrative business field; at all levels of government there were still men with great organizational abilities. This talent was displayed most dramatically in the cities, where batteries of competent, opportunistic men answered the challenge to maintain the social order in the face of inadequate legislation for doing so.[31]

The failure of state legislatures to respond to urban problems gave rise to a new type of urban leader, a manager who was not always an officeholder. Known as the "city boss," he was forced by social dysfunctions to act unofficially as often as he was called in an official capacity provided by the law. He and his political machine served as agents of transition from the ideological politics of the old society to the organizational politics of the new.[32] No longer could voters, particularly those in the cities, be rallied by any clarion call to such issues as freedom, civil rights, majority rule, and the bloody shirt. City dwellers could not afford to be preoccupied with the abstractions that had motivated the generation of the Civil War and Reconstruction. Their own ever-expanding needs and problems represented a

seemingly endless emergency. Any boss pragmatic enough to satisfy their
temporal needs became a locus of urban power. Of course, the boss was always
anxious to extend this power onto the state scene where he expected to find
the antidote to most of his city's ills. At this point he faced the most
formidable obstacle to the realization of his ambition—the state boss who, in
terms of urban objectives, was a "counter-boss." To the degree that a counter-
boss could neutralize city power at the state level, he could retain control of
state patronage; both Platt and Quay thoroughly understood the technique
and were instrumental in keeping the political power of cities submerged.

Conditions that created a city boss or a state counter-boss varied according
to place and time. Explanations for the success of some and the failure of
others were not always discernible. Any leader was judged in terms of
interaction with his particular environment, both human and physical. His
followers and the area over which he exercised control were as critical to
evaluating his success as were his personal characteristics. The chemistry of
leadership suggests that the effectiveness of a leader depended on his ability to
project himself into the lives of his followers who, in turn, could see their
needs and ambitions reflected in his solicitous words and promised deeds.
Thus a leader in one environment might not have succeeded in another. Quay
and Platt, for example, might have been failures if thrust into the role of a city
boss. They belonged to the same political genre as their city counterparts, but
their distinctive traits might not have sparked the interaction necessary in an
urban community.

The city boss was a first- or second-generation American who lived and
trained in a tenement area for as long as twenty years, amid factories and
industrial plants, before taking it over as his own bossdom. Quay spent an
even longer period (1856–1885) in more varied positions while preparing for
his role as "King Matthew" of Pennsylvania. To both state and municipal
bosses, however, current status was primary and ancestry was secondary
because the constituencies of both lived predominantly in the present, not the
past. An immigrant background merely implied that a boss had experienced
the hardships of the socially and culturally uprooted; when influential, this
trait was always favorable. In urban surroundings the immigrant boss seemed
more compassionate in the minds of the ethnics than a native American such
as Quay, but Quay's heritage was an asset for a politician appealing statewide
in the Pennsylvania environment where the impact of immigration was less
marked than elsewhere in the Northeast.[33]

During his apprenticeship the would-be city boss discovered much about
the attitudes and ambitions of those he ultimately came to dominate. He
learned that, in their formative years in America, these newcomers did not
appreciate philosophical arguments and justifications. Thus he moved

pragmatically to personalize government, recognizing the voter as an individual totally engrossed in the pursuit of his own livelihood without concern for the social implications of the many life-styles around him. In every personal crisis confronted by the city dweller after debarkation or arrival from the countryside and before the grave, the boss was there. He and his lieutenants worked to make themselves indispensable to the citizenry. As George W. Plunkitt of Tammany observed, they turned out at fires, sometimes faster than the equipment, to minister to the unfortunate victims. On other occasions they provided jobs, groceries, housing, and other essentials when they were not busy scanning obituary columns to identify funerals to attend. There was much political capital to be gained by making a public display of extending condolences to those regarded as constituents. Their emphasis on face-to-face contact engendered a system of politics minimizing public issues and stressing personalities with whom the electorate could readily identify.[34] Quay never related to the voter on such a one-to-one basis, but he did use this technique effectively in communicating with legislators and later with members of the U.S. Senate.

The depreciation in the importance of issues signaled an end to the day of the stump orator. Change came partly because the new generation of leaders adopted the philosophy that the less one said publicly, the less one would have to explain at a future date. The few spellbinders who remained were largely ornamental. Leadership passed to those who "practised keepin' their tongues still." This was a conclusion the state bosses shared with municipal leaders; adherence to this maxim was in accord with both their executive talents and the nature of their objectives.[35]

Tom Platt in particular realized that, if he wished to succeed in the role of party broker, he could not afford to express provocative ideas and premature preferences. Local Republican leaders across the state of New York were divided by conflicting issues and ambitions. Success in gaining their trust as an arbiter in behalf of party harmony meant, as George B. McClellan, Jr., observed, that Platt could have "neither likes nor dislikes that he could not easily overcome when necessary." In order to appear free of faction identification, Platt organized his celebrated "Sunday School Class," composed of the party's statewide local leaders. Through "class" discussions he attempted to learn local priorities, reconcile differences, create a harmonious party, and convey the impression to the public that his organization was effective. This was not dictatorship, but quiet management. Even when dissatisfied, he did not speak out, but discreetly prompted others to express the organization's displeasure. At the national level this strategy generally elicited favorable results, because Platt frequently controlled a portion of the vote that was crucial to Republican success.[36]

Quay was a manager, similar in style to Platt, but because Pennsylvania was virtually a one-party state, he was forced to assert more direction and inject more personal preferences. Quay did not enjoy the enviable position of controlling votes that could clinch a presidential election. In every national campaign, the Republican party confidently concluded that Pennsylvania was safely in the fold. Even when Quay and anti-Quay factions were actually attacking each other, the party's national leaders could be assured of a Republican margin from the Keystone State. This handicapped Quay in his quest for the same deferential treatment that Platt enjoyed, forcing him to work harder to retain control.

He was further committed to a free-lance policy by the fact that both Philadelphia and Pittsburgh remained overwhelmingly Republican. In most Northeast cities of comparable size, the Democrats were providing the basic challenge; neither of these Pennsylvania municipalities was severely threatened by immigration and its accompanying disorders, and their Democratic organizations remained weak. Nevertheless both cities wanted and needed government reform. According to an *Atlantic Monthly* appraisal in 1901, the need in Philadelphia was long overdue. Conditions had so deteriorated that it was "the most native-born and most evil large city in America."[37]

Superficially Quay supported better urban government, but his actions demonstrated a lack of sincerity, if not calculated deceit. At one point, in order to "correct" major defects in Pittsburgh's governmental structure, he proposed a revision in the charter which, in part, would have changed the city's status from second to first class. This manipulation would have placed Pittsburgh and Philadelphia in the same category, and the legislature would have been required to treat them equally. This possibility aroused no brotherly love in Philadelphia because the city's leaders recognized that their specific reform recommendations could only be compromised by Pittsburgh's input.[38] Thus the cities were rather cleverly set against each other; the Pittsburgh charter bill went down to defeat, and the Philadelphians were looked upon as the culprits.

In the name of reform the fertile minds of the Quay lieutenants in the legislature also conceived of a charter revision for Philadelphia. It required that all municipal appointments be confirmed by two-thirds of the members of the Select Council; one-third plus one could then reject every nomination. As Philadelphians analyzed this piece of legislation, they discovered an unstated purpose: to assure the Quay minority at least a decisive, though negative, voice in the city's government.[39] Although the governor's veto killed the measure, it served Quay well. In order to prevail in the state, it was not necessary that he dominate the urban blocs, only that he neutralize them by having them either divided within or competing with each other. When he felt the need to kindle a little dissension, charter revision was one of several topics that could be relied upon to produce factionalism.

As early as 1885 Philadelphia was suspicious of Quay's "reform" motives, had come to expect little from "his" legislature, and had actually received less. The city could always be counted upon to support at least one active, anti-Quay Republican faction, either boss-dominated or reform-minded. Reformers like Henry C. Lea, Rudolph Blankenburg, and John W. Wanamaker were sporadically antagonistic, but Quay's more consistent opposition came from the city's bosses. The most persistent of these leaders, who had to be held in check and kept from the state scene, was "King James" McManes, who converted his position as a trustee of the gas works into one of political importance. Elected a trustee in 1865, he quickly dominated the total board and transformed it into the most potent political force in the city. By 1879 his control of patronage was so extensive that an estimated 5630 individuals were dependent on his whims. He saw these jobs not as public service positions, but as the backbone of his political organization. In every one of Philadelphia's more than seven hundred precincts, there was an organization manned by McManes' subalterns.[40]

Self-assured by this urban network, McManes ventured into state and national politics and proceeded first to rebuke his long-time competitor, Simon Cameron, in public. At the Republican National Convention in 1880, in direct opposition to Cameron's edict, he read a manifesto against a three-term president. To the state boss's annoyance McManes received extensive newspaper coverage for this display of independence and was credited in many circles with being the individual most responsible for Grant's failure before the convention.[41] If the journalists catapulted McManes to political stardom, they just as quickly cast a cloud over his status. About this same time a New York paper ran a story on the graft within the gas trust that McManes so autocratically dominated. When it was revealed that the city's debt had escalated from $20 to $50 million over the twenty years of McManes's reign— while the people faced higher taxes, unpaved streets, inadequate water and gas supplies, and uncollected garbage—the city fathers became indignant and formed the Committee of One Hundred to promote reforms. Cameron recognized this as an opportunity, allied himself with the reformers, and together they quickly collapsed the McManes empire.

Although stripped of his appointment as a gas trustee, McManes rebounded as soon as the Committee of One Hundred disbanded. He recaptured the city and again attempted to thrust himself on the state and national scenes by refusing to endorse Quay's presidential choice in 1888. Another bitter battle ensued; Quay tried to dethrone King James by promoting dissension within his realm. He declared a sometime McManes henchman, David Martin, to be the boss of Philadelphia; success for Quay in this maneuver did not mean that Martin had to reign as an undisputed leader, only that he had to be aggressive enough to keep the city divided between himself and McManes. Quay made him a full member of his state organization and even advanced him to the Republican National Committee in 1891. Martin willingly took orders until 1895 when he too felt independent enough to oppose the counter-boss's choice of Boies Penrose to be mayor of Philadelphia.[42]

Quay then chose Israel "Iz" Durham, a ward politician, as his new citywide leader and assigned him the task of managing the Penrose campaign. Durham had been elected to his first public office, that of police magistrate, only ten years before. Noted for his leniency to offenders and for a willingness to oblige his friends, Iz became known as an "easy boss" and handily won reelections in 1890 and 1895. These victories were made possible primarily because of the loyalty of his district's Negroes, who constituted the bulk of the clients in his court. He was the kind of subordinate with whom a state boss could feel comfortable. Unlike McManes and Martin, he had no ambitions to enlarge his kingdom, but demonstrated an indefatigable dedication to success at the local level. Despite the 10,000 jobs that he eventually dispensed, he willingly accepted Quay's orders and once commented, "What do I care who is President, so long as I carry my ward?"[43]

With Durham content and successful in this role, Quay was able to prevent Philadelphia from presenting a united front either within the Republican party or before the state legislature throughout the remainder of his career. This proved that to divide was indeed to conquer because the counter-boss's power over rural areas was potent enough to sway most legislative proposals and recommendations. His only other urban challenge was in Pittsburgh, where the dynamic Republicans Christopher L. Magee and William Flinn came to dominate the local political scene by the early 1880s. Although Pittsburgh was much smaller than Philadelphia, the opposition was no less formidable. The state boss could not rely wholly on division tactics to suppress these two because in many ways they held Pittsburgh and Allegheny County in a tighter grip than either McManes or Martin ever enjoyed in Philadelphia.

Wealth, business connections, popularity with the masses, and good political instincts combined to make the Magee-Flinn team a dangerous adversary. Of the twenty city leaders surveyed in Harold Zink's classic study, only these two were listed in the social register. Both were noted for their benevolences although Magee's were more dramatic. During one Christmas season he displayed his generosity by announcing a gift of $100,000 "to the children of Pittsburgh" to establish a zoological garden in Highland Park; on another occasion he provided funds to build the Elizabeth Steele Magee Hospital as a monument to his mother.[44]

Both men were clearly stamped with entrepreneurial success. Their fortunes were the result of an ability to identify with other business and commercial elements of their region early in their careers. Arguing that they could manage the political concerns of these economic interests "with a minimum of expense and publicity and a maximum of efficiency," Magee and Flinn were given the opportunity to become political spokesmen by and for their business colleagues. They succeeded miraculously as agents for numerous prominent companies, and even the powerful Pennsylvania Railroad was so inspired by the trackage rights, crossing privileges, and other franchises that Magee obtained that it made him its unofficial agent, first for Allegheny County and then for all of Pennsylvania.[45]

Magee and Flinn were also distinctive in that they were the only two of Zink's bosses who compiled fortunes in real and personal property in excess of $4,000,000. Their aggregate holdings of $15,793,481 reduces Quay's estate of $800,000 to insignificance. Furthermore, Quay would have needed more than money to subdue these urban rivals who were as well endowed politically as they were financially. As their fortunes suggest, they were more business oriented than any contemporary urban bosses. Magee owned stock in more than one hundred companies, including railroads, street railways, and public utilities. He served as president for two of these enterprises and as director of fifteen others. Flinn, who was even more deeply committed to the world of business, held five presidencies and seven directorships. For Magee the ultimate goal was power, but for Flinn it was wealth. Lincoln Steffens observed that "Magee spent his wealth for more power, and Flinn spent his power for more wealth."[46]

As the Steffens remark suggests, these were different, but complementing political types. Magee possessed an infectious charisma that was reflected in his two state senate contests. On each occasion he received the nomination of both major parties, and his elections were virtually unanimous. He could charm almost everyone except Matt Quay, the man whose endorsement he needed to extend his influence to the state and national levels. Earlier in their careers, when both worked in the Cameron organization, their relationship was cordial enough for Quay to borrow $25,000 from Magee, but after a quarrel with Magee over the choice for state treasurer in 1883, followed by Cameron's designation of Magee as his spokesman at the Republican National Convention the following year, Quay identified his colleague as a potential rival and schemed to keep his sphere of influence localized in Allegheny County. Motivated as much by a concern for the fortunes of his party as for his own political gratification, Magee vacillated between trying to cooperate with Quay and attempting to overcome him. Not able to resolve the dilemma, he was ultimately devoured by it. He contracted a fatal nervous and physical disorder, produced in part by his never-ending struggle with the counter-boss, and died an untimely death at the age of fifty-three.[47]

Quay did not suffer from the indecision that handicapped Magee. His aim was to limit Magee's power to Allegheny County. Their rivalry regained the limelight in 1885 when the two again differed over the office of state treasurer, for which Quay was a candidate. After his election and the emergence of legislative differences, Magee decided to bow out of politics. He intended to retire at least until the Beaver boss reached the end of his career or his natural life, but Republican colleagues brought the two together again, and Magee actually endorsed Quay for senator in January 1887. Before the end of the year, though, the rift was fully exposed once more. In another failing effort Magee opposed the senator's candidate for state treasurer. Quay viewed that as a deliberate attempt to cut off his supply of new political blood.

Although the Pittsburgher continued his antagonistic course into the 1888 national convention, Quay somewhat magnanimously extended the olive branch, but only because he needed help. Magee was endorsing Harrison at a time when Quay was still desperately trying to carry the convention for Sherman. Before the crucial seventh ballot, Quay took Magee by the arm and in a fatherly tone suggested: "Now, Chris, if you will go on with us, I will agree to let the past go, and we will pull together in the future." To Magee the proposition was both condescending and embarrassing in the face of his previous commitment. He flared: "No, I will be d____d if I do. I am going to look out for myself."[48]

In relating this exchange to a friend, Quay predicted almost dispassionately: "Magee will regret that. He and I will never be friends again. He must go down now." Harrison's nomination, however, caused Magee to think that he had gambled and won, only to have the national committee subsequently select Quay as the national chairman. With the senator's prestige enhanced by his success in the 1888 election, Magee deduced that his adversary would never again let him get a foothold in state politics, so he—ostensibly—retired from the political scene a second time. His stated purpose was to keep his henchmen from being carried into political oblivion by Quay retributions, but circumstantial evidence suggests that he merely moved his anti-Quay campaign underground.[49]

Where Magee failed in his association with Quay, Flinn succeeded, at least partially. A businessman by profession, he managed the Magee-Flinn organization with a directness and openness that did not offend the state boss. Although Flinn was a more consistent seeker of political office than Magee, he did not excite Quay's suspicious nature. He not only served as chairman of the executive committee of Pittsburgh's Republican party for twenty years, but also was elected to two terms in the state house of representatives and three consecutive terms in the state senate. Quay interpreted this political involvement as Flinn's ploy to enhance his many private enterprises by being in a position to influence government contracts. To Quay this was good business; Flinn was using politics as a means to economic gain. In contrast, Magee wanted to suceed in politics primarily to extend his political power. Every success brought him closer to challenging Quay directly. In the interest of self-preservation, therefore, Quay's strategy limited those successes as much as possible.

Flinn's business objectives were not well served by the continuous Magee-Quay rivalry. After the two differed publicly on presidential nominees in 1888 and 1892, and particularly after Magee endorsed the Democratic gubernatorial candidate in 1890 rather than support Quay's choice, Flinn decided to take forthright action.[50] While Magee was in Europe for his health, Flinn negotiated a compromise that he hoped both Magee and Quay would accept. He and one of Magee's subordinates purportedly conferred personally with Quay in Washington in late 1895 and drew up a formal contract defining in detail the political parameters of both factions.

Cooperative in tone, this document specified that Quay would face no opposition from the Pittsburgh machine in state and national politics if he discontinued his divisive activities in Allegheny County. The legal language of this agreement, identifying Quay as the party of the first part and the Magee-Flinn cohorts as the parties of the second part, was indeed explicit:

> The said M. S. Quay is to have the benefit of the influence in all matters in state and national politics of the said parties of the second part, the said paries [sic] agreeing that they will secure the election of delegates to the state and national conventions who will be guided in all matters by the wishes of the said party of the first part, and who will also secure the election of members of the state Senate from the forty-third, forty-fourth, and forty-fifth senatorial districts, and also secure the election of members of the House of Representatives south of the Monongahela and Ohio Rivers in the County of Allegheny who will be guided by the wishes and request of said party of the first part during the continuance of this agreement upon all political matters. . . . It being distinctly understood that at the approaching national convention to be held in the city of St. Louis, the delegates from the twenty-second congressional district shall neither by voice nor vote do other than what is satisfactory to the party of the first part. The party of the first part agrees to use his influence and secure the support of his friends and

political associates to support the Republican county and city ticket when nominated both in the City of Pittsburgh and the County of Allegheny and that he will discontinue the factional fighting by his friends and associates for county offices during the continuance of this agreement.[51]

The pact was to become effective when signed by Magee upon his return from Europe. Before his arrival facsimiles of the agreement mysteriously turned up in the hands of newspapermen who publicly revealed the contents. Thus the "secret treaty" to divide the spoils was exposed and never consummated; the harmony that Flinn had worked so diligently to achieve was more tenuous than ever.

Ironically, in spite of his good intentions to cooperate with Quay, Flinn subsequently triggered a factional fight that was more crippling to the Magee-Flinn machine than any previous encounter. In an unguarded moment he permitted his business avarice to dictate a political decision openly: He engineered the dismissal of E. M. Bigelow, director of public works for the city of Pittsburgh, because he was guilty of the unpardonable offense of throwing certain city contracts open to competitive bidding instead of having them go uncontested to Flinn and his associates. A wealthy Thomas Bigelow rallied to his brother's defense. Although the Bigelows were Magee's cousins, the relationship had been poisoned some years before by several traction deals. Now they decided to regard the dismissal as a challenge not to be ignored. In the name of reform they organized a Citizens' party to attack the Magee-Flinn forces and were promptly joined by the city's Democrats, and, of course, by the ever-alert Quay organization. At one point it appeared to Pittsburgh Democrats that Quay was not a serious participant. J. M. Guffey wrote to him that "no reform measures have any hope of success without your personal aid." The reform tack may have been suspect, but aid was provided, and through legislative action this coalition succeeded in amending Pittsburgh's charter. This had the effect of deposing "Flinn's mayor," and the governor appointed a recorder to serve temporarily in his stead.[52]

This situation contained all the necessary ingredients for Quay to keep the urban caldron bubbling. His organization took over the city and carried the next mayoral election against a Flinn candidate. Not content with their role in this local triumph, the Bigelows continued to attack in Harrisburg, where a cloud lined with political corruption hung over Quay's bid for a third term in the U.S. Senate. If he could not explain the charges lodged against him to the satisfaction of the Republican legislature before the balloting, it appeared that he would not be reelected. Magee, who had long coveted a Senate seat, was considered a prominent alternative, but the Bigelows were on hand to prevent, if possible, their rival's dream from becoming reality.[53] After one of his longest and most bitter battles, the state boss was reelected to his third term. As on so many occasions, his victory was aided by division within the urban ranks.

The Syndrome of Party Regularity

Such gratuitous intracity rivalries aided Quay's schemes to prevent urban areas from realizing their full potential within both the state government and the Republican party. In Pennsylvania and other states nationwide, such strategies kept state governments tilted in favor of their rural populations. The trend was further accentuated by a less tangible factor known as party loyalty. Preserving the Union, sacking rebels, rescuing democracy from the perils of slavery, and exalting the rise of the new industrial order all combined to cause many Americans to cling to the Republican party almost as though it were a religion. With the same kind of faith, many others embraced the canons of the Democratic party that proclaimed a willingness to push slavery and secession into the background, reemphasize the role of the states in the socio-political realm, and develop a tariff more responsive to the needs of the whole nation.

These perceptions of party represented two assessments of national priorities. Allegiance to party and allegiance to government were practically synonymous in the minds of many. Strengthened by such indentification, party regularity soared to a new high; "my party, right or wrong" pervaded American political thought more widely than ever before. In Pennsylvania, where immigration caused less social disturbance than elsewhere in the industrial Northeast, the Republican monolith faced few challenges. Only once between 1865 and the turn of the century did the Democratic party dominate the state senate, and then by a single vote. Over the same period the seats in the state house had a majority of Democratic occupants only twice.

This did not mean that political controversy was reduced to a minimum, even in Pennsylvania. Although loyal party members tried to avoid, if at all possible, a crisis that would prompt them to forsake the faith and join the opposition party, they frequently formed into disgruntled factions to protest party choices and actions. John Wanamaker, who by 1898 regarded Quay as the personification of all that was unholy in politics, nevertheless boasted: "From my boyhood to this day I have never voted any other than the Republican ticket, neither have I scratched it or bolted it."[54]

Evan Holben, a Lehigh County lawyer and lifelong Democrat, frustrated by his party's failure to gain power in Pennsylvania, was highly critical of such sentiments—among Republicans. He argued that if Republican reformers

really wanted to depose their leaders, they would have become Democrats
"and not set up business for themselves." Democrats, of course, should ob-
serve party loyalty. He admonished members of his party not to make
concessions to any faction of the opposition and to "keep your Democracy out
of the Republican pawn shop." He was particularly angered by the situation in
1897 when the Democratic nominee for the U.S. Senate against a Quay
lieutenant was Chauncey F. Black, "whose ability, honesty, morality,
conservativeness and all around fitness" were completely ignored. Holben
complained bitterly because "none of these would-be reformers [Republican
Insurgents] voted for him to get rid of their terrible octopus [the rule of
Quay]."[55]

Others, who climbed higher on the political ladder than Wanamaker,
shared his attitude. Theodore Roosevelt and Henry Cabot Lodge both readily
embraced Mugwump ideas in 1884, but were repelled by the thought of joining
the organization. Senator George Hoar of Massachusetts demonstrated a
similar attraction for all the tenets of the independent reformers except for
the idea that in good conscience a man might repudiate his party. He
emphasized that a party could be improved only by working within it, and by
expressing this preference he revealed that his frame of reference was the
party, not the basic problems that were demanding solution.[56]

Since near sanctification of party was widespread among rank-and-file
voters, they tolerated no less from their politicians. Hoar the statesman,
Wanamaker the amateur, and Quay the boss—all recognized this. Party
regularity was interpreted as a specific kind of trustworthiness, a general
yardstick by which the public evaluated its leaders. Keeping one's word was a
treasured asset for any politician, and the more rural the area, the greater the
politician's reliance on this concept. Rural communities were less complex
and spawned fewer special interest groups; rural politicians were therefore
more dependent on personal reputations than on pressure blocs to achieve
success. They sought power as individuals rather than as representatives of a
sophisticated structure. A state boss could more easily coerce a rural
politician because he was under no obligation to defend his vote or explain his
conduct to any pressure group.[57]

All he had to do was demonstrate that a rural politician had gone back on his
word and his political future was in jeopardy. For this reason in every contest
in which Quay was either a candidate or a principal sponsor, his enemies
reintroduced the old argument that he had not kept the faith with Curtin, but
had repudiated his word in order to support Cameron. Quay employed the
same loyalty/honesty code in his negotiations with rural politicians. From
time to time he wrote to them in their isolated hamlets requesting written
concurrence or endorsement. Once he received their replies he knew that

they were "locked in" and dared not change their decisions at a future date lest he reveal a document that suggested a lack of loyalty. The loyalty code thus enforced party regularity.

State bosses were masters of enforcement. They recognized that disagreements must end when the nominee was chosen or the party would face possible defeat at the polls. The subordinate who openly betrayed a leader's dictum or who was suspected of deliberate failure to deliver the largest possible vote in his district was marked for discipline. A punitive reaction came as swiftly from Tom Platt, an "easy" boss, as from anyone. Although he never questioned the methods of his lieutenants, even when they were corrupt, mercenary, and ruthless, he could not excuse offenses that revealed a disrespect for the "cult of party."[58]

In Pennsylvania, offenders were accorded similar treatment. Only a small dose of Quay was necessary to induce a remarkable regularity. If an anti-Quay Republican in the legislature decided to protest a crucial issue, he was threatened with having state funds for a hospital, normal school, or other public agency in his district reduced or withheld. That was generally adequate persuasion, but for those with the temerity to believe that Quay was jesting, the appropriate curtailments followed. The prospect of having the full force of Quay's organization allied against a would-be recalcitrant at the next election was another persuasive argument for party allegiance.

This kind of control, even after Quay entered the Senate, was necessary to ensure future successes. As long as he and other senators were prepared to pay the price in both dollars and organizational effort to retain such local discipline, their seats of power in the Millionaire's Club were secure.

The Making of a Candidate
1888

THE exercise of political power from the nation's capital provided Quay with a new kind of challenge. Aware that the locus of power for an aspirant as a party boss had shifted from Washington to the individual states, he knew that the senatorial appointment removed him from the source of his newly won power. Continued success was contingent upon developing a technique that would enable him to rule by remote control. He needed a competent and trusted protégé who would take charge in Harrisburg and manage politics within the state as he had done for the Camerons. His future success in both state and national politics was partially dependent upon someone else. No longer could he personally direct the legislature, advise the governor, supervise the state treasurer, and provide day-to-day attention to the state's Republican organization. But the performance of these functions was the key to his own destiny in the struggle for party power.

The selection of a junior partner at this juncture was the most crucial personnel decision of Quay's career, and his excellent choice again proved his genius at judging political talent. By choosing Harvard-educated Boies Penrose of Philadelphia to preside in Harrisburg, he tightened his grip on the Republican party of Pennsylvania. Penrose had served only one term in the state house of representatives before his election in 1886 to the state senate, but Quay deftly assessed his leadership potential. He raised him up and set him over the organization, and from that vantage point he rendered valuable service for the next decade. So successful was the Penrose leadership in state matters that no U.S. senator from the Keystone State, before or after Quay, retained the same high level of control that marked this period. When the factionalisms, exposes, and other politically embarrassing obstacles that marred these years are considered, the feat assumes an even greater significance.

In August 1887 Quay resigned as state treasurer in favor of a trusted subordinate and plotted with Penrose until December, when he moved to Washington for the first session of the Fiftieth Congress. Accompanied by Frank Leach as his private secretary, he confidently assumed his new responsibilities. With two decades of experience in state politics, he was not a typical freshman senator. Conversant on the issues, schooled in the procedures, and respected by incumbent senators, he was accepted as a veteran from the first day. Since a Democratic administration was in command, the initial session was the calmest of his senatorial career. Only when maneuvering for the 1888 convention began to unfold was there excitement that a junior senator like Quay could enjoy.

Parochial View of the Presidency

In 1888 the Republican party was completing its first four-year exile from the White House since coming into national power under Abraham Lincoln. By early that year many of the large Republican state organizations were convinced that they possessed the political personality most capable of leading the party back to the executive control that it had come to regard as an inherited right. The favorite sons were ready—Chauncey M. Depew of New York, John Sherman of Ohio, Benjamin Harrison of Indiana, Judge Walter Q. Gresham of Illinois, Russell A. Alger of Michigan and William B. Allison of Iowa. In addition, there were pockets of adherents loyal to Maine's James G. Blaine, the defeated standard-bearer in 1884. They refused to interpret his somewhat ambiguous correspondence dispatched from various points on his European junket as conclusive evidence that he did not choose to run.

Pennsylvania was absent from this list. The state's Republican convention, held in April, registered little enthusiasm for any candidate. The only decisive action taken was the naming of Matthew S. Quay as chairman of the delegation to the national convention in Chicago, with power to exercise the unit rule. In assessing the results of the state convention for Gresham, his personal choice for the presidential nomination, Erastus Brainard of the *Philadelphia Daily News* reported: "There was no strong 'drift' to any candidate. There was only a slight undercurrent towards Sherman caused by Senator Cameron's statement that he is friendly to S. on account of family ties. [He had recently married Sherman's niece.] But Cameron was wholly 'knocked out' & the command of the Republican forces was taken by Senator Quay, who is uncommitted, but has just a slight leaning to Sherman."[1]

Previously the Keystone State had touched off several quadrennial Blaine booms, but was unwilling to do so now. This reluctance had already become apparent in 1887 when the state convention gave only guarded approval to Blaine's candidacy for 1888. Although this implied that Pennsylvania Republicans were growing lukewarm on Blaine, Quay provided a left-handed endorsement that helped to keep him in the state's presidential purview. "I am certainly in favor of Mr. Blaine if he is a candidate," Quay said. "I do not know that he desires the nomination, but if he does, I think he should be nominated."[2] Comforting as these words were to Blaine's followers, they were not to be taken literally. By his own admission Quay did not believe in a serious commitment to a candidate so far in advance, but he had hoped that such comments would prevent the remnants of the state's Independent movement from mounting an attack against him before one was truly warranted.

Although Pennsylvania had no favorite son to parade before the national convention, her large population assured a major voice in the election results. The state's leaders, who had tasted few of the choice national fruits during the long Republican reign (1860–1884) despite repeatedly rolling up large party majorities at the polls, were determined to exact a price for their endorsement. To some extent, their continued prestige within the state organization hinged on the results. Quay expressed the sentiments of the leadership when he decreed that he had no intention of entrusting the distribution of the political loaves and fishes to any random arrangement again and demanded written proof that the state would be recognized in the president's cabinet. With assistance from Philadelphia trolley-car magnate P. A. B. Widener and Allegheny County Congressman Thomas M. Bayne in carrying his message to the camps of favorite-son candidates, Quay approached the Chicago convention with this goal uppermost.[3]

Quay regarded John Sherman as the strongest character in American public life and preferred him as the nominee. At the same time he did not intend that his personal wishes should interfere with his primary political objective— gaining concessions for Pennsylvania in the next administration. He wanted to trade the state's convention votes for a cabinet position, but was realistic enough to know that it might be necessary to be more subtle and "force" his political affections on one of the candidates. If he could deliver the state's votes to the leading contender, whoever he might be, at the strategic moment to clinch his nomination, Quay would likely win special considerations for the Keystone State if the general election went well.

No overtures to Sherman in this connection were necessary. Quay or his agents implied individually to supporters of Gresham, Blaine, Harrison, Allison, and even William McKinley, for whom there was a brief two-hour boomlet, that the trading season was open—especially if it became necessary to abandon Sherman's candidacy. In order to remain flexible and entertain all promising propositions, while not invoking the unit rule within his own delegation, Quay arranged for the nomination of Edwin H. Fitler, the reform mayor of Philadelphia and an unthinkable presidential candidate. This strategy was necessary to neutralize James McManes and his Philadelphia cohorts and prevent them from openly declaring their preference for Gresham rather than Sherman. Once the mayor's name was injected into the race, the Philadelphians faced political embarrassment if they voted for anyone else on the first ballot. A week before the convention opened, Quay had stretched the truth to capacity when he informed Sherman: "I write to say that I have just now had a very satisfactory interview with Mr. McManes and that he and his friends are for you." Politically translated, this statement meant that Quay had taken steps to ascertain that the McManes delegates would not vote for a major contender on the first ballot. He also decided that four Pennsylvania votes, including his own, would be cast for Congressman William W. Phelps of New Jersey in the opening round in an effort to keep him in the race, retain that state's votes as a bloc, and influence their ultimate disposition.[4]

Political Horse Trading

In spite of his preoccupation with patronage, Quay was unquestionably Sherman's most prominent sponsor outside Ohio. Aside from Pennsylvania and the "rotten boroughs" of the South where, as secretary of the treasury, he had built an efficient organization, Sherman's support was sparse. In the duel for southern delegates, his chief rival was Blaine, but in the late stages of the contest, Alger joined the competition. In explaining Sherman's decline in the South, a subordinate complained that Alger "bought up our Negro delegates like sheep." Under the guise of purchasing gallery tickets from southern blacks who desperately needed expense money, Alger literally purchased the delegates who transferred their allegiance from Sherman.[5]

Sherman also had difficulty securing the undivided support of business interests. Those in the Midwest favored Gresham while those in the East were split between Sherman and Depew. Blaine's largest following was among the less affluent Republicans, although individual business leaders such as Stephen B. Elkins and Benjamin F. Jones remained loyal to him. With railroad management in disrepute throughout the West and Midwest at this time, Depew, who was president of the New York Central and Hudson Railroad Company, did not project a favorable nationwide image; the center of his opposition was in the Granger country where Allison took the lead in dramatizing his railroad connections and rendering his candidacy hopeless.

Depew returned the compliment by neutralizing Allison's candidacy in other sections.[6]

Just as Depew spoke out against Allison, Platt denounced Sherman. Generalizing from previous experiences with Hayes and Garfield, Platt declared that he would not trust any Ohio politician in a convention. Although this was one of his few disagreements with Quay, he bluntly proclaimed that he would not vote for Sherman "if half a dozen conventions nominated him." That attitude caused Depew to conclude that the Ohioan was, therefore, eliminated from the contest because he could not carry New York without Platt's endorsement.[7]

With the ax being swung effectively against Allison, Depew, and Sherman, many New York Republicans began to focus on Harrison. When no positive word came from Blaine, Elkins joined the trend, but maneuvered adroitly before collapsing the Blaine tent. He had endeavored to hold the Blaine delegation together either to ignite a nomination by acclamation, which at one point was Blaine's strategy, or to deliver the Blaine votes intact to a particular candidate, thereby deciding the nomination contest and preserving as much Blaine influence as possible in the next administration. Blaine himself, through his private secretary, M. A. Dodge, and James S. Clarkson of Iowa, conveyed the idea that he would be responsive to a draft. Dodge wrote to Elkins: "Mr. Blaine feels that any political advantage in his nomination would be entirely neutralized by an effort to secure it, or by its failure to be unanimous and even acclamatous. His nomination, to have any superiority over others in securing votes at the election, which is the only thing a nomination is for, must seem to the party so desirable as to preclude the mention of any other name before the Convention. A defeated candidate must be strong enough to exclude every other or he is a weak candidate."[8]

Leading politicians believed that if Blaine at any time indicated his willingness under any circumstances to become the candidate, he would be nominated. Quay, Governor Joseph B. Foraker of Ohio, Louis T. Michener of Indiana, and James S. Clarkson were among the many who expressed this belief, and the latter two in particular attempted to exploit the situation. Knowing that the possibility of Blaine's noncandidacy was stronger, they sought to identify their other candidates, Harrison and Allison respectively, with Blaine's philosophy and his following. In the months preceding the convention, Michener wrote frequently to Elkins about Harrison's campaign. Pointing out that Harrison had had no intention of being a candidate until after Blaine's letter from Italy virtually removed him from the contest, Michener stressed that Harrison's canvass was proceeding on the assumption that Blaine would not reconsider. Through his writing he hoped to enlist Elkins and the Blaine bloc in the Harrison cause. And seeing Gresham as a principal competitor, Michener noted that the judge had shown himself to be a bitter enemy of Blaine in previous conventions and observed that if his election should follow,"Blaine will have no influence whatever."[9]

Clarkson followed a similar strategy in corresponding with Elkins on behalf of Allison. In a six-page letter he recalled his own correspondence with Blaine, who had expressed his "positive unwillingness to make the fight and his equally positive determination to keep out of it." Clarkson explained how he had urged Blaine not to decide against seeking the nomination until March or April, but in advance of that date Blaine announced his decision not to run "unless I should be called upon by the unanimous voice of the party," which was never heard. Clarkson concluded, in a burst of emotion: "I have no ambition in life which I would not surrender to see him President or to serve him in any way. I will die unsatisfied and with lessened faith in American sense and appreciation if he is never President." The carefully typed letter failed to state its basic purpose; that was reserved for an abruptly penned postscript: "Allision is undoubtedly the second choice of a majority of delegates." He hoped that Elkins would endorse that proposition, if not publicly, at least privately.[10]

The Sherman advocates attempted no such identification with Blaine. Quay personally was not adverse, but such a course would have detracted from Sherman's already insecure endorsement. Although Ohio delegates were unanimously pledged to Sherman, his campaign was handicapped from the beginning by rumors of eight to ten delegates abandoning him at the earliest opportunity. Quay was "panicky all the time" lest the veneer rub off, exposing true delegate attitudes. He sincerely hoped to nominate Sherman, but failing in this, he expected the Ohio delegation to be grateful enough for his efforts that they would join Pennsylvania as a unit in naming the party's candidate from among the other contenders. The delegates firmly committed to Sherman complied willingly, but the Foraker sympathizers were impossible to control. Once free to leave Sherman, they preferred to endorse Alger. Although this reduced the thrust that Quay wished to exert on the convention floor, neither his plan nor its impact went unnoticed. Sherman was the wrong candidate at the wrong time for dramatic success such as Quay envisaged.[11]

Governor Foraker stood at the corner of the distrust and uncertainty within the ranks of Ohio Republicans. During the summer of 1887, Sherman had met at Canton with a group of state leaders, including Hanna and McKinley, who were interested in pressing his candidacy for the presidential nomination. Unfortunately for the cause of party harmony, an invitation had not been extended to the Republican governor, who became suspicious and resentful. Although Sherman tried later to minimize the role of the Canton conference by telling Foraker that it was only a "social and agreeable visit," this was not

accepted as an adequate explanation for his exclusion. Regarding himself
equally worthy of consideration for the nomination, Foraker advised Hanna
that the endorsement of Sherman, in his opinion, was not in the best interests
of the party. Publicly he supported Sherman, but thereafter he was not fully
trusted by certain Sherman leaders. Foraker sensed the alienation. When the
Ohio delegation assembled at Chicago for the convention, the governor again
became piqued at the lack of deference for his position. Hanna, who was in
charge of arrangements for the delegation, assigned him to hotel rooms on the
floor above the Ohio headquarters instead of to adjoining ones and did not
consult him concerning the state's representation on the various committees.[12]

This was an unnecessary embarrassment to a governor who had worked so
faithfully in behalf of his party. More than any other Northerner during the
Cleveland years, he had attacked the Democratic president for his lack of
reverence for Memorial Day and chastised his willingness to forgive the South
for the treachery of civil war and to surrender the captured rebel flags. To
many he seemed to be the ideal candidate to lead another campaign of
recriminations against the Democrats and the South, but Foraker and his
adherents did not understand that his failure to invoke a major response in
Ohio or elsewhere was an indication that the Republicans at long last were
preparing to abandon bloody shirt tactics in favor of more positive and
constructive campaign appeals. This was a shift in basic strategy, and reaction
to it in Ohio helped to aggravate the Foraker split and weaken the role that
Quay intended for Ohio to play in the convention.[13]

By the time the convention formally opened on June 19, many political
cards had already been played. The favorite-son candidates had checked each
other's strength and made their opening bids for the large eastern states of
Pennsylvania and New York. Early maneuvering in the race for delegates
projected the contenders from Ohio, Indiana, and Illinois into the forefront.
Victory obviously belonged to the one capable of capturing both Platt and
Quay, whose conflicting ambitions made the task all the more challenging.
With his desire to nominate Sherman and procure a cabinet post for the
Keystone State, Quay exhibited a positive approach. Platt, on the other hand,
was a negative force. He feared the railroad and money philosophies
advocated in Allison's Granger country and opposed Sherman, whom he
dubbed the "human icicle" because of his lack of popular appeal. Republican
disagreement concerning Sherman was destined to doom his candidacy.
Gresham's declaration that he wished to remain as free of commitments "as I
was the day I stepped on the bench" left Harrison alone at the head of the
list.[14]

Depew had been the first prominent New Yorker to support Harrison openly. Platt was converted to that point of view as the result of a pledge by Elkins, who had transferred his support from Blaine to Harrison. Platt believed that he was promised the portfolio of the Treasury Department in exchange for delivering a solid New York delegation to Harrison. Working successfully toward that end, he congratulated Harrison after his nomination in glowing terms: "No other result could have been so generally approved. I fail to find a 'kicking' Republican in the whole length and breadth of our State. Mr. Blaine's friends are perfectly satisfied and the anti-Blaine element, which four years ago was quite potent and poisonous, are now enthusiastically supporting the ticket." Later both Elkins and Harrison positively denied that any such promise had been made, and Platt was left to conclude that Indiana politicians were no more worthy of trust than those from Ohio.[15]

Aware of the power of the anti-Sherman forces as the Republicans assembled in Chicago, Quay realized that his options were unavoidably being narrowed to one. George Frisbie Hoar of Massachusetts, who also had originally endorsed Sherman, helped Quay to reach this conclusion. Forsaking his first choice, Hoar decided that Harrison represented the best compromise and quietly conveyed this message to eastern delegations. Learning of these visits, Quay demanded, "What is old man Hoar up to?" and received his answer in time to start bargaining for another candidate.[16] Like Hoar and the New York delegation, he identified Harrison as the most likely compromise choice and sent his emissary, Thomas Bayne, to negotiate with the Harrison managers, John B. Elam and Louis T. Michener. Bayne freely admitted to them that there were divergent views within the Pennsylvania delegation and that Quay was prepared to relinquish his personal choice in order to unite the delegation behind another candidate if he could procure recognition for his state in the cabinet.

Although Harrison had cautioned them against such commitments, Elam and Michener respected Quay's position. They also realized that Harrison's nomination might well be hanging in the balance. An arrangement with Pennsylvania could virtually assure his nomination, while rejection might end all hope of procuring the state's sixty convention votes. Since New York's position was not crystallized at this date, the decision was indeed a significant one. Unwilling to assume full responsibility for it, Elam and Michener outlined the proposal and dispatched it by special courier to Harrison in Indianapolis. They informed him that Quay wanted a general endorsement in writing and pointed out to their chief, "He is rather practical as you know."[17]

Bayne had already drafted a response that was acceptable to Quay, and the Harrison managers included it with their explanation. If Harrison agreed with the contents, only his signature was necessary. The draft, to be addressed to Bayne, read as follows: "I appreciate the kindly feeling of Senator Quay and his colleagues of the Pennsylvania delegation and I fully realize the claims of the great state of Pennsylvania. I write this to assure you and through you Senator Quay that in the event of my nomination and election to the Presidency, I shall regard the state of Penn. as entitled to representation in my cabinet—and shall freely confer with Senator Quay and his conferees in making such selection."[18] Elam and Michener concluded their letter, to which this draft was appended, with a request to "let us know your views." Harrison promptly obliged by scrawling a blunt "I said 'No'" across the proposal and returning it to his convention headquarters. Harrison thus won the first of his many political skirmishes with Quay. He went on to gain the nomination, but Quay managed to salvage a little prestige from the final decision. On the eighth and decisive ballot, Pennsylvania voted solidly for Harrison, thereby ending the contest, but the impact was not as dramatic as Quay had intended.

The analysts understood, and Harrison realized immediately, that victory was at hand. When the telegraph line from convention hall to his Indianapolis residence carried the message that Pennsylvania had swung over, Harrison remarked: "That settles it. I shall be nominated." And he was. To balance the ticket, Levi P. Morton of New York was named as his vice-presidential running mate, and the convention was promptly adjourned. John Sherman was disappointed in the outcome, but had only admiration for the manner in which Quay conducted the canvass on his behalf. At the end of the convention he wrote: "I wish I could find fitting words to express to you my thanks for your manly and honorable course in this matter. Rarely have I been so much impressed with any man on so short an acquaintance as with you."[19]

The Making of a President
1888

EXHAUSTED from more than a week of intensive convention maneuvering that demanded a daily routine of four hours of bed and twenty
hours of bedlam, Quay hastened to Washington to handle a few emergencies
and then escaped to Brigantine Beach, north of Atlantic City, to relax. Even
this retreat to his favorite New Jersey fishing haunt was not without its
political overtones. The Republican National Committee was scheduled to
meet in New York on July 10 to select a new national chairman and organize
for the coming campaign, but Quay deliberately stayed away. Although a
member of this committee, he planned to be absent because he was considered
a leading contender for the chairmanship. Not certain that he should accept
the challenge, he was nevertheless determined that he was not going to be on
hand to submit to questioning. Either he would be named to the post without
qualification or he would willingly see it pass to someone else.

In preliminary discussions concerning the chairmanship held at the
convention, there had been a division of opinion. Western Republicans did
not want to see responsibility for victory pass into the hands of an easterner
whose primary interest was the tariff. Assuming that the electoral votes of
New York were easier to corral than those of Indiana, they feared that a
chairman from an industrial state would misplace the campaign emphasis,
downgrading their desires for regulation of the railroads, public land subsidies
and so forth. Thus Quay's absence from the committee meeting was a direct
result of his desire to avoid this controversy, particularly since he regarded
New York as the key to success in the fall. As a safeguard to western interest,
William W. Dudley and John C. New, both of Indiana, were named to the

executive committee. But when the positions of chairman and secretary were assigned to Pennsylvania and New York respectively, these two states which would inevitably bear the major financial burden were actually in control.[1]

With Republican rank and file disheartened because the party's communication network had broken down under a discouraged and retiring national chairman, and with the Democrats confidently entrenched behind a wall of executive patronage, victory was not a foregone conclusion. The new chairman had to have the ability to harmonize the dissonant elements of the party and instill an esprit de corps that would attract the necessary financial and voting resources. Recalling the disastrous experience that befell Benjamin F. Jones, the Pittsburgh industrialist who managed the preceding national campaign, Quay pithily described the dubious distinction that went with the appointment: "If successful, no one remembers the national chairman who achieves the victory. If unsuccessful, no one forgets." Nevertheless, he planned to accept the challenge if it came on his terms.[2]

Blaine's defeat in 1884 had been attributed, in part, to the chairman's lack of political acumen, and the general feeling throughout the party, to which the Republican National Committee was most sensitive, was that this mistake should not be duplicated in 1888. The national chairman had to be the most astute, resourceful organizer within the ranks, possessing political ability in which "party leaders and prominent business men have every confidence." James M. Swank, general manager of the American Iron and Steel Association, believed that Quay met these specifications and sought to influence the committee to appoint him. Sherman, Platt, and Elkins all agreed that he was "a shrewd, able and skillful political manager" with a "wonderful facility in gaining the good will of those with whom he comes in contact." Swank wrote to Michener suggesting that, if Harrison personally had no objection, every effort should be made to place Quay at the head of the organization. He stressed that the East was the key to a successful campaign and that the funds required for victory could be raised there only if the chairman were a man in whom its leaders had confidence. By definition no westerner was acceptable.

The campaign in the East had to be waged primarily on the tariff plank. To be eligible in the minds of the business leadership, a candidate for party chairman had to demonstrate not only a solid voting record on the tariff, but also a political career integrally related to its success. In general, Harrison agreed. Although he offered no specific recommendations for the chairmanship, he insisted that the composition of the national committee be "a Republican and not a personal one." Declaring, "There will be no clique or ring about me," he urged that the committee be constructed without considering whether the members had voted for him in the convention "first, last, or not at all."[3]

With Harrison expressing this attitude, Michener proceeded to the July 10 organizational meeting of the national committee determined to support Quay if Morton and his New York cohorts were agreeable. Platt saw to it that they were. Western members favored Clarkson, but Michener was strategist enough to realize that if Quay were nominated by the Harrison camp, all opposition would melt away. John C. New, publisher of the *Indianapolis Journal*, Indiana committeeman, and personal friend of the presidential candidate, proposed Quay's name, and he was elected chairman by an overwhelming margin.[4]

Republican Machiavelli Takes Office

Widely acclaimed in Republican circles, this selection forecast a campaign of practical politics. Quay was recognized to be lightning quick in decision, able to gauge accurately the changing popularity of issues, and capable of altering campaign emphases a half dozen times if need be. He possessed a keen eye for detecting the enemy's weak points, for scenting trends in public opinion, and for conciliating all classes of voters. Although such personal qualities in themselves did not register votes and ensure victory, they did preclude the inevitable mistakes of an amateur and did promise an exciting political autumn for all Republicans.[5]

Unable to contact Quay at Brigantine Beach, the national committee proceeded to appoint the executive committee without consulting him. Although they were primarily men with whom he had not worked (e.g., Clarkson, New, Dudley, J. Sloat Fassett), his vigorous and amiable personality knit the band together "as a family of brothers." After he accepted and reported for duty, Quay informally reinforced the group with a number of personal choices, mostly from Pennsylvania. In time the New York press came to resent this ·contingent. Dubbed Quay's "hessians" or "kitchen cabinet," the temporary transplants included John Wanamaker, Thomas Dolan, Hamilton Disston, James A. Rutan, Thomas Bayne, his secretary Frank Leach, and his son Richard, who served as a special messenger. These Pennsylvanians were an embarrassment to New York. Normally visitors came to wonder at the city's greatness and admire its vast enterprises or to seek the assistance of its able publicists and celebrated statesmen. But that was not true of Quay's mercenaries. They came to take charge of New York's own election and institute a "political revolution whether the New Yorkers wanted one or not."[6] What followed marked the most dramatic interference of a national chairman with the campaign techniques and voting procedures of a single city in the history of American politics.

By the time Leach's telegram informed Quay that he had been named chairman, it was too late for him to decline gracefully because the national committee had already adjourned. There is no evidence, however, to suggest that he entertained such thoughts. Before leaving the Atlantic City area, he mapped preliminary strategy and issued his first requests. Messages were sent to Wanamaker and Dolan suggesting a meeting in Philadelphia to evaluate the general level of financial assistance that could be subscribed for the campaign. A third request for a meeting went to John I. Davenport, the supervisor of federal elections in New York, to whom he expressed the urgent need for cooperation in developing an efficient organization in New York City and in ensuring a fair vote and an honest count.

The pledge to minimize election fraud was lifted from the text of the Republican platform. But instead of relating it to the party's commitment, most observers considered it a part of Quay's personal modus operandi. Within that framework it had a peculiar ring, but Quay was convinced that in 1884 Blaine had received more votes in New York than Cleveland did and that the Democrats had altered the count so that their candidate carried the state and, by that margin, the presidency. Quay's campaign strategy was designed to frustrate this "skillful jugglery with the ballot boxes," and he publicly threw down the gauntlet: "I do not propose that the Democrats shall steal New York from Harrison. The false registration must be stopped. The recount and the change of votes from Harrison to Cleveland must be prevented at all hazards."[7] These were bold words, but Quay offered no hint of the means that would be deployed to ensure a more honest election. He simply declared that he proposed "to make a complete study of New York City. The election will be won or lost right there. Before I get through I shall know as much about every precinct as I now know about the borough of Beaver." But this generalization only added to the mystery of his strategy; the meaning was not fully understood until election day.[8]

As his statements implied, Quay had specific ideas about the conduct of the campaign, and he held the political leverage necessary to carry them to fruition. The campaign was stamped with his imprimatur from beginning to end. Issues of strategy and items of detail received personalized attention. He even studied the banners decorating the Fifth Avenue headquarters and insisted that the large flag displayed on the outer wall be redesigned because it expressed sentiments that the Republican party could not endorse. Attempting to unite labor, Republicanism, and patriotism, the banner portrayed the emblem of labor—a brawny arm, bared to the shoulder, swinging a ten-pound hammer—above the American eagle, but the juxtaposition upset Quay. He queried John New: "Suppose that arm should take a notion to strike and that hammer should come down, what would be the result?"

New did not immediately understand the question. When he did see what was bothering the chairman, he exclaimed: "Matt, it would hit that eagle right on the head and knock out its brains."

"Now tell me in all candor, dear John, whether we can endorse the sentiment as expressed in that picture? In fact I do not think it policy to allow
the hand of labor to knock out even one tail feather of that noble bird." The
banner was changed, the eagle was excused from further duty, and a larger
arm swinging a larger hammer was painted to fill the space.[9]

On the substantive side of organization, Quay and the national committee
were immediately confronted with the question of issues to be emphasized.
Taking their cue from the party platform, they decided to haul down the
bloody shirt and end the sectionalism that had characterized all national
elections since 1860. Complaints pertaining to this capitulation were received
from Senator William E. Chandler of New Hampshire and Governor Foraker
of Ohio, who waged self-styled campaigns condemning the South. But the
party generally focused on the tariff and the protection of domestic production.[10]

The tariff was a natural issue for the Republicans. In his annual message to
Congress in 1887, President Cleveland had stressed the need for tariff reform,
and a dutiful Democratic House responded with the Mills bill. Sponsored by
Roger Q. Mills, chairman of the Ways and Means Committee, this measure
proposed few drastic tariff curtailments, but the Republicans saw it as the
proverbial camel's nose in the tariff tent. They needed an issue to attract the
votes of workingmen in large numbers and the dollars of the industrialists in
large amounts; the tariff was certainly more timely for both purposes than a
rehash of the thirty-year-old misdeeds of the South.

Although Quay, Swank, and Wanamaker knew the fund-raising potential in
the tariff argument, the idea had to be diffused through the nation's business
leadership in order to be meaningful. In the initial stages that was not a simple
task. The Philadelphia business community, suspicious of Quay because of
the city's many previous skirmishes with him, maneuvered to establish direct
communication with Harrison. Since their financial support was essential to
the campaign, Quay reluctantly agreed that a small advisory board of
businessmen, dominated by Wanamaker, could be formed to raise funds. But
he did not know the extent of the group's involvement with the candidate.
These Philadelphians had actually demanded a promise, similar to that
suggested by Quay during the national convention, that a cabinet post be
allocated to Pennsylvania. Although Harrison did not respond directly, a
letter from Michener to Charles Emory Smith was interpreted as such a
promise. Quay remained unaware of this agreement, and after the election
Smith reminded Harrison of the wisdom of keeping it secret from him.[11]

With Thomas Dolan, a street railway and gas tycoon, serving as an
intermediary between Quay and Wanamaker, the select committee took form.
Wanamaker, the pious Sunday school superintendent who had developed a
facility to accommodate God and Mammon side by side, was above suspicion,

and was, therefore, a good choice to serve as the unofficial chancellor of the party's exchequer. To initiate the campaign for funds, he and Dolan met with eight of their fellow Philadelphians, and within ten minutes, each had subscribed $10,000.[12]

This may have set a record but it did not set the pattern. According to Quay's spending plans, this Philadelphia sum had to be multiplied many times, but in the early stages of the campaign the prospects were dim. Industrialists generally suffered from an acute case of apathy. From statements at campaign headquarters, they deduced that Quay was charting the most expensive national campaign ever conducted. From the debates in Congress, they gathered that the average 7 percent tariff reduction proposed by the Mills bill would not be catastrophic. In keeping with sound business practice, they questioned whether the defeat of the Mills bill was worth the asking price. Quay responded by urging the Republicans in the Senate to defeat the Mills bill and adjourn until after election, but Senators John Sherman, George Edmunds, John Ingalls, and others committed to the tariff issue disagreed. They preferred to take the offensive by framing a tariff bill of their own and introducing it on the floor for discussion and action. Quay argued that, whatever its merits, a Republican-sponsored tariff would take away half the thunder of the campaign. He wanted positive tariff legislation to hinge on the outcome of the election. With that dependence he would be better able to solicit larger contributions from the industrialists.[13]

Powerless to muzzle the senators, Quay was handicapped in his campaign for funds. Emphasizing the potential free-trade threat in the Mills bill, he hoped to frighten businessmen out of their money in the name of a successful campaign. At one point he privately concluded that it might be necessary to "put the manufacturers of Pennsylvania under the fire and fry all the fat out of them." This statement, published in a solicitation circular by James P. Foster, president of the Republican League of the United States, did not escape the notice of the opposition press. "Fat" became synonymous with contributions to the Republican party, and "fat frying" was depicted as Quay's major preoccupation. One headline emblazoned "MATT WANTS 'FAT'," and another proclaimed "NEW GOES WEST FOR FAT."[14]

Iron and steel barons in particular were slow to accept their share of the responsibility. When the need was great and his agents reported their lack of success in western Pennsylvania, Quay packed his bag. He went personally to supervise the fat frying, and Pittsburgh manufacturers were kept on the fire, under his watchful eye, until they contributed a total of $100,000. This was one-fourth of the sum expected from Philadelphia, and both cities raised their quotas in full. Since campaign records were systematically destroyed by bonfire, not too much can be said authoritatively about the sources of

Republican contributions, but the half-million dollars raised in Pennsylvania represented approximately 40 percent of the total funds supplied to the national committee. By coincidence 40 percent of the committee's $1,252,500 disbursement was consigned to New York, with most of those funds being allocated to three major endeavors. More than $150,000 was granted to Boss Platt for his statewide programs, $100,000 was invested in the city directory project, and a similar amount was expended to court the ethnic vote.[15]

The Keystone State proved itself to be the financial capital of the Republican party, contributing much more—perhaps five times more—than New York to the party's coffers. The leading agencies were the Manufacturers' Club under the direction of Dolan, Swank's Iron and Steel Association, and Joseph Wharton's Industrial League. In other states the Home Market Club of Boston and the Republican League of the United States in New York performed similar functions. Fry-the-Fat Foster's Republican League, which had 300,000 members enrolled in 3,625 clubs, took the lead in canvassing the rank and file, asking workingmen to contribute one dollar. The responses poured in, prompting a psychological, as well as a financial, tie to the Republican party. Gradually, and with much effort, the apathy gave way despite the protracted tariff debate in Congress. At last Quay had the funds necessary to conduct the kind of political campaign he considered essential to victory.[16]

Rhetoric as a Liability

Convinced that success depended partly on the proper balance between campaign rhetoric and campaign silence, Quay viewed the loquacious senators as only one phase of his problem. The two most troublesome individuals were the two most prominent—the presidential candidate himself, and James G. Blaine, the "Plumed Knight," who in the minds of many was the uncrowned party chieftain. Since newspapers made a monotonous habit of printing campaign speeches in full, they always provided opposition writers and speakers with statements to attack. Quay wanted to minimize the need for party responses to charges by the enemy and recognized that a prudent use of oratory was the best means.

With the disruption of Blaine's 1884 campaign by Rev. Samuel D. Burchard's three little words (Rum, Romanism, and Rebellion) still a vivid memory, the chairman declared his dislike for spouting candidates. Throughout the campaign, always fearing that something unwise had been said, he opened the morning newspaper with trepidation. This concern was obviously conveyed to the Harrison camp, but how directly is not certain. Henry L. Stoddard insisted that it was categorically agreed that Harrison would stop making speeches if Quay objected. No public confrontation on this point ever occurred, but in the heat of the campaign Harrison invited Blaine to speak in the Midwest and even expressed a willingness to go to New York for Blaine's gala at the Polo Grounds. Since Quay regarded the campaigns in the East and the West as separate entities, he saw both Harrison proposals as potential sources of embarrassment. Newspapers speculated that he interceded, explained the facts of political life to the candidate, and effectively applied the muzzle.[17]

From his front porch in Indianapolis, the candidate made short, happy speeches. He captured the spotlight in the early weeks of the campaign and held it effectively while Quay was still organizing in New York. In August when Michener called at Republican headquarters, Quay asked if Harrison "would continue making those wonderful speeches to the end of the campaign." If he has "the strength to do that," Quay predicted, "we could safely close these headquarters and he would elect himself." These words hardly reflected Quay's inner feelings: he did not consider the Midwest crucial to the election outcome, yet he did not view the candidate's speeches as a deterrent. Harrison responded with a similar show of respect, praising Quay for his management of the campaign and declaring, "My ambition will be not to put any stumbling blocks in your way."[18]

Quay could not accept Blaine's involvement with the same cavalier spirit. The uncrowned king was returning early in August from visiting the crowned heads of Europe. With the help of his legion of admirers, he made a dramatic reentry on the New York scene. A naval parade was planned to escort the vessel bringing him home, but had to be abandoned in favor of a one-boat (1,500 capacity) welcoming delegation that went out in the harbor to accompany him to the dock. An elaborate dinner with highly charged speeches was included in this extraordinary attempt to honor the man who had led the party to defeat in 1884. The overall display plainly expressed the dissatisfaction of his hard-core adherents with the candidate chosen by the Chicago convention.[19]

Quay was among the greeters. As chairman of the national committee, he could not do otherwise, but he was thoroughly disgusted at a spectacle that threatened the unity of the party by placing Blaine's popularity in competition with Harrison's. The old-line Stalwarts who had fought Blaine for years denounced the reception as the launch of a Blaine-for-secretary-of-state movement rather than an incident in a Harrison-for-president campaign. Those leaders already committed to Harrison, such as Sherman and Clarkson, feared that a Blaine-Harrison entente would place Blaine, whom they had vigorously opposed at Chicago, between themselves and the would-be president. Visibly upset by the pageant, Clarkson left town rather than witness it. Conceding that "a certain amount of this hero worship is pardonable because unavoidable," Sherman vented his feelings in a note to Harrison and sneered at "the folly and flummery of this Blaine reception."[20]

If Quay had any doubt whether Blaine would be a campaign asset or liability, it was erased as soon as the Plumed Knight returned home to Maine. In a speech at Portland, reported widely in the press, he spread consternation among the managers at campaign headquarters by assuring his audience that trusts "are largely private affairs with which neither President Cleveland nor any private citizen has any particular right to interfere." This was counter to both public sentiment and the Republican platform, which clearly stated the party's "opposition to all combination of capital, organized in trusts or otherwise, to control arbitrarily the conditions of trade among our citizens." Newspapers at once pounced on the inconsistency. Dubbing Blaine as Harrison's Burchard, they predicted that this utterance would do more harm to the Republican cause than anything that the Democrats could initiate.[21]

Quay privately conceded the wisdom of their comments and quietly found a way to turn the Blaine faux pas into an advantage; in fact, without realizing it, the newspapers helped. One writer suggested waggishly that Quay modify his Beaver note to read: "Dear Blaine: Don't talk; don't write." Like the mice that wished to bell the cat, the Republican press, in general, insisted that the wings of the party's bald eagle had to be clipped. The mice could find no one willing to accept their assignment, but the press found Quay. Although Blaine was hailed as a great orator and possessed a devoted following clamoring to hear him speak during the campaign, his espousal of an unpopular, protrust attitude threatened the party with irreparable damage and provided Quay with the necessary wedge. Prior to Blaine's most prominently billed speech, at the Polo Grounds in New York, Quay successfully curtailed his freedom of speech for the duration of the campaign and confined him to glittering generalities. In the Polo Grounds address he discussed two innocuous topics—the evolution of the tariff (scarcely getting beyond 1861) and Cleveland's plot, with the aid of the South, to bring disaster to the nation. Blaine's change in style was apparent; he had been transformed from an exciting orator to an ordinary stump speaker. One reporter characterized his speech as "Foraker-ism tariffized, the bloody shirt in a new form." Another saluted Quay because "who but he could have stopped Blaine." Still another memorialized: "The Republican Committee have squelched the orator. . . . He will soar no more." Then in dramatic conclusion he added, "The eagle's scream is hushed, the eagle's soul is crushed, and he will simply roost on a barn yard fence and sing of Grover Cleveland's vetoes and the tariff of the last century."[22]

The editing of his ideas solved only part of the Blaine problem. He had accepted speaking engagements through the West, but Quay knew that he was a campaign liability in certain of these states because of the publicity given to his trust statement. In Illinois, Iowa, Kansas, and Nebraska, antitrust sentiment ran high, and Blaine's appearances there could only imperil Republican chances for victory. Forced to limit his western trip to Michigan, where he had been requested by Alger, and to Indiana, where he had been invited by Harrison, Blaine hailed the tariff as the all-important issue. Harrison was particularly eager to have Blaine make an appearance that would seem to endorse his candidacy. After witnessing the lavish reception for Blaine in New York, Quay approved Harrison's request, but was vexed by the number of appointments scheduled. Over Blaine's vigorous protest Quay reduced his Indiana appearances to six. Since Blaine could not publicly refuse to comply without seeming to resist the national committee, Quay was able to control his itinerary and have him quickly returned to the doubtful states of the East (New York, New Jersey, and Connecticut), where a warm welcome was assured and the possibility of campaign damage diminished.[23]

Quay's Manhattan Project

Even in the East, Blaine was on the periphery of the campaign strategy. Ranking members of the national committee knew of Quay's scheme, but the presidential candidate did not have the slightest idea of what was being planned. From the inception of the campaign, Quay had recognized that the state of New York would be the principal battleground and that in New York City the issue would be resolved in hand-to-hand fighting. But as late as the third week of September, he was unwilling to admit to Harrison's chief deputy, Louis Michener, that he had any particular surprises for the people of New York. To Michener's inquiry concerning the progress of the canvass, he responded with a superficial untruth: "We are banking in the city campaign here largely upon an anticipated change in the Customs-House."[24]

The Republicans' emphasis on "the integrity and purity of elections" in their platform implied a certain dissatisfaction with the results of the 1884 election in which Blaine was defeated by a few votes in New York City. But Quay's decision to engage in a little intrigue to carry the city was not conditioned wholly by this experience. When he was editing the Beaver *Radical*, he concluded that election fraud was peculiar to cities and that New York was the most wanton example. He denounced elections there as little more than useless trouble. Even if only legitimate votes were cast, predetermined majorities could be manufactured by a system of false counting. Using the Grant election of 1868 as an example, he noted that in one division of the Sixth Ward, with a population of 850, there were 934 votes cast, "more votes than there were men, women, children, aliens, and dogs."[25]

The outlook for 1888 was indeed bleak. For the first time since 1853, "The

Democrats have the national and state patronage and also complete control of the municipal machinery in N. Y. City & Brooklyn." This was a great advantage for any party, especially for the Democratic party, but Quay accepted the challenge. He established a precedent by assuming direct control of the campaign in New York City. For the first time in the party's history, the national committee directed a local campaign in order to make certain that "the Republicans shall not only cast their votes, but those votes shall also be counted."[26]

To show his determination, Quay established a fraud fund through which the Republican National Committee offered $25,000 in rewards for the conviction of election offenders. For the first person judged guilty of illegal registration or illegal voting, the committee promised to pay $2,000 to the informant, $1,000 for the conviction of the second offender, $500 for the third, and $250 for all subsequent convictions until the fund was exhausted.

New Yorkers were indignant. Within two days a clerk at party headquarters presented Quay with a bushel basket filled with letters from irate citizens. One proposed to pay his way back to Pennsylvania if he would agree to stay there. Another offered a reward of his own—a stipend of $100 to anyone who would put Quay in the penitentiary "where he belonged." After sampling these uncomplimentary reactions, the wily chairman sighed: "I have come to the conclusion that the Democrats do not love me." Unperturbed, he turned his attention to the problems on his desk.[27]

The *New York Times* led the denunciation, defending the election laws of the state as the best in the country and condemning Quay's proposals as "both needless and impudent." It assured the nation that "the vote of this state and city will be honestly cast, fairly counted, and accurately returned without his help." New Yorkers, however, were not alone in their humiliation. The announcement of the fraud fund also disturbed Philadelphians. Aware that the major contributions to the Republican campaign were coming from their city, they resented being called upon to pay what they considered the full cost of preserving the purity of the New York ballot.[28]

The psychological advantage accruing from the fund was apparent with the first conviction. When a New York detective, who by good fortune was a Democrat, provided the evidence necessary to convict a Rhode Island Republican of illegal registration in New York City, the impact was stunning. Even skeptics were convinced. They would have scoffed at Quay as the missionary of political purity if the first victim had been conniving to vote for Cleveland. Although they may have had no respect for his motives generally, they could not deny that his fraud fund converted every supportive citizen into an election watchdog and intimidated anyone contemplating false registration or illegal voting.[29]

In spite of these efforts to promote election purity, there were frequent charges by both Republicans and Democrats that men were unlawfully brought in from other states to cast illegal ballots on election day. This method of vote control, known as colonization or pipe-laying, required the perpetrators to supply assumed names and false local addresses to the city's registering officers. Quay feared this maneuver more than any other and took his most dramatic steps to prevent it from ruining the Republican chances for victory. He had learned from John Davenport that a private census of New York City was an essential prerequisite to an honest election. Quay agreed to this prodigious task, which Davenport was asked to oversee. In order to remove any hint of politics, an apolitical individual was hired to direct the total project. Under the guise of a business venture to develop a new city directory, a building was rented on Broadway, and a sign inscribed "New York City Directory" was hung on the door. Outwardly the enterprise had no political connections, and viewed as a speculative endeavor, it attracted no newspaper attention. With the exception of the director, whom Davenport had placed in charge, none of the hundreds of employees knew that he was engaged in a master political plan. Davenport never entered the building and received only written reports that were forwarded, in turn, to Quay.[30]

For some weeks this was the busiest place in New York. Thousands of names were collected by canvassers, processed by clerks, and charted by draftsmen. The final result was a picture of New York's population, plotted by geographic location rather than listed alphabetically. The distribution of the city's male residents was detailed on hundreds of maps, each a drawing of a city block with every house, hotel, tenement, and saloon designated. Every dwelling was coded for the number of both actual and possible inhabitants. When these charts were checked against the list of registered voters, inaccuracies were noted and investigated, with the result that numerous bogus registrations were discovered before election day.[31]

In order to delineate New York's voting public still further, a second survey, totally independent of the first, was undertaken. Ostensibly in behalf of realtors who were seeking a composite list of all vacant rooms, apartments, and buildings, this fact-finding mission was designed to detect colonizers by providing a preelection tabulation of all housing vacancies. Knowing that thousands of names could be illegally assigned in certain wards of the city which were crowded with cheap lodging-houses and tenements, Quay had those areas analyzed with particular care, and upon completion of this second survey, pointedly outlined the total project to the nation's press: "We mean to look carefully after any one who registers or attempts to vote from any of these rooms or buildings which have been occupied only recently, especially from those where a considerable number of those new occupants appear in the same building, and more especially if, as seems to be the case, these new occupants are all inflamed with such a burning zeal for the good of their country that they have promptly registered."[32]

As additional fact and rumor concerning the "innocent" city directory leaked and spread, New York Democrats broke into laughter. Tammany poked fun and called it a desperate bluff to snatch victory from certain defeat. Quay was rebuked for his clumsy attempt to perpetrate such a hoax, and the Republican party was chided for not knowing "better than to have put a greenhorn over here to run a campaign in this town." The *New York Times* was scathing in its condemnation and gratuitously provided Quay with its sage advice:

> Don't delude yourself with the notion that New York is Pennsylvania. In your own state, where you have for years carried on a roaring trade in political corruption, there is no such thing as a public conscience. Your fellow-citizens, Mr. Quay, have been drugged and stupified with protection paregoric. The Republican Party has for years bribed your voters with the proceeds of tariff bills made in their interest and as they demanded. So it happens that in Pennsylvania your henchmen have escaped the common jail, though not the suspicion of deserving an acquaintance with it. . . . The roads to our jails are in excellent condition. We have uncommon facilities for sending convicts to Sing Sing, for instance. It will afford us great pleasure to show the interior of that famous structure to any or all of the interesting gang of Philadelphians whom you have brought to this city to aid you in securing "an honest vote and an honest count."[33]

According to Frank Leach, compilation of this unique directory had cost approximately $100,000. With an investment of such magnitude, Republican leaders could not long permit themselves to be cast in the role of political buffoons. According to Tom Platt's recollection of this crisis in the pages of the *New York Times* after Quay's death, the mastermind of the scheme challenged Tammany Hall with a sharp message: "I have the names of the bona fide voters of every election district in New York. If any fraud is attempted on election day, we are not only in position to detect it, but we will see to it that the guilty go to prison."[34] To demonstrate the effectiveness of the project, Quay invited one Democrat to observe a private but dramatic revelation of the directory as a political weapon. *McClure's Magazine* vividly described how Quay invited the selected opponent to headquarters after the draftsmen had completed the final charts. Explaining that the piles of port-folios, stacked half-way to the ceiling, contained the names and addresses of all of New York City's male voters carefully arranged block by block and house by house, Quay pulled down a typical volume to illustrate his point. With a wave of the hand, he added: "These books contain the names of the men who have a right to vote. If others vote, the jails will not be big enough to hold them."[35]

This revelation came two weeks before election day. New York particularly was tense and threatening. The Democratic newspapers directed their attack at Quay personally, and the political atmosphere quickly became charged. The chairman received menacing letters advising him to leave town or be assassinated. Whether for precautionary purposes or psychological advantage, the national committee accepted the threats as genuine, hired detectives to guard him day and night, and purchased a half-dozen Colt repeating rifles to be strategically placed in Everett House where he resided.[36]

Threats and tricks, rumors and maneuvers, all multiplied as the day of decision moved inevitably closer. Some reenforced Quay's design; others impeded it. Some opened opportunities requiring action; others exposed indiscretions requiring silence. During this final spurt for votes, the Republicans sustained the most devastating blow to their campaign. It involved Harrison's home state, and Quay moved as deftly as possible to minimize the embarrassment. The incident developed, in part, because of undercurrents of dissension between the national committee on the one hand and the Indiana Republican organization and the presidential candidate's personal advisers on the other. A poll conducted early in September indicated that unless the prevailing trend were reversed Grover Cleveland would carry Indiana. The local leadership appealed to Quay for funds to intensify the campaign, but he was not particularly sympathetic. Supplying a few thousand dollars, he noted that the Indiana leaders had made a pledge at the national convention to carry the state without assistance if Harrison were the nominee. In fact, the national committee had been advised to permit Indiana to operate independently during the campaign. Quay stated that his funds were committed and that Indiana Republicans should reach into their own pockets again. Unable to find the necessary funds there, the state's leaders turned to Chicago Republicans, who proved to be more understanding and charitable than Quay. They pumped new life into the Indiana campaign effort, but at the eleventh hour the outcome was still very much in doubt.[37]

The treasurer of the national committee at the time was William W. Dudley of Indiana, known to Democrats as "Two Dollar" Dudley because of the standard price he reputedly paid for votes in a previous election. He tried to help the cause by sending a circular to all Indiana committeemen advising them how, with the proper use of funds, they could corral the doubtful and undecided voters: "Divide the floaters into blocks of five and put a trusted man with necessary funds in charge of these five and make him responsible that none get away and that all vote our ticket." This invitation to bribe voters was reported to Indiana Democrats by a railroad mail clerk whose curiosity concerning the large number of letters going from Republican headquarters to party members in Indiana caused him to open one of them. When disclosure was made by the *Indianapolis Sentinel* on October 31, Quay was stunned. His only public reaction was to denounce it as "another Democratic lie," but he privately engaged a detective who quickly learned the name of the mail clerk. He advised both the clerk and the Democratic party that a prosecution for tampering with the U.S. mail would follow. In the meantime Dudley declared the "blocks of five" circular to be a forgery and instituted law suits against the journals that printed the story. Although the letter was unquestionably authentic, time and bombast favored the Republicans. The election came before the bribery attempt could be fully exploited.[38]

On the other side of the ledger, the Republicans received an unexpected assist, particularly in procuring the New York vote, from across the continent. George Osgoodby, a citrus grower in Pomona, California, writing under the nom de plume of Charles F. Murchison, conceived of a way to involve England directly in the election. Throughout the campaign both Republicans and Democrats were engaged in the popular American sport of "twisting the lion's tail"; stump orators argued that their respective parties were more anti-British, and thus pro-Irish, than the other. In the name of Murchison, supposedly a naturalized citizen of English birth, Osgoodby wrote to Lionel Sackville-West, her majesty's minister to the United States, expressing his sympathies for the mother country and asking which presidential candidate was more favorably regarded by England. The dull-witted Sackville-West never questioned the integrity of his petitioner. Violating one of the cardinal guidelines for emissaries, he became involved in the nation's internal affairs by replying on September 13 that Murchison should vote for Cleveland. This response appeared to resolve the issue of England's loyalties, but Osgoodby was uncertain how to divulge the results of his diplomatic probing. With help from the Republican *Los Angeles Times* and several self-appointed aides, the Murchison–Sackville-West exchange was released to the public on October 21. Whether Quay received the original, as Leach asserts, or just a copy is not certain, but he at once detected an opportunity to twist the tail of the Democratic donkey. Reproducing "millions of copies" of the exchange, he had them sent throughout the country to hundreds of newspapers. The effect was instantaneous.[39] Republicans were exhilarated and Democrats chagrined. Guilty of no act of omission or commission that deserved this turn of fate, the Democrats for the first time could fully appreciate the Republican reaction to "Rum, Romanism, and Rebellion" of four years earlier. The Republicans had Burchard, but now the Democrats had Sackville-West.

To Quay it was appropriate retribution, but some New York Democrats had difficulty accepting it as another political accident; they suspected that it was a cheap trick devised by Quay. There is no evidence to support such an assertion. President Cleveland himself attempted to treat the issue on a dignified level in spite of incessant demands from members of his own party that Sackville-West be dismissed. He laid the case courteously and dispassionately before the English government, but Lord Salisbury either did not comprehend what his minister had done or did not see the urgent need for action. When he in effect declined to intervene, Sackville-West was handed his passport, but the political damage had already been done.[40]

This incident provided the capstone of Quay's campaign to capture the Irish-American vote, especially in the state of New York. In New York City, where more than a quarter million citizens were expected to make the trek to the polls on election day, every third voter was likely to be of Irish extraction. This crucial bloc was overwhelmed with both Republican and Democratic attention. The only other ethnic groups to receive any significant Republican recognition were the German-Americans, Italian-Americans, and Swedish-Americans. The Republicans set the political worth of these groups collectively at $7,500, but the Irish vote alone was valued at $110,000. About $80,000 of this was raised by the national committee and the remainder by Wharton Barker, who took such a personal interest in electioneering among the Irish that he contributed $30,000 to assist them in perfecting their Republican organization. Although such expenditures represented a new emphasis, they did respond directly to the "up-trend" in Irish-American voting that George Hoar had earlier called to the attention of Harrison. At that time he advised the nominee to denounce contract labor, a source of growing irritation to Irish voters who, in turn, were expected to be impressed by Republican recognition of their problem. [41]

When Quay first took charge of the national committee, he too was aware of the potential votes in the Irish neighborhoods of New York City. Four years earlier Blaine had registered significant gains in traditionally Democratic Irish wards before his candidacy was crippled by the unfortunate Burchard remark, and the chairman wanted to build on the foundation that Blaine had identified. He established an Irish bureau within his committee and invited Patrick Ford, editor and publisher of *The Irish World*, to submit a realistic program, with an adequate budget, for a successful Republican campaign among the Irish-Americans of New York City. The editor accepted the invitation, responding with a plan for a fourteen-week campaign to which he assigned a price tag of $73,465. Consisting primarily of ward organizers, speakers, mass rallies, and special mailings, it was approved and funded for $55,000 by the national committee. To cover other approaches to the Irish vote and at the same time quiet Barker, who questioned Ford's leadership, the committee expended an additional $25,000.[42]

Barker argued that many Irish voters were recent converts from the Democratic party and that the leader responsible for that trend, which he hoped to encourage, was Dr. William Carroll. Barker contributed his funds through Carroll, but Quay was suspicious of this faction and worked primarily with Ford. Barker complained to Harrison that Quay's tactics only caused dissension among the Irish. At the same time he conceded that his own work had been so successful that Quay's ineptness would not deter the Irish from voting the Republican ticket.[43]

Quay paid little attention to Barker's intrusiveness. He quietly pursued his own predetermined course with the Irish as he did with the city directory project. Not permitting himself to be deflected by Barker's laments or Dudley's absurdity, or by less personalized threats and rumors, Quay was prepared with still another innovation by election day. He regarded the successful completion of the city directory as a worthless exercise if not reinforced by an equally valid technique to ensure an honest count. With the cooperation of certain police officials and dedicated young Republicans, Quay arranged to have the election returns from all New York and Brooklyn precincts reported to him as soon as they were tallied. He persuaded the police, who had been in the habit of collecting the returns and carrying them to city headquarters dominated by the Democrats, to provide him with certified copies of the results from each precinct. Since the New York polls closed at 4:00 P.M. and the returns were quickly sent to City Hall, changes, if deemed necessary, might be made there without anyone from the outside being aware of them. With certified copies in his hand, Quay thought that he could effectively discourage such alterations.

The police did their work flawlessly. Before midnight both Republicans and Democrats had an accurate reading of local and state voting, but the latter did not know that Quay had a precinct-by-precinct tabulation of the city vote. Calvin S. Brice, Quay's counterpart in the Democratic organization, issued a statement to the effect that Cleveland had carried New York and would be reelected. Since this was contrary to the trend expressed in the early results, Republicans maintained that it was proof that their opponents planned to alter the city returns, but given the element of bluff in any political leader, this was hardly prima facie evidence of any intention to engage in a fraudulent count.[44]

At Republican headquarters that election night, the scene was guardedly optimistic. In the early evening an immense canvas had been stretched above the entrance, and the first returns were flashed on it from a stereopticon. This unique spectacle attracted a crowd of inquisitive and sympathetic onlookers along Fifth Avenue, who filled the block and cheered with each new pictorial indication that Cleveland was in difficulty. Obviously eager and impatient, Quay remained secluded in his second-floor den throughout most of the day and early evening. Fitfully reading incoming telegrams and dictating a few of his own, he intermittently puffed on a cigar and paced the floor. At 10:00 P.M. he emerged, purportedly waved the certified returns above his head, declared that Harrison had carried the state of New York (although losing the city to Cleveland), and defied the Democrats of the city to alter the results.[45]

Quay's prediction of victory proved accurate. Officially the result went unchallenged, but New York Democrats charged that he had bought the state for Harrison with his large "corruption fund." Denouncing him as a thief and villain, they based their argument on the fact that Cleveland had failed to carry the state while David B. Hill, the Democratic candidate for governor, was elected. Hill's margin of victory in New York City was approximately thirteen thousand votes greater than Cleveland's, and Harrison had defeated Cleveland by a similar number of votes in the statewide race. Cleveland's supporters suspected that this was not a coincidence. A victory for Warner Miller, the Republican gubernatorial candidate, would have so increased his prestige within the Republican state organization that he could have challenged Platt's control. Thus the Cleveland advocates deduced that Platt and Quay had bargained with Hill subordinates. They further charged that it was to the mutual advantage of the two Republican bosses and certain of the city ward leaders to trade off Miller for Harrison votes.

On the other hand, it could be argued with equal force that no bargain was necessary. Influenced as they were by liquor interests, the city leaders were frightened by Miller's outspoken endorsement of more rigid liquor regulations and waged a quiet, but exaggerated, campaign against him. More and more Republicans who favored stronger liquor control were gravitating to the Prohibitionist party, and Miller believed that a forthright stand was needed to reverse the trend or at least to hold others within the party's ranks. He knew that this was a dangerous course, especially since Platt disapproved, and could imperil his gubernatorial chances. On the positive side he believed that such action was necessary in order to hold the state for Harrison; he hoped that the candidate would then be grateful enough to reward him with a place in the cabinet. Of course, Platt and Quay could not accept this theory because it would have meant their directory scheme, Irish bureau, and other tactics were either unnecessary or unproductive.[46]

Democratic ward leaders understood that if they could elect Hill and Hugh J. Grant, the Tammany candidate for mayor, they could exercise uncontested control over the city's taxing and spending power. The Cleveland candidacy weakened their chances for success, especially since Cleveland and Hill were the best of enemies. Thus Democrats who assigned priority to victory in the city were as likely to unfurl "Harrison and Hill" banners as any Republican. On November 3 the Republican high command attempted to counter the move to cut Miller in favor of Hill; a strongly worded statement was sent to leaders of every assembly district of New York City, over the signatures of the chairmen of the national, state, and county committees, advising that factions of the Democratic party were offering to vote for Harrison in exchange for the endorsement of Democratic candidates for mayor and certain county offices. Although the "Harrison and Hill" combination was not specifically mentioned, the Republican district leaders were reminded that "the safety of our party demands the loyal support of all its candidates, national, state, and county," and violations would result in having the leaders of any offending district "personally held in strictest accountability." Officially this placed the Republican organization squarely behind the whole ticket, but it did not erase the possibility of collusion, especially since Quay's allocations of $125,000 to Platt in the last two weeks before the election is unexplained by existing evidence. In the ledger entries of the national committee's disbursement statement, the chairman was vague, noting only that the funds were assigned to Platt for the "city" campaign or for "special" purposes.[47]

Shortly after the election the *Cincinnati Enquirer* reported on the extent of Platt's political funds, a story the Republicans had endeavored to keep secret. Quay took notice of this report, which appeared in other newspapers as well, by writing to assure Harrison that all funds spent by Platt during the campaign were allocations "made upon consultation with me, at my request, and under my direction and that he used & received no money for any illegitimate purpose or which was not accountable for—to my satisfaction."[48] Quay did not deny that Platt had received an overly generous war chest and did not elaborate on the purposes for which the funds had been authorized. This, of course, was characteristic of his treatment of Harrison. He told him as little as possible about the conduct of the campaign; in all probability no presidential candidate ever knew less. Coming from a person as direct and concise as Quay, this response was suspect and by its nature suggested that the charge by Cleveland advocates that certain New York wards were purchased could not be summarily dismissed.

On the other hand, there was a mountain of evidence to demonstrate that Quay and Platt were not culprits, only the fortunate recipients of the fruits of Democratic dissension. Conditions within Democratic ranks were no more serene than within the Republican. Like Platt and Miller, Cleveland and Hill feuded over patronage and control of the state organization, but their differences became more public and affected the fortunes of the party more directly. The fact that Hill enjoyed a popularity among labor groups not sympathetic to Cleveland was a notable distinction. In New York City he alone profited from the diverse campaigns waged by Tammany and the county organization, both of which ignored the national ticket in their canvass.

Cleveland admitted that there had been two relatively distinct campaigns in his home state. The presidential race focused almost entirely on tariff issues, while the state contest highlighted such charged local topics as liquor regulation and ballot reform. Since Hill hoped for a presidential nomination in 1892, his future could be best served by Cleveland's reelection in 1888. He should, therefore, be above suspicion in any plot to bargain away support for Cleveland.

Contrary to Democratic emphasis, the Republican campaign in the city had given the presidential election the highest priority. Quay and the national committee had assumed primary responsibility for the New York campaign. In their eagerness to provide Harrison with "a fair vote and honest count," they minimized the state and local contests to the detriment of Miller's candidacy. They did not attack Hill with the same vehemence that characterized their assault on Cleveland. The argument that Republican success in the Harrison-Cleveland and Miller-Hill races was directly proportionate to the campaign effort could thus be substantiated with equally valid documentation.[49]

In November 1888 most Republicans did not have time for such postmortems; they were too eager to celebrate their victory. Party leaders applauded Quay as the "greatest political general" in the nation's first century of partisan politics. One declared that he deserved "a monument of 18 carat gold." The party press eulogized him as a master strategist, and James S. Clarkson paid tribute to "the magnitude of the triumph," which, he passionately claimed, "no one can at this time either estimate or comprehend. It will affect and perhaps control the politics & the policies of the nation for half a century."[50]

Through this election success the Republicans recaptured control of the central government and infused new life into the party. Victory always implied a kind of success, but in the presidential triumph of 1888, the scope was definitely limited, and the popular base of the Republican party was not broadened. In many ways the victory was the greatest smoke screen of political accomplishment in the annals of American history. In spite of larger campaign expenditures than in any previous election and thousands of speeches prophesying doom if the Democrats were permitted to control tariff policy, Harrison was a minority president. Nationally he received 100,000 fewer votes than Cleveland, and in percentage of total vote cast, the Republicans dropped from 49.8 percent in 1884 to 49.5 percent in 1888. Only two states in the nation changed their electoral vote designations from those of 1884; New York and Indiana, both by narrow margins, were converted to the Republican fold, and by that thread victory was achieved.[51]

In New York City, where Quay had labored so vigorously, the Republicans captured 39.7 percent of the total Democratic-Republican vote. Four years earlier the party had garnered 40.4 percent of that vote. In New York state the party had 50.5 percent, an increase of less than six-tenths of 1 percent above the 1884 count in which the Republican total was supposedly handicapped by the Burchard blunder. In contrast the Republicans registered notable gains in certain southern states. Although they did not punch any holes in the solidly Democratic electoral wall of the South, Harrison obtained more southern votes than any Republican candidate since the end of Reconstruction. Through Quay's "spot" campaigning within certain of these states, his party captured nineteen seats in the House of Representatives—three in North Carolina, three in Tennessee, two in Virginia, two in Kentucky, two in West Virginia, one in Louisiana, four in Missouri, and two in Maryland.

These congressional triumphs were important. The Republican majority was only five, so a switch of three would have given the Democrats the opportunity to organize the House. Under such circumstances, more than luster would have been subtracted from the Harrison victory. The Republican administration of that body launched Thomas B. Reed on a distinguished career as speaker, introduced William McKinley as chairman of the Ways and Means Committee, and brought the McKinley tariff to passage. For the first time in sixteen years, the Republicans had complete control of both houses, a significant achievement considering that the Democrats had controlled the House of Representatives for six of the preceding seven sessions. Thus success in Congress enhanced both Harrison's popularity and the legislative status of all his proposed measures.[52]

Quay had limited his southern expenditures primarily to four states— Virginia, West Virginia, Tennessee, and North Carolina. George W. Delamater, with help from William "Bull" Andrews, both Quay henchmen from Pennsylvania, disbursed approximately $63,000 in the first three; but Frank Leach, dispatched to North Carolina with only $5,000, met the most Democratic hostility. He operated in the Raleigh area during the two months preceding the election and engaged Pinkerton detectives, who fanned out across the state as organizers and supervisors. Their tactics appeared to win adherents, but were unappreciated by the Democrats, who suggested that they desist or be lynched. As a result, some of the Leach out-of-state workers left early, but he himself remained until election day and expressed considerable pleasure in capturing the three seats.[53]

In most southern districts where the Republicans were victorious, the margins were slim and the Democrats did not surrender without a struggle. Knowing that each seat was crucial in determining control of the House, Democratic leaders in Washington alerted their subordinates in districts where the elections were hotly contested to juggle the vote in order to "count out" the Republicans. Under normal circumstances the offended GOP candidates would have challenged such conduct before the local election boards, charged with the responsibility of ferreting out election frauds and verifying the returns. But many southern Republicans were too poor to bear such an expense or an even more costly court battle if that should be necessary to resolve the issue. It was expected that by such intimidation some would be forced to relinquish legally won seats to their opponents; but Quay, who had gone to the nation's capital, learned of the scheme and moved quickly to frustrate it. Telegraphing a crisp, "Come to Washington. The Democrats are trying to steal Congress," he summoned Leach to initiate a counteroffensive. Together they hired detectives to watch the schemers while assuring the challenged candidates that the national committee would assume all costs incurred in securing their elections before election boards and in the courts. This in itself provided the major deterrent to the Democratic maneuver. When Southern leaders threatened not to certify the election of Republicans to the clerk of the House of Representatives, Quay retorted: "We do not care what the Democratic governors . . . may do. They are not dealing with children and old women. The Republican Party will hold with a mailed hand all that it fairly won on Nov. 6."[54]

In tying up these dangling political ends and preserving the victory, Quay assumed that the basic assignment of the office to which he had been appointed was successfully discharged and took note of his accomplishment in a modest telegram to the president-elect: "The National Committee is closing its headquarters, and its last act is to congratulate you and the country upon your election."[55]

Altruism Versus Practical Politics

1889-1890

SURPRISINGLY, Quay and Harrison had never met. They had both been delegates to the 1880 national convention, but moved in completely different circles; Quay was among the Immortal 306 while Harrison maneuvered to nominate Garfield.

With the 1888 election over, Harrison received congratulatory messages from all parts of the nation, and well-wishers with either gratuitous advice or the desire for political recognition thronged to Indianapolis. Quay meanwhile remained busy in Washington, securing the loose election ends so that the Democrats could not "steal Congress." He too received accolades from partisans in all states of the Union, and in the Republican press he was compared to every hero from Cato to Napoleon, from Washington to Lincoln. Depicted as the only public man, other than U. S. Grant, who had achieved political leadership through the eloquence of silence, he was approached, in person and by letter, by nearly every politician who had rendered service during the campaign. To these seekers he was certainly a more prominent figure than the president-elect, but he endeavored to turn all overtures aside. Declining countless invitations to dinners and receptions, he serenely explained: "I am the same Matt Quay I always was, and I don't want any demonstration made over me."[1]

Harrison expressed his appreciation to Quay for the "brilliant work done during the campaign" and extended an invitation to visit Indianapolis "at such time as suits your convenience." Being a practical-minded politician, Quay assumed that the president-elect would recognize his accomplishments, as the nation had, and would freely respond with practical rewards. When, without prodding, Harrison advised him that he would conclude nothing "in which you are likely to be interested . . . before our conference," the chairman continued to be optimistic.[2] Delaying for six weeks, he learned what he could from others who had discussed the incoming administration with Harrison and mapped his own strategy accordingly. He concluded that he would not suggest any topic for discussion, but would willingly talk about any subject initiated by the president-elect. Everyone expected the general topic of the conference to be the composition of the cabinet. When asked by a newspaper correspondent to comment on the purpose of his visit, Quay replied with his usual grim humor that he "came to Indianapolis simply and solely to perfect with Gen. Harrison the details of the inauguration festivities."[3]

The details of this historic meeting were never publicly released, but the press popularized its occurrence nationwide. Accompanied by Leach, his private secretary, and several others, Quay arrived in Indianapolis shortly before midnight on December 18 with little ceremony. No one met him at the railroad station, and only two of Harrison's subordinates extended a welcome that evening at the New Denison Hotel. His appearance in town coincided with the national meeting of the Loyal Legion, a veterans' organization for commissioned officers who had served the Union during the Civil War. In the morning after breakfast a crowd composed mostly of local politicians and Loyal Legionnaires swarmed about him. "All kinds of fulsome flattery were showered upon him, but he never as much as smiled." During this display of respect and admiration, a former president of the United States and current grand commander of the Loyal Legion, Rutherford B. Hayes, sat almost unnoticed and unattended in an upstairs bedroom. Quay, who had shown little deference for his abilities when he was in the White House, made no effort to greet him. Taking note of the incident, the *New York World* sarcastically asked why Hayes had been ignored by the national chairman. Condemning both, the paper charged that "the former accepted a presidency which other men stole; the latter bought a presidency for another man to accept. The difference is hardly great enough to warrant the President-maker in snubbing the President-taker."[4]

Colonel John New, a member of the victorious Republican National Committee, drove Quay and his entourage to their appointment at General Harrison's home on North Delaware Street. Welcomed at the door by his private secretary, they were escorted to the parlor, where Harrison met for the first time the man who had successfully managed his campaign. Grasping Quay's hand, he said solemnly: "Providence has given us the victory." Outwardly polite and placid but inwardly chilled and shaken, Quay made no immediate comment about Harrison's blind faith in the doctrine of foreordination. Believing that religious methods were not among the most persuasive, particularly in a city election, he related the incident to A. K. McClure some time later, referring to the pious president-elect as a "political tenderfoot" for suggesting that the Almighty had wrested New York from the Democrats. To the journalist he exploded: "Think of the man! He ought to know that Providence hadn't a damned thing to do with it" and suggested that Harrison would probably "never learn how close a number of men were compelled to approach the gates of the penitentiary to make him President."[5]

After an exchange of pleasantries and attention to detail, the subordinates left the president-elect alone with the man who did not talk for publication. They conferred for two hours, shook hands amicably, and Quay returned to the New Denison. The lobby crowds gathered around him again. Excusing himself almost at once, he went upstairs with a thumping headache that the attendant journalists suggested had been brought on by Harrison. In the room of Colonel William Goodloe, Kentucky's member of the Republican National Committee, who was in town for the Loyal Legion convention, ice was put on his head for an hour or more to relieve the pain. When the afternoon train to Washington arrived, Quay was at the station; his short stay and sudden departure surprised everyone. He gave no verbal hint of his impressions except a prudent: "I don't know how other people get along with General Harrison, but I can get along with him all right." The *New York World* found this disheartening because, in its opinion, any president with whom Quay could "get along" would hardly be able to inspire public confidence.[6]

Failure as a Cabinet Maker

To Tom Platt, his trusted ally, Quay was more candid. Upon returning to Washington, he confided that he had been unable to reach any agreements in Indianapolis. According to Platt's description of the senator's report, "the President-elect was all ears and no tongue" and "turned a frigid and contemptuous shoulder." Although reluctant to admit it, Quay had learned from that brief encounter that it would be exceedingly difficult to dictate any appointment to Harrison. From an earlier incident in the campaign, he had already received almost incontrovertible evidence that the Hoosier would not bargain. In 1884 James J. Hill, who was constructing a railroad empire and amassing a fortune in the Northwest, had contributed $5,000 to the Democratic campaign fund, but apparently had become disillusioned with the return on his "investment." In 1888 he offered the Republicans ten times that amount on the condition that, in the event of victory, he be granted the right to name a cabinet officer. He was obviously seeking special favor for his railroads and wanted Harrison to agree to appoint, as secretary of the interior, one of three men whose names Hill would submit after the election. Harrison not only rejected the bargain, but also stipulated that no contribution be accepted from Hill, even without conditions.[7]

Quay made it clear that he did not seek a cabinet post for himself. It was equally apparent, however, that he did expect to control federal patronage in Pennsylvania and influence suitable appointments for a few colleagues who had worked diligently during the campaign. He held no dogmatic preferences concerning the assignment of individuals to specific positions; he knew only that certain types of recognition were appropriate. He had gone to Indianapolis with an open and constructive attitude concerning the cabinet; he had wanted to impress on the president-elect the wisdom of having the Keystone State and the South represented—the former out of respect for past services and the latter in anticipation of future contributions. To Quay the election results had exposed potential weaknesses in the Democratic South, and he wanted Harrison to exploit them. Republicans could at last make great strides toward becoming a truly national party if they hung out a sign of encouragement. The appointment of a southerner to the president's official family would be interpreted as such a sign.

Quay did not consider his responsibility for promoting individual appointments to be nearly so crucial. He planned only to recommend Platt, Clarkson, and Sherman for proper recognition of their services and to carry out his obligation to Wanamaker. Since Platt believed that he had received a positive preelection pledge from Harrison through Elkins whereby he would become the secretary of the treasury, there was little for Quay to do except acknowledge his continued confidence in the New York leader. After the election Platt expected his appointment to be announced at any time, but the report on Quay's visit and a month of additional silence caused him to become impatient and suspicious. Without mentioning the treasury post specifically, Platt wrote a threatening letter addressed to Michener but intended for Harrison. Expressing his analysis of the power and preferences of the Republican masses in New York, he charged that "the whole power of the party in this state, which is able to bring about results, is at my back." Whether or not Harrison understood is uncertain, but he refused to be coerced. Declaring that he had never made such a commitment, he appointed William Windom of Minnesota as secretary of the treasury and created a credibility gap with New York Republicans that he was never able to close.[8]

The chairman's wishes concerning his other colleagues were no more adequately respected. He personally preferred to send both Blaine and Wanamaker to diplomatic posts, but they were ultimately assigned to the cabinet. Quay's nominee for the state department was John Sherman, but since Harrison had always belonged to the Blaine wing of the Republican party, his resolve to appoint Blaine was no surprise. Blaine's supporters and detractors, however, contended so vigorously for the president-elect's ear on this matter that delays and uncertainty prevailed. When the appointment was finally announced, Harrison was attacked from both sides. While the anti-Blaine leaders, particularly those of Pennsylvania, were perturbed because of his choice, the Blaine advocates, and most assuredly Blaine himself, were perturbed because Harrison required even the semblance of pressure to reach his decision. That hesitation apparently prevented complete harmony between the secretary of state and the president from ever developing.[9]

On the other hand, the relationship between Wanamaker and Harrison grew more harmonious than Quay preferred. As a Republican National Committee nominee for a cabinet position, Wanamaker had the senator at a disadvantage; Quay could not appear less than supportive without arousing suspicion and misunderstanding. The Philadelphia merchant prince had provided the party with the largest war chest in history, and only an ungrateful party or chairman could oppose his appointment. When neither Harrison nor Wanamaker snapped at the bait of a diplomatic assignment for the latter, Quay did not disclose his personal feelings, but publicly promoted Wanamaker's entry into the political arena. After his Indianapolis visit, he surmised that he had few alternatives. Since Harrison was more favorably inclined toward Wanamaker than toward any other Pennsylvanian, and since Quay desperately wanted cabinet recognition for his state, Quay decided to play the political cards as they were dealt. His endorsement of Wanamaker, however, was a Pyrrhic victory because it sapped his political strength for almost a decade. Quay had reached the zenith of his power and prestige with the Harrison victory, but in achieving this distinction, he had relied, in part, on Wanamaker's direction of the special Republican finance committee. It now became necessary to "pay the piper" whose price could not be calculated in terms of dollars. Having developed an appetite for politics, Wanamaker demanded the right to sit at the table. He wanted recognition, but only succeeded in becoming the senator's "bitterest and most dangerous foe."[10]

During his deliberations over the cabinet, Harrison invited Wanamaker to Indianapolis, but Quay in his cautious manner did not regard this as conclusive proof that he had finally been chosen. He caustically referred to "his call to Mecca . . . as resulting from Harrison's desire to meet and measure one he had never yet encountered." When he did designate Wanamaker as postmaster general, Harrison considered the appointment as a concession to the national committee and was determined that he would make only one such allocation. Quay did not appreciate this attitude, and during February 1889 he addressed several letters to the president-elect conveying as much. He wrote specifically in behalf of James Clarkson of Des Moines, the deputy chairman of the national committee and owner of the *Iowa State Register*. The committee had originally recommended him for a cabinet assignment, and Quay reiterated the reasons for that action, but Harrison replied with a firm no. He explained that he had already filled the only slot to which he could have appointed him—that of postmaster general. Since Clarkson was Quay's personal preference for that position, the rebuff was particularly irritating. Somewhat conciliatory, Harrison expressed a willingness to appoint Clarkson to a less significant post. When he offered that of assistant postmaster general, he reluctantly accepted, but gradually became obsessed with the idea that he had been victimized by Harrison.[11]

Harrison's decision against Clarkson was due, in part, to the excessive pressures to which he was subjected. Since the Republican party had been denied access to executive patronage for a term, the demand for spoils was greatly intensified. Harrison was aware of the continuing newspaper reaction to the lavish Republican campaign expenditures and wanted to be certain that cabinet appointments were not stigmatized as political payoffs. On this basis he concluded that no more than one post should be filled by a close associate of the national committee.

Newspapers speculated wildly concerning the cabinet choices. Names and sources of information were tossed about indiscriminately, and Harrison realized that the only expedient course was to say nothing; he was reluctant even to issue denials or defend himself. In spite of his preference not to respond, Wharton Barker's allegation that Wanamaker's appointment was a sop to Quay drew a retort. He pointed out that one appointment did not constitute an alignment, "a cabinet selection from a state did not mean the crowning of a boss, and should not put any barrier between me and any other friend." In response to Barker's insinuation that he had strayed from his avowed goals, Harrison righteously reproved him: "You did not need to quote from my former letters, for I had not forgotten their import and a perusal of the extracts you give me does not show anything that I would desire to retract or modify." The president-elect also demolished Barker's argument that it would be better for Pennsylvania not to be represented in the cabinet than to be represented by a Quay protégé. He pointed out that in every state there is some opposition to every appointment and that, if Barker's advice were systematically followed, there would be no appointments at all. Throughout the period in which Harrison was formulating the cabinet, he remained extremely sensitive to public opinion. He wanted to avoid any suggestion that the cabinet appointments were a series of rewards for services rendered. He therefore bypassed the prominent state leaders who had contributed to his election success and selected a politically obscure cabinet. By so irritating the state power-brokers, he isolated his administration from his party at the outset.[12]

Harrison showed his hypersensitivity to the power of the bosses in his reaction to the charges brought by Carl Schurz, an itinerant journalist and political reformer, regarding Wanamaker's campaign integrity. Assuming that his designee as postmaster general was guilty until proved innocent, he at once summoned Quay to his apartment in the Arlington Hotel. It was March 3, the eve of the inauguration. The senator, accompanied by Leach, who remained in the carriage, arrived as soon as possible. Harrison reported that Schurz was protesting Wanamaker's inclusion in the cabinet because he had made a deal with railroad promoter Henry Villard. Reputedly Villard had been promised, in the presence of New York banker Jesse Seligman, that his railroad empire would not be antagonized by the Harrison administration if he contributed generously to the campaign. Harrison insisted to Quay that either he receive a denial of the charge from Wanamaker, corroborated by Seligman, or he would not appoint him to the cabinet.[13]

When Quay returned to Leach on the street, "his face seemed ashen in the gas-light, and his lips trembled as he spoke." This was one of the few times in his life that he was visibly angry and excited. He began by blurting out: "Harrison is going to cheat us," but he quickly regained his composure and proceeded to map a strategy to carry out Harrison's dictum before the inauguration at noon the following day. Leach was sent to Philadelphia on the midnight train to brief Wanamaker and bring him back to the capital. The senator's son, Richard, was commissioned to locate Seligman, who luckily had come to Washington for the inauguration. At 11:00 A.M., an hour before the swearing-in ceremony, Quay assembled all the principals of this frantic interlude in his house at 1518 K Street—Harrison, Wanamaker, Seligman, and members of the Republican executive committee. Wanamaker declared that the charge was totally without foundation, and in supporting his statement, Seligman confessed that he "always had had a very poor opinion of Carl Schurz's veracity and that Henry Villard was worse than Schurz." Harrison was satisfied, but with the executive committee still present, he addressed himself to his host: "I want to have a chat of about 15 minutes with you and then, if you feel as you do now, I will appoint Mr. Wanamaker." When the others had retired, he elaborated on his position. "Senator Quay, I will appoint Mr. Wanamaker if you insist upon it, but you are making the political mistake of your life. It will be a great mistake for you to have anyone from Pennsylvania between me and you, and I will not appoint him unless you insist upon it." Quay promptly uttered words that he lived to regret: "I am willing to take that chance." At least on this occasion, Harrison was more politically astute than the boss.[14]

The problem of appointments continued to plague the Harrison-Quay relationship long after the inauguration. The president's personality and lack of understanding concerning the role of a national chairman, complicated by

Quay's own political ambition, kept the party leadership in turmoil. Possessing a "cold, distant temperament," Harrison had difficulty in establishing personal friendships. He was a good public speaker with a convincing presentation, but could not sustain favorable impressions if they evolved into across-the-table relationships. From the standpoint of those who had personal contact with him, he was one of the most unsatisfactory of American presidents.[15]

Totally unsympathetic to the spoils element in government, Harrison refused to admit the existence of certain practical realities. When convenient to his purposes, he ignored his debt to the politicians, denied their role in his election, and occasionally depicted himself as the chosen instrument of the Almighty. James N. Huston, chairman of Indiana's Republican Committee, was flabbergasted by such assumptions and found it impossible to influence Harrison's attitude toward appointments. The president felt that party members had no justification for making demands because they had done nothing for him. Rolling his eyes piously toward the ceiling, he told Huston that "it was the Lord that made that nomination and caused that election." Doubting that the Lord had outmaneuvered Gresham, Blaine, Allison, and Sherman at the Chicago convention, or had solicited a huge campaign fund from business leaders, or had compiled a city directory in New York, Huston bluntly observed: "Well, Mr. President, in future campaigns Republican workers had better sit down at home and let the Lord carry on the fight." Quay's experience in Indianapolis had prepared him to cope with this theme. In the course of a White House conference, when he was advised that "the Lord did it," he with characteristic silence "took his hat, cast upon Harrison a look calculated to spoil milk, and left." This attitude nevertheless served the president well. It was an ingenious device for keeping politicians at arm's length, but gave rise to numerous snide remarks of which Quay supplied his quota. When he tried to discourage one office seeker by telling him that the president would probably not consent to his appointment, the man was mystified. Incredulous that the president would not happily comply with a request from the national chairman, he demanded: "Doesn't he know that you elected him?" Shaking his head, Quay was quick to explain: "No, Benny thinks God did it." When Harrison questioned the integrity of another of Quay's designees for appointment and then formally rejected him, Pennsylvania's junior senator concluded: "They are now so damned pious over at the White House that they even open oysters with a prayer."[16]

Driven in part by a naive ambition to convert the Republican party to a Bible class and in part by a determination to soar above the party, Harrison assumed sole responsibility for its destiny, an assumption that shaped patronage struggles. The bosses had staked their reputations on campaign promises which they could not now fulfill. Content to watch them squirm, Harrison retained all appointments firmly within his own grasp. They were forced to admit openly that the president did not accept them as equal stockholders in the party. Quay sarcastically confessed that only "Ben and his creator" controlled the appointments and that one was as conversant on the topic as the other.[17] Blinded by patronage needs, Quay and the other bosses disagreed with Harrison's attempt to raise the selection of office holders to a higher plane, scan a broader political horizon, and act as a president responsible to the total nation. They wanted Harrison's role as elected head of the government subordinated to his role as titular head of the party. In his more reflective moments Quay agreed with Harrison. "Patronage," he admitted, "is a positive disadvantage to a party and particularly to a politician. Everybody cannot be gratified, and for every single appointment a dozen or more who have been disappointed become disgruntled and indifferent." Yet he was unwilling to practice what he professed. Although he knew that patronage could not long prevail over principle, he would not concede that the time for principle had arrived. On this he differed with Harrison, and the appointments battle continued.[18]

Quay was not alone in his dissatisfaction with the president. To Wisconsin, New York, and Illinois, where Henry C. Payne, Tom Platt, and Shelby Cullom, respectively, exerted forceful leadership, Harrison turned his political back with equal consistency. In the smaller states it was his general policy to defer to the senatorial and congressional delegations, but in the well-organized states he wanted to escape the charge of surrendering to the powerful bosses. To Quay this was politically embarrassing because he was repeatedly forced to yield to Wanamaker, whose power was thereby inflated. An open rupture between them came when he refused to accept Quay's candidate for postmaster at Philadelphia and was sustained by the president. Wanamaker nominated John Field, an able businessman who had served on the Committee of One Hundred. Disregarding the established custom for a president to make no appointment to office in a state unless acceptable to its U.S. senator(s) of the same party, Harrison concurred in the nomination. Senator Cameron, who had no faith in Harrison's political usefulness, joined Quay in lodging a protest, but to no avail. Their thirty-minute interview with the president succeeded only in permanently widening the breach between Quay and Wanamaker.[19]

In a token effort to pacify the senator, his nominee for collector of internal revenue in Philadelphia, David Martin, was approved, but the *North American* seized the occasion to criticize Harrison for succumbing to the boss's persuasive influence. Newspapers across Pennsylvania repeatedly classified every federal appointment in the state as either a victory or a defeat for Quay, and their interpretations were reprinted nationwide. With every commission that was signed, both Quay and Harrison thought that their prestige was at stake. The Republican party, and perhaps the nation as well, would have benefited immeasurably if neither Quay nor Harrison had kept score by reading the newspapers, but they did the human thing, and the struggle became even more heated.[20]

The fundamental difference in philosophy between Quay and Harrison was clear, but it was further accentuated by misunderstanding. The president was never able to comprehend Quay's role as national chairman. During the campaign he had issued orders to the individual state chairmen, and they complied to the best of their abilities. They had served him, and when the subject of patronage came to the forefront, they expected him to serve them. This was particularly true of chairmen from states that did not have potent Republican organizations, such as those in the South. He was their contact, and they made their requests known to him.

At times with comment and at times without, Quay forwarded proposals to the president, who believed that to comply was to reward Quay personally. When he became completely obdurate, Quay had the patronage requests accompanied by endorsements to emphasize that they were not his alone. One request from Mississippi was sponsored by a host of the party's luminaries— McKinley, Allison, Hoar, Sherman, New, Dudley, and others. Another from Pennsylvania was signed by both Quay and Cameron, along with a note to the effect that the state's total delegation was willing to support the request. Through such means Quay hoped to demonstrate to the president that he operated from a position of power and would use political muscle if necessary, but Harrison could not be persuaded to cooperate.[21]

As Harrison continued to organize the administration, Quay's letters became more offensive, and their relationship inevitably deteriorated. After attempting unsuccessfully for months to goad the president into action on the matter of Pennsylvania patronage, the senator read an account of an interview, given at the White House to a Pittsburgh news correspondent, in which Harrison was quoted as being ready to take up the Philadelphia appointments, but could not do so because the state's senators were not available and he had no idea when they would be. Quay immediately interpreted this statement as a presidential trick to shift the blame for the delay. He dispatched a caustic telegram to the president, reminding him: "I have received no intimation from you that my presence was desired or that you were ready to act." To show that he was ready to proceed, the senator identified the six positions to be filled, nominated six individuals, and urged "that the appointments be made at once." This reaction only served to foster additional delay and strain the lines of communication.[22]

When one aspirant asked Quay to endorse him for a consular post, his reply, with a copy to the president, was far from encouraging. "My recommendations for consular appointments in behalf of my own constituents have received very little consideration since the 4th of March, 1889. Indeed, I do not believe any of the persons whose appointments I have requested have been successful." Until the spring of 1892 there seemed to be no indication that the president wanted to alter the impression outlined by the senator; on that occasion, however, he advised Quay that he needed a candidate for consul at Birmingham. He pointed out that the incumbent had been recommended by the iron and steel industries and concluded that "it would be well in filling the place to have regard for the same people." Quay was invited to review the situation: "Let me know who you think should be appointed."[23] This new approach, contained in the most favorable letter pertaining to appointments that he ever received from the president, caused Quay to suspect ulterior motives. With the national convention and possible renomination only a few months away, Harrison obviously wanted to mollify both the senator and the iron and steel interests, but his overture was too weak and too late.

The Bargain Hunter

Celebrated as the party's president-maker, Quay had no intention of losing his momentum or having his influence limited to executive appointments. When the Fifty-first Congress convened in December 1889, there was still a modicum of doubt concerning control in the House of Representatives because of contested seats. The senator wanted to make certain that the individual selected as speaker would be sufficiently autocratic to retain the slight Republican margin while resolving the seating problem. Together he and Cameron controlled all but four or five of the Pennsylvania representatives in the House, and they agreed that the entire delegation would support Thomas B. Reed of Maine for the speakership. Although it was considered improper for members of one house to interfere with the organization of the other, this did not inhibit Quay. His sub-rosa work with representatives from Pennsylvania and other states surfaced at times and prompted newspaper retorts. The *Boston Herald* complained that he was a "pretty big toad in the speakership puddle." Others predicted that the resentments and antagonisms engendered by his intervention would handicap Reed's selection by his House colleagues.[24]

Reed's competition for the speakership came from William McKinley, with whom Quay had a minor altercation concerning a vacancy as solicitor of internal revenue. Sherman had first presented the name of an Ohio candidate and then withdrawn it in favor of Quay's nominee, but McKinley took up the case and ultimately the Ohio applicant received the appointment. Although Quay was angry and vowed to even the score with McKinley, the incident had little bearing on Quay's speakership preference. He was probably drawn to Reed because of his greater innate ability to command. McKinley was not as brutally partisan as the Maine representative, who proved to be more dominating than Quay himself. To the senator partisanship was a business; to Reed it was more an inner feeling, more a way of life. Quay wanted someone in the chair who could be relied upon to dominate the House despite the near balance between Republicans and Democrats. By his standards Reed was an excellent candidate; he was a "rough rider" who never pulled rein because someone was in the way or could get hurt. In an emergency he could recklessly disregard right and justice to achieve the desired result, for example, in the seating of a requisite number of Republicans.[25]

Some observers believed that Reed's tactics on the seating of members, more than the documentary evidence, gave the Republicans their final margin in the House. On this and subsequent issues, he assumed an omniscient ability to determine majorities with his eye and to rule motions out of order indiscriminately. Coupled with his refusal to entertain appeals from the chair and his arrogant recognition of members of his own faction only, this conduct threatened the House with anarchy. Quay was depicted as the power behind the speaker and charged with part of the blame. He was particularly indicted for advising Reed on how to invent a majority where none existed, how to manufacture a quorum in cases of political exigency by counting as present members who were not voting.[26]

Quay's interest in selecting the speaker was not merely to establish strong leadership, but also to exert his personal influence on the makeup of committees and develop leverage in dealing with a recalcitrant president. He was not able to overturn the time-honored practice of seniority, but he did exhibit a significant negative control. He succeeded in keeping his enemies from key committees on which they had not yet served, and the four Pennsylvania representatives who refused to support Reed in the party caucus were denied all the committee assignments they requested. Quay also spread the word to the various executive departments that they were to receive no favors.[27] In utter frustration the *New York Saturday Globe* fumed: "This man runs the Republican Party. He is now running it in Congress, as he has hitherto run it in the greatest Republican state of the Union. He has organized the House in the interest of trusts and the tariff monopolies. His speaker disgraces the chair by his tyranny. His Ways and Means Committee is framing the alleged revision of the tariff, which is to be brought in and passed when a sufficient number of Democratic seats shall have been filled by Republicans."[28]

Newspaper critics and political opponents alike exaggerated Quay's power. Through his silence he accepted credit for all the deeds and misdeeds that his detractors wished to heap upon him. The *New York Star* denounced as myth the statement that John D. Rockefeller was the richest man in the United States, proclaiming in an editorial that Quay was the "king plutocrat" because he owned a president, vice-president, and a speaker of the House, in addition to holding a grip on the postmaster general and exercising dominance over Pennsylvania. In fact, the senator from Beaver had much less influence with the president than had been claimed; he could sway Vice-President Morton only through his "partnership" with Boss Platt; his hold on Wanamaker was extremely tenuous; Reed remained more or less independent; and his dominion over the Keystone State was severely threatened before the end of 1890.[29] Early in the year, however, all publicly visible signs identified him as a Republican superman.

Quay's critics could not attack his legislative program—he had none—so they denounced what they considered the sterile functions of a senator. Ignoring their concept of the legitimate duties of his office, he engaged in political exercises that were only partially understood, but thoroughly condemned. Although he spoke a language of commitment to the protective tariff, which was the breath of political life in Pennsylvania, he did so as one doing his job rather than out of conviction. More clearly than any of his contemporaries, he grasped two fundamentals of the legislative process: power was centered more in the flow of legislation than in its substance, and a bill usually passed not because it was meritorious and equitable, but because its sponsor was shrewd and ingenious. Armed with these discoveries, he became the manipulator of the process. Successful conduct of this role precluded any close identification with the substance of legislation, a condition totally compatible with his personality. Not gifted as an orator, he was required to sponsor no bills and make no speeches.[30]

Although the days of Clay-Webster oratory were long past, the *Congressional Record* was still filled with speeches, mostly not given, but if given, inflicted on unattentive legislators and empty benches. Eloquence was no longer a major highway to legislative action. Quay was in step with the trend. He regarded the speechmakers as those providing the facade for the real march of legislative progress occurring in committee rooms, cloakrooms, and hotel dining rooms. In these more relaxed surroundings, he calmly but persuasively planned, schemed, and debated with his colleagues; there his most effective work was done, often in a whisper between cigar puffs.

The Fifty-first Congress provided Quay with ample opportunity to exploit his backroom techniques. With both houses under Republican management, party leaders were determined to proceed at once to remove an apparent contradiction: they were confronted with a treasury surplus, yet during the campaign of 1888 they proclaimed the need for additional income from protective tariffs. To Americans who perceived no relationship between themselves and foreign imports, this was an unnecessary inconsistency. Rather than attempt an explanation, the Republicans resolved the problem by declaring war on the surplus. They looked to the military past (veterans) and to the military future (navy) as the principal beneficiaries of their largess. The Pension Act of 1890 was so beneficial that it rendered the veterans' organizations almost speechless, and the total spending program was so extensive that these two legislative years were labeled the "Billion Dollar Congress."

Victory in 1888 left the Republicans with other legacies. They were committed to redeem three major campaign pledges: to ensure a free and honest ballot, to provide increased protection for domestic production, and to adopt a monetary plan for the effective use of both gold and silver. In spite of the diversity of these topics, they became intricately related, particularly in the Senate, before legislation on any of them could be enacted.

Since separate Republican factions gave three different emphases to these issues, logrolling began before any legislation was assured passage. With six northwestern states (North and South Dakota, Montana, Washington, Idaho, and Wyoming) admitted to the Union in 1889–1890, the power of the West in Congress was enhanced, and silver legislation was quickly brought to the floor. Ideally, this section wanted the free, unlimited coinage of silver. Alert to the inflationary character of such legislation, the debt-ridden South provided additional support. In the Senate a coalition of Democrats, mostly southerners, and fifteen Republicans comprised a bloc that enacted the Sherman Silver Purchase Bill, which obligated the treasury to buy a total of 4,500,000 ounces of silver monthly and pay for it in notes redeemable in either silver or gold at the discretion of the secretary of the treasury.

Buoyed by their new western allies, Senators Wolcott and Teller of Colorado had urged support for the Sherman proposal and set the tone for negotiations by declaring that the silver interests of their state were entitled to as much consideration as the iron interests of Pennsylvania. Convinced by neither the substance of the measure nor this comparison, President Harrison had opposed it. Quay, on the other hand, never got beyond a consideration of the practical implications of the comparison. He needed western votes for the tariff legislation and knew that endorsement of the silver proposal was the best insurance policy he could buy.

William McKinley, as chairman of the House Ways and Means Committee, along with Senator Nelson W. Aldrich, assumed the primary responsibility for framing tariff legislation, but critics of protectionism detected other influences at work. They maintained that, at the instigation of party managers, "the strongest and most reckless of whom is Matthew Stanley Quay," the House committee was packed with the friends of industry. Known as the "high priest of high protection," McKinley was more chronicler than designer of the tariff. Manufacturers were invited to testify before the committee and state the level of protection they considered desirable; a dutiful committee generally recommended those approximate rates. Inevitably protection was boosted to its highest level—an average of more than 48 percent on durable goods. In fact, protection took a variety of forms: certain duties curtailed foreign competition and slowed the rate at which a surplus could be accrued; other schedules tended to eliminate competition and launch domestic industries in tin plate and armor plate; and still others hushed the outraged cries of the farmer by adding almost meaningless duties to such agricultural products as wheat, corn, barley, and potatoes that entered the American market in only limited quantities.[31]

Quay was vitally concerned with the legislative progress of the tariff because of his many promises to industrialists during the 1888 campaign. If he hoped to conduct future "fat-fries" at their expense, he had to fulfill the commitments that were still outstanding. Thomas Dolan, president of the Philadelphia Manufacturers Club, which had contributed most generously on the assumption that higher rates would accompany a Republican victory, had no intention of permitting him to forget. He wrote to Quay, reminded him of their understanding, and predicted that foreign imports would flood the American market if the McKinley tariff were not enacted at once. Although such letters pressured Quay, he nonetheless welcomed them. They contributed to his mystique by perpetuating the fundamental tariff fallacy—that protection must always be promoted and that manufacturers are at the mercy of the politicians who control legislation. Both financially and strategically this fallacy did much to retain Quay and his colleagues in power. Anyone who attacked them was denounced as an enemy of the tariff and debaser of American industry.[32]

The third issue before the Congress was an administration measure known officially as the Federal Elections Bill and unofficially by its opponents as the "force" bill. Sponsorship in the Senate rested with George Hoar, chairman of the Committee on Privileges and Elections, and John C. Spooner of Wisconsin; and in the House direction was given by Henry Cabot Lodge and Speaker Reed. The most highly partisan of the three Republican proposals, it aroused the bitterest of sectional antagonisms and threatened the total legislative program of the session. The bill gave federal circuit courts, rather than governors and state election boards, authority over congressional election procedures and returns; it was in theory applicable to all congressional districts in the nation, but in reality was aimed at the South alone. Its endorsers described it as a reaffirmation of the Fifteenth Amendment and a reassertion of the principles of national citizenship. To its opponents the bill was a thinly veiled attempt to undermine white control, reimpose Reconstruction, and reestablish carpetbag rule in the South.[33]

Advocates of the bill represented the remnants of bloody-shirt Republicanism, and their reasons for sponsoring such legislation ranged from altruism to practical politics. Typical of the altruistic element, President Harrison believed that this measure offered the most effective means of protecting the constitutional rights of blacks to vote and to have their votes counted. Senator Hoar also was motivated by the concept of purity in elections. Incidents during the 1888 congressional elections—shootings, terrorism, and ballot box stuffing—had shown that blacks of the South were being denied political equality. This group maintained that a federal elections law was absolutely necessary; if no action was taken, Democrats and journalists would taunt the Republican party with its failure, when in power, to right a grievous wrong, about which it had persistently complained.

Lodge and Reed were no less adamant in their endorsement, but their motivation was quite different. The latter fully explained the basis of his support when he addressed the Americus Club of Pittsburgh. Invited to speak at the 1890 observance of General Grant's birthday, Reed suggested that the elections bill was designed primarily to secure party ascendancy, not to remedy an injustice. The tone of his remarks revealed that the fundamental purpose of the measure was to drive a wedge into the Democratic South and at the same time devise a plan to perpetuate Republican control of the House of Representatives for an indefinite period. The speaker's comments were painfully clear to the business leaders, both those assembled and those who read the newspaper accounts of his address; Reed's intention was to make the elections bill, not the tariff, the leading issue of the session. He declared that there was nothing radical in the House proposal. Without interfering in state elections, it merely sought to place the election of representatives and presidential electors under federal control. There was no fear of black domination of the Congress, but with such a procedural revision the Republicans could expect to be reinforced by approximately thirty congressmen from southern states because there were that many districts in which Negroes outnumbered whites.[34]

Since the Negro was now counted equally with the white in the determination of congressional apportionment, the black population entitled the South to greater representation than it had enjoyed before the Civil War, when the three-fifths clause operated. This change, which prevailed from the days of Reconstruction, encouraged the Republican party to compete for the black vote in the South. The Democratic response was to intimidate blacks and keep them away from the polls every election day. To the extent that suffrage was denied, the white Democratic South gained an improper number of seats in Congress. This so frustrated Reed and other partisan Republicans that they demanded federal action, through the elections bill, to prevent the Democratic South from again being overrepresented.

Reed implied to his Americus Club audience that, if the South wanted to deny blacks the right to vote in *state* elections, that was a *state* decision beyond his concern. Cautioning that the practice should not be extended to congressional elections, he was nevertheless willing to overlook the franchise principle that had dominated Reconstruction thinking, turn his political back on the bloody-shirt argument, and view the South simply as a section with votes to be won. This in essence was the philosophy of the elections bill. The Republican party, he maintained, was entitled to the Republican vote of the South whether that vote was "ignorant or sensible. If ignorant, we need it to offset the Democratic ignorance which votes in New York and other large cities. Why should they poll their ignorance and we not ours?" Thus denying that the bill was sectional, he called upon the federal government to sever its ties with state elections and conduct its "own registration, [its] own counting, and [its] own certification." He predicted that the bill would pass the Senate within ten days after being introduced.[35]

Seated at the speaker's table, Quay shook his head at this pronouncement. Although Harrison personally asked for favorable action in the Senate and although an illustrious array of Republican senators supported the measure— Orville Platt, George Edmunds, William P. Frye, and Joseph R. Hawley, in addition to Hoar, Spooner, Sherman, and Allison—Quay understood what Reed did not. He not only expected southern sensitivity, he also counted northern numbers, not reputations.[36]

Lodge was in general agreement with Reed's arguments and pointed out the bill's procedural merits. Too much energy was expended simply to ensure fair elections; the efficiency of Congress was gradually being reduced by the embarrassing number of contested election cases rising from the suppression of the Negro ballot in the South. He estimated that from thirty to sixty working days per session were devoted to resolving conflicts that belonged in the courts rather than in the House. Adjudication by the courts would tend to keep incidents localized and prevent the engendered bitterness from becoming nationalized.[37]

Southern Democrats agreed completely with the interpretation of the elections bill that Reed presented to the Americus Club, but they could not have agreed less on the justification for that position. Not only was the measure a frontal assault on white supremacy, it also suggested that the central government exercise final control over the definition of a voter, a denial of a state's right as old as the Constitution itself. Convinced that federal court actions pertaining to voters and elections in the South could not be sustained without popular consent, southerners assumed that the North would resort to armed intervention. The experience of Reconstruction had taught the vivid truth of this possibility, and they denounced the measure as a "force" bill. This argument in itself did not win many adherents among northern Democrats, but when the bill was seen as an instrument for Republican power in the South, it assumed a vital meaning for Democrats above the Mason-Dixon Line. To undermine the party in the South was to invite national Democratic disaster.[38]

Certain influential Republicans also found the bill repugnant to their economic and political aspirations. Led by Secretary of State Blaine and Murat Halstead, editor of the *Cincinnati Commercial*, one group rejected the proposal because it was inconsistent with the 1888 campaign strategy that agreed to ignore the Negro and forget the bloody shirt in favor of courting the white, protariff voters in the South. Quay accepted this view and believed that further legislation in behalf of Negro rights was hopeless and could only incite the sectional controversy anew.[39]

The national chairman also endorsed the economic position advocated by the nation's business leadership in regard to the elections bill. The peace, prosperity, and industrial growth that began to emerge in the South shortly after the withdrawal of the demoralizing carpetbag governments of the Reconstruction era were financed, in part, by northern capital which now stood shoulder to shoulder with southern enterprise. The economy of the former confederate states was flourishing. Northern bankers were growing secure in their southern investments, and sectional cooperation was becoming a reality. The "force" bill threatened that development. In the opinion of the business interests, it would produce ill feeling between the sections and disrupt the conditions necessary for economic cooperation. Senators sensitive to the demands of investors argued that the bill could only frustrate southern industry and deny the North an investment market. They pleaded, with the "election purity" adherents, for "peace and patience." As the days and weeks passed, their argument gained in acceptability. New York, Philadelphia, and Boston gradually understood that the cause of Atlanta and New Orleans was properly the cause of all.[40]

Quay foresaw the tangle into which the Senate could be thrown by the elections bill and realized that it could imperil all legislative action. Particularly concerned with the progress of the tariff bill, in which Pennsylvania and the total business community had an important stake, he worked to prevent an impasse. The Democrats feared that Republicans favoring the elections bill would unite with those supporting the tariff to enact both measures. If a choice existed, Democrats certainly preferred protection to the regulation of elections. Its southern faction, however, was more positive; it demanded a guarantee that the latter be removed from the realm of possibility. Business leaders, largely within the Republican party, agreed. They viewed the tariff as an urgent need and the elections bill as an economic liability. The advantages accruing from the tariff were expected to be offset by the decline in southern investment opportunities that would accompany passage of an elections bill.[41]

Quay understood that neither the southern Democrats nor the business leaders would compromise. Accepting this premise, he endeavored to sway enough northern Democrats and enough "pure election" Republicans to accommodate these nonnegotiable demands. Since he also believed that subsequent attempts at Negro legislation were exercises in futility, he had no qualms, political or otherwise, in subordinating Senator Hoar's bill to the McKinley tariff. This became his strategy. Although vilified as a sponsor of white supremacy in the South—and denounced for favoring manufacturers who had contributed generously during the 1888 campaign over Negroes who had no such gifts to bestow—he proceeded on a dangerous course that threatened to split his party.[42]

Since the Senate had no rules limiting debate, Quay had to negotiate a set of guidelines for the conduct of legislative business in the session or face a Democratic filibuster. Suspecting that the Democrats sought either to force an understanding on the elections bill or convert the entire first session of the Fifty-first Congress into a Senate talkathon, he decided to bargain first with the opposition and then with his own party. After the tariff had been before the Senate for two months in the summer of 1890 without any apparent end to the discussion, he went to a personal friend, Senator George G. Vest, a Missouri Democrat. Together they agreed on a plan whereby the tariff could be passed and the elections bill killed. He then consulted the Democratic floor leader, Arthur P. Gorman of Maryland, who, like Quay, did his most effective negotiating informally, off the Senate floor. Gorman regarded this as a propitious moment to strike a deal. Fearful of the threat posed by the legislation to his own party's cohesiveness, he was willing to maneuver to accentuate the tariff and table the elections bill.[43]

In mid-August, with Democratic cooperation assured, Quay presented a resolution to the Republican caucus that enumerated specific topics to be discussed during the remainder of the session. With the tariff heading the list and the elections bill conspicuously absent, Hoar and his colleagues protested. He and Spooner "read the riot act to the Senators," declaring that, as a party, Republicans were committed to both protection and election purity. They wanted a floor fight before surrendering, but in this instance

Quay believed that half a loaf was preferable to a whole. He knew that certain Republicans, strongly opposed to the elections bill, did not want to register their opposition in a formal vote because there was considerable sentiment for it among their constituents.[44]

Senator Orville Platt called Quay's proposal "a weak and cowardly surrender," and Louis Michener, the Republican chairman in the president's home state, declared that "the party will take a club to every Republican senator who fails to do his duty in that connection." Not perturbed by such vigorous vocabulary, the Pennsylvania senator concentrated on securing the endorsement of his resolution specifying that debate on the tarriff would be cut off on August 30, and that a vote would be taken at that time on all pending amendments and on the bill itself.[45]

Hoar and Quay jockeyed for position for more than a week; their maneuvering reached from the party caucus to the Senate floor and into the public press. Rarely incited to respond to his critics, the latter was forced during this political finessing to acknowledge an article in the *Washington Post*. Accused of criticizing members of the House, Quay felt compelled to correct the record; he read aloud to the Senate that part of the article which declared: "That he objected to having Southern Republicans in the House set upon him by Speaker Reed to yelp at his heels like a pack of dogs in favor of Senator Hoar's measure." He denied making such an allusion to either Reed or southern Republicans and pointed out that he would not have mentioned the statement if it had affected only himself. Implying that it may have touched a tender spot, Hoar commented that no explanation was necessary, but because of the ethics involved, Quay differed with him. He thought that he had to set the record straight because it charged him with casting "an unwarrantable reflection upon an officer and members of another branch of Congress."[46]

Hoar insisted on a revision of the resolution to include assurances that the elections bill would be given priority in the next session. Quay readily agreed to such a provision, and a conference of Republicans signed an agreement, drawn up by Hoar himself, that the measure would be kept before the next Senate session "to the exclusion of other legislative business until it shall be disposed of by vote." With this amendment Quay's resolution prevailed, although it never came to a vote. By tacit agreement its terms were carried out. Recognition of the arrangement between the Democrats and the requisite number of Republicans was sufficient indication of what was destined to happen.[47]

In keeping with the intent of the resolution, the way was cleared for the McKinley tariff to pass the Senate. Quay was hailed for rescuing the measure from the Senate dilemma; without the bargain he had arranged, both the tariff

A cartoon on the Federal Elections Bill,
Philadelphia Press, April 23, 1892.

and the elections bill would have been doomed to the wordy eloquence of a Democratic filibuster. Business interests and southern leaders were particularly gratified by the results, but Hoar and his colleagues, including the president, were disappointed over their failure to fulfill the "purity in elections" plank in the 1888 platform. Although he had credited God with his election, Harrison was now firmly convinced that Quay was responsible for the defeat of this administration measure. He was as hard pressed to document this conclusion as the first. Quay had never stated his position on the elections bill per se, but his maneuvering to advance the tariff legislation implied his dislike. In his heart he probably did oppose it, but for political reasons he appeared to endorse it.[48]

The elections bill made an anticlimactic reappearance in the December 1890 session of the Senate, and the Democrats realized that their only hope of defeating it without the help of a Quay was to talk it to death. They cleverly announced that they planned no filibuster, but immediately entered into one. Republicans, primarily from the West, anxious to consider what they viewed as more pressing issues, became impatient with the debate and moved that the bill be set aside. Forgetting their pledge to carry the issue to a floor vote, enough Republicans joined the jubilant Democrats to pass the motion, and thereby render the postwar generation's coup de grace to the civil rights effort.[49]

Trial by Newspaper
1889-1890

T HE 1889–1890 session of Congress had been a shaky introduction for Harrison and a personally troubled one for Quay. They had problems and differences in the legislative field and were bombarded by journalistic outbursts that reflected unfavorably on both. The attack was leveled at the senator, but the president also suffered, partially by association.

As early as 1885, when Quay was a candidate for state treasurer, the *Philadelphia Press* predicted that incidents from his past would become a Republican liability. Editor Charles Emory Smith expected every Democratic stump and newspaper across the Commonwealth to ring with echoes of riots, bribery, and other scandals if Quay persisted in extending his personal domination. At first the state's newspapers stood docile before this kind of evidence; there were many murmurs, but few fights. Those who fought came to an early grief. Quay rose from state treasurer to U. S. senator and to national chairman within three years without serious threat of an exposé. He grabbed patronage in Washington with one hand and dispersed it in the Keystone State with the other. This audacity caught his enemies off guard and enthroned him as the absolute proprietor of Pennsylvania before resistance could be organized. But after his success in the campaign of 1888, the *Press's* prediction began to materialize. Newspapers soon caricatured him as a sinister power behind Harrison's throne. In fact, this picture was false: the national chairman was forced to scramble for all the executive patronage he received and to endure an uncertain relationship with the president, although both kept their attitudes moderately quiet.[1]

Captivated partially by Quay partisans hailing him as the century's "greatest political general" and partially by their own words, the journalists never accurately understood the Quay-Harrison relationship of these years. Not only did this place many of their own reports in an improper setting, but it also stirred the Democrats, reform Republicans, and anti-Quay practical Republicans to a greater resentment and distrust of the party boss. Within a short time, critics of the administration, directly or indirectly, attributed most decisions to the national chairman. They were distressed by the resilience of a man who could live in the shadow of corruption and yet remain so influential that he could be called upon to make so many mistakes.[2]

Republicans accused Tammany leaders, in league with the Democratic press, of charting the personal attack on Quay because they feared that the long-range ramifications of his city directory tactics would destroy their power. Reform Republicans, led by Wharton Barker and Henry Lea of Philadelphia, joined the vendetta against Quay and the president. Disillusioned because Harrison had not reformed the civil service within twenty-four hours after his inauguration, they cited him for abusing his appointive powers and permitting Plattism and Quayism to continue. Barker had been dueling politically with Quay for a decade, but Lea was a comparative newcomer to the fray. A prominent publisher who had retired in 1885, he had contributed labor and money to help defeat Quay's candidacy for state treasurer and now wanted to renew his anti-Quay activities. Having completed a three-volume history of the *Inquisition in the Middle Ages* in 1888, he was anxious to judge the heresy that he found within the Republican party.[3]

In an open letter to Pennsylvania Republicans, published in McClure's *Times*, Lea appealed to the voters to ignore the contest for state treasurer in the November 1889 election in order to reduce the Republican margin of victory and embarrass Quay. In response to this maneuver, Quay urged Harrison to delay all Pennsylvania appointments, except the change in postmasters at Philadelphia, until after the election. Estimating that this one change was worth several thousand votes, he pointed out that if the Democratic postmaster were replaced with a Republican, the postal employees, who were mostly Democrats, could be kept at their jobs on election day rather than assigned electioneering duties. Harrison concurred, and the Quay candidate carried the election by 60,000. Although this did not equal Harrison's 80,000-vote Pennsylvania plurality the year before, it did reflect an exceptional off-year turnout, represented the largest margin of victory in the brief history of balloting for state treasurer, and gave no comfort to Quay's enemies.[4]

The Bowen Report

Although Lea failed to ignite a widespread attack by reformers against the national chairman, he did discover that Quay's opponents were becoming increasingly vocal and more diverse in their charges. Some were journalists who simply smelled a good story; others were politicians dwarfed by Quay's hastily achieved power. The most prominently overshadowed individual was Chris Magee, who by 1884 had pictured himself as succeeding Quay as the Camerons' state lieutenant. This illusion kindled great expectations, but within a year, this man of recognized ability and unquestioned achievements discovered that Quay was not stepping down, but up, and that he was in a position to suppress Magee's ambitions.[5]

Magee was bitterly disappointed, particularly according to the opinion of William Shaw Bowen, a reporter for the *New York World.* In December 1889 Bowen received an anonymous note, postmarked in Pittsburgh and handwritten on ordinary newspaper copy paper, that he suspected had been prompted by Magee. On the basis of his previous political exposés, Bowen was invited to investigate Pennsylvania: "There is a good chance for you in this state. Come to Pittsburg and see some of the leading politicians here." And then, "It affects the junior U.S. senator."[6] After discussing the suggestion with Colonel John A. Cockerill, the editor in charge of Joseph Pulitzer's *World,* Bowen agreed to investigate the possibility of a story. During a visit to Pittsburgh in January, he received a second anonymous note identifying specific individuals to be interviewed. From the available evidence, he concluded that both notes were in the handwriting of George Welshous, a Magee subordinate, and that Magee himself had encouraged the contact.

Bowen traveled throughout the Commonwealth to interview individuals who could detail aspects of Quay's relatively unknown past. His subjects ranged from casual passersby on the streets of Beaver to former Governor Hoyt and included Lea, Barker, Magee, Welshous, and a host of other political opponents, not the least of whom was the mistress of Wilson Norris, a former business partner of Quay's. Almost all were eager to vilify the senator, but some were afraid to talk while others wanted assurances that their names, the names of friends involved in particular transactions with Quay, or specific facts embarrassing to them would be withheld. Generally Bowen agreed with their conditions in order to get his story. Except for the "testimony" of John A. Hampton, solicitor for the Pennsylvania Railroad (who hated Quay but declared his only interest was "purification of politics") and that of Norris's mistress, the accounts were all verbal. Rumor and misstatement were so mingled with fact that the accuracy of the case against Quay was still in doubt after Bowen's ultimate revelations. Whereas the accounts of Quay and his henchmen tended to underexpose the facts, Bowen and his informants provided an overexposure of the incidents themselves. Although the reporter realized that he had been deliberately guided to certain forewarned individuals, he demonstrated no objectivity, only a desire to expose Quay as flamboyantly as possible.[7]

The results of Bowen's investigations were published in the *New York World* on February 10 and March 3, 1890, but he received financial encouragement to continue his quest. Sometime after publication of the second article, he received an envelope postmarked New York containing three $500 gold certificates, along with an anonymous typewritten note reading: "You are doing a good job in the Quay matter. Keep it up." On June 13 he was the beneficiary of a second envelope from the same source enclosing a single $1,000 gold certificate. Without speculating about their origin, Bowen pocketed the certificates and recorded, on the same page of the report that described this windfall, that he had reason to believe William C. Whitney and Daniel S. Lamont, trusted advisers of former President Grover Cleveland, "were greatly pleased with the publications and would put up money to have them go on."[8]

In introducing Bowen's sensational findings to its 300,000 daily subscribers, the *World* claimed that its purpose was "to expose the methods by which managing politicians gain and exercise power and accumulate vast fortunes." Since Quay's word, in the editors' opinion, weighed "more at the White House than that of any other member of his party," it seemed appropriate to focus attention on him. In a twelve-column spread, divided into chapters like a dime novel, Bowen attacked the public character and the personal integrity of the Beaver senator. Every incident in his biographical sketch was reported from the vantage point of the boss's enemies; Bowen simply painted the most lurid picture of financial and political pilfering that could be wrung from the informants' descriptions. He analyzed only those actions with which one or more of the interviewees strongly disagreed. Since the list of his revelations was extensive, but not totally accurate, the public reacted with shocked indecision. The charges did succeed, however, in sowing the seeds of rebellion against Pennsylvania bossism and in arousing the public to the need for an investigation. But without a confession or at least some explanation from Quay, no specific action could be undertaken except to renounce boss-dominated candidates at the polls at the earliest opportunity. The election was still months away. While frustration reigned and incriminations spread, Quay relaxed with a fishing line on Florida's Indian River.[9]

Bowen's account began with incidents from Quay's early life that were wholly in bad taste and partially in error. He moved quickly to the boss's political career, and in attempting to explain Quay's source of funds, he revived the negative emotions that had accompanied the betrayal of Curtin in the 1867 senatorial struggle with the elder Cameron. Purportedly Quay accepted $13,000 to muster legislative support for Curtin and $20,000 to do likewise for his opponent and then threw his personal influence behind the larger sum. Bowen then recited an incident from 1868–1869 in which Quay had been charged with offering $1,000 per week in a sealed envelope to Alexander P. Tutton, an Internal Revenue supervisor, if he ignored his responsibility and did not seize a particular distillery that was operating illegally in Philadelphia; for his maneuvering with Tutton, Quay supposedly received a $60,000 commission from the owners. Quay had temporarily ignored the rumor, but when the *Pittsburgh Commercial* accused him of malfeasance, he had instituted a libel suit. The case was heard before a Pittsburgh alderman with John Hampton representing the newspaper. Hampton supplied Bowen with many of the direct questions he had posed to Quay at the time, most of them irrelevant to the bribery charge. In a series of non sequiturs, Hampton asked if Quay had extorted the $13,000 from friends of Curtin in exchange for his support during the Senate fight, questioned him concerning the source of funds for a commercial building that he was constructing in Beaver, inquired about securities of any description from any source that he possessed during 1867, and asked about stock in the Union Passenger Railway of Philadelphia acquired during his tenure in the legislature. Quay's counsel objected to these and similar questions, and when the alderman sustained his objections, Hampton moved reluctantly to the alleged Tutton incident, asking: "Had you a conversation with Mr. Tutton relative to the seizure of a distillery in Philadelphia which did not comply with the law?" When the plaintiff's counsel objected to this as an attempt to promote self-incrimination and was sustained, Hampton rested his case. The alderman rendered a judgment against the *Commercial*. Hampton at the time, and Bowen more than twenty years later, denounced the decision.[10]

Jumping eight years in his biographical presentation, Bowen next interpreted the railroad strike of 1877 to prove that Quay, though politically bold, was physically an "arrant coward." He had falsely stated earlier that Quay had gone on active duty during the Civil War because he found "association with the upright Curtin irksome." Now he mentioned that there were "rumors" of bravery that he could not verify (Quay had been awarded the Congressional Medal of Honor in 1888), but suggested that they be discounted because of his conduct when the striking trainmen paralyzed the Pennsylvania Railroad system in Pittsburgh.[11]

When traffic on the railroad was halted during the summer of 1877, the company requested that the militia be summoned to the scene. Governor Hartranft was in the West at the time, and Quay, as secretary of the Commonwealth, was in charge. According to Bowen's evidence, he seized the opportunity to play governor and win a reputation for himself by issuing a proclamation mobilizing the militia. Philadelphia units were dispatched to Pittsburgh, where a confrontation resulted in the death of sixteen strikers. Further violence caused several million dollars in property damage. Bowen's report charged Quay personally with this loss because he ordered the troops to the troubled area where their presence incited the emotions of the strikers. When Quay came to Pittsburgh, according to Bowen, he was so frightened by the mob that he was afraid to appear in public. With face pale and hand trembling, he peered at the angry strikers from the Pennsylvania Railroad offices in the Union Depot through a crack in the window covering. Fearful that the offices would be invaded, he wanted to sneak out of town the first night. The company officials concluded that he was of no assistance to them, so they arranged for John Dalzell, who was familiar with the paths over the hill from the depot to the Monongahela River, to guide him to a skiff that took him safely to Beaver.[12]

More than a year after Bowen's publication, Quay referred to this account as the "wondrous lyric of my escape from the Pittsburgh rioters." Bowen himself admitted that he later learned that this episode was a fabrication spun by a congressman from Pittsburgh who was a friend of Dalzell's, and an ally of Chris Magee's. Dalzell, who hoped to challenge Quay for the Senate seat in 1893, never denied the tale and thereby increased the latter's displeasure as newspaper after newspaper reprinted it.[13]

The aftermath of the strike provided additional issues that threatened Quay's reputation and gave Bowen some of his choicest material. Quay was identified as the mastermind behind the riot bill of 1890, which proposed that the state legislature appropriate $4 million to indemnify the Pennsylvania Railroad for property loss during the strike. Bowen charged that only half the money would reach the company's coffers; the other half, he claimed, was earmarked for the lobby supporting the bill, with Quay named as the principal beneficiary. In order to attract votes and facilitate logrolling, a companion measure known as the border raids bill, designed to indemnify citizens of Franklin, Adams, York, and Lancaster Counties whose property had been plundered by the Confederates during the Civil War, was simultaneously introduced. A group of five legislators, headed by William Kemble, worked vigorously to win their colleagues to the riot bill, but a grand jury in Dauphin County indicted them for attempted bribery. To avoid examination in open court, four of the five pleaded guilty, and as Bowen pointed out, the guilty pleas interfered with attorney Frank Gowan's desire to implicate Quay.[14]

Two days before Kemble and his associates were to be sentenced, Quay, as chairman, called the State Board of Pardons into special session. He recommended that the four be pardoned before their sentences were pronounced, but two of the other three board members refused to acquiesce in this highly irregular action. Confronted with the penitentiary, Kemble and his colleagues jumped bail and fled. After nearly a month they were persuaded to return and accept their sentences; it had been demonstrated to their satisfaction that the recalcitrant members of the board would be more amenable to pardons after their punishments were meted out. They appeared, were fined $1,000 each, and ordered to spend one year at hard labor in the penitentiary. In less than twenty-four hours the Board of Pardons convened and set aside the prison terms. Quay explained that in the opinion of the attorney general of Pennsylvania the sentences imposed by the court were illegal and that the board acted on his recommendation. The public was indignant. Neither the board nor the attorney general was vested with the function of judicial review, but they usurped it to protect the guilty. Quay had defied the public, and the public never let him forget.[15]

Simultaneously with this incident, Quay was cited for his involvement in the first raid on the state treasury (described above, chapter 5). Although Quay maintained that his share of the investment capital had come from private sources, the best evidence supported Bowen's contention that the funds of all three investors—Quay, the retiring state treasurer, lumberman Amos C. "Square-Timbers" Noyes, and the cashier of the treasury, J. Blake Walters—had been advanced from state deposits. Quay's willingness to accept responsibility for restitution of all the funds implied more than an altruistic gesture to make certain that no public funds were lost.[16]

At this point Bowen's account, probably embellished by his informant, Chris Magee, assumed the character of a melodrama. Since Quay needed $100,000 more than he personally could raise in order to cover the state deposits, he faced public humiliation and possible legal action. Magee claimed that he found the Beaver boss drunk and despondent at his Harrisburg hotel, debating whether to cut his throat or jump into the Susquehanna. (This was not typical of Quay—normally the more grave the circumstances, the more heroic his response.) Magee purportedly sobered him up, instructed him to remain calm, then rushed to Washington and implored Donald Cameron to provide the funds to save him from political disaster.[17]

Cameron's generosity, however procured, rescued Quay's career, but neither Noyes nor Walters recovered from the shock of the exposure. Bowen attributed the deaths of both men indirectly to Quay because they had been his followers in the speculation. The primary evidence he cited was a suicide note left by Walters, who confessed that "a will stronger than mine own led me on." Claiming that the note was seen by only four individuals, of which he was one, Bowen maintained that its tone clearly indicated Quay as the "stronger will" that had directed the venture and hastened the untimely consequences.[18]

Failure in this first treasury raid, and Quay's obligation to repay Cameron, induced the need for a second—a relationship overlooked by Bowen. Quay's nomination and election as state treasurer in 1885 not only implied public acceptance of his innocent plea in the first raid, but also placed him in an ideal position to launch a second attack. Perfecting his technique and eliminating his accomplices, he transferred $400,000 in state funds to the Peoples Bank of Philadelphia. With William Kemble as the bank president, Quay knew that all bank impediments would be brushed aside. According to his revised scheme, the funds physically remained in the bank, but were assigned to the North Chicago Railroad Company for the purchase of company securities. Quay, in turn, resold the securities at a higher figure, pocketed the profits, and then returned the embezzled funds to the state treasury. On May 19, 1886, the capital gain from this venture went to repay Cameron.[19]

With this incident Bowen concluded his indictment against the Beaver senator. Although much that he presented was known previously, publication in the influential *New York World* tended to advertise Quay's indiscretions nationally. Noted by journals across the country and reprinted with editorial comment, these two articles shocked both friend and foe. All expected Quay to retaliate with either a sweeping denunciation or a libel suit; silence would be interpreted as an admission of guilt. But Quay failed to heed that advice. Irritated by his lack of response, editors challenged him to defend himself or surrender to the nearest prison warden, but he refused to comment. In spite of being labeled liar, briber, embezzler, and drunkard, taunted by related infamous epithets, he fished quietly in Florida.[20]

In April 1890, Henry Lea addressed an open letter to President Harrison that sent a second shock wave throughout the nation. He castigated Harrison for giving Quay such control over federal patronage in Pennsylvania that he had become the state's Republican dictator. He construed the appointment of Wanamaker to the cabinet as "the only cloud on the political horizon" at the outset of the administration, but concluded that, because of continued favoritism to Quay, "that cloud, then no larger than a man's hand, has spread til it covers the firmament."[21] Although he admitted that Quay's alleged crimes pertained wholly to his state career, Lea argued that Harrison's close association with him, without demanding either an acceptable defense or his resignation as party chairman, gave the scandal a national focus. His sharpest words, however, were reserved for the president:

The elections of last November [1889] were a warning that the people would not tolerate your methods. You have refused to heed this lesson, and the election of next November will emphasize it. The narrow Republican majority in the lower house will be swept away, and your path for the latter half of your Administration will be a path of thorns. You have rewarded the magnificent majority of 80,000 given to you by Pennsylvania by riveting upon her the chains of Quayism. . . . Let me counsel you, Mr. President, as a friend, to reflect that this has been your work in one short year of misused power.

Then he audaciously called upon the president to repent:

Discard the advisers who are luring you to your downfall. Recognize that the truest political expediency lies in the application of conscience to public affairs, and that you can serve your party best by stimulating the nobler aspirations of the nation, rather than by pandering to the baser appetites of spoilsmen.

Cease to expect to gather figs of thistles or to touch pitch without defilement. Apply to your public duties the high standard of morality to which you adhere in your private life.[22]

While this letter was still providing the nation's newspapers with both news copy and a fresh basis for editorial comment on Quay's alleged criminal career, the *New York Evening Post* published the results of its own investigation. This version differed only slightly from Bowen's; the *Post* declared that it had felt compelled to verify his charges before endorsing them. The editor pointed out that the *World*'s articles had failed to provoke the public outcry that such a disclosure should because its reputation for sensational journalism automatically caused the public to doubt the accuracy of its charges. This allegation catapulted the exposure of Quay's conduct more prominently than ever into the national limelight; it at once became the rope in a newspaper tug-of-war for national recognition. The *Post* asserted that its imprimatur on the charges would definitely force Quay and the administration to react because, as a thoroughly trustworthy newspaper, it would stimulate public response. In mid-May it reprinted its version in pamphlet form, but like the *World*'s charges and Lea's letter, its assertions encountered only silence.[23]

Certain newspapers, particularly in Pennsylvania, were so deeply committed to Quay, his programs, and cohorts that they felt compelled to respond to the *Post* and *World* charges. Without the information necessary to deny the charges, these defenders merely speculated and explained that "dignified silence" was the only reasonable recourse open to the senator. Through these friendly sources the Quay camp revealed its suspicions that the *World*'s strategy was to provoke a libel suit in the interest, not of honesty and good government, but of increased sales. The Quay papers argued that the

World faced no financial embarrassment, even if it lost a libel suit, because the Democratic National Committee would advance all the funds necessary to reap the political capital accruing from such anti-Quay, anti-Republican publicity.[24] Some of the attempts to defend Quay boomeranged against him. The first paper to sound off was the *Helena Journal*, edited by Russell B. Harrison, son of the president. He declared that the charges had awakened his father's sympathy, and he falsely maintained that the senator had "never stood so well in the White House" as he did after the scandals broke. Actually the contacts between the two men diminished with each passing week because Harrison realized, as Lea so aptly pointed out, that the exposure was destroying his reputation along with Quay's. In a more realistic attempt to explain Quay's conduct, Murat Halstead of the *Cincinnati Commercial* acknowledged that Quay had utilized state funds for personal advantage and that there had been a "temporary depletion" of the treasury. Since all the state's cash was in the treasury at the time he wrote, Halstead accepted the statement: "Someone says a part of it absconded once—blown into Wall Street, we believe—well, it's all solid now." This remark accentuated the current condition, registered no regard for principle, and provided the opposition with the inspiration for another round of editorial blasts, emphasizing that "temporary depletion" was a euphemism for embezzlement.[25]

At the height of the campaign against him, Quay attempted to demonstrate his firm position within the Republican party by calling a meeting of the Republican executive committee. A gracious host, he entertained the members at dinner in his Washington home before convening a parlor conference; in the face of this hospitality anyone inclined to react negatively to his conduct was placed at a disadvantage. What the group discussed has never been revealed, but with public pleas for him either to answer the charges or resign the party chairmanship, the major issue should have been his continuance in office. Either implicitly or explicitly the committee gave him a vote of confidence to continue as the party autocrat. When members of the press asked about the topics of discussion, he responded in characteristic brevity and arrogant generality: "Why, I only entertained a few friends at dinner."[26]

Demands that Quay answer the charges came from all segments of the nation. They ranged from those who believed him innocent but misguided by the decision to remain silent to those who knew that he was a scoundrel unless the charges were successfully refuted. Never before did a political leader holding such high positions and wielding such power stand before the American people accused of such malfeasance in office. Because of the gravity of the charges, most newspapers, including those that were sympathetic, demanded that he either speak out or get out. The more outraged editors believed that, with the mountain of evidence against him, he was guilty until proved innocent. Personally he was in a dilemma: if he resigned, he was politically disgraced; if he remained as party chairman, the Republican party was disgraced. Not pleased with either alternative but supported by the party's high command, he again went fishing and waited for the political climate to change.[27]

More incensed than ever, the press refused to accept this apparent indifference and hammered at all possible variations of the theme; Quay was taunted and goaded until the public tired of the constant reiteration. One journal suggested that Quay reverse the advice he himself had earlier given to Governor Beaver: "Dear Quay—Don't be a clam. Yours, The Public." Another explained to its readers that the senator had not made a five-minute speech in the last twenty-seven years because he considered actions more expressive than words. As proof of this generalization, the editor pointed to the $250,000 and $400,000 sums in state funds that had been deployed for his private use. Rudolph Blankenburg, a Philadelphia reformer, tried a different approach. With political tongue in cheek, he wrote an open letter to Quay stating that all Republicans were suffering because of the New York newspaper attack on him. To relieve the siege, he recommended a national appeal to the party faithful for funds to institute suits for civil and criminal libel against the accusers. He asked Quay if this plan to vindicate his honor as chairman of the Republican National Committee and as U.S. senator met with his approval. Recognizing Blankenburg as an ally of Lea, the *World*, and his other attackers, the senator did not break his public silence, but privately predicted to Governor Beaver: "Every dog has his day and the present seems to be the day of the dirtiest dogs in Pennsylvania politics. I think it will be short."[28]

The "day of the dirtiest dogs" did not readily pass; it lingered until after the November elections. On September 3 the charges against Quay were repeated in a new setting—the Congress of the United States. In one of the "most bitter vituperations that has been heard in Congress," Representative Robert P. Kennedy of Ohio referred to Quay as a "branded criminal" whose failure to justify his conduct was a "confession of guilt." He not only called on Pennsylvania's junior senator to resign the party chairmanship, but also to emulate the example set by Judas Iscariot, who after his betrayal hanged himself on a tree. This outburst of indignation was not activated by the newspaper charges to which he alluded, but by the sidetracking of the Federal Elections Bill in the Senate. Perhaps if Quay had not blocked this measure, which Reed had rammed through the House, he would not have incurred Kennedy's wrath.[29] The speech came in the late afternoon, after the usual hour of adjournment; most of the members had already gone to dinner, and the prepared address was delivered before an almost empty House. In Speaker Reed's absence, J. C. Burrows, a supporter of the elections bill, presided and made no effort to curtail Kennedy's remarks. He explained that technically, since no one challenged the Ohio representative's conduct from the floor, he had no alternative but to allow him to proceed. Individuals and newspapers in sympathy with Senate action on the "force" bill were suspicious and maintained that the speech was contrived by Reed, Lodge, and McKinley to gain revenge for the Senate's action on the measure. At any rate the speech did demonstrate the volcanic condition of the Republican party.[30]

Although criticisms of a senator were inappropriate when offered by a representative, Quay received little sympathy because the public was losing patience with his campaign of silence. After the speech had been telegraphed throughout the nation in the crude form in which it was delivered, Kennedy withheld it from publication in the *Congressional Record* so that he might revise it. Neither discreet in tone nor diplomatic in language, the speech in its original form was perhaps the most unparliamentary in congressional annals and was desperately in need of emendation. The revised edition omitted Quay's name and in two places dropped the word *criminal* where the reference was obviously to him; with a few other changes, it was presented for the *Record* on September 14.[31] Not satisfied with this version, Quay supporters in the House proposed a resolution addressed to the Senate condemning Kennedy's language, but it failed to carry. A second, more successful maneuver recommended that the revised speech be referred to the House Judiciary Committee to determine its fitness for publication in the permanent edition of the *Congressional Record*. After due deliberation the committee decided to eliminate it. Thus the most controversial speech of the session, discussed for two days on the House floor and longer in the Capitol corridors, did not become a part of the official record.[32]

Quaystone or Keystone State?

Although this action removed the Kennedy incident from the spotlight, the campaign against Quay was already becoming more diffuse. As senators and representatives struggled to conclude the work of the first session of the Fifty-first Congress on a constructive note and turn their undivided efforts to the 1890 elections, the boss became an even more accessible target. Ostensibly Kennedy was supplementing the New York newspaper attack decrying the senator's alleged misdeeds in Pennsylvania, but basically he was angered by the Quay maneuver to put aside the elections bill and distressed by the party's failure to fulfill its platform pledge to enact legislation in behalf of election purity.

In addition to both disguised and open criticism from supporters of the elections bill in the final weeks before the election, Quay was confronted by critics of the McKinley tariff across the country. Prodded by Democrats and antitariff, anti-Quay Republicans, the public was encouraged to relate the McKinley bill to the unconscionably high campaign expenses in 1888. The prominent identification of Quay's name with the management of the bill in the Senate caused many to wonder if it was designed to protect American labor and infant industries and raise government revenue, as they had been told, or if it was "a deed of conveyance by the Republican Party to a combination of manufacturers and trusts in consideration of money advanced by them" to purchase the election of Benjamin Harrison.[33]

This possibility was pondered in Pennsylvania as elsewhere, but Pennsylvania voters had an even more fundamental concern. There the issue was Quayism in the broadest sense. The senator had emerged from the 1888 campaign with a reputation as the shrewdest politician in the United States; within Pennsylvania he ruled as the most absolute dictator who ever rode the neck of a political party. The task of gaining such power had been simplified by his senatorial colleague, Donald Cameron, who was content to allow all federal patronage to flow through the state's junior senator. Cameron's unwillingness to compete, or even participate, made possible Quay's conquest of the state's Republican organization. He had been prominent in state affairs for years because he had conducted operations for the Cameron machine prior to establishing his own machine in the mid-eighties. By 1890 he knew most of the Keystone legislators personally; in contrast, a large majority of them did not know Cameron even by sight. Although the legislature to be elected that year would determine if Cameron would serve another Senate term, he was indifferent to the issues and concentrated on his own election. With ample personal funds available, he appointed his own state chairman to conduct a separate campaign among the legislative candidates. He was obviously content to accept the Senate seat as a sinecure.[34]

Surprised by this turn of events, the Cameron forces were completely leaderless for the first time. Lieutenants, particularly Magee and Dalzell in Pittsburgh, along with James McDavitt in Lancaster and anti-Quay stalwarts in Philadelphia, realized that they had to fight for political survival. Their best opportunity was to unite with the Independents, who based their opposition to Quayism not on factional supremacy, but on morality. To them the contest was between political virtue and political vice, between the conscientious and intelligent masses and a combination of Quayism and the corporations. Although the philosophy of the abandoned Cameron subordinates was not in tune with these sentiments, they joined the Independents in declaring their determination to oppose any gubernatorial nominee whom Quay endorsed.

Already stung by adverse publicity, Quay was not inclined to exhibit weakness in the face of this challenge. He concluded that he would suffer a worse defeat in not securing the nomination of his candidate at the party convention than in having him beaten in the general election. On this assumption he formally identified State Senator George Delamater of Meadville as his preference. Opposing Republicans rallied behind a popular hero, Adjutant General Daniel H. Hastings, who had rendered distinguished public service in 1889, when he was ordered to take charge at Johnstown after flood waters had devastated the city. Because of his popularity he expected the nomination, but discovered that it was easier to command the waters of Johnstown than to control Republican politics at Harrisburg. The political tide of the state ebbed and flowed according to no natural law, but according to the tactical edicts of Boss Quay.

In forcing the nomination of Delamater, who was stigmatized as the Standard Oil and Pennsylvania Railroad candidate, Quay demonstrated his determination to rule by force, but to have negotiated for another candidate would have been construed as a lack of self-confidence. In so defying the sentiment of the Republican masses, he gave added credence to the unanswered charges still hanging over him, but he believed that victory for his personal candidate would be answer enough to the New York newspaper exposé. Harrison had carried Pennsylvania by 80,000 votes two years before, and Quay thought that margin adequate to absorb all dissidents; but he underestimated both their numbers and their state of desperation. To prove their case against the senator and vilify his name, they quoted widely a politically calamitous statement attributed to him: "I have been making governors all my life, but I have never had one of my own. I am going to nominate Delamater and know how it feels to own a governor just for once." The Republican party was indeed sick, and the dissemination of such comments scattered the germs of revolt across the state.[35]

Hastings wisely refused to be drawn into the intraparty strife and thereby cleared the way for a coalition of anti-Quay Republicans and Democrats. Through their combined efforts the former Democratic governor, Robert Pattison, was nominated for a second term. The individual most responsible for convincing him to be a candidate was Independent Republican Henry Lea, who was again lured from his ivory tower to lead the fight against boss rule.[36] In response to a request from Pattison, Lea wrote to the Republicans of Pennsylvania, declaring that a vote for a Democrat on this occasion was the "truest fidelity to party and the highest duty of patriotism." Pattison was depicted as a defender of the people, not only against the bosses, but also against the corporations. The writer challenged his fellow Republicans to respond to duty and honor:

A vindication is truly needed at the coming election, but it is not the vindication of tainted politicians who dare not vindicate themselves.

You are called upon to vindicate your own manhood, to vindicate the
honesty of your own party, to vindicate the honor of your own state.
You are called upon to show that you do not wear the collar of Mr. Quay,
that your votes are not to be bought and sold by the manipulation of
patronage, and that you are not to be driven to the polls like cattle to
make good the bargains of your bosses. You are called upon to teach a
lesson to your self-constituted masters, and to show the country at large
that the grand old party may still be trusted to manage the affairs of the
nation.[37]

The combination of political obstacles heaped in the path of Quay and
Delamater was insurmountable. The Republican candidate's record as a
legislator demonstrated a bias toward corporate interests which as a class were
now in public disrepute. Independent oil producers, the Grangers, the
Knights of Labor, and others who considered themselves victims of corporate
interests were allied against Quayism. In a July 4 address, Terence V.
Powderly, the Grand Master of the Knights, told the workingmen of
Pennsylvania that they were slaves of the monopolists who ran the state. To
prove his point, he noted that not a single workingman had been consulted in
the nomination of Delamater, whom he described as the favorite son of
Standard Oil.[38]

If Quay had not heard the death knell before, it tolled unmistakably when
ex-Senator Lewis Emery brandished affidavits charging Delamater with
bribery, forgery, and perjury in a previous election. Like the charges against
Quay himself, these were challenged by deafening silence, but to rank-and-file
Pennsylvanians the coincidence was too much to accept. They feared Quay
was involved in a plot to transform the Republican party into "The Society for
the Encouragement of Felony."[39]

The Emery disclosure prompted Lea to write an open letter to Delamater a
month before the election, calling upon him to defend himself or withdraw,
but he did neither. The possibility of his withdrawal nevertheless remained an
active rumor in the press until two weeks before the election despite an
attempt by three Quay journals—the *North American*, the *Philadelphia Inquirer*, and the *Harrisburg Call*—to offset Emery's accusations with similar
charges against Pattison. They maintained that during his term as governor he
had been bribed by the Vanderbilts in 1883 and on another occasion had
accepted $30,000 in stock to give his approval to a measure. When Pattison
responded immediately by instituting criminal proceedings against the
proprietors of the newpapers, Quay's effort to gain the offensive once again
failed ignominiously.[40]

The campaign against the Republican candidate and his sponsor was
relentless, and their attackers continued to enjoy support from kindred

elements outside the state. Ohio and New York supplied much of the "foreign" ammunition. Congressman Kennedy had his vitriolic speech reprinted and made thousands of copies available for circulation to Pennsylvania voters. Through a series of cartoons by Thomas Nast, the *Illustrated American* in New York added a pictorial dimension to the attack. But more important than either of these was the second exposé of Quay in the *New York World*.[41] In a major story on October 4, the *World* linked Quay with a scheme to redistribute the black population and at the same time keep the Republican party in power nationally. The central figure in the plot was Daniel M. Lindsey of North Carolina, the secretary of the Southern Emigration Company. Ostensibly both Lindsey and his company were motivated by an altruistic desire to relieve the oppression and persecution of the blacks in North Carolina and neighboring states by assisting them to move elsewhere. The tendency of these poverty-stricken blacks was to migrate to the southwestern part of the country. But Lindsey recognized the advantages of organization and planning; home sites and employment should be determined in advance in order to prevent worse dislocations than those experienced in the Old South. He took charge and, with financial assistance from northern philanthropists, supposedly prepared to divert this great flood of people to northern and northwestern states. Since these Negroes would be the "safest voters in the world" for Republicans, he proposed that the party's national committee join in funding the project.[42]

According to the *World* account, Lindsey had explained to Quay that the politically doubtful states could be quietly stocked with enough black Republican voters to ensure the party's success in 1892. By settling 10,000 Negroes in Indiana, 4,000 in West Virginia, and 3,000 in Connecticut, these states could, it was argued, be placed beyond the reach of Democratic control. Remembering that the Republicans had lost Connecticut and West Virginia by 336 and 1873 votes respectively in 1888 and had carried Indiana that year largely because it was Harrison's home state, Quay was said to have encouraged exploration of the plan. By "putting wheels on the suffrage" and rolling enough people about the country to alter the Republican electoral outlook, the colonization plan potentially offered all the advantages of the force bill without reverting to bloody-shirt tactics.[43] During 1889 and 1890 Lindsey discussed his scheme with Republican congressmen from all three states, as well as with Quay, Clarkson, and Dudley of the national committee and James Huston, treasurer of the United States, who was from Indiana. Huston was so impressed with the idea that he proposed to call it to the attention of the president. Lindsey's arguments in behalf of the plan varied according to the attitudes and backgrounds of his listeners. To the Negroes themselves he stressed the challenges of employment in the North. To humanitarians he emphasized that the blacks were not being uprooted against their will, but welcomed an opportunity to rise above their economic and political depression in the South. To politicians he described how political liberty for the blacks could be converted into their own security.

Details of the scheme were discovered by the *World* when J. B. Whitehead, Lindsey's principal assistant, became "crazy drunk" one night while working in West Virginia and attempted suicide by jumping into the Kanawha River. During the ensuing rescue, correspondence containing the secret political implications of the scheme was found in his pockets and by some unknown means gravitated to the *World*, which then added its own interpretation and made the information public. Described as Quay's substitute for the elections bill, the colonization plan was also denounced as a conspiracy to steal three sovereign states. It was interpreted as a plan to transfer control of electoral votes and congressional delegations from the people and the states themselves to the Republican National Committee. This suspected tampering with the composition of state representation did not directly affect Pennsylvania, but it did provide the state's voters with another basis for judgment on election day.[44]

Such intrigue testifies to Quay's ingenuity, but ingenuity was not enough to influence that election outcome. Fundamentally concerned with vindicating their own conscience, Republican voters registered a stinging rebuke to Quay and Delamater; the latter lost the gubernatorial contest by approximately 17,000 votes while the remainder of the Republican ticket swept the state. With Harrison's 80,000 majority in Pennsylvania in 1888, the election showed a shift of nearly 100,000 votes, indicating how decisively rank-and-file Republicans had reacted to Quayism. Unquestionably Henry Lea's letters were among the most persuasive documents in leading the voters in this about-face. The returns were obviously *against* Quay and Delamater rather than *for* Pattison; despite that victory, Pennsylvania was not even temporarily a Democratic state at the congressional and legislative levels.

Nationally the trend was otherwise; a Democratic cyclone swept away the tenuous Republican control in the House of Representatives. The Quay critics assigned the blame to him, charging that, as national chairman, he had squandered the party's resources in Pennsylvania in a hopeless attempt to vindicate himself instead of concentrating the funds in doubtful states and doubtful congressional districts. The charge was partly correct, but not particularly relevant in explaining the final result. The unfortunate handling of the McKinley tariff in the Senate, the sudden rise of the Farmers' Alliance in the Midwest, and the failure of thousands of Republicans to vote were the primary factors responsible for the Democratic victory in the House and the party's major gains through the Midwest.

Those most exhilarated by the election outcome proclaimed that the Quay machine was a total wreck and proceeded to write the boss's political obituary. The senator himself remained the same imperturbable sphinx he had been throughout the newspaper barrage and provided no comment for his enemies to attack and no concession in which they might revel. He withdrew from the scene to fish in Florida and regroup his thoughts. En route he was asked to what he attributed Delamater's defeat, stoically replied, "a lack of votes," and continued on his way.[45]

The Unmaking of a President
1891-1893

I
N late January 1891 the first rumors that Quay would definitely reply
to the *World*'s charges began to circulate. For almost a year he had been
hounded and maligned by those who suspected his guilt, partly because of this
unresponsiveness. His allies had kept the faith by repeatedly justifying his
"dignified silence" while vainly scanning the horizon for some evidence that
he would refute the charges. After the long silence even the announcement of
a forthcoming defense, to be presented on the floor of the Senate, created a
sensation. When there was no heated political conflict raging, when he felt
that neither hope nor fear could be deemed the inspiration for his revelation,
the Beaver boss decided "to confront accusation with truth."[1]

Late on the afternoon of February 16, he stood at his desk and addressed the
Senate for exactly ten minutes on the subject of the celebrated incidents in his
Pennsylvania career. In spite of his spectacles, he held his typed manuscript
close to his face and read in a low, clear voice distinguishable even in the back
rows of the gallery. During this brief rendition there was profound silence.
Although he was a veteran of more than four years in the Senate, this was his
first real utterance, except to vote, and there was a certain curiosity to see how
he would handle himself as a speaker.[2] His tone was calm and his style
reserved, with less fire and fury than one would expect from one so accused,
but his explicitness and apparent frankness overwhelmed many of his
colleagues. He answered the charges individually, first by identifying the
incident and disclosing hitherto unknown details, and then by denying the
specific accusation: it was part of the "mass of direct falsehood, confused
statements, innuendo, insinuation, and cunning implication that . . . has

been gathered together for my destruction." All the allegations were, he concluded, "false and foul to the core."[3]

Quay's disclosures amounted to a contradiction, not a refutation. To his
accusers, who had cast themselves in the role of judge and jury, this did not
exonerate him. They noted that he had admitted involvement in all the
incidents and thereby established some plausibility for each of the specific
charges. These critics again challenged him to present irrefutable proof of
innocence. Others felt relieved and at least mildly satisfied with the senator's
delayed rebuttal, largely because of numerous references to living individuals
who could corroborate parts of his story. This group now attacked Quay's
accusers, arguing that if they considered their charges true and provable, they
were remiss for not instituting legal proceedings months before and seeing
that he was punished through the courts. Still others were critical of Quay's
decision to remain silent over this extended period, because all the information provided could just as easily have been released a year earlier. Reluctant to accept the senator's reasons for the delay, they criticized him for
permitting party prestige to deteriorate to the point of the election debacle
in 1890. The senator himself did not elaborate. He left colleagues, newspapermen, and the general public to appraise his statement without further
explanation and returned to Florida.[4]

Still unappeased, his enemies shifted their thrust from bribery and embezzlement to political ineffectiveness. After the defeat of 1890, they maintained that Quay was a detriment to his party and should resign from the
chairmanship of the Republican National Committee. This suggestion had
been heard intermittently for months. In fact, after Harrison had been in
office about a year, he was thoroughly frustrated by Quay's tactics and hoped
for his resignation. According to Walter Wellman, Washington correspondent for the *Chicago Times-Herald,* he summoned James Clarkson, Quay's
first assistant on the committee, to the White House and calmly asked, "On a
motion to depose Quay as chairman, how many members of the committee do
you think will vote yea?" Clarkson's answer made the committee's position
very clear: "Mr. President, Senator Quay has for a long time wished to resign
the chairmanship, and if such a motion were put in committee, he might cast
his vote in favor of it. He is the only man that would. Between you, the President of the nation and the official head of our party, and Senator Quay, the
committee to a man will stand by Quay."[5]

In spite of this declaration of support, the resignation was being urged more
persistently with each passing week. Quay realized that in the best interests of
his own political future he should heed the call, but hesitated to resign
because it appeared to be a surrender to the attacks of the newspapers on his
personal and political record. He examined his limited alternatives: either
weather the political storm or construct a setting in which he could resign on a

dignified and positive note. During a visit to the White House, he tried to bluff Harrison into coming to his defense by requesting the president's candid opinion concerning the demands for his resignation. Before responding, Harrison wanted to be certain that his opinion was earnestly desired, and Quay replied in the affirmative. Then with a smile Harrison said: "I believe it would be for the best interests of the party if you would resign the chairmanship of the Committee."[6]

The senator had bluffed and the president called him. Resignation under favorable circumstances was the only remaining alternative. In mid-June he took the first step and announced that he did not intend to serve as the chairman in the next presidential campaign. Noting that he had directed a successful campaign, he said, "There is nothing more in the chairmanship . . . for me." This suggested that he had accepted the assignment as a challenge rather than a service to his party. To some his announcement was a relief; to others it was an expression of doom for 1892. To his hard-core enemies the disclosure that he would not be a candidate to succeed himself was not enough. They demanded an immediate resignation.[7]

Quay's most vocal critics at this time were Pennsylvania's Independent Republicans, concentrated primarily in Philadelphia. By joining forces with the Democrats in 1890, they had succeeded in ousting the Quay machine from the governorship, but to their chagrin this had produced no change in the high command of the state's Republican organization, which they had hoped to inherit. Quay did not abandon his stalled machine, but remained at the throttle. Insurgent Republicans were thus forced to accept only half the victory they coveted. Although they had helped to "cleanse" the state government, the task of cleansing the party was still before them. Republican insurgents had to shoulder that burden alone—the Democrats had a stake in government reform, but they could muster no enthusiasm to assist in reforming the Republican party.

To launch their offensive, a group of 150 business and professional leaders, under the direction of Rudolph Blankenburg, issued a manifesto to the citizens of Philadelphia. Stressing the need for honesty and political purity in government, they denounced Quay because of the newspaper charges and because of his leadership, characterized as unscrupulous in method and disastrous in results.[8] They declared that neither Quay nor Cameron was a Republican because they had opposed an administration effort to revive the elections bill. Quay retaliated by questioning their Republicanism for supporting such a manifesto. "All of them voted for Pattison for governor, many of them voted for Cleveland for President, and you will find among them a large number who are free traders and whose sympathies are with the free traders. I can stand attacks coming from such Democratic sources."[9]

In early July, Quay sources spread the word that his health was too uncertain to permit him to take charge of the 1892 campaign for which preparations had to be initiated in the near future. With this brief, indirect notice, he submitted his resignation when the Republican executive committee met at the Continental Hotel in Philadelphia on July 29, 1891, but even to those who read the signs clearly, his action contained an element of surprise. He resigned not only the chairmanship, but also his membership on the national committee. When the resignation was presented, Clarkson promptly proposed a resolution of acceptance stating that the committee was reluctant to accede to his request because it is "against our judgment." In this manner he hoped to convey to those who were clamoring for Quay's political scalp that the sympathies of the committee were with him and not with them. The committeemen had been more favorably impressed by Quay's success in managing Harrison's campaign than by any considerations of morality. They would probably have been happier to reelect him to another term as chairman than to accept his resignation. The implications of Clarkson's resolution accurately expressed the sentiments of the committee members who were present, and it was unanimously adopted.[10]

The Independents were not concerned with the inference. They rejoiced in their apparent victory and exulted: "Quay has actually gone. The Republican voters from Maine to California will breathe one simultaneous sigh of relief." Thinking that he had given up the battle for his political life—its national aspect at least—and that an era had ended, a reporter asked Quay to recall and comment on certain incidents in his long career. He retorted: "So you want to print my obituary, do you? Well, I am not ready to have it written just yet," and he moved at once to prove his point.[11]

The Blaine Revival

Quay's resignation removed him from further association with the downward trend of the party's fortunes. It also freed him for certain positive actions at the state and national levels. Within Pennsylvania the time was rapidly approaching when attention had to be given to the 1892 elections, which included balloting for the legislature that would consider Quay's reelection to the Senate. In many counties the senator had to prepare for hand-to-hand combat with either the Independents or dissident Stalwarts who indicated their intention to challenge him. On the national scene he was no longer content with the neutrality to which he had been more or less confined by the nature of the chairmanship. He wanted flexibility to maneuver with individual state and congressional leaders to prevent the renomination of Harrison. Within days he moved on these fronts, and his opposition quickly realized that he was still politically alive and scrambling.

Months before his resignation, Quay had actually moved from the neutral pose expected of a national chairman, but any time that he was challenged, he explained that his words did not mean what they appeared to mean. On one occasion he and several lieutenants called on Harrison to impress him with the urgency of making certain Pennsylvania appointments. Indifferent to their pleadings, the president gave them little encouragement. In desperation Quay said to him: "Mr. President, you cannot afford to ignore those people who made your election possible." Harrison assumed his most solemn pose, lifted himself as high as possible on his toes, and replied: "Senator, God Almighty made me President." Quay was speechless, not from choice but astonishment. He and his henchmen made an indecorous exit and headed for Chamberlain's in the hope that a little liquid refreshment would restore their sense of political balance. En route they met the celebrated agnostic Robert Ingersoll and blurted out the details of their encounter with the president. "Well," exclaimed the profane Ingersoll, "I have heard some pretty tough charges preferred against God Almighty, but I don't think that I ever heard that he was guilty of anything so bad as that."[12]

Probably because it illustrated his own point of view, Quay came to enjoy the Ingersoll retort. In political conversations he repeated it with gusto, and every time that he did, his attitude toward Harrison became more obvious, although he never directly said that he opposed his renomination. When others inferred an anti-Harrison bias from such remarks, he countered with oblique statements, such as, Blaine "can have the Pennsylvania delegation whenever he wants it." In fact, at this point he intended for Blaine to have the endorsement of the Pennsylvania delegation in 1892 whether he wanted it or not.[13]

Speaking for Blaine, Stephen Elkins declared that he flatly refused to be a candidate, but Quay gave him little choice. Once again he reverted to a letter-writing campaign requesting assistance; this time the Republican committees of the various Pennsylvania counties received his appeal. Since they were responsible for selecting and instructing delegates to the state convention, he urged them to pass resolutions endorsing Blaine and to send delegates who would campaign actively on the convention floor for his nomination. The reaction was encouraging both for the candidacy of Blaine and the reestablishment of Quay with leaders at the county level. Typical of the response was the resolution adopted by the Lawrence County committee, declaring "that in James G. Blaine, that American of Americans, who by his matchless diplomacy and his championship of the principles of reciprocal commercial intercourse to our financial advantage, with full protection to our home industries, has proven himself the statesman of statesmen, we recognize one preeminently fitted to lead the Republican party to victory in the presidential contest of 1892."[14]

Quay publicly affirmed his position at the state's Republican convention in

August 1891, although the national convention was almost a year in the future. Having shed the national chairmanship a few weeks before, he formally proposed that the convention endorse Blaine for the presidential nomination: "It has been with especial gratification that the Republicans of this Commonwealth have observed the brilliant administration of the State Department by one of Pennsylvania's native sons, whose superb diplomacy has electrified the hearts of all Americans, extracted from foreign powers a degree of respect and admiration for the American flag hitherto unequalled, and opened wide to us in other lands commercial gates hitherto barred. In view of his magnificent achievement in diplomacy and statecraft, we earnestly express the hope that the Republican National Convention of 1892 may place in unanimous nomination for the Presidency . . . the Honorable James G. Blaine of Pennsylvania and Maine."[15]

This resolution contained the essence of all that Quay hoped to accomplish at the convention. He and Cameron had been at work for several weeks attempting to convert the state convention into an embarrassment for the president. Dissatisfied with Harrison's conduct of his office, they wanted to undermine his support and demonstrate their own power. Their technique for achieving this goal was a Blaine boom, a simple device that required little imagination. In each of the four preceding presidential campaigns, there had been movements in numerous states by rank-and-file Republicans in behalf of the Maine statesman. This dormant legion, known to observers and antagonists alike as Blainiacs, was easily awakened for another campaign. Particularly in Pennsylvania, the cradle of previous Blaine crusades, the name was still magnetic. Blaine's endorsement by the state convention was considered the most dramatic way to snub the president and tell the nation at large that the most powerful Republican state of the Union did not favor his renomination.[16]

The convention did not adopt Quay's plank as proposed because it was regarded as politically premature. A revision praising Blaine, but stopping short of formal endorsement, was adopted and unmistakably proclaimed Pennsylvania's preference. This caused the senator's enemies to conclude that the convention was unwilling to follow his leadership. They failed to comprehend, however, that he merely wanted to create an impression, not dictate the phrasing of the resolution. Intent upon defeating him on a secondary matter, they missed the basic point of his strategy. The resolution accomplished Quay's objective and brought a sense of unity to the convention proceedings. The tone still implied a Blaine convention with a Quay prominence, but not dominance. Through this submission he regained much of his lost power and prestige with local party leaders; in a single stroke he had stamped his mark, as well as Blaine's, on the convention. Temporarily the boss convinced the delegates of his willingness not to boss.[17]

The convention openly selected its candidates, but the Quay influence was prevalent. In previous elections when he thought the tide was against him, he had rallied the soldier vote. During a recent encounter with the Independents who had denounced his machine tactics, he laid the foundation to exploit this bloc of voters again. By noting that not one of the Philadelphia signers of the Blankenburg manifesto had served as a soldier during the Civil War, he painted them as warriors of the home front who fought "valiantly for large profits on sugar and other merchandise." Because the delegates included a significant number of veterans, he was able to maneuver them to nominate a significant number of ex-soldiers for office and at the same time slap the wrists of his Independent critics. He had not employed this "soldier racket" in absorbing the 1890 defeat, but now reverted to it in an effort to spark a Republican resurgence.[18]

The master strategist further distracted the Independents by setting up a straw man for them to attack in the weeks before the convention: a rumor that he was seeking the state chairmanship. Factionalism flared over this issue because both Independents and Stalwarts demanded the right to name the state leader. The Independents were shocked by his audacity; according to their interpretation, he had resigned the national chairmanship because of the cloud hanging over his conduct of state affairs. To their chagrin, however, when they proposed Lieutenant Governor Louis A. Watres as their candidate, there was no reaction from the Quay camp. His election went uncontested, and the Independents were left to unload their guns because they had no target; they could not prove that Quay was the political ogre they proclaimed him to be. For the Beaver senator there was little at stake in the 1891 elections, and he was pleased to make this conciliatory gesture. By the following May, however, before an election of major significance, mysterious pressure caused Watres to become undecided about continuing. He wrote a letter stating that he wanted to resign, but did not formally commit himself. His indecision was all that the Quay forces needed. Moving cautiously in order to preserve party harmony, they successfully brought about his withdrawal and maneuvered to name General Frank Reeder, a loyal hench-man, as chairman, and with this success the party machine swerved back into its comfortable rut.[19]

With the defeat of 1890 and the vicious newspaper assault on Quay only months in the background, the Republican party in Pennsylvania was badly scarred as it approached the 1891 election. In addition, the Independents were poised to renew their vendetta against the boss, the man whose call for Blaine's name to head the next presidential ticket provided the only adhesive for a badly disunited party. Throughout the campaign Quay charted a course that intermingled promoting and withdrawing, cooperating and standing firm, advising and remaining silent, in order to help reverse the party's fortunes. He knew that the campaign in every county should be as vigorous and thorough as possible and that "every one of our voters should be warned out" because "it is very important for next year."[20]

Only days before the election, the boss appeared to be deep in trouble again and that, in turn, signified that Republican unity was threatened. The Independent press suddenly accused him of complicity in the Philadelphia treasury scandal, but on this occasion his response was prompt and direct. He sued the *Pittsburgh Post* and the *Beaver Star* for printing the charges. In subsequent court actions two of the *Star*'s editors were fined $600 each and sentenced to six-month terms in the county jail, with lesser penalties for the president and editor of the *Post*, as well as for the publishing company itself. Reenforcing Quay's contention that the newspaper witch hunt against him was unwarranted, these decisions materially brightened his personal prospects for the future.[21]

Failing to read the signs of a Republican revival and believing that popular indignation against Quay still prevailed, the Democrats expected to carry Pennsylvania easily. On the eve of the election one of their party journals declared that if they were not victorious, public sentiment in Pennsylvania was "utterly debauched." If true, it follows that the political conscience of the Keystone State was thoroughly depraved, because the Democrats were hopelessly overwhelmed. In 1890 they had a majority of 17,000 for Pattison, but now just one year later the Republicans rallied to carry the state offices by approximately 57,000 votes. They exhibited strength in all sections of the Commonwealth, and even without the benefit of a presidential election to swell the totals, the GOP was rebuilding at an impressive rate.[22]

Quay's campaign to embarrass Harrison was reenforced by the election results in New York, where the party organization was controlled by Harrisonites. After a campaign designed to justify renominating the president, New York voters registered a majority for the Democratic opposition. Thus the election struck a new Blaine-Harrison balance in these two pivotal Republican states, and the results seemed to indicate that Harrison would be forced to retire after one term. The preliminary phase of the Blaine boom succeeded admirably. The Harrison forces had been publicly challenged, and Quay had reestablished himself with the party's rank-and-file. The most dramatic evidence of his newly acquired strength was the newspaper "revolution" in Pittsburgh. To varying degrees the *Dispatch, Commercial Gazette, Times, Chronicle-Telegraph, Leader,* and *Press* had denounced Quay and Delamater in 1890, but a year later they all boarded the Blaine bandwagon being steered by Quay, who profited handsomely from the joint exposure.[23]

The Pennsylvania and New York victories gave fresh impetus to the Blaine movement, and Quay sought to exploit it fully. The extent of his actual commitment to the candidacy of the secretary of state in the months that followed was a moot point. His promotion of Blaine's nomination was not a goal, but a strategy to achieve a goal, namely, the defeat, or at least control, of Harrison. Quay actually preferred to switch his allegiance to an unnamed candidate at the crucial moment, but would certainly have accepted Blaine if he were the only alternative to Harrison. Thus Blaine was being used as a political stalking horse to undermine the president, and Quay hoped to re-align the Republican forces nationally behind the most promising challenger.

Quay wanted all the advantages that would accrue from having Blaine's prestige at his command, but did not feel particularly comfortable with the prospects of having him as a presidential candidate. Identifying several battle lines where he could temporarily maneuver before being forced to endorse Blaine, he moved at once to test their strengths. His first preference was to generate enough Blaine support to convince Harrison that renomination was a forlorn hope and that he should withdraw from contention. This alternative permitted Quay, Platt, and Clarkson, known as the Grievance Committee by the Harrisonites, to negotiate with other prospective nominees. At one time or another in this pre-convention juggling, the names of Alger, Allison, Cullom, Gresham, McKinley, Reed, and Sherman were all considered. Quay was willing to sanction any one of them who could demonstrate an ability to defeat Harrison in a convention showdown. When none was able to generate that level of support, he fell back to his second line of defense—a vigorous campaign to nominate Blaine.[24]

The Grievance Committee proceeded to build up Blaine in spite of his failing health and his declarations in a February 6 letter to Clarkson: "I am not a candidate for the presidency, and my name will not go before the Republican National Convention." They turned this aside as the usual disclaimer and noted that Blaine had not threatened to decline the nomination if it were offered to him. They insisted that this posture was quite different from saying that he would not be a candidate. In effect, they reconstructed the circumstances that had surrounded the letter from Florence in 1888 and proceeded with their plan.[25]

Quay also heard a more dramatic version of Blaine's decision. He had been approached by an unnamed newspaper correspondent who wanted to sell him "a sensational piece of news," the substance of which was that Harrison had compelled Blaine to write to Clarkson declining to be a candidate. The president supposedly shook certain documents pertaining to his Chilean diplomacy in Blaine's face and threatened to publish them if he actively sought the nomination. There is no evidence that Quay purchased the letter containing this bit of political blackmail. Written by one of Harrison's Indiana confidants to a relative in Illinois, the letter by some unexplained process had passed into the hands of the newspaperman, who then revealed the contents to a Quay investigator. Although not as valuable as the letter itself, knowledge of the existence of the Chilean documents offered several advantages to the Pennsylvania manipulator. It gave him an insight into Blaine's private position on the presidential nomination and also provided a potential weapon against both Blaine and Harrison if either insisted upon being a candidate against a strong third possibility.[26]

Quay expected that Blaine's health would force him to decline the nomination and that Harrison would refuse to be the second choice. With these options prevailing, the Grievance Committee believed that it could stop both candidates and at the same time acquire the necessary leverage to determine the ultimate nominee, but this procedure was more hazardous and uncertain than they preferred.[27] Quay automatically set up a third, more realistic, possibility. Although not optimistic about preventing the president's renomination, he hoped that his flurry of activity would frighten Harrison into a patronage agreement that would permit the Grievance Committee to live in peace and power in a second Harrison administration.

Armed with this understanding and without any prodding from Quay, John Wanamaker undertook a peace mission to the White House. Hoping to promote a Quay-Harrison entente, he wanted specifically to ensure tranquility at the April 20 state convention charged with the selection of Pennsylvania's delegates to the national convention at Minneapolis. He urged the president to come to terms with Quay so that his own renomination might move forward behind a solid Pennsylvania delegation. To his surprise Harrison was totally negative to the suggestions of compromise and advised him firmly, "The less you have to do with Mr. Quay, the better it will be for yourself. He is not a fit man to associate with."[28]

The substance of that interview, without having the wording authenticated, was reported widely in the press and served more to inflame than to restrain. For Wanamaker personally it appeared to tip the political scale. In the interest of party harmony, he had endeavored for more than three years to maintain a rapport with Quay in spite of accusations and political snubs, but now he gave up all pretense of camaraderie. He had been maligned from the outset of his cabinet appointment because the public had erroneously concluded that his office had been purchased. Simultaneously the nation was shocked to learn about Quay's fat-frying techniques and the uses to which the funds had been put. Unfortunately for Wanamaker he was identified with both, but opted to remain silent even in the face of caustic criticism.[29]

Following a Democratic administration, Wanamaker, a Republican postmaster general, had an opportunity to make many changes. The boss disapproved of having patronage power in the Post Office—a department that controlled more jobs than any other in the federal hierarchy—concentrated in the hands of Wanamaker, who was intent upon keeping it and asserting his own preferences. With Clarkson, a staunch ally of Quay, serving as assistant postmaster general, Wanamaker was politically squeezed by both his own department and the party headquarters. Since he was unwilling to share this control in a manner acceptable to Quay, numerous crises, heightened by partisan newspaper coverage, were carried to the president before they could be resolved. Certain journals kept score, noting the number of victories for Quay and the number for the postmaster general. The boss added to Wanamaker's embarrassment and discomfort in 1890 when he dictated the gubernatorial nomination of Delamater and made it manifest that the cabinet member was without any voice in the Republican affairs of his home state. After the president's admonition, the Quay-Wanamaker feud was in the open. The senator never again enjoyed "unchallenged suzerainty over Pennsylvania Republican politics," and for the next seven years, the postmaster general appeared as a personal challenger.[30]

Although this unforeseen result sharpened the Quay-Harrison rivalry, its impact on the state convention was slight. Resolutions praising both the senator and the president were passed, and no attempt was made to commit delegates for or against Harrison. Quay likewise made no effort to press for a formal position on Blaine. The only discordant note was sounded in response to a proposal to endorse Quay for reelection to the Senate in January 1893; with Magee leading the opposition, this resolution went down to defeat. Although a revision thanked the senator for his eminent public and party services, the incident had overtones which reached the floor of the national convention. There, against the counsel of Quay, Magee became the Pennsylvania spokesman for the renomination of Harrison. Not only had he favored Blaine at the state convention, but also reaffirmed to Russell Alger his commitment to work harmoniously with Quay in behalf of the secretary of state's candidacy. Magee altered his political course by 180 degrees within two weeks.[31]

Quay's decision not to insist upon the nomination of Blaine delegates was based more on his general strategy than on any effort to promote goodwill among the state's Republicans. This unexplained course of action, plus Senator Frank Hiscock's biased report of a conversation with Quay, caused Platt to write and ask if the Pennsylvania boss was resigned to Harrison's renomination. On the assumption that the pro-Harrison Hiscock had slightly strained the truth, Platt recommended that if Quay were still determined to lead the opposition he should proceed with the plan that they had discussed earlier, namely, a conference of a few of those opposed to the perpetuation of the administration. Quay had received a somewhat similar recommendation from Harrison Gray Otis, proprietor of the *Los Angeles Times*. He favored holding a small convention of all unpledged Republican delegates in either Chicago or Minneapolis, prior to the national convention. To avoid bluntly requesting a meeting of all anti-Harrison Republicans, he suggested that the call go to all delegates who were not "irrevocably committed" and who were interested in selecting the nominee best equipped to carry the party to victory. This was obviously euphemistic language because, with the party leadership so hopelessly divided on Harrison's candidacy, any group that looked objectively beyond the nomination to the election would conclude that Republican chances for success were greater with either Blaine or a compromise choice than with Harrison. Quay definitely wished to convey that point of view to a majority of the delegates, but relied on the small conference technique to do so.[32]

The Grievance Committee, supported by many distinguished senators and prominent party leaders such as Thomas Reed of Maine, Samuel Fessenden of Connecticut, Warner Miller of New York, J. Donald Cameron of Pennsylvania, Joseph Foraker of Ohio, and Russell Alger of Michigan, met in several closed sessions in New York and Washington during May to map a successful course of action. At one of the stop-Harrison conferences in Washington, the Pennsylvania senators listened attentively as Reed, Platt, and others denounced the president. During a lull Quay said to Cameron, "Senator, I'm afraid that if we nominated Harrison we couldn't elect him."

"Humph!" grumped Cameron, "my only fear is if he's nominated, he will be elected."[33]

Not only does this exchange dramatize party frustration, but it also expresses two fundamentally different evaluations of Republican power in the spring of 1892. Cameron apparently considered victory to be a foregone conclusion while Quay, who regarded the president as a campaign liability, was anxious to select a candidate who might elevate the party to a competitive position. Quay's appraisal was certainly more realistic.

Experience in the preceding months, however, had demonstrated to these anti-Harrisonites that no single, widely accepted compromise candidate between Blaine and Harrison existed at that time. In January Quay had privately indicated that he would support Judge Gresham if he were convinced that he could carry Indiana at the general election. This information was conveyed to the judge by a personal friend, P. A. B. Widener of Philadelphia, whom Quay had asked to intercede. He inquired directly about the judge's availability and received an equally direct reply: "The question is a fair one, and I answer it in the negative." Later Quay personally discussed the candidacy with Gresham, who refused to alter his position, partly because he considered the cause hopeless. He argued that it was impossible to prevent the president's renomination because with only office holders, and not a party in the South, "any Republican administration that will use its power can renominate itself."[34]

Time confirmed the accuracy of Gresham's analysis. But before it was fully accepted, other presidential balloons were launched and readily collapsed. Cullom, Reed, and Alger in particular attempted to excite the imaginations of the leaders and would-be delegates, but without success. Alger was convinced that, with sentiment in Pennsylvania so favorable to Blaine, Harrison could not receive a second nomination. In asking for Quay's support he declared "You, I am satisfied, can name the candidate."[35] Objective enough to brush this comment aside, Quay was nevertheless reluctant to accept Gresham's decision. He knew that a single challenger probably could not prevent the Harrison forces from gaining a majority of the delegates, but was confident that a series of challengers could achieve that objective. On this assumption, he and the Grievance Committee concluded their conferences with a determination to launch a two-pronged offensive: the Blaine boom was to continue to receive vigorous support and the individual states were to develop as many favorite-son candidates as possible. Although both prongs succeeded, the latter caused certain harmful side effects. There were as many factional fights as favorite sons because Harrison, through the patronage system, was able to shore up his own supporters. This, in turn, left the party more hopelessly divided than at any time in its existence.

Phase one of Quay's master plan, designed to sidetrack Harrison, contained ingredients potentially destructive to the party, but phase two was scheduled to erase all such possibilities by focusing on the identification of a candidate capable of uniting the various state groups. Pursuit of this goal caused the national party leadership to split into aggressive foraging factions that sallied forth to restore order out of the division that had been consciously created by phase one. Handicapped further by attempting to fight Harrison without an issue, the task proved insurmountable.[36]

Blaine was flattered by the spoilsmen's enthusiasm and found satisfaction in Quay's prediction that he would be nominated on the first ballot and triumphantly elected in November. This was more optimism than he had heard expressed in any previous campaign by the individuals capable of electing a President. But his acceptance of their solicitations was "a dying man's last gasp at a lifetime's ambition." His poor health and his family's ambition for him to be a candidate again pulled him in opposite directions and blurred his ability to judge the motives of his new allies. They supported him for selfish reasons without any sincere desire to see his nomination pushed to a logical conclusion. As anti-Harrison opportunists, they regarded all candidates expendable in their frantic desire to defeat the president. It was a cruel game to play with a man not fully capable of making his own decisions.[37]

In the four previous convention skirmishes, the movement in Blaine's behalf was inspired by the masses and resisted by the politicians. Now for ulterior motives politicians, such as the Grievance Committee, endorsed him. In certain respects this alignment was analogous to that in 1880 when the political machine under Cameron had endorsed Grant, a popular hero, for machine purposes. Cameron had no reverence for Grant and Quay none for Blaine. In both instances the politicians were only interested in exploiting the prestige of the names, but the endorsement of the secretary of state was more absurd than that of Grant; the Stalwarts had never opposed the general, but they had worked against Blaine with varying degrees of vigor in the four previous nominating campaigns.[38]

Harrison's Final Fling

The Grievance Committee was so blinded by hatred of Harrison and so engrossed in strategy to defeat his renomination that it failed to ask the most fundamental question: did the president intend to seek a second term? Unfortunately for the committee its total program was based on the false premise that he was eager to run again. Quay's failure to ascertain the facts was perhaps the most costly blunder of his career. With Harrison out of contention, he could, as Alger observed, have named the candidate. Anyone other than the president could optimistically have looked toward the campaign with a united party behind him.

Early in 1892 pressure for the president to stand for renomination began to mount. He gave guarded responses, misinterpreted by the committee, to all such appeals and never actually agreed to be a candidate. In March, when the Republican party of his home state of Indiana instructed its delegates to support renomination, he remained noncommittal. He even requested that cabinet members and other administrative officials not become active in his behalf, and on May 10 he wrote to Governor P. C. Cheney of New Hampshire that he was not seeking nomination. To Michener he was more explicit and privately confided that he did not want to be reelected and that at the appropriate time he would formally decline. This delay in facing the issue publicly helped to promote party discord. His inaction discouraged his own supporters from organizing while the opposition vigorously jumped into the contest.[39]

Unaware of Harrison's decision not to run, the Grievance Committee pursued their frantic search for delegates pledged against him. Their attack became so defiant that the president realized he had only two choices: become a candidate or "forever wear the name of a political coward." Insulted by their tactics, he told Michener on May 23 that he felt compelled to become a candidate in spite of his strong desire not to be one. "No Harrison," he said, "has ever retreated in the presence of a foe without giving battle, so I have determined to stand and fight." The president therefore entered an unnecessary contest, relying primarily on his federal appointive power to subdue the opposition. The potency of this weapon increased through the years of his administration, and by the time of the national convention, his appointees had an unshakable grip on many of the state delegations.[40]

Pennsylvania was an exceptional case. In late 1891 Harrison had lamented that in Pennsylvania, in spite of all his appointments to the post office, customs house, and other departments, there did not seem to be one man friendly to him who could be elected as a delegate. This was discouraging to him, embarrassing to Wanamaker, and gratifying to Quay. Although the delegate picture changed only slightly in the months that followed, Harrison's skillful use of patronage produced significant delegate gains in other states where he did not face as keen party competition as Quay provided. With 453 votes necessary to nominate, approximately one-third of that number proved to be federal officeholders committed to Harrison. Other officeholders who were not delegates appeared on the floor of the convention and lobbied in behalf of the president. This spectacle, according to one newspaper reporter, was almost enough to convert Quay to a civil service reformer.[41]

When Harrison entered the convention fight, Michener became his personal liaison with the various state delegations, and Chauncey Depew of New York was asked to lead his forces on the convention floor. Depew hesitated because, being a loyal organization man, he did not want to compromise the position of the state boss. But believing that no one could help Harrison, Platt approved the appointment. He thought that Depew could conduct the campaign "in a better spirit" than anyone else.[42] Michener also needed a prominent party leader to nominate the president, and in seeking one he uncovered part of the intrigue against him. Harrison's first choice was Governor William McKinley of Ohio, who was invited to deliver the address, but he ignored the overture. After a reasonable delay Michener telegraphed a second invitation, but this also failed to elicit a response. Michener deduced that the governor himself intended to be a candidate. Harrison was amazed but seriously doubted the possibility. "McKinley was the first man of prominence," he said, "to ask me to be a candidate, and every time since then that he has been in Washington, he has . . . voluntarily promised me his support. I cannot believe he will oppose me in any way. I expect his support."[43]

More than six months earlier, Blaine had expressed a more accurate analysis of McKinley's position in regard to the presidency. In a letter to Russell Alger, he asked, "Won't McKinley be an important factor in the presidential election? He is ambitious for it, and if you will notice, Ohio has always had a presidential candidate. When Hayes was through, John Sherman has been at it every convention since, and now it will be McKinley."[44]

When the Ohio governor arrived at the convention, Michener called upon him and treated him as a Harrison supporter, but the governor appeared uninterested and offered no comment on the proposed nominating speech. Michener observed that McKinley attended all the anti-Harrison conferences and also learned that a number of boxes, addressed to a Minneapolis man, arrived from Cleveland and were taken to the loft of a building near the convention headquarters. Through a friend who procured admittance to the loft, Michener discovered that the boxes contained portraits of McKinley, badges, pennants, flags—all the accoutrements for a McKinley parade. This was convincing evidence of McKinley's objective, but the Harrison leaders decided not to disclose their discovery publicly. Instead, they devised a strategy of their own. Suspecting that the plan was not to have McKinley nominated on the convention floor, but to have him seem to receive votes as a result of delegate spontaneity, the Harrisonites were determined that he would not be allowed to repeat the Garfield tactics of 1880. They decided to advance his name for the honorific post of permanent chairman of the convention from which he could neither mingle freely with the delegates nor otherwise promote his own cause. In this capacity his acclaim could be limited to two occasions: his selection by the delegates and his address to them. After that he would be relegated to the humdrum role of "making rulings and doing things that would cause discontent—always the lot of a presiding officer— and thus put him out of the hero class."[45]

When the endorsement of McKinley for permanent chairman was announced, Quay immediately understood its purpose and realized that he and his cohorts could not be placed in the position of opposing this honor for the Ohio governor. He told a conference of anti-Harrison leaders, "We will have to support McKinley for the place, although we had planned that he should be on the floor." This made it impossible for him "to Garfield the convention." Detoured into the chairmanship, McKinley maintained that he had never wavered in his support of Harrison. By casting his own convention vote for the president, he hoped to convince everyone that he had entertained no personal ambitions at Minneapolis.[46]

Blaine also joined the eleventh hour maneuvering. On June 4, just three days before the national convention convened, when his own boom was beginning to wane, he dramatically resigned from the cabinet in a cold, formal note to Harrison, who accepted it with an equally cold, formal acknowledgment. This action shocked the political world, but no clear explanation for it emerged. Illness could not have prompted his decision because for a year he had been physically incapable of meeting the demands of his office. He could not have desired political freedom in order to spark a campaign for the nomination or he would have resigned months earlier. Perhaps he subscribed to Quay's outward optimism, or as McKinley's stock began to rise, he became convinced for the first time that together the two of them could overcome the president's strength.[47] But there was no single motive. In the preconvention excitement a combination of lesser issues probably stirred him to make a spur-of-the-moment decision. Politically isolated in Bar Harbor, Blaine discussed private feelings and grievances with his family. His wife had had a bitter encounter with Harrison when he refused to promote their son-in-law over twenty-nine army officers who outranked him. She had left in a rage, slamming the door behind her. Their son Walker had also been disappointed by the president, who refused to appoint him assistant secretary of state as recommended by his father. When Harrison assumed some of the responsibilities normally entrusted to the secretary of state, Blaine felt slighted. These family tussles with the president may have weighed more heavily than any of Blaine's political feelings. Probably not by coincidence, Blaine's wife telegraphed another son, Emmons, in Minneapolis on the same day that he resigned: "PA WILL ACCEPT." The fact that the convention received no word from Blaine himself also suggests the strong family involvement.[48]

The public viewed Blaine's resignation as a forthright bid for the presidential nomination, but contrasted this action with his letter to Clarkson on February 6. They were not certain which to believe. About a month before the convention, Clarkson himself decided that Blaine's true ambition had been modified to fall between the two extremes. He thought that the aging leader was now "largely governed by his desire to hold Maine & New England from Reed, whom he hates even more than he does Harrison."[49] Some, who had always implicitly trusted Blaine's motives, feared that he was turning his back on the Republican party in order to serve Quay and his Grievance Committee, that he too was more interested in Harrison's defeat than in his own victory. Others, without reference to the Grievance Committee, believed that his candidacy was dictated only by bitter, implacable hostility for the president.

To the Blainiacs explanations did not matter; they were ecstatic because he was no longer a phantom candidate. But to the other alignments, the resignation struck a temporary note of alarm. The Harrisonites felt betrayed, and the Grievance Committee discovered that it had a more serious candidate on its hands than some of its members had ever intended. Clarkson immediately recommended that both Harrison and Blaine withdraw to prevent a bitter fight. This reflected the general preference of the Grievance Committee, which was more than willing to sacrifice Blaine if Depew and the administration forces would drop Harrison, but the proposition was not acceptable.[50] Clarkson, who had been advocating Blaine's nomination for months, now shifted his ground and argued that his health would make it impossible for him to discharge the duties of the presidential office. A week before the resignation announcement, Blaine had told Clarkson that he probably could not stand the labor and excitement of a campaign and that he suspected he had only a short time to live. The national chairman had replied, "Even suppose all you say is true, Mr. Blaine, I should think that if you die as soon as you say . . . the height of your ambition would be to die in the White House." But now that Blaine's candidacy had become a reality, Clarkson wanted to stifle it. In contrast the Blainiacs were willing to gamble with Blaine's life even after the resignation. According to one partisan newspaper report, "They say that they would rather see Blaine the presidential candidate of his party for a month than that Harrison should have the satisfaction for a brief moment of taunting Blaine with his own renomination."[51]

Amid this new Blaine optimism, the national convention opened. The first two days were devoted to preliminaries, but on June 9 two incidents, one formal and the other informal, determined the fate of the candidates. The formal report from the Committee on Credentials noted that its members could not agree on the seating of delegates from Alabama and that there would be a minority report. This provided the first test of strength for the contending forces, and in this instance the Grievance Committee opposed the majority report, which endorsed the seating of Harrison delegates. A roll call of the delegates favored acceptance of the majority report, but the formal vote to substitute the minority report was delayed until the following day. Since the vote demonstrated that most Southern delegates concurred in this decision, Quay could see that his faction was decidedly in the minority in the South and that Blaine could therefore not be nominated. When asked if this assured Harrison's nomination, Quay murmured: "I do not know. The Harrison people have bought up the colored fellows, and we must try to get them back." Toward this end he quietly maneuvered to persuade delegates to transfer their allegiance from Blaine to McKinley in the hope that others who had favored Harrison would also switch to McKinley.[52]

The informal incident further strengthened Harrison's hold on the convention. His managers sponsored a secret caucus designed to achieve a threefold purpose: convince doubting delegates in their ranks that Harrison would be nominated, prevent desertions to Blaine or McKinley, and augment their strength by recruiting converts from the opposition. Without disclosing the aims of the meeting, each of the Harrison leaders was assigned to invite specific delegates, some of whom seemed attracted by the mystery surrounding the invitation. Depew was elected chairman of this rump session, and Magee was chosen secretary. To those in attendance the meeting succeeded in removing all doubt concerning Harrison's strength and demonstrated conclusively that he controlled more delegates than the minimum needed for the nomination. Realizing this, the leaders encouraged the participants to discuss the deliberations openly with fellow delegates after adjournment. When the first report of this behind-the-scenes session, with a description of the president's delegate support, reached Quay, he refused to believe it. Finally convinced, he said only: "The fight [in behalf of Blaine] will go on just the same." But he really did not mean that. Through various avenues, particularly his henchman, David Martin, from Philadelphia, he was already plotting the switch to McKinley.[53]

The next morning the convention chairman turned the delegates' attention back to the unfinished business pertaining to the report of the Committee on Credentials. Convinced that there was little merit in attempting to substitute the minority for the majority report, the Beaver boss was applauded by the delegates for his decision not to "prolong the contest on these lines." Both time and maneuvering space were rapidly eluding him, but he was left with one last ploy—the candidacy of McKinley—with which to excite the imaginations of the delegates and stem the Harrison tide.[54]

Harrison and Blaine were promptly nominated on that same day, June 10. According to the plan McKinley's name was not formally placed before the convention, but in seconding the nomination of Blaine, Stephen W. Downey came close by turning to the Ohio governor and promising, "When four more years roll around, we will make you President of the United States." This produced thunderous applause, and Quay momentarily thought that he had held off the Harrison onslaught. He had, in the meantime, arranged for Alabama, leading off the presidential roll call, to cast seven of her twenty-two votes for McKinley, and he went from delegation to delegation in an effort to encourage similar changes from Harrison and Blaine to McKinley, but his primary objective, of course, was to move Harrison's support to any other candidate.[55]

The battle ended with the first ballot. Quay had failed to prevent the president's renomination, but he did succeed in demonstrating delegate strength that did much to create a favorable atmosphere for McKinley in 1896. The official tally gave Harrison 535 1/6 votes, Blaine 182 1/6 , McKinley 182, Thomas B. Reed 4, and Robert Lincoln 1. For the most part the Pennsylvania delegates performed like dutiful Quay puppets and voted McKinley 42, Harrison 19, and Blaine 3. Aside from the Keystone State, the only concentrations of McKinley votes were in Ohio (45) and Michigan (19). The senator gave his personal vote to the Ohio governor, while Magee led the contingent that supported the president. As Gresham had warned, Harrison's patronage power, particularly in the South, was the decisive factor. From that section alone administration forces compiled approximately 50 percent of the delegate strength necessary to nominate; and in competition among the northern and western delegations for the other 50 percent, they also enjoyed the patronage advantage which was not available to any candidate brought forward by the Grievance Committee. In the South, for example, Blaine could attract only 10 percent of the delegate support necessary to acquire the nomination and had no asset comparable to patronage when he went forth to corner the other 90 percent. With the Republican electoral potential of the South almost nonexistent, Quay commented that "the President has been renominated by the powers which cannot give him an electoral vote," and left for home.[56]

As an anticlimax to the presidential intrigue, the convention selected Whitelaw Reid, editor of the *New York Tribune,* as the vice-presidential nominee. He had actively promoted Blaine's candidacy, and the Blainiacs insisted on the right to name Harrison's running mate. With New York an obvious key to victory in November and with Quay no longer on the scene to duel with Tammany, his selection at first seemed politically astute, but the opposition exposed him as a liability, not an asset. Reid was closely identified with the *Tribune's* bitter battles against the typographical union, and his presence only succeeded in making the Republican ticket suspect to organized labor across the country.[57]

The selection of Reid did nothing to mollify the Grievance Committee, embittered by the failure to sidetrack Harrison. Having feuded, sometimes openly, with the president for more than three years, members of the committee were not easily reconciled to their public defeat. Although they were not about to oppose him actively, they viewed his possible defeat in the general election with stoic indifference, if not secret gratification. In spite of their thirst for revenge, they were too shrewd to be identified with any overt scheme that would permit the Democrats to be victorious in November. Quay, in fact, declared his intention "to work for the ticket," but obviously had no desire to show much enthusiasm for the Harrison nomination, which had been "received very coldly at Pittsburgh" and elsewhere in Pennsylvania. On the other hand, he knew that the triumph of Harrison could only cloud, if not disrupt, his own political future. If the president were reelected, Pennsylvania patronage for the next four years would be distributed by Magee, not Quay. He was Pennsylvania's foremost advocate of renomination and would undoubtedly inherit control of state patronage. In spite of this prospect and its threat to Quay's future, he could not openly bolt the party candidate without imperiling his standing within the Republican party.[58]

The men responsible for the success of the Republican ticket recognized that reconciliation with the bosses was a sine qua non. Harrison and Reid both sought to involve the Grievance Committee in the campaign. They were particularly solicitous of Platt; with the electoral vote of New York in doubt, but crucial to victory, they made a concerted effort to pacify him. Harrison wrote at length and personally consulted him. How they placated Quay was never publicly revealed, but Michener complained that Harrison's willingness to cooperate with the bosses was the most serious blunder of the campaign. Quay's appearance at Republican national headquarters on October 24 marked his first general acknowledgment of the presidential contest being waged around him. With the campaign in its final stages, he announced a willingness to assist in raising money. The combination of his appearance and his desire to cooperate was hailed as a major conquest and offered as proof that the Republicans were a united family again.[59]

In attempting to shift responsibility for the subsequent Republican collapse to Harrison's long-time enemies, Michener obviously oversimplified the case. Although they shared the burden of defeat, it was not directly attributable to their campaign conduct. The principal indictments against the Grievance Committee are a lingering bitterness over its failure to dictate cabinet appointments in 1889, a three-year running battle over the control of patronage, failure to answer the press's attack on Quay, and the vicious contest to prevent Harrison's renomination. Although these incidents sapped the party's strength, it was beaten largely on the basis of the administration's unresponsiveness to the challenging economic issues of the day. Failure to recognize the legitimate protests of labor, an inability to design a more effective control of corporate power, and an unwillingness to relieve the monetary "squeeze" by either of the more widely advocated means (the free coinage of silver or the graduated income tax) caused dissatisfied voters, particularly in the South and West, to defect to the new Populist party. Indicative of this failure to heal the economic ills was the handling of the Homestead strike, which raged during the campaign and noticeably handicapped the drive for votes. The strike implied a weakness in the McKinley tariff and the policy of high protection that it represented. It also identified the administration with the corporate interests of the nation while remaining indifferent to the demands of organized labor.[60]

Surprisingly, the nation's corporate interests also cooperated in bringing about Harrison's downfall. The general unpopularity of the McKinley tariff in its early stages and the administration's spending program, coupled with Grover Cleveland's demonstrated ability to work effectively with Wall Street during the Harrison years, prompted the corporations to conclude that he was the "safer" candidate. Henry Clay Frick wrote to Andrew Carnegie: "I cannot see that our interests are going to be affected one way or the other by the change in administration." In a reply written after the election, Carnegie concurred: "Cleveland! Landslide! Well, we have nothing to fear and perhaps it is best." As further proof of their changed attitude, the Carnegie-Frick interests, which had contributed $50,000 to defeat Cleveland in 1888, subscribed far less four years later. Only the delay in trans-Atlantic correspondence provided the Republican party with as much as $25,000 in 1892; on his own initiative Frick had decided on the reduction, but Carnegie, absent in Scotland, thought $10,000 more appropriate.[61]

This combination of forces at work among the voters succeeded in returning Cleveland to the White House. His 277 electoral votes to Harrison's 145 constituted a stunning victory, and as Quay had predicted, the president did not receive a single electoral vote in the southern states that had been largely responsible for his nomination, nor did he carry any of the doubtful states of the North, including his home state of Indiana. This was a blow to the prestige of the Republican National Committee, which believed that it had taken all the steps necessary to secure Indiana. In addition, the party had fully expected to carry New York because both the city and state organizations there received all the financial assistance they requested.[62]

Vindication by Election

Paralleling this contest over the renomination and reelection of Harrison was the Pennsylvania battle to determine whether or not Quay would be reseated in the U.S. Senate. Both had been launched in the summer of 1891, alternately heating up and cooling off over the subsequent eighteen months. Throughout much of the period Quay and Harrison obviously needed each other. They recognized that fact, but were never able to come to an amicable agreement.

In the months preceding the national convention, the president had coveted control of the Pennsylvania delegation, not so much because this bloc was essential to renomination, but because of the prestige in having the unqualified endorsement of the largest Republican state in the Union. Only Quay could provide the votes that could make his ambition a reality. On the other hand, the senator needed certain patronage promises in order to ensure his reelection by the state legislature in January 1893, an advantage that only the president could grant. Harrison's principles and personal coldness impeded all compromise efforts. Coupled with Quay's determination to defeat the president's renomination, at the cost of his own reelection if necessary, these attitudes produced a political standoff that went unresolved throughout the campaigns. Nationally the Republican party was weakened by the duel, but in Pennsylvania the Beaver boss again demonstrated his mastery.[63]

Opposition to Quay was centered in Philadelphia. The faction of Independents that had spearheaded the successful defeat of the Quay machine in the gubernatorial election of 1890 planned to resume where it had left off. Directing the attack at Quay personally, it regrouped under the banner of the Reform Republican League of Pennsylvania, with Herbert Welsh as president. The league's manifesto declared that its goal was to crush boss rule and its dishonorable political methods so that the control of public affairs could be returned to the people.[64]

The league developed support in other parts of the state, particularly in Pittsburgh, where Chris Magee yearned to use on Quay the same dagger with which he had helped to stab Delamater. But like the Philadelphia Independents, he discovered that by going outside the party to elect Pattison in 1890, he had weakened his position within. Under pressure from rank-and-file Republicans, Magee and the Independents were forced to share the leadership with those who had been more faithful.

Dissatisfaction with the efforts of Magee and the Independents to assume sole control of the anti-Quay forces prompted the rise of the Pennsylvania Republican Association, a collateral organization designed to prevent Quay's nomination to the Senate and to secure the choice of "some able and loyal Republican" as his successor. Whereas members of the league had been battling the party machine for years, the association was composed of business and professional people, plus a contingent of artisans, who had uniformly supported the Republican party but had never taken an active part in politics before. It represented the emergence of a neomugwumpism. Its influence likewise spread across the state, meeting its most favorable reception in Pittsburgh, where a large number of merchants, bankers, and lawyers joined the battle of the "Sunday-school politicians" against the bosses. In a pamphlet entitled *Republicanism vs. Quayism*, the association outlined for the voters its complaints against the senator, arguing that Republican voters, not the legislature, should have the right to determine the senatorial candidate. With that right they were expected to choose someone other than Quay because in more than five years he had failed—partly due to absenteeism—to originate a single piece of legislation significant to either the state or the nation.[65]

Eager to attend Quay's political funeral, Magee attempted to cooperate with both the league and the association. His most significant contribution to their campaign was the identification of John Dalzell, a congressman from Allegheny County, as a worthy challenger for the Senate seat. Since Dalzell was a member of the Magee faction, his relationship with Quay was already strained. Long before this contest began, the senator had described him as a qualified lawyer, an excellent speaker, and a self-styled "unappreciated great man" who was "narrow between the eyes."[66] Dalzell was a willing candidate, acceptable to the league and the association because he had succeeded where Quay had supposedly failed. He had been elected to the House at the same time that Quay entered the Senate and had compiled a distinguished record for attendance at, and participation in, the discussions on the floor. The senator could make no similar claim. In the first session of the Fiftieth Congress, he was present for only 36 roll-call votes and absent for 108, and in the second session, his attendance improved only a few percentage points. Responding on less than 37 percent of the votes in the Fifty-first Congress, he was still conspicuously delinquent. Since Cameron, the senior senator from Pennsylvania, had failed to answer the roll call almost as frequently, Quay's opposition charged that the state was without representation in the Senate much of the time and that, when these two were present, they contributed nothing to the proceedings.[67] The *Philadelphia Press* had excoriated them and their performance: "Pennsylvania is now voiceless in the Senate, for neither of its members can advocate, explain, or defend any measure in the interest of the state or present in plain and simple English reasons why any particular measure prejudicial to this Commonwealth should not become a law. No man in his senses would employ a dumb counsel, much less two dumb counsels, to plead for him at the bar, yet Pennsylvania is practically in that position in the Senate."[68]

This absenteeism could not be denied, but the Dalzell faction went a step further, attributing it to a "lack of ability, . . . the enforced silence of incapacity." In this respect the comment was mere campaign bravado because Quay, in attendance or not, exercised more influence over legislation than almost any other senator. Legitimately the Dalzell advocates could have denounced the nature of that influence, but to deny it or to imply incompetence and indifference was totally capricious.[69]

The Quay forces, however, were prepared to retaliate. The senator's absenteeism was explained in two campaign pamphlets, *The True Story About Senator Quay's Occasional Trips to Florida* and *The Great Conspiracy of Four Years Ago.* Largely the work of Clarkson, the Republican national chairman at the time, with a few tactical suggestions from the senator's secretary, Frank Leach, this literature traced Quay's health problem directly to the strenuous campaign of 1888. By implication his chronic illness was incurred in the line of party duty. For a Republican to assail "the man who elected Harrison" for making such a sacrifice was denounced as base ingratitude, but this too was an oversimplification for political purposes: Quay's physical difficulties predated that campaign by many years. In January and February 1892, however, he suffered one of his most severe attacks. Having caught a cold and developed a cough in Washington, he went to St. Lucie in a weakened

STRANGERS IN THOSE PARTS.

A SCENE THAT MAY BE WITNESSED WHEN THE JUNIOR SENATOR RETURNS.

Fisherman Quay, meeting Sportsman Cameron in the Corridor of the Capitol:—"Pardon me, sir, but can you direct me to the Senate Chamber?"

Sportsman Cameron:—"Sorry, Sir, but I'm something of a stranger in these parts myself."

A comment on absenteeism from the *Philadelphia Press*, March 8, 1892.

condition to recuperate, but there he contracted pneumonia. His wife Agnes was called to his bedside, marking for her an almost unique appearance away from Beaver with her husband. Whether he had been politicking in Harrisburg or Washington or vacationing in Florida mattered little; she had generally remained at home with their unmarried children. He communicated frequently through cheery notes inquiring about and reporting on various members of the family, but rarely did he express even a hint of his political dealings. Now because of his illness Agnes hastened to Florida, and under her care he rallied and regained his health. Recovery was dramatic and came in the early stages of his campaign when the Quay strategists used it effectively to explain his total record of absenteeism.[70]

In another pamphet, entitled *Corporation John,* Quay demonstrated an offensive of his own. Since the term *corporation* had a generally unfavorable connotation in the American mind at the time, he exploited it against Dalzell who was posing as a champion of the people and defender of farmers. Quoting Dalzell's autobiographical sketch in the *Congressional Directory,* the senator portrayed his opponent as a friend of corporations, not of the people. In a poor choice of words the congressman had described himself as "one of the attorneys for the Pennsylvania Railroad Company . . . and for many corporations in Allegheny County."[71]

Leaders of the Dalzell campaign discovered early that the task of defeating Quay the man was far more complicated than defeating the Quay machine. Realizing that the senator would have to be beaten within the Republican ranks without the assistance of a Democratic coalition, Herbert Welsh of the Reform Republican League suggested that all Republican candidates for the legislature be required to declare their attitude toward Quay's reelection in advance. Those who refused to pledge themselves against his return to the Senate were, according to the league, to be challenged in the primaries. Although this plan was never fully activated, Quay endorsed a modified version of it whereby in certain counties where there was a contest between Quay and Dalzell, both names would appear on the Republican primary ballot. Republican members of the legislature elected the following November from these districts would be bound by the results of the primary vote. This procedure was a quasi-direct election of a U.S. senator. It tended to involve masses of people directly, and the locus of power in the determination of a senator shifted from the legislature to the polls, marking the first time in the history of Pennsylvania that any of the people cast a direct senatorial vote.[72]

If the procedure in Chester County was a valid index of his statewide design, Quay conducted an elaborate campaign to win the voters in this test of the direct election process. A subordinate in that county reported the completion of his assignment in vivid detail:

In conformity with your request, I personally visited the Republican editors of our county during the past week, and find we can secure the active support of the "Daily Republican" for $200, "Coatesville Times" for $50, "Spring City Sun" without cost. . . . Of course I did not connect you in any way with my visit when in conversation with the editors of the above papers, but led them to believe should any material aid be forthcoming, it would come from an entirely different source than yourself. . . . I do not anticipate all of these papers would be against you without any move being made as the "Malvern Item" is now pouring hot-shot into Dalzell, and will publish any editorial matter we furnish, but it might spur them on to renewed effort.[73]

Farmers and soldiers voted solidly for Quay, who won by lopsided margins in almost all the county contests. In a number of counties the primary vote was larger than that cast for Harrison in November. As the only ex-soldier ever sent by the Keystone State to the Senate, Quay received an almost "blind" endorsement from the veteran press, not only in the state, but also across the country. These journals had already defended him against the protracted charges of the *World* and in his running patronage battle with President Harrison; now their Pennsylvania subscribers had an opportunity to react personally at the polls. They did so with such decisiveness that Dalzell never recovered—exactly the response that Quay wished to achieve. Even the 134th Regiment of Pennsylvania Volunteers, which Quay had commanded briefly during the Civil War, formed a campaign committee in his behalf. In a flyer sent to all its members, the committee noted that twenty-three of the nation's eighty-eight senators had served in the Confederate Army and only sixteen in the Union Army. Stressing the fact that Quay was one of the sixteen, the committee urged his endorsement for reelection and exhorted his former comrades to go to the polls and "stand with a soldier's pride for a soldier's rights."[74]

Through such efforts a legislature firmly committed to support him was elected, and his vindication was complete, except for the formal ratification. Elated with the returns, Clarkson wrote gleefully from his vacation retreat at Hot Springs, Arkansas: "I see by the dispatch in the St. Louis papers this morning that you have only 'carried every county in the State and gained a 200,439 majority over Dalzell in the popular vote in the Repu primaries.' I should have thought that with the help of the administration and Bro. Wanamaker you would also have carried a good many of the counties in Ohio and New Jersey."[75] In spite of this overwhelming victory, Quay admitted privately to A. K. McClure that he really did not want a second term. But, like Harrison, he "was compelled to this contest" by his relentless enemies.[76]

In December the senator fell ill again. Rushing in vain for the healing rays of the Florida sun, he was stricken for the second time within a year with a nearly fatal pneumonia attack and did not return north until March. This illness shifted responsibility for the final stage of the Senate battle, which was almost perfunctory, to his capable secretary. When the legislature convened in January, Leach made the arrangements necessary to assure victory in the formal balloting. By this time the Dalzell boom had collapsed so completely that in the Republican caucus Quay won the party nomination on the first ballot with 146 votes to Dalzell's 14. In a subsequent, strictly partisan, vote in the total legislature, he defeated the Democratic nominee 165 to 80 and was forced to turn his attention to the question he had posed to McClure: "What shall we do with the victory?"[77]

The Sphinx Speaks
1894-1896

AMID a setting similar to that which marked his initial entry into the
Senate, Matt Quay took his seat for a second term. Grover Cleveland was again
in the White House. The initiative for legislation rested with the Democrats,
but they had difficulty in exercising it. With his party divided on both the
tariff and monetary issues and further handicapped by the Panic of 1893, the
president was unable to move with confidence. He chose to make the repeal of
the Sherman Silver Purchase Act his highest priority. Revision of the tariff,
to which his party had devoted most of its campaign oratory, was temporarily
deferred.

This decision worked to the advantage of Quay and the other protectionists.
Although the Democrats controlled both houses of Congress and the
presidency simultaneously for the first time since the Civil War, they failed to
make the most of this advantage. Since their majority in the Senate was slight,
it was imperative that they move at once. If Cleveland had summoned a special
session of Congress on March 4, 1893, and insisted upon appropriate
adjustments in the tariff schedules before any executive patronage was
dispensed, he would have been better able to force all the Democratic senators
to adhere to the administration position, but this he did not do. Belatedly
aware of this loss of political leverage, Daniel Lamont, Cleveland's most
trusted confidant, admitted to Quay that it was a mistake to "distribute your
plums before you secure your legislation."[1]

The special session was not called until early August 1893, when repeal of
the silver purchase law was requested. Debate on this issue did not follow
party lines in either house. Republicans from silver-producing states in the

West joined agricultural Democrats of the South to sustain the law, while Republicans from the industrial North united with the presidential forces in order to bring about complete repeal. After extended deliberation the act was put aside, and the government's purchases of silver ended; but the Democratic party was split into two antagonistic factions, one gold and one silver.[2]

The Senator and Tariff Manipulations

With the money problem resolved, Congress directed its attention to the tariff. In the process of deliberation, however, the tariff issue became tainted with scandal that reflected unfavorably on the nation's political and business leadership.

In keeping with the Democratic promise to rewrite the McKinley tariff, William L. Wilson, chairman of the Committee on Ways and Means and a former university president, pushed through the House a bill that revised the rates downward, but the measure met a roadblock in the Senate. Using the unlimited debate rule to full advantage, the protectionists launched a vigorous attack. Before the battle began, Quay admitted privately to James Swank, secretary of the Iron and Steel Association, that the bill was a threat to American industry. "I have no hope of accomplishing anything for the iron interests," he said, "except by the absolute defeat of the Wilson Bill." His plan to bring about this defeat was circuitous. In cooperation with other tariff senators, specific schedules were attacked, 634 changes adopted, the protective principle restored, and the president's efforts crushed.[3]

In achieving this end Quay exceeded his normal methods of "thinking and scheming." To gain the tariff concessions desired by protectionists, particularly those of Pennsylvania, he threatened to talk the Wilson bill to death. Since he had not spoken in the Senate on any substantive issue during his entire first term, his threat was not taken seriously, but he discovered a voice, collected suitable material, and launched into a filibuster that lasted two months and two days. He held control of the floor from April 14 to June 16, 1894, during which he personally spoke for fourteen legislative days against aspects of the bill. In an almost inaudible tone, he read, day after day, from copy provided primarily by Thomas Dolan of Philadelphia. His long-awaited concluding remarks, addressed to his Republican colleagues of the North, noted that both party and nation would benefit from the defeat of the Wilson tariff: "In all of the southern states the Republican Party is incapable of achieving success. The great northern states alone can be relied upon to support the principles of that party. Therefore, it is our duty as patriotic citizens to stand firmly by the grand old party which piloted us through the storm of rebellion and landed us safely in the harbor of peace."[4]

The speech, which covered more than two hundred twenty pages in the *Congressional Record,* achieved its purpose. Arthur Gorman, the Democratic leader in the Senate, understood clearly, as he listened to Quay, that the sphinx-turned-orator intended to stall the passage of any tariff measure until he received certain concessions. He was also bombarded from other quarters concerning the same tariff schedules. Motivated more by political necessity than tariff convictions, Gorman endeavored to work out a compromise and halt the filibuster. He agreed to schedules for the various types of iron that satisfied industry's demands; in fact, the amendment pertaining to bar iron was written for Quay by Swank.[5]

Gorman's compromise brought Quay's marathon to an end and moved the Senate toward a consensus. Although the House version of the bill expressed good Democratic tariff theory, it could not overcome protectionist sentiment and pressure. Observant senators in both parties, including Quay and Gorman, understood this, and each in his own way undermined the measure in the schedules accepted by the Senate. As a result the House-Senate conference committee accepted the modifications advanced by the Senate. The president was so disgusted that the Wilson-Gorman bill became law without his signature. Particularly in the face of Cleveland's dissatisfaction, the Republicans hailed the measure as a triumph.[6] William McKinley later recalled for a delegation from Beaver that visited him in Canton during the 1896 presidential campaign that he had been favorably impressed by Quay's "unfaltered devotion to Republicanism" during the Senate fight over the Wilson-Gorman bill. "I remember well that, when the Wilson Bill went from the House to the Senate, Senator Quay stood resolutely for every interest of his state and prevented the destruction of great industries by his famous speech, which was the longest ever delivered on the tariff in the history of the Republic. He kept on without apparent diminution of manuscript that lay before him until victory crowned his efforts. It certainly was a master stroke."[7]

During his filibuster, Quay had been frequently chided by Democratic Senator Isham G. Harris of Tennessee. After speaking for an hour and forty-five minutes on May 3, Quay sent to the desk of the Senate secretary an article analyzing the sugar bounty systems in foreign countries and requested that the secretary read it to the Senate. Harris pointed out that a senator must read his own material. Quay countered, saying "I am not well today, or else I should not have asked the secretary to read the article." The presiding officer ruled against Quay, who then agreed to continue reading himself.[8] Noting that the sugar bounty systems employed by foreign nations offered their producers an export bounty expressly for the purpose of securing the American market, he stressed that a sugar tariff, adequate to offset this bounty, was a necessity. Earlier he had informed the Senate that the sugar schedule was of utmost importance to Pennsylvania because Philadelphia alone had $30,000,000 invested in the industry. The city's board of trade had petitioned him to support their interests, and he was prepared to respond affirmatively.[9]

In the course of the Senate's deliberations, attention was temporarily diverted from the economic to the ethical aspects of the tariff schedules, particularly those pertaining to sugar. In New York, *The Sun* reported that bribes had been offered to two senators to induce them to vote against certain schedules. Almost simultaneously the *Philadelphia Press* charged that the sugar interests had been accorded the privilege of writing the sugar schedules because of large contributions to Democratic campaigns. In addition, it was rumored that senators were using information gained in the Senate as a basis to speculate in certificates of the American Sugar Refining Company, known otherwise as the Sugar Trust. This implied that a seat in Congress was preferable to a seat on the New York Stock Exchange, and the press sensationalized the charges. They were reprinted widely in urban and rural newspapers across the country. For several weeks the gossip mounted until it reached the Senate chamber, where it could no longer be ignored.[10]

Largely because of the alleged conflict of interest, Senator William A. Peffer of Kansas proposed a Senate investigation. On May 17, 1894, his resolution passed. Five members were appointed by the president of the Senate to conduct the investigation of their colleagues, and during the summer months that followed, the Senate proceeded to wash its dirty linen in the presence of all who cared to watch. The committee, chaired by Henry Cabot Lodge, reported to the entire Senate on August 24. The charges of bribery and graft were dismissed as groundless. The eighty-five senators examined in regard to their personal conduct were all acquitted of unethical practice although two—Quay and John R. McPherson of New Jersey— admitted dealing in sugar stock while the bill was pending. Others were suspected of similar involvement, but found it convenient to give forthright denials. The press and other critics were willing to accept such statements and dwell on the two who "confessed their sins."[11]Under questioning by Lodge, Quay admitted having bought and sold stock of the American Sugar Refining and other companies as recently as the current session of Congress. His last transaction, on the same day that the Senate adopted the sugar schedule, was, in his opinion, a gesture of conscience. "I closed out at some loss to enable me to vote without having any interest in the stock." He then added, "I do not feel that there is anything in my connection with the Senate to interfere with my buying or selling the stock when I please; and I propose to do so."[12] Interpreted as a challenge flung in the face of the Senate, this last sentence was quoted widely in denouncing Quay for both avarice and arrogance. To him it was a statement of fact and his behavior was less mercenary than

Donald Cameron's just a few years before. At that time Cameron had purchased large quantities of silver and then voted in the Senate to increase its cost to the Treasury. Arguing that as a member of Congress he had a right to speculate like other people, the senior senator from Pennsylvania had met no rebuff. Since Quay had participated neither in the framing of the sugar schedule nor in sponsoring the legislation, he thought that he was guilty of no misconduct. He would certainly have found senatorial office less attractive if he had had to suppress his speculative passion in order to retain it.[13]

To Quay politics and the stock market were twin magnets. They had both been an integral part of his life for more than thirty years. Aside from the Senate, the market was his only livelihood. The inner motivation that inspired him to the one inevitably attracted him to the other. Both contained elements of uncertainty and risk that made life continuously exciting. Quay dealt as deftly in one area as in the other; winner or loser, he was rarely upset. When a turn in the market caused him to lose $10,000, in a single day, he laughed heartily at his bad luck. Since the funds he had ventured often belonged to a private bank or the Commonwealth, why shouldn't he laugh?[14]

Revolt in the Ranks

While Quay was engaged in these tariff wars, jealous state leaders were regrouping their forces for another attempt to reduce his power. The senator tried to avoid a confrontation with them, but his antagonists knew that only by provoking a crisis could they hope to cripple his hold on the party.

Their first opportunity to strike came in the gubernatorial contest of 1894. Quay was compelled either to accept a candidate he could not completely control or to face an intraparty battle that might assure the Democrats another term in the state capitol. The Republican rank-and-file were still indignant because the party had gone down to defeat in 1890, when the Beaver boss had foisted his own candidate on them. General Hastings, now more popular than ever, had no reason to be grateful to him for the nomination; but in order to avoid a divisive struggle, Quay acquiesced in Hastings's candidacy and remained outwardly supportive throughout the successful campaign. Hastings, in turn, had made a pledge to Quay when he was first selected as a gubernatorial candidate by the Philadelphia Republicans: "If I live, you will have proof of my gratitude, my loyalty and fidelity to you." After the election, still in awe of Quay's power, he expressed a willingness to submit to the senator's authority: "I am exceedingly anxious to have everything in connection with the Harrisburg business going to your liking, and my determination is to do it if you will not be too modest with me." He declared that he had no ulterior political ambition, such as succeeding Cameron in the

Senate in 1897, because he had observed that other young men ruined their lives by going too fast. Concluding on a friendly note, he encouraged Quay never to go to Harrisburg "without making our home your home. These are boss orders No. 1, and you will please take notice."[15]

This expression of friendship never became a reality. A group of Republican leaders in Philadelphia, headed by David Martin and Charles A. Porter, were dedicated to the proposition that it should not. When Quay had been forced to submit to the Hastings nomination, they knew that they had him off balance, and they intended to keep him that way. Philadelphia's Republican organization was already divided. The Martin-Porter forces had drifted away from the Quay-Penrose-Durham group, but the division was not considered irreparable. In late 1894 and the first weeks of 1895, when Boies Penrose was advanced as a candidate for mayor, the prospects for unity brightened. With his ever increasing popularity, it seemed that his nomination and election would bring peace to the warring factions. Steady progress toward these goals was noted until a few weeks before the nominating convention. Various religious groups began to express their doubts about Penrose's personal qualifications. In a short time it was apparent that the Martin-Porter forces had decided to challenge him at the party's formal meeting. No specific challenger was announced, however, until the morning of the convention when City Solicitor Charles F. Warwick was named.[16]

The startled Quay faction requested an explanation. Martin, the spokesman for the group of ward leaders whom Quay subsequently dubbed "the Hog Combine," smugly volunteered that the situation was "perfectly simple. We're nominating Charlie Warwick. We're ditching Penrose." Speaking in a triumphant tone, he unveiled a large photograph of Penrose leaving a house of ill repute at daybreak. An editor standing conveniently nearby declared his intention to print the picture if Penrose insisted on being a candidate. He did not insist.[17]

Martin, the mastermind of this stratagem, was a rotund, bullet-headed man who had once been a faithful Quay lieutenant. The Beaver boss had promoted him "through the chairs" from a driver of wagons to membership on the Republican National Committee. Having enjoyed the fruits of power and wealth along the way, he sought to use the mayoralty as the first step in wresting control of the state from his benefactor. Quay did not want the Republicans to wash their dirty laundry in public again and hoped to avoid a fight with Martin and his cohorts, but A. K. McClure, the editor of Philadelphia's Republican *Times*, pressed for a showdown. Exercised at the betrayal of Penrose, which he called "assassination, nothing more nor less," McClure launched a newspaper campaign against the Hog Combine, concentrating mostly on Martin. At one point, according to McClure, Penrose expressed a willingness to withdraw in the interest of party harmony, but from the moment Martin realized that it was possible to defeat Quay's protégé, he schemed to keep him from stepping aside without an incident. Martin's primary goal was to remove Penrose as a factor in both city and state politics, as well as in the party generally. This particularly angered McClure, but Quay, who did not object to the editor pillorying the Combine generally, appealed to him to halt his attack on Martin personally. McClure hotly refused—"you might as well ask that *The Times* shall stop publication"—and argued that to condemn the Hog Combine and not Martin would be like "the play of *Hamlet* with Hamlet omitted." Quay had no love for Martin; he was only trying to prevent a more disastrous party rupture. Other colleagues, like McClure, either did not understand his purpose or were more interested in having Martin reprimanded than in having the party reunited. Josh Nobie, who misread discretion as sympathy, advised Quay that his one weakness, "too much sympathy" for his rivals, was destroying the prestige of his friends, who were threatened with being "wiped from the political battlefield." Within weeks the boss had to rally to their defense and his own by taking a forthright stand against Martin and his Combine.[18]

This Republican rift caused the Democrats to think that conceivably they could elect a mayor. They dangled the nomination before former governor Robert Pattison, but he refused to claim it without being assured of the support of the Quay-Durham Republicans. McClure was certain that Pattison would be elected if endorsed by Quay, and he urged the senator to lend his support because "the force you could wield here is much greater than you even imagine."[19]

Quay refused to be drawn into a coalition with the Democrats. He realized that such a combination had little or no meaning beyond the initial purpose for which it was created; at best it was a temporary expedient. He had once declared: "Sooner or later the lure of party will be too strong, and men with whom you have made hard and fast agreements will desert you and join their party associates." He understood not only that his future was independent of the Philadelphia mayoralty outcome, but also that this was only the opening volley of the Martin-Porter attack. Knowing in his heart that his enemies had frustrated the election of a competent mayor, Quay was determined to chastise them; for the first time he thought about slating Penrose as a successor to Cameron in the U.S. Senate. And when Penrose actually took the Senate oath in 1897, Quay had redressed the balance between Penrose and his Philadelphia rivals in a self-satisfying manner.[20]

During the winter and spring of 1895, the state legislature became the battleground for renewed efforts against the Quay forces. Although the next opportunity for a formal encounter did not occur until the Republican state convention on August 28, both sides sought to achieve an advantage before the party council met. In the legislature the Quay contingent was led by the disappointed Penrose and "Bull" Andrews, the Crawford County "Machiavelli"; the Combine's legislative strength rested primarily in Philadelphia's bosses and Pittsburgh's Magee-Flinn faction.[21] In the interest of their constituencies, the party leaders from both cities established channels of communication with the Hastings administration, and all the governor's responses to them were categorically denounced by Penrose and Andrews as evidence of his alignment with the Combine. This was exactly the public impression the Combine wished to create; it wanted to convince the rural districts and towns that Quay's star was fading and Hastings's was rising independently. By this maneuver they actually succeeded in siphoning off much of Quay's support. For a time his ranks were noticeably ragged.

A large fraction of Pennsylvania's wealth and power was concentrated in the state's two major cities, and in both, the leadership overwhelmingly supported Hastings. Although he sought no quarrel with Quay, circumstances drew him inevitably into the orbit of the Pittsburgh and Philadelphia politicians. Martin and Magee were in command, and they pushed the governor to the forefront, where he became a reluctant and misunderstood figurehead. Penrose and Andrews heartily distrusted him, while Josh Nobie described him to Quay as a "weak piece of human flesh." More affirmative reports on him were supplied by Frank Reeder, secretary of the Commonwealth, who made a passionate plea for Quay not to start a feud with Hastings because it would wreck the Republican party in Pennsylvania. To demonstrate that the governor did not oppose the senator, Reeder disclosed that Hastings was willing to appoint anyone to the vacant judgeships that Quay would name, even if he personally were not fully convinced of the individual's fitness. He even claimed that the governor said: "I would be an ungrateful dog if I did not grant any request the senator would make. He is my benefactor. I would not now be governor except for his kindness."[22]

Reeder and Hastings were probably more objective than either the Combine leaders or the Penrose-Andrews group in analyzing the party crisis. Unfortunately Reeder carried less influence with Quay than Penrose did, and Hastings was not equal to the political challenge of conveying his neutrality. He was not in sympathy with Quay, but knew that as governor he should remain aloof from factional fights, except to attempt to minimize them. On one occasion while traveling together by train from Philadelphia to Harrisburg, Reeder suggested to Penrose that, if the governor made a particular appointment that the Quay faction was requesting, Penrose should convince the newspaper not to report the action as a Quay victory because the governor should not be placed in the position of taking sides. After reporting this incident to the Beaver boss, Penrose concluded with his own evaluation: "I do not think that Reeder is much better than Hastings."[23]

Several times the factions came to the point of an open break, but moderating influences prevented a complete rupture. Quay knew, however, that a showdown was inevitable. When Penrose urged him to bring the fight into the open by announcing his support of Andrews for chairman of the Republican State Central Committee, he responded more dramatically than Penrose expected. He announced that he, not Andrews, would be the candidate for chairman against B. Frank Gilkeson, whom the Combine wished to continue in the post. If he lost, Quay would be confessing that his leadership in the state was subordinate to another power and that his final overthrow was only a matter of time. If, on the other hand, he won under these conditions, his leadership would be unquestioned. The Combine understood this gamble. Its objective was to defeat and humiliate him in his home state while undermining his power and prestige as a national leader. Believing that Quay was particularly vulnerable at this point because the last vestiges of the federal patronage he had enjoyed under the Harrison administration were disappearing, the Combine considered this a propitious time to challenge him. For men like Chris Magee and Charles Emory Smith, it was a renewal of a long-standing feud, but most of the others who confronted the senator were ex-colleagues who had entered the political arena under his tutelage or endorsement.[24]

Since the factions were engaged solely in a power struggle and not in the interpretation of a substantive issue, the crisis appropriately came over the state chairmanship. The battle was strictly for control of the party machinery and for the spoils that it could command. Control meant jurisdiction over the state's delegation to the 1896 national convention and any patronage that would accrue if a Republican president was elected. Cynics among the observers viewed the challenge differently—as one between "the master of corrupt politics" and "his recalcitrant pupils," or as a contest between one great boss and a combination of smaller bosses.[25]

The prognosis for Quay's recovery was not good. The city bosses, in league with the railroads, were against him. Most of the state's newspapers—owned and controlled by corporations—were also listed among his enemies. And many rural politicians, anxious for state patronage, were attracted to the Combine by propaganda that identified the governor with the scheme to oust Quay. The steel industry, although not as hostile as the railroads, was somewhat unsympathetic. Its spokesman, James Swank, reasoned that Quay "has made mistake after mistake and is the author of his own troubles. Nevertheless, two thoughts concerning him are constantly in my mind; first, our manufacturers are under great obligations to him, and second, what is to be gained by a change of bosses to Magee, Martin & Co.?"[26] J. W. Gates, a director of the Consolidated Steel and Wire Company of Allentown, confirmed that appraisal of the senator's contribution to the steel industry. He wrote to the company's plant superintendent, who supported the Hog Combine, reminding him of Quay's service: "When our company wanted a friend in Washington, he was the first to speak and work for us day and night." Because there was so little time to suppress the Combine rebellion, Swank concluded that the senator would be beaten in the convention battle, but predicted that he would recover and take command in 1896.[27]

The task before Quay would have daunted a less combative politician. The Combine had boasted that it would tear him apart and convert the state convention into a burial ceremony, but Quay was a reluctant corpse. He again exhibited his ability to extricate himself from almost certain political oblivion. His strategy was to eschew all former preachments and adopt the role of reformer. In the past he had had only sneers and contempt for reformers, whom he had labeled "theorists, purists, and cranks." Before a startled constituency, he now parted company with that philosophy. He wrapped himself in the white robes of reform, and as a self-crowned champion prepared to slay corporate giants, stall political machines, and bring professionalism to government services.[28]

With the shrewdness that had marked his hegemony in Pennsylvania politics for more than a quarter of a century, Quay appealed first to rural politicians. Asserting that the city combines were trying to extend their influence into the countryside by using the same methods that had made city government synonymous with corruption and extravagance, Quay captured rural imaginations and, in due time, their votes. One county chairman proclaimed that his delegates were "ready to fight God, man or the devil if it is necessary" to procure the chairmanship for Quay. The Northeast Republican League also endorsed the senator, and from the northwest Samuel B. Dick of Meadville reported that he had visited the leaders in all the counties of that section with uniform success. In addition, Dick stressed that Quay's prestige among the organized Civil War veterans was still strong: "The North West Association of the Grand Army met here . . . and had a large representation from this entire section of the state and I found everyone outspoken in your favor."[29] Quay also pledged support to the masses of urban dwellers. If installed as state chairman, he promised to bring relief from the machines and corporations that dominated their politics. By these assertions he figuratively left the ranks of the Republican party and extended his hand to the "demi-mugwumps." In rural areas he defined the issue as one between country votes and city rings, and in the urban communities, as bosses and corporate agents versus the masses.[30]

Quay could offer one precedent for his new declaration of goals. The previous year he had recommended that Galusha Grow, a recognized Republican opponent of machine politics, be nominated for congressman-at-large. That recommendation had been accepted, and by the outbreak of the 1895 controversy, Grow was established in Congress to the satisfaction of the independents.[31]

When the sun went down the day before the convention, the opposing forces were drawn up in battle array. A general brawl complete with bloodshed was forecast. The seating of delegates was expected to ignite tempers because in the past the chairman on his own initiative had certified those entitled to seats. In districts where seats were now contested by Quay and anti-Quay delegates, it seemed that Gilkeson, the incumbent chairman, would undoubtedly rule to exclude all of the former, and the battle would begin. The prospect of two separate conventions, with two sets of delegates, resulting in two tickets, seemed inevitable. The opposing forces were so evenly matched that Frank Leach, who once again joined Quay to assist in this fight for survival, declared that "it was the toss of a copper" as to which controlled the more delegates. After bringing the party to this edge of disruption and looking over the brink into the dark political chasm, the leaders wisely stepped back to more solid ground and avoided the greatest crisis in the history of Pennsylvania Republicanism.[32]

On that convention eve both sides caucused, and the Quay contingent demonstrated that it had a slight majority. The senator's caucus was no star chamber proceeding; in contrast to the Combine caucus, which met behind closed doors, its deliberations were open to all. The names of those participating were published the next day, and all their procedures were open to inspection. This approach, hailed as a victory for the people as well as for Quay, seemed to explode the myth of machine domination. In addition, the Magee-Martin faction, which Quay now called "the municipal thieves of the two great cities of our State," was "inspired" toward compromise by Quay's announcement that his colleagues possessed evidence implying the misappropriation of funds by the Martin group. John P. Persch, who held the incriminating documents, dangled them before Martin and suggested that they would be surrendered if the Combine capitulated to Quay. To the senator, however, Persch revealed his personal conviction: "This evidence must always be held; they (Latta, Porter, and Martin) will do anything to have it destroyed." Quay advised Gilkeson that he would request the issuance of a writ of mandamus compelling Gilkeson to produce his accounts. To publicize the issue, Quay supporters cavorted about Harrisburg before the opening of the convention wearing large badges reading "What Did He Do With It?" Rather than tell, the Combine preferred compromise.[33]

Before noon on the day of the convention, peace was formally achieved. In counties where there were contending delegates, both were seated, each with one-half vote. Because of the demonstrated majority behind the senator, it was agreed that Gilkeson should step aside in favor of Quay as state chairman. So that the Combine might retire with grace, Hastings was named permanent chairman of the convention. A hastily called peace conference on that convention eve had also concluded that only delegates, the press, and 100 friends of each faction would be admitted to the convention.[34]

The convention that opened on the morning of August 28 in the Harrisburg Opera House was a farce. Quay moved that Hastings be named permanent chairman, and Gilkeson nominated Quay as the chairman of the party's State Central Committee. William A. Stone, a Pittsburgh congressman, seconded the latter in a speech characterizing the senator as "a poor country boy with nothing but the pious example of his Presbyterian father and the prayers of his Christian mother for his inheritance." Although no rebuttal to this polemic was offered from the floor, hostile editors suggested brightly that Quay must have squandered his inheritance at an early age.[35]

Providing this brief but hectic convention with another jolt, Quay moved for adoption of a platform that committed the party to reform. The document not only decried the increased use of money in politics and the power of corporations over state and municipal affairs, but forthrightly advocated civil service reform in all branches of government. In accepting this position, Quay sealed his victory over the Combine, won the hearts of the people, and again became the unquestioned leader in Pennsylvania politics. The perfect illustration of a machine leader, he defeated the machine in behalf of popular government, and in doing so demonstrated the value of a machine in defeating a machine.[36]

The reform element of the party was elated. Ignoring their earlier vilification of Quay as the incarnation of bad politics, many now greeted him as a regenerated sinner who had turned his back on the past and was born anew. The senator's espousal of reform had come not so much from seeing the light, however, as from feeling the heat. Not the wisdom of the movement, but the desire for public acceptance had convinced him to champion reform ideas. The reformers believed that, fighting to win their support, Quay had accepted their program. They knew that this was the same man who constantly thirsted after power, who schemed to dictate nominations, who plotted the fate of legislation, and who maneuvered to dominate the party. But they were optimistic concerning his intrusion into their midst because he was demonstrating that "he who would have political power must reckon with the people." They argued that the greedier he became, the safer he was, because he was more likely to heed the wishes of the masses.[37] Despite this questionable logic, Quay had become the nation's leading mugwump. George Curtis, Carl Schurz, and E. L. Godkin never achieved acclaim that approached such heights. Paradoxically, Quay was at the same time the greatest boss throughout the land. With his victory being one of the most complete and significant in the political annals of America, the *Kansas City Star* caustically sermonized: "And now abideth Gorman, Brice, and Quay—these three, but the greatest of these is Quay."[38]

Party leaders at the national level were relieved that Pennsylvania Republicans had not declared war on each other. In the brief, half-day convention, Quay had won the state chairmanship that he coveted, but did not attempt to misuse his power. He established an entente cordiale with the Combine by supporting incumbents for all positions on the party slate. That courtesy and generosity were not wasted on the Republican masses, who compared his conduct to that of Grant when he triumphed over Lee at Appomattox. A. K. McClure went even a step further, purporting that Quay's "opponents came on their knees to beg for permission to follow him." Although there was no outward sign that his victory was that compelling, valid parallels to the Confederate surrender could be drawn. As Grant had been magnanimous and allowed Lee's army to retain its rations to keep from starving on the homeward trek, Quay too granted honorable terms and thereby met the test of an effective leader. Obviously gratified by Quay's conduct, Andrew Carnegie told him that "no man has rendered such service to Pennsylvania in my time." The sincerity of his compliment was amplified when he confided to Swank that Quay's defeat "would have been more than a state—a national calamity. It is necessary . . . to keep him in the Senate as long as he can be induced to serve."[39] Consistent with his conduct in previous situations, Quay showed that he could be conciliatory even when he possessed the power to be otherwise. Amalgamation had long been a part of his success formula, and he again demonstrated that it paid high dividends. At the same time he acknowledged the delegates who made his victory possible and heartily congratulated them for their efforts: "You have fought a great battle, and you fought it fairly and won it bravely. It was a contest in the interest of good government and purity in Republican politics."[40]

A Reluctant McKinleyite

On Sunday afternoon following the convention, a Pittsburgh newspaper sponsored a special train to Quay's hometown of Beaver, twenty-seven miles down the Ohio, so that the citizens of Allegheny County could personally endorse his platform calling for governmental reform. A thousand demonstrators took advantage of the opportunity. At Beaver fifteen hundred more joined the ranks, and together they marched to the senator's residence. He met the throng on the lawn, where spokesmen presented congratulatory remarks. Then the senator forcefully reaffirmed his allegiance to the principles of good government: "Those principles were embodied in the platform upon which I was elected. It is the written law of the Republican party in Pennsylvania, and as chairman of the State Committee it is my duty, in addition to my pleasure, to enforce it, as I intend to do, as well in the counties of Allegheny and Philadelphia as in other portions of Pennsylvania."[41]

The public, both state and national, recovered from the initial shock of seeing Quay as a reformer to discover that the political reverberations from the convention had produced several casualties in addition to the Combine. A dark shadow had fallen over the future careers of both Senator Cameron and former President Harrison. Throughout the hand-to-hand combat with the Combine, Cameron had remained stoically indifferent. His silence affected party subordinates across Pennsylvania. Quay became aware of local disenchantment with his senatorial colleague when he wrote to Republican leaders in the various counties to enlist their support against the Combine. Some who volunteered their unqualified endorsement of the Beaver boss felt compelled to add that their cooperative spirit did not extend to Cameron. One actually noted that Quay's enemies realized that Cameron had fallen from popular favor and were trying to curtail Quay's strength by arguing that support for him was support for Cameron. On the same theme, and without any prodding, a second declared that his constituents were "unalterably opposed to the placing of further political honors on the shoulders of Don Cameron, a Democrat at heart." Even more emphatically another wrote that the Republicans of his county were for Quay against the Combine, for McKinley for president, and "not for J. Donald for anything."[42] Through such reactions Quay learned that he could not long afford to be identified politically with his state's senior senator. In addition to Cameron's withdrawal from participation in the affairs of the party, his advocacy of free silver made him a liability. Quay had never challenged his right to pursue such a course, but when Republican delegates clamored for a sound money plank, Quay concluded that the people wanted no more Cameronism. By accepting the plank, he cut himself loose from Cameron, who, in turn, found the door to reelection to another Senate term being closed in his face.[43]

Harrison too was looking forward to an election. In 1895 he was considered a strong presidential possibility for 1896, but had made it clear that he would not engage in a struggle for the nomination. If Quay remained as a power within the party, a struggle was inevitable; so Harrison had hoped for a Combine victory. He argued that a Quay defeat would be "a good thing for the party"—and incidentally for his own future. With Quay's success in Pennsylvania, and with Platt irrevocably anti-Harrison, the two largest Republican states were aligned against him. Quay actually prided himself on his anti-Harrison stand. In an autobiographical statement for the *Congressional Directory*, he tersely wrote: "Was a delegate to the National Republican Convention in 1892 and voted against the renomination of Benjamin Harrison."[44]

Consensus held that the Quay victory eliminated Harrison and left McKinley as the primary candidate for the nomination in the Midwest. In the Northeast the Pennsylvania result was considered as a boost to the candidacy of Thomas Reed of Maine, who was endeavoring to outdistance McKinley. Theodore Roosevelt, the youthful chairman of the Board of Police Commissioners for New York City, who was already showing a major interest in national politics, advised Henry Cabot Lodge to try to get control of the Reed canvass "so that it won't look as if he was being nominated by Platt and Quay." Throughout the nation speculation that Quay was going to be a major factor in the 1896 national convention began to mount. The prediction—that the rivalry between the aspirants from Maine and Ohio would be so bitter that both would be left on the field after the smoke of the convention battle cleared—caught the imaginations of numerous would-be candidates, and the political tug-of-war began.[45]

Those who believed this prediction failed to appreciate the comprehensive campaign that was already being waged by the McKinley forces. McKinley's conduct as presiding officer at the Minneapolis convention in 1892 had rekindled the attention of Mark Hanna, a Cleveland financier. Without objection from McKinley, Hanna became his self-appointed patron. With his personal patronage prior to the national convention estimated to run into six digits, many doors were opened and many issues closed before other candidates could concentrate their energies on the 1896 campaign. This initial advantage was possible not only because of the crackling of Hanna's checkbook, but also because the established bosses underrated Hanna as a political foe. They knew that he had "hardly a single political acquaintance outside of Ohio," but with the proper mixture of money, enthusiasm, and naiveté, he was able to overcome that. Even his lack of political sophistication was excused because he was laboring for McKinley, not for himself. In retrospect, Platt lamented that "Hanna really began his campaign to make McKinley president immediately after the defeat of Harrison in 1892. He had the South practically solid before some of us awakened."[46]

Although both Hanna and McKinley had probed the political pulse of the South prior to 1895, they now decided to make a concerted effort to control it. In March, Hanna arranged to have Governor McKinley spend three weeks at his winter residence in Thomasville, Georgia, and then quietly invited prominent Republicans from all parts of the South to come, meet the governor, and discuss patronage and other political possibilities in a relaxed atmosphere.[47] In the South, as elsewhere, McKinley maneuvered to make the tariff the only campaign issue because that would catapult him into the forefront as the one logical candidate. Southerners who were invited to exchange ideas with him were impressed not only by his political style but also by his hospitality. This technique, reenforced by emissaries dispatched by Hanna to carry the McKinley message throughout the South, succeeded in gaining convention pledges from an overwhelming majority of that section's delegates. Months later, when other candidates joined the race and threatened to undermine this delegate strength, Hanna hastily wrote to Swank of the American Iron and Steel Association for funds to resist such efforts. Naively he thought that the steel industry regarded McKinley as its sole benefactor. Swank corrected that conception, responded with a friendly but negative note, and reported the incident to Quay, on whom the industry had relied most heavily for the legislation it sought. The convention results proved, however, that Hanna's fears were unfounded. His missionary work passed the test of competition; there were no backsliders, and McKinley won 197 of the South's 222 convention votes.[48]

When Hanna returned north, he was visited by Russell Alger of Michigan, who was functioning as an agent for Quay and Platt. His mission was twofold: to confront Hanna with suspected collusion between McKinley and Platt's Republican opposition within the New York state organization, and to explore the possibilities of an undefined "deal." On the first he was assured that "no pledges, understandings, or encouragements" had been or would be given to Platt's intrastate rivals. Hanna maintained that the governor held Platt in high esteem even though Alger had reported that the anti-Platt feeling had taken "strong root" with the McKinley faction. On the second item, Hanna insisted that "the Governor should stand without a single fetter, before the people, if he receives the nomination." From this expression of confidence Alger deduced that Hanna's dragnet for delegates had been cast far more extensively and profitably than he and his colleagues suspected.[49]

Hanna made his purity statement before Quay's late summer showdown with the Combine, but once the Beaver boss had demonstrated his dominion over Pennsylvania's Republican organization and had thereby strengthened his bond with Platt in New York, Hanna came to view the idea of concessions more favorably. It then became McKinley's turn to send an emissary. The lot fell to Hanna, who was commissioned to visit Platt and Quay in order to enlist their support of the McKinley candidacy. When he returned to Ohio, he reported their demands to the McKinley inner circle.

Hanna: You can get both New York and Pennsylvania, Governor, but there are certain conditions.

McKinley: What are they?

Hanna: They want a promise that you will appoint Tom Platt secretary of the treasury, and they want it in writing. Platt says he has had an experience with one President [Harrison] born in Ohio, and he wants no more verbal promises.

The governor, who had remained seated, now rose, paced the floor for a few minutes, and finally dissented. "There are some things in this world that come too high. If I cannot be President without promising to make Tom Platt secretary of the treasury, I will never be President."[50]

McKinley's refusal to bargain sparked a bitter struggle for control of the Republican convention. Quay and Platt met with leaders from other states in an effort to sidetrack McKinley. Their two-pronged strategy was to flood the scene with a host of favorite-son candidates in order to prevent a ground swell for the Ohio governor, and to battle vigorously to recruit delegates in the South. They failed on both fronts, but their ignominious defeat in the South provided the decisive blow to their plan. They sadly learned that Hanna had already scouted the southern territory and staked out irreversible claims on an overwhelming number of delegates.

The campaigns in behalf of favorite-son nominees were full of sound and fury, but in the end they signified very little. Reed of Maine was expected to restrain all New England from joining McKinley, while Allison of Iowa was to charm the Plains and Rocky Mountain areas. Along with the elderly Shelby Cullom of Illinois, former President Harrison, now recognized by the bosses to have nuisance value, was counted on to keep the Midwest from coalescing on Hanna's protégé. In New York, Levi Morton was Platt's nominee to subdue McKinley, and Quay personally took on that assignment in the Keystone State.[51]

These campaigns were launched amid great expectations for the local candidates. Politicians in general accepted the thesis that, after the first convention ballot, the "also-rans" always worked harmoniously against the one receiving the largest number of votes, and rarely was he able to retain his coveted position on subsequent ballots. The candidates' immediate task was to prevent McKinley's nomination on the first ballot. If successful, each one would then have a relatively equal opportunity to win the nomination. With Platt and Quay the obvious leaders in this maneuver, rumors concerning their private preferences abounded, particularly in their home states. Some doubted the sincerity of their stated endorsements, but no one questioned the fact that they were in league with each other. In Pennsylvania many argued that Morton's candidacy was only a cover for Platt's design to throw the New York delegation behind Quay. In New York the rumor was reversed; Quay was depicted as the Pennsylvania manager of Morton's campaign. In reality both bosses favored Reed, with Allison as second choice. The Iowan had been catapulted into prominence through the efforts of Clarkson, who convinced the bosses that, in addition to Iowa, Allison would carry Illinois, Minnesota, Nebraska, and Kansas. On that assumption they favored him, but time proved that he was unable to fulfill any part of such a strategy.[52]

Quay's own state organization "manufactured" a favorite-son boom in record time. Almost as soon as his name was mentioned in conjunction with the presidency, groups clamored to climb onto the bandwagon. Support came from the halls of Congress, from county conventions, from political clubs, and even from the Combine press. Livy S. Richard of the *Scranton Tribune*, a Combine editor in 1895 who had since been converted, righteously told the public: "As the leader of his party in the state, proved such by the walloping he gave us Combiners last year, Senator Quay is entitled to the support of the state delegation at St. Louis; and if he wants it, he ought to have it."[53] A more formal demonstration greeted the senator on February 19 when he returned from a Florida vacation. On behalf of twenty-five Republican members of Congress from Pennsylvania, Alfred C. Harmer of Philadelphia presented him with a petition urging him to be a presidential candidate and pledging their support. Quay's acceptance came immediately. The next day the press published this appeal, along with a statement of his decision to run. In his personal acknowledgment to Harmer, he claimed that "in deference to friends whose wishes could not be disregarded, I signified my willingness that my name should go before the Republicans of this country."[54]

Almost simultaneously the various counties began holding their conventions to select and instruct delegates to the April 23 state convention. The idea of a Pennsylvania nominee immediately excited the imaginations of locally minded Republicans. The Erie County resolution expressed some of the strongest, most lavish support for the idea and the man:

> Whereas the Republicans of Pennsylvania have never faltered in giving their electoral vote to the Republican candidate for President during almost forty years of its existence, and yet have not, during this time, been awarded a name upon the national ticket, . . .
>
> . . . The Republicans of Erie County, in convention assembled, do unite in the spontaneous movement which from the Lakes to the Delaware has so grandly joined in the choice of their matchless leader and patriotic statesman, Matthew Stanley Quay, as a candidate for the President of the United States.[55]

Two of the most influential black organizations, the J. D. Cameron Club of Harrisburg and the Matthew Stanley Quay Club of Philadelphia, also endorsed Quay for the presidency. Remembering that in 1895 Quay had appointed the first Negro ever to serve on Pennsylvania's Republican State Committee, they pledged their efforts to convert the black delegates of the South to his cause. Since the blacks constituted approximately one-third of the Republican delegate strength in that section, the outlook was optimistic. In addition, Quay's major role in the defeat of the elections bill led him to expect the endorsement of many southern whites. In neither instance did such support develop.[56]

Support among Pennsylvania delegates, however, was never in doubt. From the moment Frank Leach's gavel called the state convention to order on April 23, delegate sentiment overwhelmingly favored Quay. Leaders of the Combine, almost completely stripped of their followers, tried desperately, but in vain, to frustrate the senator's candidacy. At the behest of Martin, Magee, and Wanamaker, Congressman John Robinson attempted to introduce McKinley's name, but the convention refused to consider any second choice. As the floor manager of the Quay forces, Penrose led the convention to this decision, and his rebuttal of Robinson's proposal in behalf of McKinley was greeted "with unbounded enthusiasm and vociferous applause."[57]

Hardly had the delegates returned to their homes than the Combine struck again. This time Martin reported to the press that the state's delegation was not the cohesive unit Quay's selection implied and that twenty-seven of the Commonwealth's sixty-four delegates would vote against him on the first ballot at the national convention in St. Louis. Confronted with such crises in the past, the senator had gone directly to the people; on this occasion, however, he went directly to their representatives, the delegates. Quay sent telegrams to all sixty-four, stated Martin's charge, and requested a reaction to his candidacy from each. He received sixty-one replies, fifty-eight of which clearly indicated their preference for him, and three that were vague and noncommittal. In general the responses expressed indignation at Martin's charge. Israel Durham vowed: "Quay, first, last and all the time. Martin lies." A more verbose John Elkin pledged: "I am for you on the first and every other ballot until you are nominated. Should you decide at any time to help nominate any other candidate, I will follow your lead." Another who was equally willing to follow added the proviso: "unless you would ask me to vote for Harrison." Governor Hastings, a delegate-at-large and former colleague of the Combine, assured Quay: "I will vote for you on the first ballot and on every other ballot so long as your name is before the convention."[58]

Having thus reaffirmed his strength in Pennsylvania, Quay more confidently turned to negotiate with McKinley. In order to gauge the force and direction of the political winds, he visited the Ohio governor in Canton, although some state leaders were critical of his action. They feared that it magnified McKinley's importance and weakened the favorite-son movement that Quay himself had helped to foster against him. The two lunched together and appeared to part on friendly terms, but the details of their meeting were left to speculation. According to Platt, Quay was given undefined "assurances," none of which, he predicted, would materialize. Still distrustful of Ohio politicians as a class, the New York boss cynically argued that McKinley was "much too amiable and much too impressionable to be safely intrusted with great executive office." At least in the financial field, this attitude was shared by Quay's sound money colleagues who wanted assurances of the Ohioan's commitment. They knew that he had thus far studiously avoided the issue that they believed could present the next president with his most grave crisis. The "gold bugs" feared that, no matter which presidential candidate was nominated and elected, the silverites could control both houses of Congress. They wanted a president who would veto any silver legislation that came to his desk. They doubted that McKinley had the necessary firmness; if he did, they wanted assurances.[59]

Another of the purposes in Quay's visit to Ohio was to repair the McKinley-Platt relationship, but he was unsuccessful. Platt was constantly concerned lest McKinley aid his Republican rivals in New York and thereby embarrass him. He wanted the Ohio governor at least to demonstrate publicly that he recognized him as the "senior" leader in New York. Quay thought this could be accomplished simply by having McKinley summon Platt to Canton after the convention, supposedly for a strategy conference. But the governor refused, saying that Platt was welcome at any time, but that he would not ask him to come.[60]

Quay's proposal that the McKinley-Platt rendezvous take place after the convention signified that he had already accepted McKinley's nomination as inevitable. Before leaving their homes for the June convention, the better informed delegates anticipated this result. The trains carrying easterners to St. Louis were loaded with disappointed and unenthusiastic disciples of Reed, Platt, and Quay. They knew that Hanna had already secured enough support to provide McKinley with victory. Divided delegations from several New England states, the commitment of nine state conventions for McKinley, and the "rotten borough" delegations from the South supplied the Ohio governor with a strength that no other combination could counter. Such an alignment was a tribute to Hanna's genius, which only a year before had been discounted by the eastern bosses. Without assistance from either the entrenched leaders or the large delegate blocs of Pennsylvania and New York, he had placed his candidate beyond the reach of all rivals.[61]

Although the outcome was foretold, the Republicans nevertheless acted out the convention ritual. Five candidates (McKinley, Reed, Quay, Morton, and Allison) were formally nominated, with Governor Hastings eloquently placing Quay's name before the delegates. Extolling the senator as patriot, soldier, and party hero, the governor emphasized his direction of the 1888 presidential campaign. Quay was acclaimed for having "throttled the Tammany tiger in his lair" and for having "rescued the country from the heresies" of the Democratic party; in fact, he made himself so powerful and dangerous to the enemy that "the order went forth to assassinate him."[62] Hastings's dramatic language, like that of the other nominating speakers, was wasted on the convention. The delegates knew what they were about before they went to St. Louis, and no purple oratory was going to change their minds. Only one ballot was required to demonstrate McKinley's strength and Hanna's organizing ability. The tally showed McKinley with 661.5 votes, Reed with 84.5, Quay with 61.5, Morton with 58, and Allison with 35.5. All Quay's votes—except 2 in Georgia, 1 in Mississippi, and .5 in Louisiana—came from Pennsylvania. The bosses were deeply disappointed and with some justification. McKinley had done nothing to warrant such overwhelming support or to inspire confidence. They thought they had reason to question his ability and did not regard this conclusion a partisan judgment. William L. Wilson, a member of President Cleveland's cabinet, an anti-protectionist, and one of many who shared this opinion, grieved in his diary that "of all the candidates, he [McKinley] is the weakest."[63]

In spite of his disappointment, Quay sent McKinley the customary note of congratulations, and in due time received an acknowledgment that endeavored to establish a spirit of goodwill and cooperation. The governor expressed his gratitude by asking the senator to "accept my warmest thanks for your kind words," and assuring him that "in the campaign, which is upon us, I shall necessarily have to look for help and strength from my good friends among whom I place you; and I trust that you will feel free at any time to make any suggestions that may occur to you."[64]

This was quickly followed by an invitation from Hanna, the new national chairman, for Quay to serve on the party's executive committee. Giving health as his reason, the senator hesitated and had to be coaxed. In his third letter to persuade Quay to consent, Hanna confided that he would be embarrassed if he could not announce Quay as a member of the committee. The senator understood the nature of Hanna's impending embarrassment, but was not sympathetic. The New York–Pennsylvania combination had to be prominently represented on the committee, but under no circumstances would Platt consent to serve. Quay's own reluctance kept Hanna dangling. Hanna meanwhile reminded him that he had served on the advisory

committee for him in 1888 against his will and that "turn about is fair play."
Returning to the theme of the senator's health, Hanna extended his personal
hospitality: "I will put you and your family on one of our steamers and send
you to Lake Superior and anything else you want—only don't go back on me. I
have a pretty good 'resort' at my house here on the lake where you can hide
for a week or two. Unless you *positively say no*, out goes your name."[65] On the
day following this appeal, McKinley wrote Quay expressing his personal concern at his reluctance to serve. In an effort to sway the senator, he resorted to
flattery, telling him that his own disappointment was shared "by Republicans
generally throughout the country," and forcefully concluding, "Your
experience and splendid services would inspire a confidence that with you on
the committee the pathway to victory in November would be made clear. You
must not decline Mr. Hanna's invitation."[66] Quay did not decline, and
apparently backed onto the executive committee in the manner suggested by
Hanna, who published his name as a member. Although he did not become
particularly active during the campaign, he nevertheless fulfilled the basic
desire of the national chairman to have his name on the committee's
stationery.

Since the Republicans faced two almost distinct campaigns—one in the
East and one in the West—Hanna established two headquarters, New York
and Chicago. Quay was assigned to the New York office, which also had
responsibility for the campaign in the South. Impressed by Republican
possibilities in Florida, Tennessee, and Alabama, Quay recommended to his
colleagues on the national committee that allocation of their funds should
include these states. Hanna reviewed his plan, but authorized funds only for
Florida. Aside from this one overture, the senator offered no positive
suggestions, faded into the background, and permitted Hanna and his cohorts
to direct the canvass.[67]

Preparing to spend several months in Florida immediately following the
election, Quay sent McKinley a note on October 20 containing several
predictions, both optimistic and precautionary. He evaluated trends in the
campaign and forecast, "If the Chicago people understand themselves, your
victory will be overwhelming though the labor vote will go pretty largely
against us." To reenforce his point, he said that the Pennsylvania Railroad, in
anticipation of his election, was already preparing to place a special train at his
disposal to move him and his family from Canton to Washington prior to the
inauguration. Quay also predicted that the same Pennsylvania clique that
had driven a wedge between him and President Harrison (Dolan, Wanamaker,
Smith, Blankenburg, and a Pittsburgh contingent) would endeavor to
produce an estrangement between the two of them: "They will be after you
briefly after the election—and you will know what the approaches mean."[68]

As Quay had implied, the states of the Plains and Rocky Mountains provided the key to McKinley's margin of victory. This section surrendered to William Jennings Bryan and the silver craze and tarnished the Republican record. In popular vote the party received 51 percent of the total;[69] the electoral distribution, however, was a convincing 271 to 176 triumph. The Pennsylvania results justified Quay's use of the term *overwhelming;* McKinley registered a 295,070 advantage over Bryan and thereby accounted for 49 percent of his total margin over the Democratic party nationally. The Republicans also made remarkable gains in the percentage of the state's total vote that they controlled.

These results made it possible for Quay to depart with satisfaction and relax in confidence at his St. Lucie estate. Not caring whether the fish took his bait or not, he rested comfortably in the knowledge that the Pennsylvania voters had done so. He was still very much the political proprietor of the Commonwealth.

Exercises in Defensive Power

1897-1900

McKINLEY'S presidential victory blunted Quay's aggressiveness, although he himself did not admit it publicly for several years. No longer concerned with the development of a national political empire of his own, he was nevertheless determined to retain control of the Republican machine he had built in Pennsylvania, at least through the remainder of his senatorial term. If he had not been in the midst of a running battle with John Wanamaker and the Republican insurgents, he probably would have retired in 1898. But in that instance, like so many others in his career, he would not withdraw while under attack.[1]

The entry of Mark Hanna into the new Congress eclipsed Quay's senatorial power. Taking his seat in the Senate for the first time in 1897 (a vacancy had been deliberately created so that the governor of Ohio could appoint him), the chairman of the Republican National Committee rose to prominence more rapidly than any of his predecessors. He had nominated and elected McKinley, and this feat alone commanded immediate respect from his senatorial colleagues. At the same time it gave him an entree to the White House that no other senator enjoyed. When an appointment or project lay unnoticed on the corner of the president's desk and a gentle nudge was needed, Hanna was most frequently sought out by the impatient legislator and asked to call the item to the president's attention. Graciously responding to such requests, he quickly developed more power in the White House and in the Senate than any of his fellow senators.[2]

Quay accepted Hanna's new leadership with characteristic silence and perfunctorily went about the task of protecting the interests of his constituents. When the Republicans decided to rewrite the tariff in 1897, he negotiated those schedules vital to the industrial life of Pennsylvania. His questions and comments concerning both the free list and dutiable items were penetrating, but he permitted others to take charge of the legislation itself. He spoke simply for the Keystone State. At one point the trend in the deliberations was so favorable to Quay's prescription that Senator Richard F. Pettigrew of South Dakota, mindful of the Pennsylvanian's filibuster on the Wilson-Gorman tariff, angrily charged that the duty on china clay was increased from two to three dollars per ton solely on the scientific ground that "the senator from Pennsylvania has four bushels of manuscript which he has told the committee he would bring in and read for a week and has thereby obtained these concessions. The rest of us," he concluded, "had better get four bushels of manuscript." The Beaver boss denied making any such threat; protectionist sentiment was so strong in the Senate that no pressure was necessary. By contrast, his political energies were urgently needed in his home state, where the restlessness of the insurgents was continuing unabated.[3]

Wanamaker Renews His Attack

To Pennsylvanians the 1896 election had major significance aside from the presidency. The legislature elected that year was called upon either to return J. Donald Cameron to the U.S. Senate for another term or to designate his successor. Cameron had been a member of that body for almost twenty years, and Quay had been his partner over the last decade. This two-man domination had not provided much opportunity for other senatorial aspirants, but 1897 offered a strong possibility for change.

Circumstance had effectively removed Cameron from consideration even before the 1896 campaign began. He had strayed from the Republican fold with his espousal of free silver, and this alone was sufficient to make him a vulnerable target for intraparty snipers. Frank Leach, who had assisted Quay in his 1895 fight for control of the party organization, further contributed to the decline and fall of Cameron in an interview given to the *Philadelphia Inquirer* on November 7, 1895. Both Quay and Leach were on most cordial terms with the senior senator, but regarded him as a political liability. Leach's strategem, unknown to Quay at the time, was to remove Cameron as gracefully as possible. Having accidentally stumbled on the fact that Philadelphia, which possessed one-fifth of the state's total Republican vote, had not had a senator since George Mifflin Dallas served a partial term in the 1830s, he demanded in the *Inquirer* that the legislature redress this inequity in its 1897 choice. Thus without reference to Cameron, who was a Harrisburger, he directed the attention of the legislature to other possibilities. To simplify the task he named five qualified Philadelphians: Boies Penrose, John Wanamaker, George S. Graham, John Russell Young, and Charles C. Harrison. Although intended for the legislature, this argument also awakened the Philadelphia Combine and the Pittsburgh bosses, who saw another opportunity to wrest control of the party from Quay.[4]

The *Inquirer* interview came on the eve of Leach's departure for a little postelection relaxation in Florida. He was a guest in Quay's private railroad car, but to his chagrin Cameron was enjoying the same hospitality. On the second morning after the interview, while the train was stopped at Jacksonville, a newsboy passed through the car, and Quay purchased a paper that reported Leach's comments. Reading the account as he sat at breakfast, Quay lowered his gold-rimmed glasses, looked at both Cameron and Leach who were seated at the table with him, and said, "Frank, I see you have taken up the job of making senators." When Cameron requested an elaboration of the comment, Quay read the article aloud. By Leach's own confession, "the silence which followed . . . was sufficient to dislocate or detonate any ordinary eardrum." He suddenly lost his appetite, excused himself, and stood alone on the station platform until the train was ready to proceed. Quay was not angry, but grateful, for what Leach had done. Several days later in the relaxed atmosphere of St. Lucie, he used the incident to inquire about Cameron's senatorial plans, and in the course of the discussion he tactfully pointed out that he thought reelection was doubtful. He advised Cameron that his only chance to escape his critics' abuse was to write a letter declining to be a candidate for reelection. Through such a maneuver, Quay argued, Cameron could prevent the violent attack that would inevitably be aimed at him over the next fourteen months if he were to remain as an incumbent to be dislodged. In this scenario a scramble for the position would follow an announcement of Cameron's retirement, and at the proper psychological moment, after the party failed to agree on a successor, the senior senator could step back into the contest and carry off the prize if he so desired.[5]

Although the possibility of such a scramble existed, it did not take place. Quay did not expect that it would. When he, Leach, and Cameron returned north, the anti-Cameron movement was already under way. For some time the business leaders of Philadelphia had considered the advantages of having a businessman such as John Wanamaker, Thomas Dolan, or Charles Smith represent them in the Senate. Since Cameron's silver heresy had already antagonized the public, they regarded this as the opportune time to replace him with their own choice. They needed a resourceful manager, and the name that came to the forefront was that of the Wellsboro editor, Edwin A. Van Valkenberg. A staunch Quay supporter, he was secretly invited to

Philadelphia to discuss possible direction of an anti-Cameron campaign. The group's emphasis was primarily negative. Concentrating on getting Cameron out, the businessmen had not yet focused on a candidate of their own. With evidence of this Republican revolt mounting, Quay summoned Van Valkenberg to Washington and requested the facts. The editor admitted that he had accepted an assignment to dramatize all the weaknesses in Cameron's political armor, but at the same time assured Quay that Wanamaker and his allies meant no disrespect for him. They believed that they were saving the senator from the personal embarrassment of having to put Cameron aside. Quay listened and was apparently impressed. He asked Van Valkenberg to call a temporary halt in his campaign against Cameron, and within forty-eight hours the senior senator announced his retirement. If Cameron expected a general competition to ensue, he was to be badly disappointed. There was never an opportunity to reenter the race; his name was totally lost in the vicious two-way struggle between Wanamaker and Penrose that followed.[6]

Throughout most of 1896 Quay permitted the senatorial contest to progress without interference. He personally favored Penrose, but realized that political expediency could force him to accept another alternative. This, plus his technique of not identifying his preference at an early date and thereby keeping the opposition from focusing its attack on that individual, permitted him to explore the state's political drift objectively.

John Wanamaker was openly ambitious to become a U.S. senator. He courted Quay both directly and indirectly. After the 1895 showdown over control of the state's Republican organization, Wanamaker had written on two occasions and suggested that they meet. In his second note, before leaving for Europe, the former postmaster general blithely suggested, "I trust the old friendship still stands, and if there are any broken links . . . there ought not to be." Quay apparently did not respond to either letter, but his pursuer would not be turned aside. Shifting to the indirect approach, he sought to interest Quay in his candidacy through the influence of A. K. McClure and Henry Clay Frick. To Frick he confided his admiration for Quay and expressed the desire to be his partner in the Senate. To McClure he was even more explicit, asking him to intercede by arranging an interview with the senator. Not adverse to seeing the Philadelphia merchant in the Senate, McClure advised Wanamaker that a senatorial appointment was unthinkable without Quay's imprimatur because his power over the legislature would be decisive in the final choice. The editor quickly learned, however, that the boss was suspicious of Wanamaker's motives. Quay thought that the merchant might attempt to control the state organization, but as a result of McClure's intervention, he nevertheless agreed to explore the issues with Wanamaker, who left for Washington the very next day.[7]

The two exchanged views, and according to Wanamaker they came to terms, but time proved that they had different perceptions of what those terms were. The "applicant" was to contribute the funds necessary for Quay to maintain the state organization, and he, in turn, was to put together the necessary legislative combination to procure the Senate seat. This understanding existed for six or eight weeks without becoming public knowledge. Then for unexplained reasons, the two suddenly declared political war on each other rather than on rival candidates. Obviously defensive about his control of the state organization, Quay may have become alarmed by the support Wanamaker received in recent battles from his old enemies—Magee, Flinn, and Martin; or he may have been disturbed by Wanamaker's attempt to operate through an intermediary in financial negotiations and keep his identity with the machine a secret. On the other hand, Wanamaker may have initiated the break when he discovered the extent of the campaign funds (rumored to be $200,000) that Quay desired. He may also have drawn back because he realized how complete his submission to Quay and the party machine would be if he provided the funds under the terms requested.[8]

Another unknown was the sincerity with which Quay entered the agreement with Wanamaker. He was certainly receiving pressure from machine politicians, notably Bull Andrews and Iz Durham, to endorse Penrose, who was one of their kind, but at the same time he knew that the business interests preferred a Wanamaker. Undecided between these two alternatives, he may have been willing to hold back Penrose in order to receive the financial assets that he thought a Wanamaker tie could produce. When the Wanamaker deal went sour, however, Quay forthrightly endorsed his Harrisburg leader of the past ten years, and as Penrose's biographer noted, made it perfectly clear at the outset that the election would cost $200,000. Penrose went to New York at once and returned within forty-eight hours with the campaign chest oversubscribed.[9]

The funds were needed because a more hotly contested senatorial campaign than Pennsylvania had ever witnessed was about to ensue. Wanamaker announced his intention to defy the party machine and seek the Senate seat as an independent Republican. Van Valkenberg broke with Quay and was recruited to lead the Wanamaker fight. His anti-Cameron arguments were quickly converted to pro-Wanamaker propaganda, and like others before him, he was delighted at the challenge of clashing with the great Republican chieftain. The Penrose-Wanamaker rivalry turned the Commonwealth upside down and raged into every senatorial and representative district that could reasonably be expected to elect Republicans. Van Valkenberg was assigned the task of managing these many local campaigns designed to bring about the election of legislators sympathetic to Wanamaker, whose checkbook

simplified the assignment. Funds were needed even after the 1896 elections—
either to keep legislators committed until the January selection of a senator or
to win them from their indecision or opposing point of view.[10]

Amid this commercialized campaign, Governor Hastings, who had a
lingering hope of receiving the senatorial appointment, became alarmed at the
lavish expenditure and hired a detective agency to trap and expose Van
Valkenberg as a purchaser of votes for Wanamaker. The enterprise succeeded
admirably, and on December 31, 1896, the editor was charged with soliciting a
legislator. When the grand jury handed down an indictment ten days later,
Wanamaker's bid for the senatorial appointment was crushed. The legislature
nevertheless showed no disposition toward Hastings, who then called off the
attack on Van Valkenberg. Quay successfully insisted that the charges be
prosecuted, but he knew the evidence was insufficient to bring about a
conviction: "I have an elephant on my hand and dont [sic] know how to feed
him." By the fall of 1897 the Quayites concluded that the editor had been
pilloried enough by the arrest and indictment and that "the cause of justice
would not suffer by letting off a small fish while other bigger fish were beyond
our reach." They dropped the charges, hoping to transfer the onus to
Wanamaker and Thomas Dolan, who were accused of subscribing the funds
and condoning their improper use.[11]

The dismissal argument implied that Wanamaker had escaped all taint from
the Van Valkenberg episode, but this was not true. His senatorial campaign
had been enveloped in a cloud of bribery and corruption in January 1897
when the state's lawmakers were considering the Senate choice. Legislators
who were undecided between Wanamaker and Penrose were presented with a
lofty moral reason for endorsing the latter. This alone may have been
decisive; the vote in the Republican caucus was 133 for Penrose and 76 for
Wanamaker. The Quay nominee was victorious, but again the cost of victory
was staggering. The incident caused a political rift with Wanamaker that
absorbed almost all Quay's political energy for three years.

The seventy-six Republican legislators who supported Wanamaker in the
party caucus retained their cohesion throughout that session of the
legislature. Opposing the program of the Quay machine, this determined
minority kept the reform spirit alive and provided a nucleus of power with
which to challenge the boss in the gubernatorial election of 1898. In February
of that year more than four hundred leading anti-Quay Republicans met in
Philadelphia to chart their strategy. These insurgents recommended John
Wanamaker to the voters as their candidate for the Republican gubernatorial
nomination. Prior to this action, Wanamaker had declared his determination
not to be a candidate for any office. He insisted that his decision did not
preclude his willingness "to help clear the atmosphere in order to help people

to do better thinking and reach out for better work for the public good." In a matter of weeks this tortured verbiage was translated to mean that he was pleased to accept the gubernatorial nomination.[12]

Wanamaker reentered the Quay wars with the same gusto that had marked his senatorial efforts. In a preconvention campaign of seventy-two days, he delivered sixty-seven speeches, all on the theme of "Quayism and Boss Domination in Pennsylvania Politics." During this whirlwind stumping tour, he charged that for forty years politicians had been building walls to shut out inquiry and erecting barriers to hide their official delinquencies and criminal acts. He promised to tear down such walls, remove the barriers, and place political activity in full public view. Wanamaker was countered in most communities by William A. Stone, an Allegheny County congressman who was Quay's choice for the nomination. This marked the first and only time, while candidates were chosen by state conventions rather than primary ballot, that candidates for the gubernatorial nomination carried their campaigns to the people. Wanamaker initiated this approach because he assumed that the public favored him over a candidate privately selected by Quay two years before the election. Concluding that the politicians constituted his enemy, he believed that only through such a direct approach could he influence the choice of convention delegates.[13]

This contest for delegates coincided with the outbreak of the Spanish-American War. Wanamaker had no military record, but Stone had been a Union soldier. His advocates quickly capitalized on the international developments to claim him as a qualified "war governor." Slating veterans was a regular Quay technique, and with the magic of Civil War duty now losing its voter appeal, the war with Spain supplied a new emphasis. A veteran whose judgment Quay respected, Stone was a typical machine candidate. Delegations pledged to others lobbied to enlist Quay's support, and when one of them sensed the boss's preference for Stone, he exclaimed in all earnestness that his nominee "will do just as you tell him, the same as Stone would." Quay was quick to agree, but suggested that there was a subtle distinction: "I would have to tell him, and I would not have to tell Stone. He would know what to do without telling."[14] Although this response had explicit meaning for both Stone and his 1898 competitors, it suggests an important key to Quay's candidate selections. He was always less interested in *what* a candidate thought about specific issues than *how* he approached the whole spectrum of problems that came within his purview. Also characteristic of his own conduct in the Senate, this emphasis helped to explain his analysis of the issues; ramifications of a decision were always considered more carefully than the substance of the issue itself.

Opposition to Stone was not united. Other reform Republicans were attacking the image of "pious John Wanamaker." They recalled that he had voluntarily raised $400,000 for Quay in 1888 and had willingly served as the "post office spoilsman" in the Harrison administration. To these critics the only way by which Wanamaker could reconcile his past conduct with his current denunication of Quay's expenditures was to maintain that it was sinful *to use* money in politics, but saintly *to raise* money for political purposes. By so burlesquing his conduct, they questioned the sincerity of his reform confessions and charged that he was a reformer not by conviction but by design, that he preferred to cooperate with the machine and had been cast out, and that, smitten by the desire for high public office, he joined the reform camp only to fulfill a selfish ambition.[15]

In a limited sense these accusations were justified, but they did not identify the basic motivation for Wanamaker's action. Fundamentally and emotionally he was anti-Quay. On the eve of the Republican state convention at Harrisburg, when it was apparent that the antimachine forces had to coalesce or submit to Stone without a serious challenge, Wanamaker unhesitatingly withdrew in favor of another Stone (Charles W.), who was also an anti-Quay candidate. The final phase of the contest appeared to be Stone versus Stone, but behind the scene lurked the Quay-Wanamaker feud, and again the boss demonstrated his superiority. Although his margin was slim, he knew that it was reliable. Convinced that the machine had been properly programmed to nominate the ticket and adopt the platform desired, he returned to Washington before the convention was formally called to order.[16]

The closeness of this preliminary test, however, caused Quay to realize that a majority of the state's voters were opposed to his candidate. This prompted another display of his shrewdness as a political manager. Quietly using his influence within the Democratic party, he assisted in maneuvering the nomination of George A. Jenks, an advocate of free silver with no support among Pennsylvania Independents. Their support was given to Dr. Silas Swallow, a Methodist book publisher, who also won the endorsement of the Prohibition and Honest Government parties. His was a gallant but unsuccessful campaign as was that of the Democrats. Conservative Republicans who were anti-Quay preferred "to hold their political noses" and vote for Quay's candidate rather than endanger the sound money system by switching to Jenks.[17]

Quay's genius in keeping the Democrats and Independents from uniting on a common candidate was essential to victory. Although Stone registered a plurality of more than 117,000 over Jenks, the combined vote of Jenks and Swallow showed a majority of 14,000 over the Quay candidate. This indicated clearly that the Republicans generally were dissatisfied with the boss's choice for governor, and inspired the Wanamaker faction to keep up the fight.[18]

The Final Struggle

Within the Republican party the struggle against Quay had been the ongoing preoccupation of a minority since 1882. Always scheming or battling, the insurgents were always beaten. Always coming closer to success, they always collapsed before the boss's gentle coup de grace. By 1898 the intensity of their efforts reached crusade proportions. Indifferent to Republican organization and principles, they sought alliances with Democrats, whenever possible, to produce an anti-Quay majority. John Wanamaker emerged as their statewide spokesman. The two local machines in Pittsburgh and Philadelphia, still under Magee and Martin, occasionally joined the strategy, but they were primarily concerned with carrying their own plans to fruition and only secondarily with either the state boss or the insurgents.

In the campaign of 1898, as in the preconvention competition, Wanamaker provided the anti-Quay missiles. His speeches in the fall campaign failed to defeat Stone, but they brought the issues to the people of Pennsylvania more effectively than to any element of the American public since the Lincoln-Douglass debates forty years before. His tactics succeeded in undermining machine strength in many legislative districts and in seating Democratic and insurgent legislators. To the insurgents this was the first step toward a significant victory—the unseating of Quay. William Stone became the governor, but the legislature that took office in 1899 consisted of more Democrats and insurgents than machine Republicans. It possessed the power to frustrate the reelection of Quay when his senatorial term expired on March 4, 1899. Wanamaker was fully aware of the potentials. Having failed because of Quay to win one Senate seat two years earlier, he was now determined to wrest the other from Quay himself.[19]

The oft-repeated charge of the misuse of public funds was again revived and became the focus of Wanamaker's attack against Quay in the general election. On March 24, 1898, the Peoples Bank of Philadelphia had closed its doors, declaring bankruptcy. Shaken by the incidents that had brought about this collapse, John S. Hopkins, the cashier, left his unlocked desk, walked to his home on Spruce Street, and put a bullet through his head. James McManes, the bank president and one-time boss of the Gas Trust, issued a statement four days later indicating that he had been severely ill for months and that unlawful and unauthorized transactions had taken place in his absence. This effectively transferred the onus to the deceased Hopkins and those associated with him, the most prominent of whom was Matthew S. Quay.[20]

Quay was a major depositor in the bank, and for years Hopkins had handled most of his personal stock transactions through the bank. He dealt in a variety of securities, but particularly in Metropolitan Traction of New York,

Philadelphia Traction, Duquesne Traction, United Gas Improvement, and Consolidated Traction of New Jersey. At the time of Hopkins's death, private letters and telegrams pertaining to these stock operations were found in his desk. In the opinion of the insurgents, the most significant discovery was a telegram from Quay to Hopkins: "If you buy and carry a thousand Met. for me, I'll shake the plum tree." This was interpreted to mean that Quay would shake loose the funds from the state necessary to cover the speculations. This was perhaps a free translation, but it was the most convincing version that they could offer to tie Quay, the bank, and stock speculation together.[21]

Since the Peoples Bank was the favorite repository for state funds as established by a line of Quay-controlled state treasurers, it had been the focus of previous scandals involving the use of such funds for personal speculation by Quay and his colleagues. The insurgents were determined to relate the telegram to similar misuse. They knew that questionable practices prevailed, but concrete proof eluded them now as it had for years. If politicians had not, in fact, been accorded the use of state funds, the record shows that they were certainly favored by loans not supported by collateral. In June 1893 Quay himself had loans in excess of $250,000 from the Peoples Bank. Although it was uncertain whether these were private or public funds, at least part of this total was without security, because Hopkins had warned him: "Please send me down something to make the collateral up, as the bank examiner is liable to drop in at any time."[22]

When the Peoples Bank went into receivership, McManes called in friends of Martin to advise him. Among these was James Gay Gordon, a judge of the court of common pleas in Philadelphia, who served as special counsel and obtained possession of certain Quay letters relative to his stock purchases. Gordon at the time was a candidate for the Democratic gubernatorial nomination, and when Jenks was chosen over him, he publicly accused Quay of preventing his nomination. He and the Martin faction recognized the possibility afforded by the stock correspondence and hoped to exploit it to strike at Quay.[23]

Whatever the character of that information, it was available in March, but was not revealed until the final weeks of the 1898 campaign when it was calculated to have the most devastating effect on Stone and Quay's legislative candidates. Without question the disclosure was politically inspired. It cut into Stone's margin and contributed to the legislative strength registered by the Democrats and the insurgents. On October 3 indictments charging conspiracy to misappropriate and misuse Commonwealth funds were returned against Quay. But since he retained a personal account in the Peoples Bank, his adherents promptly pointed out that he was only a customer and that the bank, not he, was responsible for the state's money. Without prima facie evidence to the contrary, this was a difficult argument to counter and had been confidently relied upon in previous years to protect Quay's stock operations.[24]

Once the November elections were over, Quay petitioned the supreme court of Pennsylvania to assign a judge from the court of the quarter sessions to hear the indictments against him. He was eager for an immediate trial because the composition of the legislature and the impending indictments jeopardized his reelection.[25] The legislature convened and began to ballot for senator on January 17. Although Quay was the caucus nominee of the Republicans, the party's minority refused to be bound by the caucus decision, and a deadlock was in the making. Ballots were taken daily until the legislature adjourned on April 20; in all, seventy-nine ballots were cast. Conflicting ambitions between Democrats and anti-Quay Republicans prevented agreement on a compromise candidate. The final unproductive tally gave Quay ninety-three votes, Jenks eighty-five, and B. F. Jones sixty-nine. The sixty-nine insurgent votes for Jones could have elected Quay. Frank Leach pointed out that ironically they were given to the former Republican national chairman "who had permitted the Democrats to cheat Blaine out of the presidency in 1884" when they should have gone to the former national chairman who not only elected Harrison in 1888, but also prevented the "Tammany marauders" from repeating their contemplated rape of the ballot box in New York City.[26]

The deliberations of the legislature tried men's patience and tired their minds. To those directly involved, the frantic efforts to make successful combinations or convert individual legislators turned the protracted struggle into a reign of terror—physically, mentally, and morally. The tension was heightened by Quay's success in having his case brought to trial in Philadelphia. For almost two weeks the balloting in Harrisburg and the trial in Philadelphia overlapped.[27] Quay was defended by an able battery of attorneys headed by A. S. L. Shields, Rufus E. Shapley, and David T. Watson. The prosecution was handled by the newly elected district attorney for Philadelphia, Peter F. Rothermel, who was anxious to make a reputation for himself by winning a conviction against such a notable figure as the state boss. The prosecution obviously had a weak case that had been patched together primarily to discredit Quay in political circles. He may have been guilty, but Rothermel had neither the documents nor the witnesses to prove it. Miscellaneous statements and the implication that Hopkins had something to hide when he took his life were the best evidence that the district attorney could uncover. The indictments, charging that Quay conspired to misuse public funds, were dated November 17, 1898. Although the statute of limitations on such offenses expired after two years, the prosecution was prepared to base the senator's guilt on the "plum tree" letter of July 31, 1896, which was more than three months beyond the statue. The judge was about to rule that the statute affected only the crime, and not the evidence, and that the letter in question, plus all the records of Quay's stock transactions through the Peoples Bank from his days as state treasurer in 1885 to the present, could be subpoenaed as evidence. This ruling, by which Rothermel and his supporters might have found some concrete evidence, would have dramatized the political overtones of the case.[28] But before the judge could hand down such a ruling, Watson, with his calm, dispassionate logic, asked the court to consider that the prosecution had failed to show any specific conspiracy within the statutory period and that this should be done before the general question of conspiracy and the evidence from preceding years could be introduced. The judge accepted Watson's argument, which sealed the prosecution's doom. Rothermel continued with his case, but that decision rendered it hopeless.[29]

The legislature adjourned on April 20 without choosing a senator. To the surprise of Quay's friends and enemies alike, within an hour of the Harrisburg adjournment, the prosecution rested its case in Philadelphia and thereby added to the suspicion that the charges against Quay were first and foremost a conspiracy to prevent his reelection. The defense attorneys pointed out that no case had been made against the senator and his fellow defendants and urged that the jury return a verdict of acquittal. This was done with such dispatch that the jury was charged and given the case that same afternoon. Although no verdict was reached until the next day, the fact that Quay's attorneys offered no defense further convinced the public that the case was not rooted in the law, but in politics. To the consternation of the insurgents, this chain of events reflected favorably on Quay and attracted sympathy to his cause.

Quay had returned from Florida for the conspiracy trial still suffering from insomnia, a malady that had afflicted him since the first Harrison campaign. His face was pale, his drooping eye more lusterless than ususal. As the trial proceeded, however, he underwent one of those sudden changes that his colleagues had known him to experience. Calling him "a wonder," Israel Durham diagnosed the trial as therapy for Quay because it "acted like a stimulant. He is sleeping soundly. For years after the Harrison campaign sleep refused to come to him until daylight. His appetite has returned. His color is good, his eye bright, and he looks younger by many years than he looked before the trial began."[30]

When the "innocent" verdict was announced, pandemonium, unparalleled in the courts of Philadelphia, broke loose. Men shouted, tossed their hats into the air, and surged about the silent but happy man. Hailed as a conquering hero, he moved from the courtroom into the corridor where he faced a second uproarious demonstration. A crowd drunk with joy and mad with enthusiasm greeted him. Instead of attempting to quell the tumult, the court guards joined in the yelling and cheering. By the time Quay reached the corner of Broad and Chestnut, en route to his hotel, the throng of well-wishers had swelled to more than a thousand. As quickly as possible he reached the Walton, packed his bag, and took the first train to Washington, confident that Governor Stone would appoint him to the Senate seat.[31]

Earlier Quay had declared that Stone knew what to do without being told. His confidence was fully justified. Within minutes after hearing of the acquittal, Stone wired Quay that he was giving him an interim appointment to succeed himself, at least until the legislature next met to confirm or reject his action. According to strict constitutional interpretation, this was not an option available to the governor. His only recourse under this theory was to call the legislature back into session on the assumption that the acquittal would make it possible to reach a decision. But in his haste to rebuke Wanamaker and "the hypocritical psalm singing element in politics," he took unilateral action to make the appointment as an executive endorsement of Quay.[32]

The favorable response of Philadelphia to the court decision echoed throughout the state and nation. A jubilant writer recalled the scene in the town of Liberty in Tioga County. "We got out our drum core [sic] and paraded the streets in your behalf, cheering for the victory you have wone [sic]." In Atlantic City the keeper of Innlet House unfurled an American flag and a white flag bearing Quay's name and treated his customers to free clams all day. On the Pacific Coast the cities of Portland, Tacoma, and Seattle wrote that they were as interested and as spirited as any followers in Pennsylvania; and in Alexandria, Virginia, the trustees of the Normal & Industrial School for Negro youth promptly and unanimously named their library the "M. S. Quay Library."[33] By the time Quay retired that night in Washington more than four hundred telegrams of congratulation had arrived, primarily from Pennsylvania constituents and congressional colleagues. A New York newspaper quoted Senator Edward Wolcott of Colorado as saying: "The animus of the whole proceedings was shown when the state ceased its prosecution within an hour after the legislature adjourned. He [Quay] was the object of as villainous a conspiracy as was ever conceived by man."[34]

To commemorate the acquittal numerous individuals planted plum trees. A man from Gettysburg was either more energetic or more elated than the others because he planted 50 plum trees and invited Quay to visit him in a few years and "shake all of them." Others, like a Uniontown citizen, demanded revenge. He called upon the senator "to exterminate the Bolters who are, as I have said before, sired by Nobody and damned by Everybody." A typical public reaction came from a stranger in Savannah, Georgia, who confessed: "I do not know why I write this! But I cannot resist the desire to convey to you the heartfelt congratulations of a perfect stranger (and always a Democrat) in your victory over what the whole U. S. is perfectly convinced was a dastardly political persecution. And I with them am D—— glad you have 'downed' the canting hypocritical scoundrels."[35]

For those who concluded that Quay's return to the Senate would inevitably follow his vindication in the courts and appointment by Governor Stone, the jubilation was premature. Their expectations suffered a severe jolt when Senator Penrose formally presented his colleague's credentials to the Senate on December 4, 1899. Objection came from Senator Julius C. Burrows of Michigan, who announced that he had received a resolution signed by a large number of Pennsylvania legislators protesting the governor's action. He suggested that this remonstrance, along with the letter of appointment from Stone, be reviewed by the Committee on Privileges and Elections. This challenge came as no surprise to Quay's inner group. On the very day of his acquittal, J. L. Hampton of Ohio had frankly lamented, "We cannot see under the present rulings of the Senate how you are to be admitted." Yet the Quayites believed that the Senate would disregard the precedents to which Hampton referred, since Quay was held in high esteem by Senate Republicans and Democrats alike. In contrast to the many scars he had left on members of both parties in Pennsylvania, he had established a reputation for graciousness and cooperation among his Senate colleagues. Although there was no doubt in the minds of most state politicians that they were working for him and not with him, he always respected his fellow senators as peers. Thus it seemed that there would be enough goodwill in the Senate to compile a majority in his favor.[36]

In the Pennsylvania legislature Quay's election had been contested largely on political grounds. In the Senate his actual seating was contested primarily on constitutional grounds, though not without political overtones. The relevant clause in article I, section 3, of the Constitution states: "If vacancies happen by resignation, or otherwise, during the recess of the legislature of any state, the executive thereof may make a temporary appointment until the next meeting of the legislature, which shall then fill such vacancies." Those who endorsed the seating of the controversial senator based their argument on the theory that a vacancy "happens" whenever it happens to exist. In this case it existed after the adjournment of the legislature, as well as while it was in session. Speaking in defense of this position, Senator Elkins argued that, when the combination of a recess and a vacancy coexist, a state's governor may appoint as Stone proceeded to do after the Pennsylvania legislature adjourned on April 20.[37] Those opposed to permitting Quay to take his seat followed a more strict interpretation of the constitutional clause. Senator Thomas B. Turley of Tennessee maintained that the Constitution did not explicitly declare that under all conditions of a vacancy a governor may make an interim appointment. If that had been the intent, Turley argued, it would have been so stated. These advocates also claimed that the vacancy did not occur during the recess, but was merely continued into the period of the recess. Both groups believed that they spoke for the intention of the Constitution. One argued that each state should be represented by two senators at all times, and that Governor Stone, in appointing Quay, was discharging a duty intended by the Founding Fathers. Turley contended that the failure of a state legislature to fulfill its duty and elect a senator had never occurred to the framers of the Constitution. The Pennsylvania legislature, in his opinion, was simply derelict in its duty, and the state would have to bear the consequences.[38]

On January 23, 1900, the Committee on Privileges and Elections, after a five to four vote, declared that Quay was not legally entitled to his seat. Burrows joined four Democrats to form the majority, and the four other Republicans on the committee, including such notables as Hoar of Massachusetts and Chandler of New Hampshire, constituted the minority. In holding that the governor's right to appoint had been negated because the legislature had an opportunity to appoint a senator and failed to do so, the majority reaffirmed a Senate decision reached in 1898 when Henry W. Corbett of Oregon had been denied a seat under similar circumstances.[39]

This report initiated another three-month debate to rival that conducted in the Pennsylvania legislature the previous year. Boies Penrose managed the speaking campaign in behalf of Quay, and his principal exponents were Hoar, Chandler, and Elkins. By this time Hoar considered himself an authority on the subject; over the preceding fifteen years he had written reports and made "eight or ten elaborate speeches" defending the right of a governor to appoint. After Turley delivered a three-hour discourse against seating Quay, Penrose sought to have it answered in kind. Since Hoar had already spoken frequently, he was not anxious to reply at length again. Penrose turned to Chandler, whom he discovered to be sick in bed. Lamenting that the case suffered from lack of explanation, he asked the New Hampshire senator to write to Hoar from his sick bed and urge him to give a full reply—but to no avail.[40]

Quay personally did not think that the floor debate would win many votes, but on the basis of his Senate record he did expect major support from the southern contingent. His expectations were not realized. Only the state senate in Texas caught the spirit he intended, calling on its two senators to endorse the seating of the Pennsylvanian in return for services rendered, namely, his consistent support for measures to deepen Texas waterways and improve the state's harbors. The resolution stressed the fact that Texas should show its gratitude for Quay's efforts in defeating the elections bill, declaring that he "perhaps contributed more largely to its defeat than any other man then in public life." But the plea went unheeded.[41]

Some of the most capable Republican lawyers in the Senate favored accepting Quay's credentials, and many Democrats concurred. Senate opinion appeared to be evenly divided on the issue. Although Corbett had been denied his seat by a decisive margin, ten of the senators who voted against him ultimately voted to admit Quay. Mark Hanna surprisingly moved in the opposite direction. Since he had sided with the minority that wanted to seat Corbett and belonged to the same Republican clique as Quay, his vote for the Pennsylvanian was considered a certainty. He had spoken glowingly in behalf of Quay, and there seemed to be no antagonism between the two.[42] Hanna never explained his anti-Quay action. Some argued that he was motivated wholly by concern for his party. To seat, by a Republican vote, a man who had been rejected by the legislature of his own state was to give the Democrats ammunition for the 1900 elections. Republican newspapers across the nation stressed this point, and for Hanna, still the national chairman, this analysis had a direct and immediate message. At the same time numerous national leaders, including Hanna, McKinley, and Hoar, were pressured by prominent Pennsylvania Republicans to stand firm against the seating of Quay. Their intent was clear: to deny Quay a voice in carving Pennsylvania's patronage pie and thereby destroy, or at least limit, his political power.[43]

Confronted with another version of the same pressure, Hoar responded differently. He conceived of the Senate as a court and the senators as judges considering the credentials of an individual for membership. Letters from Pennsylvania leaders, urging him to vote against Quay because they wanted someone else appointed, showed no recognition of this function and demanded that he act on this not as a legal, but as a political, question. He concluded that "what these wealthy gentlemen are asking me to do is, in substance, to stuff the ballot box and make a false return in my capacity as a sworn judge of elections."[44]

Others interpreted Hanna's vote, as well as the votes of his colleagues who adopted a similar position, as an effort to stem the movement for the direct election of senators. In many states the tide was already against control of senatorial elections by governors and legislatures. Those who favored retention of the principle realized that a decision in favor of Quay would prejudice their case because his claim to the office had several weaknesses. With the publicity that the case had attracted, the designation of a senator by a governor alone, especially in opposition to the wishes of the legislature, would play into the hands of those who wished to place the election of senators directly with the people. Either this fear of such a constitutional revision or political expediency or a combination of the two prompted Hanna to be out of town on the fateful day of decision. Public recognition of his position did not come until the roll-call vote. When the name of Senator Depew, who favored the seating of Quay, was called, he declined to vote, announcing that he was paired with Hanna on the opposite side of the question.[45]

Quay's followers bitterly denounced Hanna, whose endorsement they believed they had reason to expect. Comment and advice to Quay poured in from many sources. One tried to console him with the idea that "they may Hannaize you and keep you out of the Senate, but they cannot rob you of your friends. Hanna, with qualms of constitutional conscience . . . is the greatest clown act in politics yet on record." The writer declared that in retaliation he would not vote for "Hanna's little man" for president in 1900.[46]

In addition to the shock of Hanna's alignment, the advocates of seating Quay received a second one from Senator Vest of Missouri, one of the ablest of Democratic lawmakers. A dangerous man to encounter in debate because of his sharp tongue, Vest was socially charming and always a gracious host. His hospitality extended to many Republicans, including Matt Quay, his most intimate Senate acquaintance. The two were congenial companions in spite of diverse backgrounds. One was a Republican and the other a Democrat, one a protectionist and the other a free trader, one a Northerner and the other a Southerner, and both were proud of the service they had rendered to their respective sections during the Civil War. The intellectual stimulation they offered each other, particularly when supplemented by good food or two fishing poles, made them kin. The Quayites considered Vest's vote certain, but there was an intellectual honesty about him that they did not comprehend. He was a rugged conservative who revered the Constitution with a religious zeal. Those who were quick to count his vote had forgotten that, in a definitive speech on the Corbett case, he had concluded that the Constitution did not allow a governor to appoint a senator under conditions prevailing in the Quay case. He could no more renounce his constitutional beliefs than he could repudiate the tenets of Presbyterianism on which he had been nurtured. Vest worked hard to line up other Democrats, particularly southerners, for Quay, and amidst this activity no one questioned his own vote, except Vest himself and perhaps Quay, who knew and respected him so well.[47]

When the sound of the gavel called the Senate to order on April 24, the section reserved for the press was filled; the spectators' gallery was also packed, with an overflow in the corridor where a surging throng was eager to learn Quay's fate first-hand. Every senator in the city was present, including elderly George Vest, who was seriously ill at the time. At first it was feared that he would not be able to attend, but on the morning of the fateful session, weak and tottering, he was helped to his seat. There was no doubt in the minds of those prejudging the result that he represented a vote for Quay. They reasoned that, if constitutional scruples disturbed him, he had the perfect excuse to remain at home, but he chose to attend; his physical condition was widely known, and no one would have questioned his motive.[48]

The senators' names were called in alphabetical order, and the votes were tallied. As the clerk neared the end of the roll, the Senate still appeared evenly divided. When Vest's name was called, almost everyone who had been keeping a record realized that this was probably the deciding vote. The Missouri senator sat motionless, almost as though he did not hear his name. When the clerk called a second time, every eye turned toward the veteran senator, and every ear strained to hear his response. He half rose from his chair, and unable to overcome his constitutional convictions, he voted, in a voice that was husky and trembling with emotion, not to seat his friend. Quay's partisans were furious, but the Beaver boss himself sat silently, speaking only once to quiet a man who was abusing Vest.[49]

Vest went home immediately, and the next morning tried to explain that the sanctity of the Constitution had a higher claim on his conscience than even their friendship:

My dear Quay,

After a sleepless night I write this only to express my sorrow over the result of yesterday. God knows how anxiously I tried to find some ground on which to honestly change my position, but I could not. I might have dodged, but this would not have changed the result—and was mere evasion.

I may have done wrong, but I could not see any other course, and I have suffered more than in all my public life over this vote. I do not expect you to forgive me, and I feel that I have lost my best friend, but I hope you will think of me charitably.

Whatever you may think, I am and will always be your friend, and sincerely pray that you will triumph over all your enemies, as I believe you will. May God bless you!

Your friend,
G. G. Vest[50]

The final vote against Quay was cast by Orville Platt of Connecticut, who had not answered to his name during the roll call. Hanna, Vest, or Platt could have tipped the election the other way because Quay was denied his seat by only one vote (32 to 33). The suspense was finally over, and the telegraph clicked the result to a waiting nation. The most dramatic incident in Washington since the decision of the Electoral Commission in 1877 was at once opened to various interpretations. On the surface the Senate had decided a constitutional issue, but underneath it had also determined the fate of the most criticized politician on the American scene. Men with motives as diverse as Vest and Penrose shared a common disappointment, but the anti-Quayites were jubilant. In their view this one action had upheld the Constitution and transformed Quay into a political corpse. The *North American* rejoiced that his foot had been "lifted from the neck of Pennsylvania" for the last time.[51]

Leader of the Anti-Hanna Forces
1900-1904

MARK HANNA quickly learned that the Quayites would not forget his affront to their leader. Penrose addressed him forcefully in the Senate cloakroom: "Senator, it probably didn't occur to you that the next legislature of Pennsylvania will send you some very disturbing news. . . . I'm simply telling you that you have some months to prepare yourself for the return of Mr. Quay who has a hell of a memory. I'd work hard during those months, senator, if I were you."[1]

As predicted, Quay was prepared to act. The first opportunity came when the Republican National Convention assembled in Philadelphia on June 19, 1900. Quay gathered a few stray political threads, cleverly wove them into a rope, and securely tied the hands of the national chairman. His comprehensive plan was a cooperative venture with Boss Platt of New York, who was anxious to transplant Governor Theodore Roosevelt, his enfant terrible, into the national arena because he was a threat to the boss's system. By muscling into the state's patronage picture, the governor was slowly wrecking the Platt machine. Platt had confidentially requested Hanna's support for a campaign to make the second position on the ticket available to Roosevelt. He interpreted Hanna's refusal as retaliation for his endorsement of Reed over McKinley during the 1896 nomination hassle, and he was stymied until Quay came to the rescue.[2]

Quay knew that the selection of a candidate for vice-president was the last and least significant function of a national chairman. Usually the slot was assigned as a consolation prize to a defeated faction or a different section of the nation. The Beaver boss decided that in 1900 the second spot on the ticket should be lifted to a new prominence in the convention, one that would at the same time bring continuing political anguish into Hanna's life. Almost a month before the convention, Quay had written to McKinley asking if he had any recommendations for the post. He volunteered none because he wanted to remain neutral and avoid antagonizing any of the individual state leaders and delegations. Quay had indicated that, without directions to the contrary from the president, the Middle States would try to identify a nominee from a doubtful state before the convention opened.[3]

With the Republican state convention of Pennsylvania slated to convene on April 25, the day after the final vote on Quay's seating, there were many suggestions on ways to register immediate dissatisfaction with the McKinley-Hanna leadership. One came immediately on the day of decision. Francis T. Tobin suggested that Quay ask the state convention to "turn down President McKinley and endorse Gov. Roosevelt for President; this would bring Senator Hanna to terms." Such political maneuvering represents the earliest recorded identification of Theodore Roosevelt with the national ticket. On the basis of his San Juan Hill fame, he had been linked with the central government earlier, but Tobin's recognition tied his utility to purely political motives. Samuel W. Pennypacker also wrote to Quay on the day after the decision and asked him to "consider the question of throwing the delegation to Roosevelt." Within the week this was reenforced by Frank A. Hower, publisher of the *Bryn Mawr Home News*, who observed that the sentiment of Republican party workers was strongly against McKinley for reelection and that he would "not be surprised to witness a stampede in the National Rep. Convention at Philada for Gov. Roosevelt of N.Y." Reaction to the vote on seating Quay thus did much to launch Roosevelt's career in national politics.[4]

These numerous impromptu suggestions that Roosevelt be substituted for McKinley at the head of the ticket were absurd because of the president's popularity and his command of the federal patronage. Quay realized, however, that he could achieve Platt's goal and humble Hanna just as effectively by having Roosevelt nominated for the vice-presidency. Achievement required finesse because the Quay-Platt combine was greatly outnumbered by the administration forces, but Quay evolved a two-part strategy aimed at disarming their opposition—one designed to conquer the West for Roosevelt, and the other the South.[5]

Throughout the North there were Republicans distressed by the power that southern delegates wielded in the party's national conventions while their ability to supply electoral strength in general elections was almost nil. One phase of Quay's plan was to exploit this discontent; on the second day of the convention, he demonstrated how it was to be done. He proposed a resolution to the effect that in future national conventions, a state's representation should be regulated by the size of its Republican vote at the preceding presidential election. More specifically, each state would have four delegates at large and one additional delegate for every 10,000 votes or majority fraction thereof cast for Republican electors in the preceding presidential election. Based on the 1896 voting pattern, for example, this system of representation would have increased the combined voting power of six northern states at the Republican convention from 286 to 354 and decreased the strength in six southern states from 108 to 40. This was not a totally new idea, and southern Republicans, immediately alert to its ramifications, rose to denounce it as an abridgment of a fundamental democratic right. On the other hand, with the new reform atmosphere gripping much of the nation, the northern delegates rallied to it as an attempt to promote honesty in politics and curtail the South's unwarranted influence. Both the packed gallery and a majority of delegates on the floor wildly applauded the suggestion.[6]

Although the resolution pertained to the South, it was directed at Mark Hanna and designed to pull down his patronage house about his ears. He controlled the southern delegates who, for the most part, were federal officeholders representing negligible numbers of Republican voters. They understood the threat to their power posed by the resolution and immediately clamored for the floor to rebut its implications. Before the presiding officer recognized any one of them, Quay magnanimously proposed that discussion of his motion be delayed until the next day. Hanna understood the message. He had less than twenty-four hours to line up behind Roosevelt for vice-president or face a floor fight on the resolution. Quay quietly leaked to southern delegates the idea that he was prepared to withdraw the resolution if they swung their support to the New York governor. At once they flocked to Hanna's headquarters asking to be released from their commitment to follow his lead on the vice-presidential nomination. There was always the possibility that, if he did not concede, they would disregard his instructions anyway. They had no positive objection to Roosevelt and were more willing to take their chances with him than with a resolution that would curtail their prestige at home. To them this was a modest concession if it would wipe the resolution from the agenda. Still reluctant to release them, a disturbed Hanna asked: "Don't any of you realize that there's only one life between this madman and the White House?"[7]

A major obstacle to Quay's plan was the New York governor himself. Roosevelt insisted that he would never be forced into accepting the vice-presidential nomination by Platt and Quay, but he did not know how persuasive they could be. Ten days before the convention he extracted from Platt a promise that his name would not be presented as the caucus candidate of the New York delegation. This concession forced Platt into the background and lulled Roosevelt into a false sense of security, while Quay took charge of converting the governor into a willing candidate and a majority of the delegates into his faithful supporters. Roosevelt arrived in Philadelphia vowing that he was not a candidate and on the eve of the convention gave a newspaper interview declaring that he would not accept the nomination. He did not know, of course, how much effort Quay was putting into the procurement of delegates. When the time for his conversion came, he managed it gracefully.[8]

The Pennsylvania delegation was almost unanimous in its endorsement of Roosevelt and became the working nucleus to win other delegates to its cause. This group was particularly useful in the second phase of the master's plan— to convert the western delegates. In that section the primary concern among the delegates was to name a known liberal as the vice-presidential nominee in order to rebuff the third-party tickets that were threatening to cut into Republican strength in individual western states. Roosevelt met those specifications, and Quay knew how to bring the two together. As the westerners stepped from their trains in Philadelphia, they were quietly advised, often by members of the Pennsylvania delegation, that dirty politics was at work to cheat Roosevelt of his rightful recognition. Accepting such statements as fact, the Westerners immediately rallied to his defense and demanded that Hanna "stop kicking their friend in the face." This reaction established an emotional alliance with Quay's candidate that was shrewdly turned into voting power. The spontaneity that accompanied his candidacy astounded Roosevelt, embarrassed Hanna, and elated Quay. Seeing the pieces of his political puzzle fall into place, he irreverently boasted: "Our babe is in the manger; the kings have seen his star in the East and are come to worship him."[9]

After an hour of plain talk with Platt, Roosevelt concluded that he could not disappoint his western friends. He did not want to appear "bigger than the party"; if they insisted—and they did—he agreed to make the sacrifices necessary to be a candidate. On the surface he was conceding to his allies in the West, but in reality he was a victim of the Quay-Platt combine. The bosses had used him to strike at Hanna, who had to admit publicly that he had been outmaneuvered. He was reluctant to yield without a fight, but McKinley, who was willing "to follow the crowd," ordered him to surrender because he wanted nothing to cloud his own nomination and election. In complying with this request not to oppose the bosses' choice of TR, whom he regarded as a political bumpkin, Hanna sardonically jested that McKinley had a special duty to his country—"to live for four years from next March" so that the affairs of the nation would never fall into the hands of Roosevelt.[10]

Hoping to salvage as much prestige as possible from the incident, Hanna decided to cooperate. Although he and Roosevelt agreed on little, they did agree that the latter's nomination had to appear to come from the West, not from New York or Pennsylvania, lest the Quay-Platt victory be too obvious. After the details were settled, Hanna returned to his suite, where a group was waiting to hear the results of the negotiations. A dejected Hanna unofficially reported: "Well, gentlemen, it is all over. Roosevelt is going to be nominated. I have done all I could to prevent it, but in vain, for Platt and Quay have outmatched me. I want to say in all candor that I fear the result. If anything should happen to McKinley and Roosevelt should become President, nobody knows what tactics he would adopt or what policies he would pursue. The best we can all do is to pray fervently for the continued health of the President."[11]

In addition to using the New York governor to repress Hanna, the two eastern bosses had exploited him for personal gain. To relieve Platt's anxiety over the future of this state machine, Roosevelt was kicked upstairs. To rebuild Quay's tarnished image in the Keystone State and assist in reestablishing him as a viable Senate candidate, Roosevelt was identified with Quay in the public mind. As the champion of the hero of San Juan Hill and an associate of a prominent governor who had developed a reputation for "honesty in government," Quay emerged from the convention as one of its most popular personages, and his home state public was indeed impressed. Several years later he laughingly told Roosevelt that he (Roosevelt) had been responsible for his return to the Senate in 1901: "When John Wanamaker and others were trying to defeat me, I declared for you for Vice President. Then the anti-Quay movement collapsed." Although his recital of the facts was not literally correct, identification with Roosevelt contributed immeasurably to the rebuilding of a favorable public impression.[12]

Campaigning at Last

After the unanimous nomination of McKinley and Roosevelt, Quay and Platt returned home to organize hard-hitting state campaigns. Quay became more intensely involved than ever before. Over the insurgents' protests, but as anticipated, the Republican state convention in Pennsylvania nominated him as its choice for the vacant Senate seat that he had occupied until March 4, 1899.

To repel the charges of bossism and suppression of popular will, the regulars invited the insurgents to name a candidate to challenge Quay in a popular vote in the various counties. The Quayites knew that their invitation could not be accepted; because of their limited numbers, the insurgents could not afford such a positive approach. Their only hope of victory was to agree with the Democrats on a compromise candidate, and that could not be discussed realistically until the legislature was elected and in session. Instead they endeavored to have their legislative candidates declare their oppostion to Quay and sign statements to that effect. This forced the regulars to adopt similar tactics. They required their candidates to agree to attend the Republican caucus and vote for the senatorial candidate endorsed by it. The insurgents learned again that you can't beat somebody with nobody.[13]

In preparing himself physically for an arduous campaign, Quay spent the last six weeks of the summer hunting in the forests of Maine. He returned about mid-September and accepted the decision of his lieutneants—supposedly reached in his absence—that he undertake a statewide speaking tour and meet the people face to face. With his innate horror of crowds and lack of faith in the powers of oratory, he undertook the assignment with a feeling that mixed trepidation with futility. When the public responded enthusiastically to the prospect of seeing the controversial boss about whom they had heard so much, these fears vanished. Quay caught the spirit of stump campaigning and fulfilled his mission admirably.[14] His swing across the state began on October 1 at West Chester, and in the course of the next thirty-four days he delivered nineteen speeches, some of them as extended appearances. In general, they were short, direct, and positive, with appeals to the Republican party and to patriotism, both state and national. During his second address, in an almost triumphant tone, he declared, "Until Monday night I had never made a speech to a public audience."[16] Despite more than twenty years in state politics and two terms in the U.S. Senate, he saw no reason to apologize. The public had become accustomed to his silence. The voters assumed that it was proper senatorial exclusiveness and took no offense. For the most part they were impressed by his humility. Spoken with conviciton and a dash of humor, his remarks assailed no one and accused no group of having deprived him of the Senate seat. Instead he stressed Pennsylvania's misfortune in not being represented when crucial national issues, with long-range ramifications, were being deliberated.[15]

On various occasions during the tour, he alluded to the specific national issues that were so vital to his state. Disagreeing with William Jennings Bryan, the Democratic candidate, who identified imperialism as the paramount issue, he warned that such rhetoric was only a smoke screen hiding the basic goal of the Democrats: "They are after your tariff and your currency system, and if they carry the country, they will give you free trade and free silver. Mr. Bryan is not a fool, as he has been called. He is a man of ability. He is stubborn and honest, and fanatical in his convictions. His under jaw and steady eye bespeak the iron will of the man. If he is elected, he will have his way, and free trade and free silver will close your mines and factories and adversely affect your wages." Recalling that the McKinley administration had lifted the nation out of the depression, Quay estimated that the wealth of Pennsylvania had almost doubled because of Republican monetary and tariff policies in the last four years. In his speech at New Castle he illustrated this point. "The tin plate industry, which is your greatest industry, is literally the creature of tariff legislation." Employing thousands in New Castle, it had sprung from a line in the McKinley tariff bill and within a few years mushroomed into a national industry that was challenging the markets of the world. Such a climate for growth, he noted, brought unparalleled prosperity at home and converted the United States into a creditor nation.[16]

His thesis had its ambiguities, but the challenge would not come from organized labor. Representatives of various labor associations met in Philadelphia late in the campaign to proclaim their endorsement of his argument. They pledged to support only legislative candidates who declared themselves unalterably in favor of Quay's reelection because they interpreted his record as a trust that he had "filled so long to our entire satisfaction, and from which we cannot afford to spare you."[17]

In several speeches the senator analyzed the Democrats' charge of imperialism. They were denouncing the commitments assumed by the United States in the treaty ending the Spanish-American War, particularly the article providing for the purchase of the Philippines. Quay admitted being partially sympathetic to the Democratic position because he could not see the purpose behind annexation of the total island chain. To him a coaling station, a shipyard, and a few acres of fortified territory around a good harbor adequately met the nation's commercial requirements in the Orient. Almost before the ink on the treaty was dry, the Republican administration was embarrassed by having to land troops to suppress an insurrection led by Aguinaldo, whose organization had no more desire to see the homeland dominated by the United States than by Spain. This unforeseen event provided the Democrats with ammunition for their political guns, and the Republicans felt the salvos. Quay defended the acquisition as normal expansion, not imperialism, and the clash with Aguinaldo he regarded as inevitable. In his final speech on the tour, he spoke as a militant nationalist who believed that the United States had an imperial destiny. Perhaps more interested in appealing to the emotions of his audience than in advancing a logical argument, he justified the presence of American troops in the Far East as the first wave of true Christian soldiers. He passionately tried to enlighten his Philadelphia listeners:

Confucians, Buddhists, Moslems, and pagans— there are as many anti-Christians in China as there are Christians in all the world. Enlightened civilization and Christianity are synonymous, and the world cannot endure one-third Christian and two-thirds heathen. The controlling forces are hostile and collide, and one or the other must perish. Christianity has failed in Asia in peaceful missionary effort, and if the cross is to prevail there, it must be preceded or accompanied by the battle flag. God in his infinite wisdom seems to have ordained that the sword shall open the bloody road for the coming of the gospel of peace and love.[18]

Intertwined with such comments on national issues was the senator's analysis of political alignments in the Keystone State. He grouped his Republican adversaries in two categories: victims of disappointed ambition such as Wanamaker, Magee, and Martin; and professional reformers such as Blankenburg, Lea, and Welsh, who were always anxious to place their altruism on parade. In some districts they rallied behind the slogan of "good government," in others behind "ballot reform," and in still others they tried to give oleomargarine a political tinge. By such local appeals, according to Quay, they hoped to have these issues construed as various voices of God's prophet calling from the wilderness, but he interpreted them as the disguised howls of a hungry wolf. He himself advocated reform, which he recognized was "as natural as human progress." But his detractors were false prophets who "erect altars where knaves minister and fools kneel." Where their strength warranted, the insurgents challenged the regular Republican organization directly. Elsewhere they formed alliances with Democrats, but under both approaches their purpose was to create another deadlock in the legislature and prevent the election of a Stalwart senator if, in fact, they could not seat a candidate of their own choice.[19]

Attempting to capitalize on the fact that Pennsylvania was basically a Republican state, Quay warned his audiences that success for the insurgents was a defeat for the Republican party. As free American citizens, John Wanamaker and his cohorts could cooperate with the Democrats, but those who joined such a coalition would have to realize that they were surrendering their Republican birthright. Quay denounced such tactics and endorsed the conclusion reached by one of Wanamaker's former Sunday school students who considered "his theology all right, but his politics . . . wretched."[20]

On several occasions during the campaign, Quay told audiences that, although nominated for the Senate seat by the Republican state convention, he was a reluctant candidate. With unabashed frankness he disclosed: "It is a matter of absolute indifference to me whether the choice of the legislature shall fall upon me or upon any good, straight, stalwart Republican." His senatorial experience had not been "exactly pleasure sailing upon summer seas," and he was prepared to see someone else represent the Commonwealth so that he could go fishing. This was hardly a positive approach, but it conveyed the mixed emotions with which Quay conducted the campaign and the understandable confusion that resulted when the public attempted to sort out the nuances. Quay was not anxious to resume the duties of a senator, but nevertheless felt a compulsion to fight vigorously to win. His goal was limited to victory; the responsibilities of the office were an unfortunate concomitant, and he said so.[21]

This two-year battle over the senatorship was the most debilitating ordeal of his career. His appearance and his attitude recorded the strain. Both Republican factions wanted desperately to win. They regarded this election as the decisive event in a controversy that had raged intermittently for a decade. Both groups supported the national ticket, but frequently contributed to the campaigns of different legislators. When the election was over, McKinley and Roosevelt were overwhelmingly triumphant in Pennsylvania, but the senatorial outcome was still uncertain. Both factions claimed victory and spent the ten weeks before the legislature convened in frantic maneuvers to fortify their positions. The results indicated that Quay would have a larger legislative delegation than either the insurgents or the Democrats. Whether a coalition could block the Quay election again was subject to debate. This uncertainty inspired a flurry of conferences and negotiations by both sides to secure a definitive majority.[22]

Quay departed for Florida two days after the election, but this did not slow his campaign to ascertain how every legislator stood on the Senate issue. Over his signature letters immediately went to each of them, asking how they would vote in the coming election. Since the letters merely inquired about the preferences of the people's representatives, no one could take offense. But Quay used them not only to force all those committed to him to declare themselves in writing so that they could more easily withstand pressure from the opposition to alter their positions, but also to identify those who would not endorse him. His note was discreet and disarming: "In view of the fact that the last Republican state convention by resolution insisted that I should be a candidate for United States senator, you will probably not consider it impertinent if I ask you whether you will support me in case I should be nominated by a caucus of Republican senators and members of the House of Representatives."[23] This probe to locate vulnerable spots in the opponent's armor was very useful. It indicated that Quay did not have a conclusive margin and that several of the weak spots had to be shored up to preserve the election. Both factions understood the realities of the situation, and both approached legislators whom they thought could be influenced. Individual legislators, in turn, recognized their own importance and maneuvered to extract personal advantage from their votes. Some who had favored Quay during the campaign agreed not to enter the Republican caucus, while others crossed the line in the opposite direction. Thomas Davis, who was unwavering in his loyalty to Quay, played a variation of this scramble for votes. He privately wrote to the Beaver boss that he had been offered flattering inducements to forsake him, but, in spite of what he might hear, he had no such intention. Davis disclosed that he had intimated to the insurgents that he might be interested in their proposition in order to "make your enemies relax their efforts to secure some other member that might be purchaseable."[24]

When a joint session of the legislature brought the marathon struggle to a merciful end on January 16, 1901, Quay was returned to the Senate by the narrow margin of six votes (130 to seat and 124 against). Conceivably the Democrats and insurgents could have blocked the election if they had agreed on a compromise candidate, but each group stayed with its own choice, as in the initial confrontation in 1899. Unwilling to accept the result, the insurgents again cried "foul," maintaining that they had achieved victory in November only to have it stolen in subsequent weeks through the machine technique that Quay knew so well. They blamed the outcome on ten pivotal votes, nine of which they charged had been bought in eleventh-hour negotiations. Four of these "conversions" were Democrats, and the others had been elected as Wanamaker insurgents. The tenth crucial vote was registered by a sick regular who was carried on a litter from the hospital to the state capital in order to cast his ballot.[25]

When the election was declared official, the regulars rejoiced wildly. The factories of Harrisburg tied down their boiler whistles and the churches rang their bells to proclaim to the countryside that the long-standing stalemate had at last been resolved. Even the stretcher bearers joined in the celebration, temporarily forgetting the sick legislator. Left in a drafty hallway for an hour before being returned to the hospital, he contracted pneumonia and died shortly thereafter. The only comfort to his family was the knowledge that "his funeral was impressive, Senators Quay and Penrose attending in silk hats."[26]

Immediately after the vote Quay left for Washington and the final scene in his struggle for vindication. The trip was like a triumphal tour, and before he retired that night more than six hundred telegrams of congratulation were piled on his desk. Other thoughtful supporters came personally to offer their best wishes, but his most important caller that evening was Governor Stone's secretary, who arrived about 7:00 P.M. with the Certificate of Election. Senator Penrose presented it to the Senate the next day, and Quay was sworn into office on January 18—the date for all party purposes that he retired from national politics, "except to finish up some fag ends."[27] The chamber was bedecked for the ceremony. "Flowers were dumped into the Senate by the wagonload," and a large floral arrangement with a streamer proclaiming "the verdict of the people" adorned Quay's desk. His followers packed the galleries as he calmly took the oath. Afterward, while a group of admirers was waiting to celebrate with him, he mysteriously disappeared for some hours. When he reappeared, a member of his family mentioned the disappointed well-wishers and asked what had happened. He replied, "I have been taking dinner with an old friend." Further inquiry revealed that "it was my friend, Vest." But the insurgents and their sympathizers across the nation could not appreciate any part of this Senate melodrama—not even the show of continuing friendship for a Democratic colleague whose constitutional scruples had extended the battle by a year.

Among the congratulations were some critical notes. The most malicious denunciation of all was an unsigned note penciled on copy paper, attached to a clipping from the *Boston Herald*, and forwarded to the senator. Disturbed by Quay's success, the unknown author contemptuously declared: "The verdict of all right-minded people is that had you your just deserts you would be in stripes and behind the bars. Your apparent success will prove a monumental failure. Justice is sometimes slow but inflexible and will overtake you. Give a rascal rope enough, and he will hang himself, says Wanamaker. Do not the flowers droop & fade in your pestilential presence?"[28] In a sense Quay heeded the warning. He knew that he could not expect to keep winning with the political odds distributed as they were. The cost of keeping a firm hand on the throttle of the party machine for so many years included an ever widening circle of "political friends" to whom he was obligated; recommendations for every appointment presented a serious problem. During this struggle for the senatorship, for example, a vacancy on the Pennsylvania supreme court occurred, and no fewer than twenty men expected his support. To have endorsed any one of them would have ignited nineteen political grass fires and would have enveloped the senatorship with an even larger cloud. But not to endorse a candidate was to permit his power to pass to others. On previous occasions Quay had been equal to the challenge, but now age and ill health were offsetting his political cunning. The combination, as he said during the campaign of 1900, made political combat no longer attractive.[29]

Rather than face possible defeat before a relentless enemy in the future, he preferred to withdraw from the competition. Speaking before the State League of Republican Clubs in Philadelphia's Academy of Music on May 14, 1901, he informed the public of his intention: "My political race is run. It is not to be understood that God's sword is drawn immediately against my life or that my seat in the Senate is to be prematurely vacated, but that with the subscription of my official oath on the 18th of January my connection with the various labors and responsibilities of active politics ceased, except in so far as I may be committed to certain measures pending in the present legislature. I will never again be a candidate for or accept any official position. I have many friends to remember; I have no enemies to punish. In this regard I put aside the past."[30]

The Roosevelt Years

Several consequences of the 1900 elections were ironic. The American public authorized a second term for William McKinley, and after a two-year fight the Pennsylvania legislature awarded Matthew Stanley Quay a third appointment to the U.S. Senate. But neither lived to complete his term. Almost as a part of his oath of office, Quay declared that he was abdicating from political competition; except for a few notable forays, he carried out that pledge and thereby became a lame duck at the outset of his term. McKinley was removed by an assassin's bullet in the late summer of 1901. The tragedy catapulted Theodore Roosevelt, a political showman full of youthful vigor, into the presidency, and Quay, even if he had chosen to compete, could not have mustered the stamina to challenge the new president. TR was a forceful figure who harbored an inner sense of inferiority behind a facade of superiority. He stood in sharp contrast to the Pennsylvania boss, who experienced no inner uncertainties and whose career had been devoted to the utilization of as few words and as little publicity as possible in swaying conventions, selecting nominees, bossing his Commonwealth, and manipulating the Republican party at large.

The elevation of Roosevelt alarmed the conservatives in general and Hanna in particular. The Ohio senator had prophetically warned the party leaders the year before that only one life separated "that madman" from the presidency. Now the conservatives and TR faced each other. The industrial and financial moguls, along with many in the Republican high command, were certain that the new president would lead the nation to destruction and the party to ruin. Quay did not subscribe to this analysis. Shortly after Roosevelt assumed the duties of his office, the boss took the pose of elder statesman, called on him, and offered his full cooperation. Admitting that he regarded most reformers as hypocrites, he told the president that he did not consider him in that category. Struck by TR's sincerity, honesty, and aggressiveness, Quay expressed his confidence in the president's ability to remedy the ills of the nation and pledged his full support to making the administration a success. The president later saluted him because "he kept his word with absolute good faith."[31]

In an effort to calm conservative fears, the new president declared his intention to carry out McKinley's policies. For the most part the conservatives were suspicious and agreed with the interpretation of the cartoon character, Mr. Dooley, who charged that Roosevelt intended to carry them out and bury them. Although they could do nothing for the remainder of the term, they believed that at all costs Roosevelt had to be replaced as the titular head of the party in 1904. Hanna, who regarded him as the most obnoxious man in politics, was eager to undertake such an assignment because numerous incidents in the McKinley years had produced bad blood between the two—one of the most significant being the Cuban controversy. Like other conservatives, McKinley and Hanna had maneuvered to avoid involvement with Spain, while TR, as assistant secretary of the navy, ignored the administration's lead and tried to steer the nation in such a way that involvement was inevitable. The war that resulted was a lingering embarrassment to Hanna, and he was eager to retaliate. He hoped to identify "a second McKinley" or possibly to direct the party's attention to himself, but Roosevelt was determined to rule as well as preside. He had the senator at a disadvantage and was unwilling to share his power. The death of McKinley was also a blow to Hanna's prestige among his senatorial colleagues. No longer able to provide the friendly words at the White House that had previously moved appointments and private bills to the president's attention, he lost the informal power he had held over many of his fellow senators.[32]

Roosevelt was a practical man who, while pacifying the progressive rumblings of both the urban and western areas, nevertheless understood the bosses. He knew their natures and their ambitions, but was not enchanted by their appeals. Instead, he adopted a flexible attitude—standing firm, compromising, or surrendering according to what he considered the most expedient course to provide for the general welfare. Except for his unfriendly relationship with Hanna, he enjoyed the bosses' respect and was able to balance their interests with those of competing pressure blocs. Because of his need for support from an organized and influential segment of the party at the outset of his tenure, and because of Hanna's predetermined hostility, the president was drawn to Platt and Quay. By embracing one of these factions and not the other, he was at least able to keep the bosses from uniting against him. In any case, his overture to the New York–Pennsylvania combine provided for his own political security.

Platt and Quay had pressed his nomination for vice-president at the 1900 convention, and they were now obliged to continue their endorsement. Roosevelt counted on this allegation, but to make certain that they did not stray, he fed their patronage appetites when such concessions did not interfere with his primary goals. In his home state he accomplished more by working with Platt than by challenging him on every issue. The same was true in Pennsylvania where, to the discomfiture of the insurgents, he provided Quay with enough federal patronage to control the state's organization. In fact, almost from the beginning the insurgents were incensed because the president's deference for the boss tended to enhance his prestige.[33]

There was, of course, another side to the coin (which the insurgents chose to ignore). Both Roosevelt and Quay were accomplished players in the game of give-and-take. In the summer of 1902 the senator explained to the president that he had a candidate for a particular position and that any other choice, especially at that time, would be embarrassing for him. TR either forgot or brushed aside the first part of Quay's message and misinterpreted the second. He simply concluded from their conversation that, if a delay could not be arranged, he should feel free to appoint his own candidate. He apparently did not construe the senator's remark as a polite command, and under pressure from a congressional committee filled the vacancy. Quay expressed his irritation, and in response the president "admitted" his mistake and offered his regrets. To his typed note of apology, he wrote a more personal postscript: "You have been so considerate and courteous that I hate to have been guilty of such forgetfulness." This the senator accepted in good faith, and four days later, in an almost unprecedented action, influenced the Pennsylvania Republican State Convention to endorse Roosevelt for the presidential nomination a full two years before the national convention.[34]

During the mid-term campaign of 1902 that followed this endorsement, Quay in a dangerous maneuver continued to test his standing with the administration. Campaign funds were solicited from federal officeholders via a circular mailed over the signatures of Quay as chairman and Andrews as secretary of the Republican State Committee, but Pennsylvania's ever vigilant insurgents protested. They invoked a law stipulating that civil service employees could not be approached for party funds by federal officials such as senators. Their pressure on the Civil Service Commission and the president prompted the latter to discuss the situation with Quay. In doing so, TR tried to be as understanding of Quay's position as possible, but stressed that the law governing political assessments was stringent and that Quay had technically violated it. The president thoughtfully but firmly explained:

> Of course, I understand that these circulars are sent, in most cases without any knowledge on the part of the man whose name appears on the bottom. The people of Philadelphia have been agitating to bring suit in the matter, and the Civil Service Commission have called it to my attention. The same thing happened in Iowa a few weeks ago, but the circular was at once withdrawn, as I think this should be. Can you not get Mr. Andrews, the secretary, whose name appeared with yours on the circular to call Mr. Garfield of the Civil Service Commission and find out exactly what ought to be done? Mr. Garfield, a son of the late President, is a thoroughly practical fellow, an active Republican, . . . and it is safe to follow him in matters of this kind.[35]

Quay promptly advised the president that the circular had been retracted, but even more promptly a second letter was dispatched to the same employees over Andrews's signature alone. Since Quay's name still appeared on the letterhead, this request for funds was also in conflict with the law and again came under the scrutiny of the Civil Service Commission and the president. Angered by the arrogance, TR nevertheless remained charitable toward Quay, but criticized Andrews for defiantly sending out another circular which he denounced as "a piece of irritating and purposeless folly, and unless instantly withdrawn, the attorney general will have to take action under it, and the good effect of the previous withdrawal is completely nullified."[36]

To reenforce his request, Roosevelt sent William D. Foulke of the Civil Service Commission to Philadelphia to advise Quay personally that the second letter also would have to be withdrawn. But the senator resolutely refused to comply: "I won't do it. I would do more for the President than for any man living. I withdrew the previous letter, but this one was written when I was off in another part of the state trying to settle the [anthracite] Coal strike. I did not know anything about the sending of the letter and therefore I will not withdraw it. I made a fool of myself once to oblige the President, and I won't do it again. Let him have me indicted if he will, but I hope he won't do that before the election."[37] When this refusal was reported to the president, he ordered the matter laid before Attorney General Philander C. Knox in order to determine whether or not criminal charges should be instituted. Knox concluded that such action was useless because there was no evidence that Quay had in any way taken part in sponsoring the second circular or even knew that it had been sent.

Quay was the victor in this incident, but he was not always so triumphant. When he asked the president to appoint Penrose or another Pennsylvanian to the Panama Canal Commission, TR was totally unreceptive. Without hesitation he issued a rejection that was both polite and firm. "You have been so kind to me in so many ways that I hate to be in any way unreciprocative. . . . When it comes to a position like this, I feel as I do when I am choosing a judge for the Supreme Court, that I must have an eye single to the way the work will be done."[38]

Despite these clashes, the president and the boss simultaneously engaged in several cooperative ventures. The most crucial of these was the task of finding a solution to the five-month-old strike in the anthracite coal fields of Pennsylvania. They accepted the challenge, realizing the political advantage that would result from a preelection settlement. Although the United Mine Workers Union was only demanding an increase in wages and a reduction in hours comparable to the gains made in the bituminous industry, the Reading Railroad, a Morgan affiliate that controlled two-thirds of the anthracite output, stubbornly refused to accept their terms. Roosevelt surprised Quay by declaring that he would solve the coal famine and end the strike if Quay would assure him that the governor would request federal troops when the president gave the word. TR conveniently failed to report what use he would make of the federal troops, and the senator neglected to ask. Like the coal operators, Quay assumed that the federal government, as in the past, would interpret the strike as a violation of the Sherman Anti-Trust Act, intervene to maintain law and order, and thereby end the harassment by the miners. He therefore assured Roosevelt that the governor would request the troops at the designated signal.[39]

Secure in this knowledge, the president used his privileged information to build public opinion behind him in order to force the recalcitrant operators to alter their position. At the psychologically appropriate moment he publicly threatened to deploy the troops to take possession, open, and operate the mines without tolerating interference from owners, strikers, or anyone else. Under this threat the operators accepted an arbitration commission through which they made the wage and hour concessions necessary to satisfy the demands of the workers.[40]

In one of his letters to Roosevelt about the anthracite crisis, Quay commented briefly on the political scene. "We are having a hard fight in Pennsylvania in some of our congressional and legislative districts." Roosevelt recognized this as a request to direct his personal attention to the campaign in the Keystone State. With nearly every state in the vicinity of Washington clamoring for his participation in their campaigns, his first impulse was to decline. Since he could not possibly satisfy all the requests, he decided not to participate in any of the state contests. He dictated a letter of regret to Quay, but after signing it, added a handwritten postscript saying that he had decided to speak in Pennsylvania and New York only.[41]

Quay was pleasantly surprised at Roosevelt's reaction, which was the kind of response he had expected, but did not receive, from previous Republican presidents. Ironically, now that he had announced his retirement from political competition, his rapport with the White House was better than ever. Contributing to the development of this congenial atmosphere, however, was Roosevelt's recognition that no "accidental" president before him had been elected to a term of his own. As he looked forward to upsetting this precedent, the endorsement of Quay and Platt could unquestionably facilitate his efforts; their approval would shrink into insignificance the opposition that Hanna was stirring.

The president's participation in the Pennsylvania contest offered certain benefits to Quay, who in 1902 was gambling for the last time in state politics. Suspecting that he would need all the assistance possible to achieve his objective, he welcomed the president's support. In addition to prompting the

Republican State Convention to endorse TR for a full presidential term, he had also dictated the party's gubernatorial nominee. In the months preceding that convention, all the evidence, including Quay's own conduct, pointed to John P. Elkin as the overwhelming choice for the nomination, but gradually word leaked out, only days before the convention, that Quay intended to endorse Samuel Pennypacker. At first this seemed incredible, since Elkin had served the Quay machine long and faithfully and had even been entrusted with the task of defending the boss's entitlement to his Senate seat in 1899. He had argued congently and eloquently before the Senate investigating committee and had won the plaudits of the state's Republicans, but Quay would not permit the past to command the future.

Although a majority of the delegates was already pledged to Elkin, Quay, as usual, took his chances with silence rather than explain his eleventh-hour switch to the public. In the absence of an official statement, party leaders who ultimately supported the boss were forced to provide their own intuitive explanations, and they ranged from Elkin's overzealous partisanship to an actual distrust of his goals. On the one hand, Elkin was so closely identified with Quay and the Republican machine that he could be a liability; times were changing, and the spirit of Progressive reform was everywhere, even in Pennsylvania. Some believed that Quay wanted a nominee of unimpeachable character, without any taint of machine politics in order to silence the demands of the party elements that listened to the beat of the reform drummer. Since Elkin did not conform to this model, the boss switched to Pennypacker, hoping that the anti-Quay Republicans would rush to his support and increase the prospects of victory. Some, on the other hand, suspected that Quay was motivated more by the fact that he detected a yearning for power and independence on the part of Elkin than by a desire to close ranks with the insurgents. One of the cardinal rules designed to keep power invested in the boss pertained to the selection of gubernatorial candidates; the individuals chosen were expected to demonstrate either mediocre ability or limited ambition or both, Elkin's tendency not to conform disturbed the boss. Furthermore, his display of independence was linked to Mark Hanna's forlorn ambition to discredit Roosevelt and capture control of the national convention in 1904. The Ohio senator favored Elkin's nomination and was quietly working in his behalf. If he should win the nomination and the election, he would inherit, in addition to the governship, control of the Pennsylvania delegation to the next Republican National Convention. If he then recognized a debt to Hanna for assistance along the way, Pennsylvania could be expected to provide convention votes to give the Ohioan the nomination leverage he coveted. Even the vaguest prospect that this could happen was enough to prompt Quay to veto the Elkin nomination.[42]

The boss tried in vain to convince Elkin of the propriety of withdrawing his name from the convention. In refusing, the latter exclaimed: "Senator, I cannot understand why you are not for me. You taught me all the politics I ever knew." Quay conceded the point, adding a cryptic insight of his own: "That's true, John, but I didn't teach you all I know." Unwilling to accept this decree, Elkin publicized the clash. When he arrived in Harrisburg for the state convention, he stepped from the train and announced to the waiting reporters that he would "be nominated on the first ballot. The fight is over. It is now a question of the majority. My friends have made a splendid fight, and the victory is complete."[43]

Within days the convention gave Elkin his disappointing answer, but the campaign and the election were necessary to determine where Quay's prestige stood on the political barometer. When Pennypacker carried the November election, the boss's prominence was apparent to all. The Republican insurgents found little satisfaction in their party's victory. Not only did the result permit the boss to continue doing "business as usual" throughout the Commonwealth, but the campaign had also linked him directly and advantageously with the president. Evaluating the political scene for the insurgents, Carl Schurz reluctantly declared that with this victory Quay had established himself among Roosevelt's "influential" friends. His domination of federal patronage was less than complete, but "he controlled enough to maintain his absolute boss rule . . . entirely unimpaired."[44]

Although the boss had taken the initiative to involve the president in the state's 1902 campaign, his friendship with Roosevelt was a two-way street. Roosevelt at times actively sought Quay's advice. In one ten-day period late in the summer of 1903, he sent the senator four letters, all inviting him to his Oyster Bay residence to discuss financial legislation. He assured him that no action would be taken by the administration in this field until he and several others were consulted and then only if they deemed it advisable. The president returned to Washington in the fall, renewing his quest for Quay's counsel: "When is there any chance of your coming to Washington? As you know, I tried in vain to get you to Oyster Bay last summer. Cannot you come down here? There are a number of things I would like to consult you about."[45]

Interpreted as indications of political preferment, all such solicitations angered the reformers, but TR did not reply directly to their attacks until after Quay's death and his own election to the presidency in 1904. Offended by the criticism of his conduct toward Quay and other bosses levied by the Carl Schurz and Charles Francis Adams groups, the president felt compelled to declare that the bosses were men "of whom I thoroughly disapprove." This was certainly a more negative attitude than his actions had implied, and it offered a pragmatic explanation of his relationships with them. He pointed out that he had not made them senators, but would have been derelict in his duty if he had not tried to get along with them.[46] Roosevelt held his own views on how best to promote the general welfare, but knew that they could become reality only through his cooperation with men of prominence in the Republican party. Although this meant an identification with Quay's methods, for which he obviously had some dislike, he concluded that forebearance was in the interest of his own legislative program which, to him at least, represented the greater good. At the same time he rebuked the reform journals that refused to recognize the necessity of such compromises. Disgusted by their naive and unrealistic outlook, the president wrote in a letter to George H. Putnam, "Quay was worth a hundred men like Miller of the New York Times, like Villard and Ogden of the Evening Post, like McKelway of the Brooklyn Eagle." TR respected power, discerned it in men such as Quay, and understood that reformers foolishly interpreted the justness of a cause as the power to achieve it. Being a man who cherished success and directness as virtues, he could not concede that the bosses were all bad.[47]

The Senator's Career Faces West
1902-1904

ASIDE from his attack on the Wilson-Gorman tariff and his explanation on sugar speculations, Quay had not taken the Senate podium to achieve his objectives. Committee rooms, private dinners, personal letters, and a group of able subordinates had served his purposes satisfactorily. But in the Roosevelt years he decided to use the Senate floor to assist the economic and political aspirations of his long-time lieutenant, William "Bull" Andrews, who had become interested in various enterprises in the New Mexico Territory. If statehood were extended to the territory, Andrews's business ventures would prosper more rapidly, and he himself could look forward to an appointment as U.S. senator, a distinction he coveted but could not attain in his native Pennsylvania as long as Quay and Penrose retained their seats.[1]

As a member of the Republican-dominated Senate Committee on Territories, Quay felt confident in advocating statehood for New Mexico, particularly since his request was coupled with bills to admit Arizona and Oklahoma at the same time. Both political parties had endorsed the principle of statehood for all three, and a bill providing for their immediate admission had already moved through the House of Representatives without a contest. Quay thus had no reason to expect a delay in the Senate, but Albert J. Beveridge of Indiana, the new committee chairman, knew well that scandals, injustice, and disappointment had marred the admission of other territories in the post–Civil War era. Determined that such practices would not be repeated under his aegis, the chairman opposed any perfunctory endorsement.[2] A relative newcomer to the Senate, Beveridge was influenced by the reform spirit and possessed the fire and vigor of youth necessary to animate it. Quay, on the other hand, was in no condition to compete; the passing of years, complicated by declining health, placed the Pennsylvania boss at a disadvantage for a confrontation with a man whose position was further enhanced by exceptional forensic skills.

Debating at Last

When the House bill pertaining to the admission of these territories was reported to the Senate, it was immediately assigned to Beveridge's committee. As chairman, he was justified in holding up the bill until he was familiar with the actual conditions in the territories. While asking questions and procuring information, Beveridge was bombarded with letters urging early removal of the measure to the Senate floor, and gradually he became aware of the personal benefits that were at stake. He concluded that the primary motivation for committee action was being stirred up by Quay, who was "anxious to help his old friend 'Bull' Andrews to a seat in the United States Senate and also to help him sell his bonds for his new railroad down there." He requested that action be postponed until the next session of Congress to permit a thorough review of territorial capabilities, and by a vote of six to four, the committee sustained him.[3]

Unwilling to accept the committee decision, Quay carried the fight to the Senate floor. In his third and last extended Senate speech, on June 23, 1902, he urged his colleagues to discharge the committee from any further consideration of the House bill and place it squarely before the Senate itself. Quoting the Republican platform of 1900, which declared that "we favor home rule for, and the early admission to statehood of, the territories of New Mexico, Arizona, and Oklahoma," he stressed the sanctity of platform pledges. He also noted that his party had made a similar declaration in 1896 and that in 1900 the Democrats denounced the Republicans for their failure to redeem that pledge. In their own platform the Democrats promised these territories "statehood and home rule." With both parties championing the cause, he believed that statehood had already "received the pretty nearly unanimous approval of the people of the United States." He reminded his colleagues that, if statehood were not to be granted, both parties would be "self-convicted of treachery." Whether or not a majority of the Senate agreed with him, he wanted the world to know that Pennsylvania "proclaims her fidelity to the declaration of the Republican platform, and no matter what others may do, extends a friendly and helping hand to the youngest children of the Republic."[4]

Beveridge, in turn, explained to the Senate that time was needed to study the political and economic solvency of the territories. He promised that his committee would not impose an unnecessary delay, but would make a definite recommendation early in the next session of Congress. In a cross-examination on the floor, Quay attempted to prove that the chairman had already retarded the progress of the territorial bill that had come from the House. He forced Beveridge to admit that the issue had never been discussed in committee, but in pressing further to know if committee members had asked to have the measure acted upon, he provided Beveridge with an opportunity to insert the political knife. The chairman frankly acknowledged that there had been two such requests, one of which had come from his interrogator "at the only meeting he ever attended." Undaunted, Quay insisted that the Senate consider the measure and declared that he and the other committee members in the minority on this question desired "nothing from the majority . . . except some assurance of a day in court." Beveridge refused to consent to have the bill taken from the committee to the floor, and the Senate sustained his position.[5]

Between sessions of the Fifty-seventh Congress, Beveridge pieced together some of the details surrounding the urgency for the statehood proposals. He accepted the validity in Quay's argument that both Republicans and Democrats had endorsed the admission of these territories, but he also noted that the senator had studiously avoided any reference to a substantive basis for the party decisions. His own assessment revealed that none of the three territories was prepared to assume the responsibilities of statehood; Arizona was a loose collection of mining camps, Oklahoma was a totally unacceptable political entity, and New Mexico could not adequately provide a system of public education for the children of its inhabitants.[6]

When the Senate reconvened in December 1902, Beveridge submitted his report, recommending an indefinite postponement of the omnibus statehood proposal. In a counterattack Quay urged acceptance of the House version favoring admission, but by pressing for an early vote, he betrayed one of his basic political tenets. In an unguarded moment—due to age, health, lack of personal commitment, or a combination of these—he exposed his political hand before he was in position to play the trump card. Beveridge at once realized that this bold challenge to a vote signified that the Beaver boss had enlisted the number of senators necessary to sustain his position. He was able to construct his defenses accordingly and prevent the boss, who normally capitalized on the mistakes of others, from registering his majority.

Beveridge's own alternatives were to delay Senate action either until public opinion could be marshaled against the statehood propositions or until the session adjourned. Both placed a premium on time, and the struggle to capture the advantage kept both men alert and tense throughout the three-month session. At no time did either dare to leave the Senate floor without a lieutenant on duty lest the other attempt to push his case. On one occasion when Beveridge was out to lunch, Quay tried to move formally toward a vote. Summoned by a subordinate, Beveridge pushed his meal aside, "dashed through the swinging doors of the Senate chamber waving his napkin, and launched into a long extemporaneous speech, clutching the napkin in his hand."[7]

With little more than a month of the session remaining, Beveridge had almost exhausted his bag of parliamentary tricks to prevent a vote. In desperation he decided to lean heavily on Senate protocol which opposed a vote on any measure in the absence of the chairman of the controlling committee, especially if he were known to be in opposition. Beveridge disappeared and spent a week in Gifford Pinchot's attic on Rhode Island Avenue. When the claustrophobia became unbearable, he escaped to an Atlantic City hotel. In time his melodramatic flight produced the desired results. To Quay's frustration, the Senate adjourned without the majority who favored the statehood bill having an opportunity to declare its position.[8]

This, Quay's most crushing Senate defeat, hurt both politically and physically. Normally during the winter months he informally excused himself from the Senate routine for weeks of relaxation in the Florida sun, but the contest with Beveridge forced him to remain in Washington throughout the 1902–1903 session. His general health suffered and from this time continued to decline steadily until his death in 1904.

The private goal that Quay hoped to achieve by his statehood campaign was the removal of the debt limitation placed on an area while it was still a territory. By federal statute, a territory, along with its individual counties and municipalities, could not contract debt in excess of 4 percent of the assessed valuation of property. With the conferring of statehood, this limitation was removed, and the new state, through bond issues and other subsidies, could aid promoters such as Andrews. In 1901 two aspiring leaders from New Mexico had come East to obtain financial support for the development of the territory politically and economically. They had met Andrews, who at once detected an emerging field for exploitation. He knew that his good friend, Senator Quay, was the master manipulator who could pilot a statehood measure through the Congress and thereby shift the burden of New Mexico's economic development from the entrepreneurs to the territory itself. Quay was amenable and even became an investor in several of Andrews's New Mexico enterprises, which included the Pennsylvania Development Company and the Santa Fe Railroad, as well as smaller timber and mining companies. Failure of the statehood bill jeopardized the future of these projects, but Andrews, Quay, and their business associates nevertheless conceived of an alternate scheme to defraud New Mexico of part of its timber resources.[9]

These intriguers arranged for employees of the Pennsylvania Development Company to take up options on valuable sections of timberland to be exploited collectively by the company. The company thus technically adhered to the law limiting the "sale" of territorial land to 160 acres per individual or corporation. Since the law did not require the recording of deeds, the company proceeded to cut timber on land for which it had options but no title. With its Santa Fe Railroad running from the town of the same name into the timber country, this group quickly exploited resources that were a part of the public domain. Beveridge had anticipated this kind of abuse and fought successfully to hold up statehood to prevent it, but the inventive minds of the Quay clique demonstrated that they were equal to the challenge.[10]

Paying a Debt to the Past

Paradoxically, at the same time that Quay was exerting himself in behalf of Andrews's partisan schemes, he was assiduously defending and promoting the cause of American Indians. With no political or economic reward on that horizon, he extended his thoughtful, devoted support to their plight. Why did he become "one of the best friends Indians ever had in Congress"? Did a desire to balance political greed with altruism motivate him to champion the native Americans who were accorded the most casual treatment by most of his contemporaries in government? Whatever the explanation, he both deserved and cherished his recognition as the protector of the "forgotten" race.[11]

Throughout his Senate career Quay had ministered to Indian needs and requests, but in his later years he was particularly attentive to their welfare. Once during the Roosevelt years a delegation of Iroquois came from Canada to seek readmission to the United States, from which their ancestors had fled during the American Revolution. They called on Quay and asked that he arrange an interview with the president to discuss their formal return. He, in turn, pointed out that their proposal was an absurdity: the federal government could not reclaim their original tribal lands and reassign title to them. But he agreed to ease their disappointment by arranging for them to meet the president. He called Roosevelt and advised him that although their errand was hopeless, the president should extend the courtesy of an interview. Roosevelt was receptive to the suggestion, and Quay accompanied the Indian delegation to the White House. After a solemn but sterile session with the president, the Indians seemed satisfied and filed out. Before following them, the senator turned to Roosevelt and said without expression: "Good-bye, Mr. President; this reminds one of the Flight of a Tartar Tribe, doesn't it?"

"So you're fond of DeQuincey, senator?"

"Yes, always liked DeQuincey," said the urbane and scholarly boss as he fell in behind the tribesmen.[12]

Almost every Indian delegation that visited Washington while Quay was senator found its way to his open door. His hospitality was genuine, and they were always grateful. In 1903 a council of the Senecas passed a unanimous resolution of sincere thanks to this "highly esteemed friend" for his untiring and voluntary efforts in their behalf "before the departments and in the United States Congress."[13] In a similar gesture the Delawares, in an annual worship service, elected him "grand chief" of their tribe, and thereafter he wrote affectionately of "my Delawares." The Nez Perce Indians also received the benefit of his largess. When Chief Joseph and his party visited the nation's capital, they expended all their funds in behalf of the cause for which they had come and were unable to pay for their transportation home. Quay arranged for their return railroad fare. On vacation trips to Florida he became acquainted with the problems and conditions among the Seminoles and exhibited a similar concern, even to the extent of paying the hospital and operation costs of a destitute tribesman.[14]

Quay's personal commitment to the Indian cause was based, in part, on his conviction that the responsible federal officials were extremely cavalier, if not woefully negligent, in carrying out their responsibilities. He was particularly critical of the Interior Department's conduct of Indian affairs and once left a sick bed to search for the department's secretary to protest a pending appointment that he considered detrimental to the Indians. With no animosity toward the prospective appointee and no candidate of his own to promote, he acted only to preserve the integrity of the Indian program as he perceived it. On another occasion he emerged from a vacation in Maine's north woods, picked up a newspaper, and learned that the Flathead Indians were being assessed a tax of one dollar per head on ponies. Believing that he had an understanding with the secretary of the interior that the tax would not be imposed until after the Senate Committee on Indian Affairs, of which he was a member, went West and reviewed the situation, he telegraphed the president, demanding that the secretary's action be countermanded: "Send for him and stop it, . . . I think you had better turn Hitchcock out and appoint me or some man of my kidney in his place."[15]

Even when he lay mortally ill in the spring of 1904, he continued to express a concern for "my Delawares." From his sick room, he requested an appointment with the president to discuss an urgent matter and told TR that he "would have himself carried round" at any time he stipulated. Although presidents do not normally make calls on senators, Roosevelt decided to make an exception and sent word that an appointment was not necessary; he would stop at the Quay residence on his way home from church the following Sunday. He made the call, which he later labeled a "most unusual experience," and on his return to the White House related the intimate details to Lincoln Steffens:

> I was admitted into the senator's sick room, and there he lay, long and still in his bed, eying me. I—well, you know how when somebody is sick or dying—you know how you feel you've got to say something cheerful, something banal. So I chirped up, all jolly and—and silly, and said, "Why, senator, how well you look! You'll soon be up and out and with us again." It sounded bad enough to me. It must have made Quay sick. He didn't say a word for a minute; just looked at me and picked at the counterpane with his long, thin fingers. Gee, I felt cheap. Then he shook his head slowly, very slowly, and said, "No, Mr. President, I'll not be with you again. I am dying. And,"—as I started to remonstrate, he lifted his hand to stop my—politeness—"that's all right, dying; only I hate to be dying here on a bed like this. What I would like would be to crawl off on a rock in the sun and die like a wolf."[16]

Quay then directed the conversation to the issue that had prompted the interview. Telling the president that he did not trust the Department of the Interior's conduct of Indian affairs, he added that he had even less faith in the willingness of any of his Senate colleagues to exert themselves in behalf of the Delawares. This led him to ask for TR's personal promise to become their protector. In describing the scene to Steffens, Roosevelt declared: "And you bet I was proud to be chosen. I promised Quay to take and fill his place, and I will." The boss-turned-humanitarian was pleased and calmly told the president: "Now I can die in peace."[17]

This was the last meeting between the two men. Shortly thereafter, Quay returned to his home in Beaver, where he grew steadily weaker. Illness was not new to him; he had never been strong physically and always prided himself on his endurance. But as he grew more feeble from a condition diagnosed as gastritis, he realized that this was one battle that he was destined to lose. No strategy, no organization, and no wire-pulling could alter the result. Unable to assimilate food, he continued to lose weight and strength. One day late in May, he asked "to see my books once more before I die." Carried into his famous library, "he fondled the volumes, read a line here and there, surveyed them lovingly and longingly until his eyelids closed, and like a tired child he was carried away from them forever."[18]

The interested public was kept informed of his condition through the newspapers and through disclosures of the senator's own correspondence, but the accounts were all more optimistic than his health warranted. On the morning of May 28, 1904, President Roosevelt personally inquired about him and later in the day was informed that the senator had just died. Without hesitation the president dispatched a telegram to his widow: "Accept my profound sympathy, official and personal. Throughout my term as President, Senator Quay has been my staunch and loyal friend. I have hoped to the last that he would by his sheer courage pull through his illness."[19]

Local friends and neighbors had kept a vigil outside the Quay residence; with the announcement of his death they dispersed to their homes, and the town prepared to mourn. By the day of the funeral, there was no home or prominent business establishment that did not reflect the prevailing spirit by displaying some emblem of mourning. Hundreds of flags hung at half-mast, and black bunting was draped from doorways and windows. Even the streetcars that plied the Beaver Valley were draped in black, and during the hours of the funeral service, industry throughout the valley came to a halt— not a wheel turned.[20]

The funeral service, held in the church that his father had served years before, was Beaver's greatest spectacle. United States senators in attendance included Boies Penrose, Nelson Aldrich, William Allison, Russell Alger, Stephen Elkins, Joseph Foraker, Thomas Platt, Arthur Gorman, and Ben Tillman. Speaker Cannon appointed the entire Pennsylvania delegation to represent the House, and Governor Pennypacker personally headed the state's official party. These dignitaries were joined by hundreds of local mourners, who descended on Beaver in conveyances ranging from a farmer's wagon to the railroad and the newest of mechanical inventions, the automobile. Together with the scores of government officials, they paid their final tribute and witnessed the senator's burial amid a spring downpour punctuated by flashes of lightning and salvos of thunder. It seemed that the elements too were offering a last salute.[21]

As the senator had requested, the slab that eventually covered his grave bore the inscription:

Matthew Stanley Quay
Son of the Rev. Anderson Beaton and Catherine
McCain Quay
Born September 30, 1833
Died May 28, 1904
Implora Pacem

The epitaph, "I pray for peace," expressed the great personal lament of the senator's career. His political life had been stormy. Constantly forced to fight foes with one hand, he had only one, in the opinion of his friends, to attend to public duties—but to his many detractors the one hand was free to engage in public plunder. Thus to the end Quay remained an uncertain quantity. Antagonists and defenders were in general agreement on his results, but more often than not both camps were baffled concerning his methods.[22]

Quay had discussed his enigmatic career with Senator Beveridge when they visited in Washington during the early stages of his illness. Although the Hoosier's parliamentary tactics had robbed Quay of success with his omnibus statehood bill, their personal relationship was a friendly one. The Pennsylvanian regarded Beveridge as a worthy antagonist and respected his ability; he suggested that his younger colleague might profit from his experiences. With this in mind he predicted that, when he was dead, the newspapers would record, "Matt Quay, boss, is dead," but he pointed out that, if he had lived his life differently, the same papers would have proclaimed, "Death of Matthew S. Quay, statesman." Realizing that he had had the opportunity to be a statesman and perhaps had squandered it, he urged Beveridge to ponder this example as he approached future crossroads in his own budding career so that he might escape the pitfalls that had dotted Quay's years of public service.[23]

When Quay entered the U.S. Senate in 1887, the nation was already engaged in "a search for order." Since there was no public outcry for a thorough search, Quay and his political contemporaries conducted none. Bold and innovative in party methods, he did not apply his creativity to policy issues. If he had displayed the same vision toward the issues that he displayed toward party organization, he might have become a statesman. Quay and his fellow politicians preferred to treat social and economic dysfunctions with verbal patches and legislative bandages instead of forward-looking statesmanship. By supplying superficial responses they permitted many of society's most crucial decisions to gravitate from the realm of party and government into the hands of the rising industrial complex. Thus the party system failed to function as an effective catalyst when the nation desperately needed solutions to basic problems.

Aside from Robert LaFollette, whose crusades in behalf of reform causes were only beginning, Quay's generation did not produce a single liberal Republican of stature. Quay was even more committed to the status quo than most legislators were. Serving Pennsylvania rather than the United States, he contributed little to the national legislative program of his party. He was content to sit in silence while senatorial disscussion resounded on all sides; he never championed any principle, not even the Republican doctrine of protection. Although he did speak on the tariff, he pronounced no theory, but merely demanded specific schedules for the iron and steel producers of his state. Once local appetites were appeased, he lapsed into legislative indifference until another issue important to his constituents arose. At the end of his career, such self-interest was disturbing to Republican leadership in the Senate. With his passing, many colleagues tacitly hoped for a successor more committed to issues national in scope and substantive in character.

Another evidence of Quay's failure as a party man in the legislative sense was his refusal to accept the chairmanship of a significant Senate committee. Although he had served as a member of such prestigious committees as Commerce, Territories, Indian Affairs, and Manufactures, his career-long duty was with the Committee on Public Buildings and Grounds, of which he did become chairman. Never in the limelight, this committee offered its own peculiar rewards that were suited to Quay's purposes. Every senator, regardless of party, was always interested in public building projects within his home state, and from time to time he needed support from the committee's chairman to push them more vigorously. Frequently a senator's prestige at home—sometimes even his reelection—depended on his success in behalf of such a project. Knowing the subtle character of this chairmanship, Quay exercised a quiet influence over all senators and, when necessary, could demand his pound of political flesh.

In contrast to his lackluster legislative career, Quay became an administrative giant. In the political realm, he added new dimensions to power, discipline, and compromise. Refining state politics to a science, he learned early in his career that nominal leaders do not always possess power, and he set about systematically to discern who did—within the state's Republican party, within the legislature, within the various state committees, within county organizations, and within the Democratic party. But knowing was not enough; controlling was essential, and his career focused constantly on that goal. In the process he discovered new uses for money which, in turn, facilitated party discipline, purchased favors, and promoted compromises.

By the turn of the century, the American public was no longer impressed with the halfhearted search for order that this generation had conducted and no longer desirous of retaining the system that Quay had so studiously helped to structure. With the tempo of industrialization and urbanization accelerating, problems were multiplying. The public recognized that issue-oriented leaders, not old-school tacticians, could better meet their needs. Thus Quay's death coincided with the nation's rejection of his brand of politics, but in Pennsylvania where his imprint was more firmly stamped, rejection has been more gradual. Like the boy who tried to throw away his boomerang, Pennsylvanians, years afterward, have discovered vestiges of Quayism in candidate attitudes, legislative programs, and election techniques. In fact, the senator—in statuary marble—is still overlooking the governmental process in Harrisburg, from the head of the imposing staircase in the capitol rotunda.

Notes

Bibliography

Index

Notes

In the notes, complete citations are given only for items not listed in the Bibliography. The following abbreviations are used; consult the Bibliography for a complete description of the documents.

MSQ Papers   Papers and correspondence of Matthew Stanley Quay, in the possession of James A. Kehl.

PC   Press Comments—newspaper clippings in the possession of James A. Kehl, cited by volume and item number.

Quay Family Papers   Correspondence and newspaper clippings in the Archives of Industrial Society, University of Pittsburgh.

Introduction

1. Theodore Roosevelt to Agnes B. Quay (telegram), May 28, 1904, MSQ Papers.
2. Quoted in Bloom, "Philadelphia *North American*," p. 566.
3. Stoddard, *As I Knew Them*, p. 168.
4. Although attributed to Quay, this statement may not have originated with him. At a much later date *Time* (May 19, 1975, p. 79) identified the late Senator Kenneth B. Keating of New York as the author. Either Keating was rewording Quay's remark or both versions had a common derivation.
5. Stackpole, *Behind the Scenes*, p. 95.
6. Orville Platt to Wharton Barker, June 17, 1891, Barker Papers.
7. *San Francisco Bulletin*, April 30, 1899, loose clipping in MSQ Papers.
8. John P. Blair to MSQ, January 19, 1887, MSQ Papers.
9. M. M. Ogden to MSQ, March 25, 1899, MSQ Papers.
10. James S. Clarkson to MSQ, February 4, 1897, and H. R. Clarkson to MSQ, February 13, 1897, both in MSQ Papers.
11. Herbert Agar, *The Price of Union* (Boston: Houghton Mifflin, 1950), pp. 237, 243;

William Bennett Munro, *Personality in Politics: A Study of Three Types in American Public Life* (New York: Macmillan, 1934), p. 73.

12. Blankenburg, "Forty Years," p. 126.

13. Kehl, "Unmaking of a President," p. 482.

14. *New York Press*, July 13, 1888, PC, II, 88.

15. Leach, "Twenty Years with Quay," July 3, 1904.

16. Gresham, *Life of W. Q. Gresham*, II, 491.

17. Leach, "Twenty Years with Quay," September 18, 1904; author interview with W. Scott Moore, Beaver, Pa., June 20, 1962.

18. Platt, *Autobiography*, p. 211; Stackpole, *Behind the Scenes*, p. 109; Bowers, *Beveridge*, p. 195; Davenport, *Power and Glory*, pp. 79–80.

19. Isaac R. Pennypacker, *Pennsylvania and Senator Quay: A Reply to Mr. Herbert Welsh* (pamphlet published in Philadelphia, 1892), p. 17; *San Francisco Bulletin*, April, 30, 1899.

20. Unidentified newspaper clipping in MSQ Papers.

21. Ibid.

22. Interview with W. Scott Moore, June 20, 1962; unidentified newspaper clipping in box 1, Quay Family Papers.

23. Leach, "Twenty Years with Quay," July 3, 1904, and October 16, 1904.

24. Pennypacker, *Autobiography*, p. 322; Davenport, *Power and Glory*, p. 81.

25. Pennypacker, *Autobiography*, p. 486; Davenport, *Power and Glory*, pp. 79–80.

26. Pennypacker, "Quay of Pennsylvania," p. 357; *New York World*, July 14, 1888, PC, II, 104.

27. Anderson B. Quay to C. C. Beaty, March 23, 1849, and Catherine M. Quay to MSQ, April 24, 1864, both in MSQ Papers.

1. From These Roots: 1833–1865

1. Phoenixville Speech, October 27, 1900, quoted in Quay, *Pennsylvania Politics*, p. 156.

2. *The Centennial Memorial of the Presbytery of Carlisle*, 2 vols., (Harrisburg: Meyers Printing and Publishing House, 1889), II, 278.

3. Stanley Quay to John W. Willson Loose, June 2, 1956, in possession of James A. Kehl.

4. *Centennial Memorial of the Presbytery of Carlisle*, II, 277–78; James McClure, *History of the Presbyterian Church in the Forks of Brandywine, Chester County, Pa., from A.D. 1735 to A.D. 1885* (Philadelphia: J. B. Lippincott Co., 1885), p. 146.

5. Leaf of births from A. B. Quay's Bible, MSQ Papers; handwritten copy of Anderson B. Quay to Joseph Quay, October 1854, MSQ Papers.

6. Anderson B. Quay to Francis McFarland, July 5 and August 9, 1839, and March 10, 1849, Typed Excerpts from Quay Letters, MSQ Papers.

7. Anderson B. Quay to Francis McFarland, June 20, 1841, Typed Excerpts from Quay Letters, MSQ Papers.

8. Anderson B. Quay to H. Malcom, August 1 and September 25, 1851, Typed Excerpts from Quay Letters, MSQ Papers; McClure, *History of the Presbyterian Church*, p. 147.

9. The college was located in Canonsburg, Pennsylvania, but later became part of the merger which resulted in Washington and Jefferson College.

10. Statement of J. C. Penney, January 20, 1853, Archives of Industrial Society.

11. William Griffin, Reminiscences of M. S. Quay, MSQ Papers.

12. Ibid.; Bowers, *Beveridge*, p. 195; Platt, *Autobiography*, p. 212; Boies Penrose, in *Matthew Stanley Quay: Memorial Addresses Delivered in the Senate and House of Representatives* (Washington, D.C.: U.S. Government Printing Office, 1905), pp. 35–36.

13. Theodore Roosevelt, *Autobiography*, p. 155; Theodore Roosevelt to MSQ, February 16, 1904, Roosevelt Papers, Personal Letter Books, XV, 373; Stoddard, *It Costs to Be President*, p. 180; Leach, "Twenty Years with Quay," July 3, 1904.

14. Griffin, Reminiscences of M. S. Quay; Lizzie Griffin Baldwin to Mary Quay Davidson, August 27, 1905, MSQ Papers.

15. Ibid.

16. Griffin, Reminiscences of M. S. Quay.

17. Ibid.

18. Ibid.

19. I. L. Fitzgerald to MSQ, April 24, 1854, MSQ Papers; Official Statement of the Court of Common Pleas of Allegheny County, Pennsylvania, endorsed by Penney and Sterrett, January 20, 1853, MSQ Papers.

20. Anderson B. Quay to MSQ, March 15, 1853, MSQ Papers.

21. Proclamation of James Pollock, April 24, 1856, MSQ Papers; McClure, *Old Time Notes*, I, 456-57; Pennypacker, *Autobiography*, p. 320.

22. Commissions of Appointment from the State of Pennsylvania, MSQ Papers.

23. McClure, *Old Time Notes*, I, 457; Alexander K. McClure, *Lincoln and Men of War Times*, ed. J. Stuart Torrey (Philadelphia: Rolley and Reynolds, 1961), p. 222.

24. Alexander K. McClure, *The Life and Services of Andrew Gregg Curtin: An Address* (delivered in the House of Representatives at Harrisburg, January 20, 1895, and published by Clarence M. Busch, state printer of Pennsylvania, 1895), p. 29; Stanton L. Davis, *Pennsylvania Politics, 1860-1863* (Cleveland: Stanton L. Davis, 1935), p. 309.

25. McClure, *Lincoln*, p. 234.

26. McClure, *Old Time Notes*, I, 458-59.

27. *Pittsburgh Gazette*, October 9, 1904.

28. McClure, *Old Time Notes*, I, 457-58.

29. *Pittsburgh Gazette*, October 9, 1904.

30. Elliott S. Quay to MSQ, September 1, 1861, and February 11, 1862, MSQ Papers.

31. MSQ to Agnes B. Quay, August 22, 1862, Quay Family Papers.

32. *Under the Maltese Cross, Antietam to Appomattox: The Loyal Uprising in Western Pennsylvania 1861-1865* (Pittsburgh: The 155th Regimental Assoication, 1910), pp. 532-37.

33. MSQ to Agnes B. Quay, September 23, 1862, Quay Family Papers.

34. Letter of Discharge from the Command of Maj. Gen. Hooker, MSQ Papers; Muster-Out Roll of Field Staff of the 134th Regiment of Pennsylvania Volunteers (certified true and correct copy from the adjutant general's office, Harrisburg, August 1, 1878), MSQ Papers; *M. S. Quay and the Soldiers* (pamphlet), p. 3.

35. McClure, *Old Time Notes*, I, 461. This account is verified by the handwritten records made by Quay in the field and extant in the MSQ Papers, along with receipts from the Adams Express Company totaling $3,954, indicating that he ultimately mailed this amount to members of the soldiers' families. In a deposition before Alderman John B. Brown on May 19, 1888 (typed copy in MSQ Papers), David Pearson placed the amount that Quay was carrying at "some twenty odd thousand dollars."

36. Winfield M. Clark to William C. Endicott, May 28, 1888, and J. M. Clark to William C. Endicott, June 6, 1888 (typed copy), both in MSQ Papers.

37. *Quay and the Soldiers*, p. 5; Oliver, "Quay," p. 3.

38. Vorin E. Whan, *Fiasco at Fredericksburg* (University Park: The Pennsylvania State University Press, 1961), pp. 47, 51, 79-80.

39. Francis W. Palfrey, *The Antietam and Frederickburg*, vol. 5 of *Campaigns of the Civil War* (New York: Charles Scribner's Sons, 1882), pp. 171-72.

40. J. M. Clark to William C. Endicott, June 6, 1888, and Winfield M. Clark to William C. Endicott, May 28, 1888, both in MSQ Papers; McClure, *Old Time Notes*, I, 461.

41. Palfrey, *Antietam and Fredericksburg*, p. 172; Whan, *Fiasco at Fredericksburg*, pp. 86–87; Edward J. Stackpole, *Drama of the Rappahannock: The Fredericksburg Campaign* (Harrisburg: Military Service Publishing Company, 1957), pp. 217–18, 224.

42. Extract from General E. B. Tyler's Report of the Part Taken by His Brigade in the Battle of Fredericksburg, December 16, 1862, MSQ Papers.

43. Winfield M. Clark to William C. Endicott, May 28, 1888, and undated letter to William C. Endicott signed by 53 officers and men of the 134th regiment (typed copy) both in MSQ Papers.

44. James A. Beaver to Matthew S. Quay, August 6, 1866, MSQ Papers; Adjutant General R. C. Drum to Matthew S. Quay, July 9, 1888, MSQ Papers. Since the first Congressional Medals of Honor were not awarded until March 1863, there was understandable confusion in the procedure for identifying individuals to be so honored, especially those whose acts of bravery preceded that date. It was not uncommon for Civil War incidents of heroism to be recognized years later. According to Bruce Jacobs, *Heroes of the Army: The Medal of Honor and Its Winners* (New York: W. W. Norton and Co., 1956), p. 37, there were 1527 Congressional Medals awarded for Civil War gallantry, more than a third of which were bestowed after 1890. According to A. K. McClure, a Quay contemporary, in his *Old Time Notes*, I, 461, "No man in the army ever more justly merited it."

45. William B. Hesseltine, *Lincoln and the War Governors* (New York: Knopf, 1948), pp. 340–41.

46. Andrew G. Curtin to MSQ, July 14, 1866, MSQ Papers.

47. Erastus B. Tyler to MSQ, September 29, 1863, MSQ Papers; McClure, *Lincoln*, p. 235.

48. Mary R. Dearing, *Veterans in Politics: The Story of the G.A.R.* (Baton Rouge: Louisiana State University Press, 1952), p. 37.

2. A Lieutenant in Cameron's Army: 1865-1867

1. West Chester Speech, October 1, 1900, quoted in Quay, *Pennsylvania Politics*, p. 22.

2. McClure, *Old Time Notes*, II, 196, 558–59.

3. Ibid., I, 461–62.

4. H. Pillow to MSQ, July 19, 1866, G. W. Kinney to MSQ, July 21, 1866, E. W. Davis to MSQ, August 13, 1866, George Y. McKee to MSQ, November 5, 1866, J. D. Cameron to MSQ, November [date illegible], 1866, James H. Webb to MSQ, November 20, 1866, all in MSQ Papers.

5. E. W. Davis to MSQ, October 13, 1866, and D. B. McCreary to MSQ, November 5, 1866, MSQ Papers.

6. E. W. Davis to MSQ, October 11, 1866, E. Billingfelt to MSQ, November 6, 1866, E. D. Roath to MSQ, November 6, 1866, all in MSQ Papers; McClure, *Old Time Notes*, I, 462, and II, 203–08.

7. J. B. Kelly to MSQ, December 19, 1866, and W. W. Watt to MSQ, December 28, 1866, both in MSQ Papers.

8. McClure, *Old Time Notes*, I, 463.

9. Ibid., I, 464–65; Kelley, "Simon Cameron and the Senatorial Nomination of 1867," p. 377; Stewart, "Deal for Philadelphia," pp. 42–43.

10. *Beaver Radical*, November 17, 1871; Blankenburg, "Forty Years," p. 118.

11. Macy, *Party Organization*, pp. 122, 155.

12. Ibid., pp. 145, 149; Keller, *Affairs of State*, p. 537.

13. Adams, *Education of Henry Adams*, p. 311.

14. *Cong. Rec.*, Senate, 53rd Cong., 2nd sess., XXVI, pt. 4, 3724.

15. "Ills of Pennsylvania," pp. 565–66.

16. Yearly, *Money Machines*, p. 127.

17. Stewart, "Deal for Pennsylvania," p. 43.

18. "Ills of Pennsylvania," p. 565.

19. Macy, *Party Organization*, pp. 149, 156.

20. F. C. Hooton to Rutherford B. Hayes, December 24, 1880, Hayes Papers.

21. To be discussed in detail in chapter 5.

22. Yearly, *Money Machines*, p. 104.

23. Ibid.; Macy, *Party Organization*, p. 111.

24. Yearly, *Money Machines*, p. 127; Macy, *Party Organization*, pp. 159–60; Rothman, *Politics and Power*, p. 261.

25. *Pittsburgh Gazette*, October 9, 1904.

26. "Ills of Pennsylvania," p. 562.

27. Ibid., p. 563.

28. Thayer, *Who Shakes the Money Tree?* p. 38.

29. Dobson, *Politics in the Gilded Age*, p. 545.

3. A Profile Low in Politics, High in Visibility: 1867-1877

1. *Beaver Radical*, January 1, 1869, and December 20, 1872.

2. Ibid., December 11, 1868; MSQ to Wayne MacVeagh, December 20, 1868, MacVeagh Papers: Wayne MacVeagh Correspondence, Historical Society of Pennsylvania.

3. Michael Weyand to Simon Cameron, January 10, 1869, Cameron Papers, microfilm reel no. 10.

4. *Beaver Radical*, January 29, 1869.

5. Ibid., December 10, 1869, January 28, 1870, and December 22, 1871.

6. Ibid., December 18, 1868.

7. Ibid., January 15, February 26, and April 23, 1869; Stackpole, *Behind the Scenes*, p. 93.

8. *Beaver Radical*, February 5, 1869.

9. Quay, *Pennsylvania Politics*, p. 30.

10. *Beaver Radical*, January 15, 1869; McClure, *Old Time Notes*, II, 255–56; Bradley, *Triumph of Militant Republicanism*, p. 33.

11. William W. Irwin to A. G. Henry, November 23, 1869, MSQ Papers; *Beaver Radical*, January 14, 1870; McClure, *Old Time Notes*, II, 257.

12. *Beaver Radical*, January 21, October 7 and 14, 1870.

13. Robert W. Mackey to MSQ, June 4, 1870, MSQ Papers.

14. *Beaver Radical*, August 19, 1870, November 24, and December 1, 1871.

15. Ibid., April 19, August 30, and September 13, 1872.

16. Lambert, *Elkins*, p. 67.

17. Thomas, *Return of the Democratic Party*, p. 34; Thomas H. Sherman, *Twenty Years with James G. Blaine: Reminiscences by His Private Secretary* (New York: Grafton Press, 1928), pp. 51–53.

18. Thomas, *Return of the Democratic Party*, pp. 28, 33.

19. Ibid., pp. 39–40; McClure, *Old Time Notes*, II, 428, 475–76.

20. Theron C. Crawford, *James G. Blaine: A Study of His Life and Career* (Edgewood Publishing Company, 1893), pp. 391–96.

21. John F. Hartranft to Rutherford B. Hayes, June 16 and July 14, 1876, MSQ to Rutherford B. Hayes, July 14, 1876, all in Hayes Papers.

22.   Copy of this letter sent to Rutherford B. Hayes, August 22, 1876, as an example of the campaign effort in Pennsylvania, MSQ Papers.

23.   Loth, *Public Plunder*, p. 212; James Ford Rhodes, *History of the United States from the Compromise of 1850 to the End of the Roosevelt Administration*, new ed., 9 vols. (Macmillan, 1928), VII, 293-94.

24.   McClure, *Old Time Notes*, II, 262-63.

25.   MSQ to Rutherford B. Hayes, December 16 and 17, 1877, Hayes Papers; Hirshson, *Farewell to the Bloody Shirt*, p. 27.

26.   Blankenburg, "Forty Years," pp. 9-10.

4. From Lieutenant to General: 1877-1884

1.   Blankenburg, "Forty Years," p. 119; McClure, *Old Time Notes*, II, 498-500.

2.   MSQ to Eugene Hale, October 11, 1878, Garfield Papers, LV, 179.

3.   MSQ to James A. Garfield, August 21, September 19, and October 18, 1878, Garfield Papers, LIV, 346, LV, 79, and LV, 225, respectively.

4.   McClure, *Old Time Notes*, II, 492.

5.   Ibid., II, 505; Simon Cameron to James N. Kerns (telegram), November 3, 1878, MSQ Papers; Loth, *Public Plunder*, pp. 213-14.

6.   Evans, "Wharton Barker," p. 32.

7.   MSQ to "Dear Sir," November 19, 1879, MSQ Papers.

8.   Ibid.; F. C. Hooton to Rutherford B. Hayes, December 24, 1880, Hayes Papers.

9.   Evans, "Wharton Barker," p. 31.

10.   Frank A. Burr, *Life and Achievements of James Addams Beaver: Early Life, Military Services, and Public Career* (Philadelphia: Ferguson Bros. & Co., 1882), pp. 169, 191, 193, and 195.

11.   McClure, *Old Time Notes*, II, 507-08.

12.   William R. Balch, *The Life of James Abram Garfield, Late President of the United States* (Philadelphia: J. C. McCurdy & Co., 1881), pp. 375, 377.

13.   Evans, "Wharton Barker," pp. 37-40.

14.   Platt, *Autobiography*, pp. 114-16, 119-20.

15.   Balch, *Garfield*, p. 483.

16.   MSQ to James A. Garfield, January 31, February 2 and 25, 1881, Garfield Papers, CXXVII, 113, 169, and CXXXII, 232.

17.   George H. Mayer, *The Republican Party, 1854-1964* (New York: Oxford University Press, 1964), pp. 205-06.

18.   John I. Mitchell to Wharton Barker, May 18, 1882, Barker Papers.

19.   Mayer, *Republican Party*, p. 206; "Republican Independents," p. 456.

20.   Thomas, *Return of the Democratic Party*, p. 74.

21.   MSQ to John R. Oursler, March 13, 1886, MSQ Papers; John Stewart to Wharton Barker, April 4, 1882, Barker Papers.

22.   Leach, "Twenty Years with Quay," July 3 and October 2, 1904.

23.   MSQ to James A. Beaver, April 25 and 28, 1882, Beaver Manuscripts; John I. Mitchell to Wharton Barker, May 18, 1882, Barker Papers; Leach, "Twenty Years with Quay," July 3, 1904; Leach, *Partial Portrait*, pp. 6-7; "The Pennsylvania Convention," *Nation*, 34 (1882), 419.

24.   Leach, "Twenty Years with Quay," November 27, 1904.

25.   "The Pennsylvania Convention," pp. 419-20.

26.   MSQ to James A. Beaver, July 12, 1882, Beaver Manuscripts.

27.   Mary A. Cook, "Matthew Stanley Quay in Pennsylvania Politics as Viewed through His Home-Town Newspapers," MA thesis, Pittsburgh, 1932, pp. 61-64.

28. Ibid., pp. 67–70.
29. Leach, "Twenty Years with Quay," April 23, and May 14, 1905.
30. Cook, "Quay," pp. 62, 79.
31. Ibid., pp. 75–76.
32. Quoted in Thomas, *Return of the Democratic Party*, p. 162.
33. Partial manuscript, MSQ Papers.

5. The Unofficial Government: 1884-1895

1. Keller, *Affairs of State*, p. 108.
2. Stewart, "Deal for Philadelphia," p. 47.
3. Keller, *Affairs of State*, p. 265.
4. "Origin of the Boss System," p. 194; *Philadelphia Press*, February 13, 1884.
5. Marcus, *Grand Old Party*, p. 72.
6. Ibid., pp. 73–74.
7. Josephson, *The Politicos*, pp. 98–99, 107.
8. "Senator Quay and the Republican Machine," p. 15.
9. "Costly Bosses," p. 455; *The Speeches of Hon. John Wanamaker on Quayism and Boss Domination in Pennsylvania Politics* (Philadelphia: Business Men's League of the State of Pennsylvania, c. 1898), p. 195.
10. Blankenburg, "Quay," p. 209.
11. Stackpole, *Behind the Scenes*, p. 105; Davenport, *Power and Glory*, pp. 70–73.
12. John F. Hartranft to MSQ, August 25, 1886, MSQ Papers; Marcosson, "House of Quay," p. 7120.
13. McClure, *Old Time Notes*, II, 503–05; *Speeches of Wanamaker on Quayism*, p. 369; "Quayism in Pennsylvania," p. 250. See also chapter 9.
14. J. Donald Cameron to MSQ, August 9, 1885, and cancelled check in the amount of $100,000, MSQ Papers; Marcosson, "House of Quay," p. 7120.
15. Leach, "Twenty Years with Quay," July 3, 1904.
16. Wharton Barker to MSQ, May 5, 1885, Barker Papers; Simon Cameron to MSQ, July 10, 1885, MSQ Papers; Certificate of Election as State Treasurer, with letter of transmittal from Thomas B. Cochran to MSQ, January 20, 1886, MSQ Papers.
17. Marcosson, "House of Quay," p. 7119.
18. MSQ to A. L. Conger, November 2, 1889, A. L. Conger Collection.
19. "Senator Quay and the Republican Machine," p. 13; "Pennsylvania Again," p. 271.
20. MSQ to James A. Beaver, September 11, 1885, Beaver Manuscripts; McClure, *Old Time Notes*, II, 563.
21. MSQ to James A. Beaver, December 24, 1885, Beaver Manuscripts.
22. MSQ to James A. Beaver, June 19, 1886, Beaver Manuscripts; Leach, "Twenty Years with Quay," November 27, 1904.
23. MSQ to James A. Beaver, May 2, 1886, Beaver Manuscripts; Leach, "Twenty Years with Quay," November 27, 1904.
24. Wharton Barker to MSQ (copy), November 10, 1886, Barker Papers.
25. Nelson P. Reed to MSQ, November 9, 1886, and C. Wesley Thomas to MSQ, December 27, 1886, both in MSQ Papers; Wharton Barker to William R. Leeds (copy), November 10, 1886, Barker Papers; Resolves of the Cameron Club of Philadelphia, March 8, 1887, Beaver Manuscripts; "The New Senators," p. 63.
26. Chidsay, *Gentleman from New York*, p. 143.
27. *Urban* is used here to describe communities of 8,000 or more inhabitants.
28. Jaher, *Doubters and Dissenters*, p. 4.

29.　Riordan, *Plunkitt*, p. 113; Haeger and Weber, *The Bosses*, pp. 2–3, 5, 34.

30.　Riordan, *Plunkitt*, p. 113; Jaher, *Doubters and Dissenters*, pp. 44–45.

31.　Dorsett, *Bosses and Machines*, p. 2; Keller, *Affairs of State*, p. 542.

32.　Keller, *Affairs of State*, p. 538.

33.　Zink, *City Bosses*, pp. 3, 9; Tarr, *Boss Politics*, p. 12; "King George; King Matthew," p. 218.

34.　Riordan, *Plunkitt*, pp. 123, 126.

35.　Ibid., p. 11; Josephson, *The Robber Barons*, pp. 406–07.

36.　Gosnell, *Boss Platt*, pp. 37, 59, 67, 72, 324; Ginger, *Age of Excess*, p. 115.

37.　"Ills of Pennsylvania," p. 559.

38.　"Senator Quay as a Reformer," p. 910.

39.　Ibid.

40.　Zink, *City Bosses*, p. 201.

41.　Ibid., p. 203; Martin, *Bosses*, p. 40.

42.　Martin, *Bosses*, p. 40; Zink, *City Bosses*, p. 204–05; Leach, "Twenty Years with Quay," June 18, 1905.

43.　Zink, *City Bosses*, pp. 208, 213–14; Martin, *Bosses*, p. 40; Cornelius C. Regier, *The Era of the Muckrakers* (Chapel Hill: University of North Carolina Press, 1932), p. 64.

44.　Zink, *City Bosses*, pp. 19, 29, 240.

45.　Ibid., pp. 234–35, 253.

46.　Ibid., pp. 37, 41, 240; Steffens, *Shame of the Cities*, pp. 153–54.

47.　Cancelled promissory note dated May 10, 1880, signed by MSQ, MSQ Papers; Zink, *City Bosses*, pp. 18, 22–23, 233, 242–43.

48.　*Philadelphia Record*, December 30, 1889, PC, V, 177–78.

49.　Ibid.

50.　*Philadelphia Inquirer*, April 22, 1899.

51.　Commonwealth of Pennsylvania, *Legislative Journal*, Senate, 1913, pt. 3, 3766.

52.　J. M. Guffey to MSQ, May 14, 1897, MSQ Papers; Steffens, *Shame of the Cities*, pp. 183–84; Leland D. Baldwin, *Pittsburgh: The Story of a City* (Pittsburgh: University of Pittsburgh Press, 1937), p. 354.

53.　Steffens, *Shame of the Cities*, p. 184.

54.　"King George; King Matthew," p. 218.

55.　Holben, *Stories and Reminiscences*, pp. 147, 155–56.

56.　Dobson, *Politics in the Gilded Age*, pp. 116–17.

57.　Patrick F. Palermo, "Gemeinschaft Politics in Nineteenth Century America: The Republican Party in the Midwest," paper presented to the Duquesne Forum, Duquesne University, Pittsburgh, Pa., October 30, 1975; Tarr, *Boss Politics*, p. 14.

58.　Gosnell, *Boss Platt*, pp. 329, 343.

6. The Making of a Candidate: 1888

1.　Erastus Brainard to Walter Q. Gresham, April 26, 1888, Gresham Papers.

2.　*Philadelphia Press*, April 30, 1887; "Pennsylvania Republicans," pp. 148–49.

3.　Joseph Medill to Walter Q. Gresham, April 19, 1888, Gresham Papers; John B. Elam and Louis T. Michener to Benjamin Harrison, June 17, 1888, Harrison Papers; Gresham, *Life of W. Q. Gresham*, II, 581.

4.　C. B. Farwell to Walter Q. Gresham, May 24, 1888, Gresham Papers; MSQ to John Sherman, June 12, 1888, and M. A. Hanna to John Sherman, June 22, 1888, both in Sherman Papers; Hoar, *Autobiography*, I, 412–13; Gresham, *Life of W. Q. Gresham*, II, 590–96; Sievers,

Harrison, Hoosier Statesman, p. 336; Leland L. Sage, *William Boyd Allison: A Study of Practical Politics* (Iowa City: State Historical Society of Iowa, 1956), p. 224.

5. Charles Foster to John Sherman, June 27, 1888, Sherman Papers; Foraker, *Notes*, I, 363, 389, 428.

6. Hoar, *Autobiography*, I, 413; Gresham, *Life of W. Q. Gresham*, II, 579.

7. Foraker, *Notes*, I, 390; Depew, *Memories*, p. 131.

8. M. A. Dodge to Stephen B. Elkins, January 24, 1888, and James S. Clarkson to Stephen B. Elkins, May 18, 1888, both in Elkins Papers.

9. Louis T. Michener to Stephen B. Elkins, March 19, May 5, and May 11, 1888, and James S. Clarkson to Stephen B. Elkins, May 18, 1888, Elkins Papers; Foraker, *Notes*, I, 340.

10. James S. Clarkson to Stephen B. Elkins, May 18, 1888, Elkins Papers.

11. M. A. Hanna to John Sherman (telegram), June 22, 1888, and Charles Foster to John Sherman, June 27, 1888, both in Sherman Papers.

12. Foraker, *Notes*, I, 316-17, 338-39.

13. Ibid., 391-92.

14. Platt, *Autobiography*, p. 111; Gresham, *Life of W. Q. Gresham*, II, 576, 578.

15. Thomas C. Platt to Benjamin Harrison, July 7, 1888, Harrison Papers; Gosnell, *Boss Platt*, pp. 34-35.

16. Welch, *George F. Hoar*, p. 140.

17. John B. Elam and Louis T. Michener to Benjamin Harrison, June 17, 1888, Harrison Papers; Sievers, *Harrison, Hoosier Statesman*, pp. 336-37.

18. Draft of proposed letter of Benjamin Harrison to Thomas M. Bayne, June ____, 1888, Harrison Papers.

19. John Sherman to MSQ, June 26, 1888, MSQ Papers; *The Great Conspiracy of Four Years Ago: An Inside History of the Remarkable Campaign in Which Harrison Defeated Cleveland* (pamphlet, 1892), p. 4.

7. The Making of a President: 1888

1. Sievers, *Harrison, Hoosier Statesman*, p. 367; Marcus, *Grand Old Party*, pp. 125-26.

2. Leach, "Twenty Years with Quay," July 3, 1904; *Great Conspiracy* (pamphlet), p. 4; Frank W. Leach to Albert T. Volwiler, July 20, 1938, box 2, Quay Family Papers; Marcus, *Grand Old Party*, p. 102.

3. Harry R. Smith to Benjamin Harrison, July 9, 1888, and John Sherman to Benjamin Harrison, July 13, 1888, both in Harrison Papers; Benjamin Harrison to John Sherman, July 14, 1888, Sherman Papers; MSQ to James M. Swank, July 17, 1888, Swank Papers; *Great Conspiracy*, p. 5.

4. Louis T. Michener, "Organization of National Committee in 1888," typed manuscript in Michener Papers; Louis T. Michener to Stephen B. Elkins, July 30, 1888, Elkins Papers.

5. *New York World*, July 12 and 13, 1888, PC, II, 79 and 83; *New York Press*, July 13, 1888, PC, II, 84.

6. MSQ to Benjamin Harrison, July 30, 1888, Harrison Papers; *New York World*, October 11, 1888, PC, II, 536.

7. *Matthew Stanley Quay, A Man of the People* (pamphlet), p. 2, Quay Family Papers; MSQ, "The Man or the Platform?" p. 514; Leach, "Twenty Years with Quay," July 3, 1904.

8. *Great Conspiracy*, p. 5.

9. *New York Evening Telegram*, August 6, 1888, PC, II, 223.

10. Hirshson, *Farewell to the Bloody Shirt*, pp. 157, 162.

11. Marcus, *Grand Old Party*, pp. 132-33.

12. Michener, "Organization of National Committee"; Gibbons, *Wanamaker*, I, 258-59; Josephson, *Politicos*, pp. 423-24.

13. *New York Evening Post*, August 22, 1888, PC, II, 305; *New York Daily Graphic*, September 14, 1888, PC, II, 381; *New York Commercial Advertiser*, September 16, 1888, PC, II, 386; *New York Morning Journal*, September 27, 1888, PC, II, 443.

14. *New York Morning Journal*, September 14, 1888, PC, II, 379; Ellis P. Oberholtzer, *A History of the United States since the Civil War*, 5 vols. (New York: Macmillan, 1926-1937), V, 44, 53.

15. Disbursements of the Republican National Committee, 1888, 26 pp., MSQ Papers; *New York Star*, September 14, 15, and 24, 1888, PC, II, 378, 384, and 412; *New York Press*, September 15, 1888, PC, II, 383; *New York Morning Journal*, September 23, 1888, PC, II, 411.

16. Oberholtzer, *United States*, V, 44, 53; *New York Star*, October 19, 1888, PC, II, 617.

17. Michener, "Organization of National Committee"; Stoddard, *As I Knew Them*, p. 169; *New York Times*, August 2, 1888; *New York Evening World*, October 20, 1888, PC, II, 778.

18. Benjamin Harrison to MSQ, September 12, 1888, MSQ Papers; Michener, "Organization of National Committee"; Sievers, *Harrison, Hoosier Statesman*, p. 378.

19. *New York Times*, August 8, 1888, PC, II, 241.

20. John Sherman to Benjamin Harrison, August 4, 1888, Harrison Papers; *New York Star*, August 11 and 15, 1888, PC, II, 258 and 279.

21. *New York World*, August 12, 1888, PC, II, 263; *New York Graphic*, August 12, 1888, PC, II, 266; *New York Evening Post*, August 16, 1888, PC, II, 282.

22. *New York Morning Journal*, August 27, 1888, PC, II, 321; *New York Evening Post*, August 28, 1888, PC, II, 325; *New York Herald*, September 30 and October 5, 1888, PC, II, 458 and 481.

23. Albert T. Volwiler, ed., *The Correspondence between Benjamin Harrison and James G. Blaine, 1882-1893* (Philadelphia: American Philosophical Society, 1940), p. 35; James S. Clarkson to Benjamin Harrison, October 1, 1888, Harrison Papers; *New York Times*, September 1, 1888, PC, II, 345; *New York World*, October 1, 1888, PC, II, 801.

24. MSQ to Louis T. Michener, September 20, 1888, Harrison Papers.

25. *Beaver Radical*, February 24, 1871.

26. James G. Blaine to Benjamin Harrison, July 10, 1888, Harrison Papers; *Great Conspiracy*, p. 7.

27. *Brooklyn Eagle*, October 8, 1888, PC, II, 488; *New York World*, October 31, 1888, PC, II, 789.

28. *New York Times*, October 8, 1888, PC, II, 489; *New York Morning Journal*, October 15, 1888, PC, II, 568.

29. *New York Sun*, October 24, 1888, PC, II, 669; *New York Times*, October 25, 1888, PC, II, 594.

30. Leach, "Twenty Years with Quay," October 23, 1904; *Great Conspiracy*, p. 7; "The Strategy of National Campaigns," p. 490.

31. Leach, "Twenty Years with Quay," October 23, 1904.

32. *Great Conspiracy*, p. 7; *New York Morning Journal*, October 22, 1888, PC, II, 636; *New York Herald*, October 23, 1888, PC, II, 644.

33. *New York Times*, October 23 and 24, 1888, PC, II, 652 and 666; *Great Conspiracy*, p. 8.

34. Leach, "Twenty Years with Quay," October 23, 1904; *New York Times*, February 20, 1905.

35. "The Strategy of National Campaigns," p. 491.

36. Leach, "Twenty Years with Quay," October 23, 1904; *Great Conspiracy*, p. 9.

37. Richard R. Quay to Isaac R. Pennypacker, March 9, 1927, copy in box 3, Quay Family Papers; Gresham, *Life of W. Q. Gresham*, II, 603.

38. Nevins, *Grover Cleveland*, pp. 436-37; Gresham, *Life of W. Q. Gresham*, II, 603-06.

39. Hinckley, "Osgoodby and the Murchison Letter," pp. 359, 361, 366; Leach, "Twenty Years with Quay," October 23, 1904.

40. New York Evening Telegram, October 30, 1888, PC, II, 764; New York Graphic, October 31, 1888, PC, II, 783.

41. Disbursements of Republican National Committee; Wharton Barker to Levi P. Morton, August 13, 1888, MSQ Papers; Welch, George F. Hoar, p. 140.

42. Disbursements of Republican National Committee; Statement of "Mr. Ford's Requirements" for organizing New York City, MSQ Papers; Dobson, Politics in the Gilded Age, pp. 154-55.

43. Wharton Barker to Levi P. Morton, August 13, 1888, MSQ Papers; Wharton Barker to Benjamin Harrison, August 6, 1888, Harrison Papers; Bernardo, "Election of 1888," pp. 296-97.

44. Leach, "Twenty Years with Quay," October 23, 1904; Great Conspiracy, pp. 11-12.

45. Great Conspiracy, p. 3; New York Morning Journal, November 7, 1888, PC, II, 979.

46. Marcus, Grand Old Party, p. 148.

47. Oberholtzer, United States, V, 71-72; Gosnell, Boss Platt, pp. 35-36; Stoddard, It Costs to Be President, p. 180; Williams, Years of Decision, p. 55; New York Tribune, November 5, 1888, PC, II, 930; Disbursements of Republican National Committee.

48. Disbursements of Republican National Committee; MSQ to Benjamin Harrison, January 18, 1889, Harrison Papers.

49. Ginger, Age of Excess, p. 116.

50. Theodore Roosevelt to Henry Cabot Lodge, October, 19, 1888, Selections from the Correspondence of Theodore Roosevelt and Henry Cabot Lodge, 1884-1918, 2 vols. (New York: Charles Scribner's Sons, 1925), I, 72-73; Bernardo, "Election of 1888," p. 297.

51. Sidney DeKay to MSQ, November 7, 1888 and James S. Clarkson to MSQ, November 9, 1888, both in MSQ Papers; M. S. Quay and the Great Campaign of 1888: What His Colleagues of the Republican National Committee Think of Him (pamphlet, 1891), Quay Family Papers.

52. Leach, "Twenty Years with Quay," July 3, 1904; Hirshson, Bloody Shirt, pp. 166-67; Lambert, Gorman, p. 145.

53. Disbursements of Republican National Committee; Great Conspiracy, p. 10; New York Tribune, November 6, 1888, PC, II, 959.

54. A. C. Thompson to MSQ, November 14, 1888, Quay Family Papers; Leach, "Twenty Years with Quay," July 3, 1904; New York Star, November 18, 1888, PC, II, 1118.

55. MSQ to Benjamin Harrison, November 8, 1888, Harrison Papers.

8. Altruism Versus Practical Politics: 1889-1890

1. New York Herald, November 11, 1888, PC, II, 1049; New York World, November 12, 1888, PC, II, 1063.

2. Benjamin Harrison to MSQ, November 22, 1888, MSQ Papers.

3. New York Times, December 19 and 21, 1888, PC, II, 1318 and 1339.

4. Ibid.; New York World, December 22, 1888, PC, II, 1349.

5. New York Herald, December 20, 1888, PC, II, 1334; McClure, Old Time Notes, II, 572-73; Gibbons, Wanamaker, I, 260.

6. New York Times, December 20, 1888, PC, II, 1328; New York Tribune, December 20 and 21, 1888, PC, II, 1335 and 1345; New York World, December 22, 1888, PC, II, 1352.

7. Thomas C. Platt to Russell A. Alger, December 25, 1888, Alger Papers; Platt, Autobiography, p. 210; Stoddard, As I Knew Them, p. 170; Ginger, Age of Excess, p. 106.

8. Thomas C. Platt to Louis T. Michener, January 18, 1889, Michener Papers; Platt, Autobiography, pp. 206-10.

9. Gresham, Life of W. Q. Gresham, II, 609; Dozer, "Harrison and 1892," p. 50.

10. Thomas C. Platt to Russell A. Alger, December 25, 1888, Alger Papers; *Matthew Stanley Quay: A Man of the People* (pamphlet, c. 1898); Gibbons, *Wanamaker*, I, 263, 339.

11. MSQ to Benjamin Harrison, February 15 and 28, 1889, Harrison Papers; Benjamin Harrison to MSQ, February 21, 1889, copy in Harrison Papers; MSQ to James S. Clarkson, n.d., box 1, Clarkson Papers; Hirshson, "Clarkson Versus Harrison," p. 219.

12. Benjamin Harrison to Wharton Barker, February 5 and 12, 1889, copies in Harrison Papers; Benjamin Harrison to Russell A. Alger, February 5, 1889, Alger Papers; Marcus, *Grand Old Party*, pp. 156–57.

13. Leach, "Twenty Years with Quay," July 3, 1904.

14. Ibid.; Frank W. Leach to Albert T. Volwiler, July 20, 1938, copy in box 2, Quay Family Papers; Richard R. Quay to Isaac Pennypacker, March 9, 1927, copy in MSQ Papers.

15. Cullom, *Fifty Years*, p. 248.

16. *Chicago Herald*, October 29, 1889, PC, III, 1; Richard R. Quay to James A. Kehl, August 3, 1959, in possession of recipient.

17. *Pittsburgh Dispatch*, November 13, 1889, PC, III, 396.

18. *Kansas City Star*, November 11, 1889, PC, III, 373.

19. Dozer, "Harrison and 1892," pp. 51–52; Mary Lucille O'Marra, "Quay and Harrison from 1888 to 1892," MA thesis, Catholic University of America, 1956, pp. 32–33.

20. O'Marra, "Quay and Harrison," pp. 36–37.

21. Joseph R. Dillon to MSQ, December 5, 1888, MSQ to Benjamin Harrison, March 11 and 18, May 9, and June 15, 1889, all in Harrison Papers.

22. MSQ to Benjamin Harrison, October 4, 1889, Harrison Papers; Williams, *Years of Decision*, p. 59.

23. MSQ to G. F. Little, September 17, 1890, and Benjamin Harrison to MSQ, April 15, 1892, Harrison Papers.

24. *Philadelphia Record*, November 19, 1889, PC, III, 529; *Philadelphia Press*, November 20, 1889, PC, III, 562; *Boston Herald*, November 29, 1889, PC, IV, 187; *Chicago News*, November 30, 1889, PC, IV, 212; *Savannah Morning News*, December 23, 1889, PC, V, 83.

25. *Hartford Times*, November 20, 1889, PC, III, 538; *Kansas City Times*, January 27, 1890, PC, V, 456.

26. *St. Louis Republican* and *Kansas City Star*, February 4, PC, V, 546 and 548.

27. *Philadelphia Record*, December 23, 1889, PC, V, 77; *Portland Argus* (Maine), December 27, 1889, PC, V, 142.

28. *New York Saturday Globe*, February 8, 1890, PC, V, 577.

29. *Kansas City Times*, December 29, 1889, PC, V, 167; *New York Star*, February 7, 1890, PC, V, 562.

30. *Man of the People*, p. 5.

31. Cullom, *Fifty Years*, p. 253; *New York City Globe*, March 29, 1890, PC, VII, 41.

32. Hirshson, *Bloody Shirt*, p. 227; "Fundamental Fallacy," p. 5.

33. Hoar, *Autobiography*, II, 151–53; Welch, "Federal Elections Bill," pp. 511–12, 514; Williams, *Years of Decision*, pp. 30–31.

34. *Pittsburgh Commercial Gazette*, April 28, 1890.

35. Ibid.

36. Oliver, "Quay," p. 7.

37. Hirshson, *Bloody Shirt*, pp. 202–03.

38. Lambert, *Gorman*, pp. 147–48; *New York World*, March 17, 1890, PC, VI, 483.

39. Hirshson, *Bloody Shirt*, pp. 222–23; *New York Post*, November 23, 1889, PC, III, 607.

40. *New York World*, March 26, 1890, and *Mobile Register*, March 30, 1890, PC, VII, 9 and 85; Ginger, *Age of Excess*, p. 76.

41. Ginger, *Age of Excess*, p. 76.

42. Leon B. Richardson, *William Chandler, Republican* (New York: Dodd, Mead & Co., 1940), p. 413; Lambert, *Gorman*, pp. 147, 149; Welch, "Federal Elections Bill," p. 516.

43. Gresham, *Life of W. Q. Gresham*, II, 813; Welch, "Federal Elections Bill," p. 515; Williams, *Years of Decision*, pp. 37, 82.

44. Dorothy G. Fowler, *John Coit Spooner: Defender of Presidents* (New York: University Publishers, 1961), p. 138.

45. Coolidge, *Old-Fashioned Senator*, p. 234; DeSantis, *Republicans Face the Southern Question*, pp. 207-09.

46. *Cong. Rec.*, 51st Cong., 1st sess., XXI, pt. 9, 8586.

47. Hoar, *Autobiography*, II, 156; Coolidge, *Old-Fashioned Senator*, pp. 231-32; *How Quay's Clever Move Saved the McKinley Bill* (pamphlet, c. 1892), p. 2, Quay Family Papers.

48. *Man of the People*, p. 6; McClure, *Old Time Notes*, II, 480.

49. Hoar, *Autobiography*, II, 156; Lambert, *Gorman*, pp. 154-59.

9. Trial by Newspaper: 1889-1890

1. *Philadelphia Press*, quoted in *New York Evening Post*, December 11, 1888, and *New York Saturday Globe*, October 26, 1889, PC, II, 1275 and 2803.

2. "Remarks of J. S. Clarkson on Accepting the Chairmanship of the Republican National Committee," box 3, Clarkson Papers.

3. Ibid.; *Philadelphia Record*, October 22, 1889, and *Philadelphia Evening Bulletin*, October 24, 1889, PC, II, 2729 and 2775; *Nation*, November 7, 1889, PC, III, 258.

4. MSQ to Benjamin Harrison, October 22, 1889, Harrison Papers; *Minneapolis Tribune*, November 9, 1889, PC, III, 284.

5. *Pittsburgh Chronicle Telegraph*, September 24, 1889, PC, II, 2186; *Philadelphia Record*, December 30, 1889, PC, V, 177.

6. "Statement of Wm Shaw Bowen made June 2, 1890," pp. 1, 9-10, MSQ Papers. This is a first person, handwritten, 33-page report detailing the places visited, the individuals interviewed, and the general character of their remarks. The results of Bowen's search appeared in the *New York World*, February 10 and March 3, 1890. How Senator Quay or his family came to possess Bowen's statement is not known.

7. Ibid., pp. 10-11, 14-18, 21, 24.

8. Ibid., p. 26.

9. *New York World*, February 10, 1890, PC, V, 596; *Shreveport Caucasian*, February 14, 1890, PC, VI, 49.

10. *New York World*, February 10, 1890 (chs. 1 and 3), PC, V, 599.

11. Ibid., (ch. 4).

12. Ibid.

13. *Cong. Rec.*, 51st Cong., 2nd sess., XXVI, pt. 3, 2731; "Statement of W. S. Bowen," p. 23.

14. *New York World*, February 10, 1890 (ch. 5), PC, V, 599.

15. Ibid.; Blankenburg, "Forty Years," p. 124; *Cong. Rec.*, 51st Cong., 2nd sess., XXII, pt. 3, 2731.

16. *New York World*, February 10, 1890 (ch. 6), PC, V, 599.

17. Ibid.; *New Haven Commercial Register*, April 19, 1890, PC, VII, 520; McClure, *Old Time Notes*, II, 504-05.

18. *New York World*, February 10, 1890, PC, V, 599.

19. Ibid., March 3, 1890, PC, VI, 295; *Matthew S. Quay: The Kind of Man This Republican Leader Is* (pamphlet, reprinted from the *New York Evening Post*, 1890), pp. 10-12.

20.   *Little Rock Gazette*, February 21, 1890, *Buffalo Times*, February 23, 1890, and *St Louis Post-Dispatch*, March 13, 1890, PC, VI, 110, 130, and 412.

21.   Henry C. Lea to Benjamin Harrison, April 8, 1890, reprinted in *Quay: The Kind of Man*, pp. 15-16.

22.   Ibid.; *New York Times*, April 14, 1890, PC, VII, 371.

23.   *New York Evening Post*, April 1, 1890, and *Newark Evening News*, April 15, 1890, PC, VII, 312 and 413; *Atlanta Journal*, April 21, 1890, and *Springfield Republican*, May 14, 1890, PC, VIII, 61 and 521.

24.   *St. Louis Post-Dispatch*, May 2, 1890, PC, VIII, 350; *Scranton Truth*, quoted in *New York World*, May 27, 1890, PC, IX, 122.

25.   *Chicago Post*, May 1, 1890, *New York World*, May 20, 1890, and *New York Post*, May 23, 1890, PC, VIII, 314, 626, and 646; *New York World*, June 17, 1890, PC, X, 52.

26.   *New York World*, June 1, 1890, and *Hacketstown Republican* (New Jersey), June 6, 1890, PC, IX, 278 and 443.

27.   *St. Louis Post-Dispatch*, May 2, 1890, PC, VIII, 350; *Macon Telegraph* (Georgia), May 27, 1890, and *Spokane Falls Chronicle* (Washington), May 29, 1890, PC, IX, 116 and 205.

28.   *New York Post*, May 7, 1890, and *St. Louis Republican*, May 9, 1890, PC, VIII, 429 and 467; *Newark News*, August 9, 1890, PC, XII, 532; MSQ to James A. Beaver, (n.d. in 1890), Beaver Manuscripts.

29.   *Atlanta Journal* and *New York Herald*, September 4, 1890, PC, XIII, 478 and 493.

30.   "Representative Kennedy's Speech," pp. 519-20; *New York Evening Post*, September 4, 1890, PC, XIII, 508; *Binghamton Leader*, September 10, 1890, and *New York World*, September 15, 1890, PC, XIV, 122 and 249.

31.   *Buffalo Express*, *New York Commercial Advertiser*, and *New York World*, September 15, 1890, PC, XIV, 241, 244, and 249.

32.   *Buffalo Express*, September 17, 1890, and *New York Times*, September 18, 1890, PC, XIV, 329 and 378.

33.   *Laramie Boomerang*, September 8, 1890, PC, XIV, 71.

34.   *New York World*, November 7, 1890, PC, XVII, 52; *New York Evening Post*, October 23, 1890, PC, XVI, 179; *Inter-Ocean* (Chicago), November 20, 1890, PC, XVII, 405.

35.   *Elmira Gazette*, June 20, 1890, PC, X, 131; *Illustrated American*, October 25, 1890, PC, XVI, 226.

36.   Bradley, *Lea*, pp. 201-02.

37.   Letter of Henry C. Lea to the Republicans of Pennsylvania, July 9, 1890, quoted in the *New York Evening Post*, July 12, 1890, PC, XII, 92.

38.   *New York Star*, June 8, 1890, PC, IX, 503; *Newark Journal*, June 28, 1890, PC, X, 265; *New York World*, July 9, 1890, PC, XII, 9.

39.   *New York World*, September 29, 1890, and *Atlanta Constitution*, October 1, 1890, PC, XV, 74 and 118.

40.   *New York Commercial Advertiser*, October 6, 1890, PC, XV, 125; *New Orleans States*, October 28, 1890, PC, XVI, 263.

41.   *Brooklyn Citizen*, October 4, 1890, PC, XV, 198; *Illustrated American*, October 25, 1890, PC, XVI, 226.

42.   *New York World*, October 4, 1890, PC, XV, 191.

43.   Ibid.; *Chicago Times*, October 4, 1890, PC, XV, 194.

44.   *Washington Post and Every Evening* (Wilmington), October 6, 1890, PC, XV, 250 and 256.

45.   *Union-Standard* (Brooklyn), November 6, 1890, PC, XVII, 2.

10. The Unmaking of a President: 1891-1893

1. *Cong. Rec.*, 51st Cong., 2nd sess., XXVI, pt. 3, 2731.

2. *New York Evening Sun*, February 16, 1891, and *Atlanta Journal*, February 17, 1891, PC, XX, 139 and 188.

3. *Cong. Rec.*, 51st Cong., 2nd sess., XXVI, pt. 3, 2732.

4. *Grand Rapids Eagle*, February 17, 1891, *Richmond Times*, February 18, 1891, and *Pottsville Miners Journal*, February 18, 1891, PC, XX, 207, 429, and 431.

5. *Chicago Herald*, October 29, 1889, PC, III, 1.

6. *St. Louis Republic*, April 20, 1892, PC, XLIII, 180.

7. *New York Times*, June 13, 1891, and *York Age*, June 23, 1891, PC, XXIV, 283 and 502.

8. *Washington Post*, June 30, 1891, and *Doylestown Intelligencer*, July 2, 1891, PC, XXV, 29 and 198.

9. *North American* (Philadelphia), June 30, 1891, PC, XXIV, 568; *Philadelphia Item*, July 8, 1891, PC, XXV, 361.

10. *Rochester Herald* (New York), July 10, 1891, and *Pittsburgh Leader*, July 21, 1891, PC, XXVI, 131 and 471; *Louisville Courier-Journal*, July 30, 1891, PC, XXVIII, 148.

11. *Buffalo Express*, July 30, 1891, and *Chicago News*, July 30, 1891, PC, XXVIII, 166 and 209.

12. *Pittsburgh Times*, April 23, 1891, PC, XXII, 357.

13. *Scranton Times*, June 3, 1891, PC, XXIV, 28.

14. Resolve of the Republican County Committee of Lawrence County, August 15, 1891, Resolve of the Republicans of Mercer County, Thomas S. Butler to MSQ, August 3 and 7, 1891, J. C. Sturtevant to MSQ, August 15, 1891, all in MSQ Papers.

15. Quoted in Muzzey, *Blaine*, p. 469.

16. Knoles, *Campaign and Election of 1892*, p. 37; "Republican Tactics in Pennsylvania," p. 154.

17. *New York Evening Post*, August 19, 1891, PC, XXXI, 315.

18. *Pittsburgh Dispatch*, July 10, 1891, PC, XXV, 433; *Pittsburgh Post*, July 23, 1891, PC, XXXIV, 421.

19. Edwin K. Martin to MSQ, May 13, 1892, and J. R. Dean to MSQ, May 13, 1892, both in MSQ Papers.

20. MSQ to Edward McPherson, October 10, 1891, XL, McPherson Papers.

21. Coral Quay to MSQ (telegrams), January 19 and 22, 1892, MSQ Papers; *Pittsburgh Dispatch*, February 2, 1892, and *New York Tribune*, February 26, 1892, PC, XXXIX, 84 and 577.

22. *Memphis Appeal Avalanche*, November 1, 1891, and *Philadelphia Press*, November 6, 1891, PC, XXXVI, 54 and 162.

23. *Jacksonville Times-Union*, February 21, 1891, PC, XXI, 158; *Doylestown Intelligencer*, August 5, 1891, PC, XXX, 45.

24. Platt, *Autobiography*, p. 246; Depew, *Memories*, p. 135; *Philadelphia Times*, December 2, 1891, PC, XXXVII, 40; *Chicago News*, February 10, 1892, PC, XXXIX, 234.

25. James G. Blaine to James S. Clarkson, February 6, 1892, quoted in Muzzey, *Blaine*, p. 471; Gosnell, *Boss Platt*, p. 112.

26. Letter to MSQ, April 25, 1892, MSQ Papers. Signature is illegible; perhaps "John McMilla."

27. "Republican Tactics in Pennsylvania," p. 154; *Santa Barbara Independent*, February 17, 1892, PC, XXXIX, 349; *Seattle Telegraph*, June 2, 1892, PC, XLIX, 8.

28. *New York Evening Post*, April 11, 1892, PC, XLII, 282; *Brooklyn Citizen*, May 30, 1892, PC, XLVII, 140.

29. *Tacoma Record*, June 11, 1890, PC, X, 1.

30. Bloom, "Philadelphia *North American*," p. 429.

31. Russell A. Alger to MSQ, April 30, 1892, MSQ Papers; *Philadelphia Bulletin*, April 21, 1892, PC, XLIII, 59.

32. Thomas C. Platt to MSQ, April 29, 1892, and Harrison Gray Otis to MSQ, April 14, 1892, MSQ Papers.

33. *Louisville Post*, May 9, 1892, PC, XLIV, 267.

34. P. A. B. Widener to Walter Q. Gresham, January 15, 1892, and Walter Q. Gresham to P. A. B. Widener, January 21, 1892, both in Gresham Papers.

35. Russell A. Alger to MSQ, April 30, 1892, MSQ Papers.

36. Platt, *Autobiography*, p. 489; Louis T. Michener, "The Minneapolis Convention of June 7th to 10th," a typed manuscript in the Michener Papers, p. 4; *New York Evening Sun*, May 7, 1892, PC, XLIII, 370; *Detroit Free Press*, May 20, 1892, PC, XLV, 248; Hirshson, "Clarkson Versus Harrison," p. 220.

37. Muzzey, *Blaine*, p. 472; *Wilkes-Barre Record*, August 15, 1891, PC, XXIX, 571; Stoddard, *It Costs to Be President*, p. 187.

38. *Doylestown Intelligencer*, August 5, 1891, PC, XXX, 45.

39. Louis T. Michener, "Harrison Prior to the National Convention of 1892," a typed manuscript in the Michener Papers, p. 1; Dozer, "Harrison and 1892," p. 53.

40. Michener, "Harrison Prior to 1892," p. 2; Stoddard, *As I Knew Them*, pp. 179-80; *Albany Argus*, May 18, 1892, PC, XLV, 184.

41. George E. Vickers to MSQ, December 26, 1891, MSQ Papers; *North American*, June 11, 1892, *Easton Express*, June 13, 1892, and *Lebanon Report*, June 14, 1892, PC, L, 204, 393, and 467.

42. Depew, *Memories*, p. 134.

43. Michener, *"Minneapolis Convention,"* p. 6.

44. James G. Blaine to Russell A. Alger, November 5, 1891, Alger Papers.

45. Michener, *"Minneapolis Convention,"* pp. 7-8.

46. Ibid.

47. Harold U. Faulkner, *Politics, Reform and Expansion, 1890-1900* (New York: Harper & Row, 1959), p. 127.

48. Michener, "Minneapolis Convention," p. 10; Peck, *Twenty Years of the Republic*, p. 285.

49. James S. Clarkson to MSQ, April 27, 1892, MSQ Papers.

50. *Savannah Press*, May 31, 1892, PC, XLVIII, 264.

51. *St. Louis Republic*, June 5, 1892, PC, XLVII, 420.

52. *Proceedings of the Tenth Republican National Convention* (Minneapolis: Harrison and Smith Co., Printers, 1892), pp. 62-63; *Philadelphia Inquirer*, June 11, 1892, PC, L, 191; *Youngstown Vindicator*, June 10, 1892, PC, LI, 377; Williams, *Years of Decision*, p. 63.

53. Michener, "Minneapolis Convention," pp. 11-13; *Philadelphia Inquirer*, June 11, 1892, PC, L, 191.

54. *Proceedings of the Tenth Republican Convention*, p. 69; Gresham, *Life of W. Q. Gresham*, II, 663.

55. *Proceedings of the Tenth Republican Convention*, pp. 98-102, 106.

56. Ibid., pp. 113-14; *St. Paul Globe*, June 11, 1892, and *Chicago Tribune*, June 13, 1892, PC, L, 5 and 380.

57. Michener, "Minneapolis Convention," p. 16; *Roanoke Times*, June 11, 1892, PC, L, 53.

58. Thomas S. Bigelow to Richard Quay (n.d.), MSQ Papers.

59. Knoles, *Campaign and Election of 1892*, pp. 147-48; Dozer, "Harrison and 1892," p. 76.

60. Frank W. Leach to A. T. Volwiler, July 20, 1938, box 2, Quay Family Papers; Stoddard, *As I Knew Them*, p. 168; Dozer, "Harrison and 1892," pp. 75-77.

61.   William E. Chandler to Edward McPherson, July 21, 1893, McPherson Papers; Josephson, *Politicos*, p. 513; Stoddard, *As I Knew Them*, p. 179; George Harvey, *Henry Clay Frick* (New York: Charles Scribner's Sons, 1928), p. 157.

62.   David Martin to MSQ, November 4 and 7, 1892, MSQ Papers.

63.   *Pottsville Chronicle*, June 13, 1891, PC, XXIV, 282.

64.   *Philadelphia Record*, October 8, 1891, PC, XXXIV, 106.

65.   Pennsylvania Republican Association, *Republicanism vs. Quayism* (pamphlet, 1892), MSQ Papers; *Washington Post*, February 18, 1892, and *Pittsburgh Dispatch*, February 19, 1892, PC, XXXIX, 381 and 412.

66.   MSQ to John Livingston, July 4, 1890, Harrison Papers.

67.   *Pennsylvania's Representation in the U.S. Senate* and *Which Is the Greater Statesman?* (pamphlets), both in MSQ Papers.

68.   *Philadelphia Press*, January 7, 1892.

69.   *Which Is the Greater Statesman?*, p. 3.

70.   *The True Story about Senator Quay's Occasional Trips to Florida* (pamphlet), Quay Family Papers; *Great Conspiracy; New York Times*, February 21, 1892, and *New York Press*, February 22, 1892, PC, XXXIX, 508 and 513; *Louisville Courier-Journal*, March 10, 1892, PC, XL, 131.

71.   *Corporation John* (pamphlet), Quay Family Papers.

72.   *Pottsville Chronicle*, December 18, 1891, PC, XXXVIII, 345; *Philadelphia Inquirer*, February 25, 1892, PC, XXXIX, 564.

73.   T. L. Eyre to MSQ, January 6, 1892, MSQ Papers.

74.   Campaign Committee, 134th Regiment, Pennsylvania Volunteers to Its Membership, March 15, 1892, MSQ Papers.

75.   James S. Clarkson to MSQ, April 27, 1892, MSQ Papers.

76.   MSQ to A. K. McClure, January 19, 1893, Autograph Collection of Simon Gratz, Historical Society of Pennsylvania.

77.   Ibid.; McClure, *Old Time Notes*, II, 585.

11. The Sphinx Speaks: 1894-1896

1.   MSQ to William McKinley, December 15, 1896, McKinley Papers.

2.   Lambert, *Gorman*, pp. 184-87, 199.

3.   MSQ to James M. Swank, March 14, 1894, Swank Papers.

4.   Clark, *My Quarter Century*, II, 325; Ida Tarbell, *The Tariff in Our Time* (New York: Macmillan, 1911), p. 228; Blankenburg, "Forty Years," p. 234.

5.   James M. Swank to Edward McPherson, September 17, 1894, McPherson Papers; Lambert, *Gorman*, pp. 210, 212-14.

6.   Lambert, *Gorman*, pp. 219-22.

7.   Unidentified newspaper clipping, MSQ Papers.

8.   *Cong. Rec.*, 53rd Cong., 2nd sess., XXVI, pt. 5, 4371-72.

9.   Ibid., XXVI, pt. 4, 3440, 3443.

10.   Ibid., XXVI, pt. 3, 2833; Senate Report No. 606, 53rd Cong., 2nd sess.

11.   Senate Report No. 606, 53rd Cong., 2nd sess.; Tarbell, *Tariff in Our Time*, p. 227.

12.   Senate Report No. 606, 53rd Cong., 2nd sess. A note to Quay from John S. Hopkins of the Peoples Bank of Philadelphia in the MSQ Papers indicates that Quay lost more than $43,900 on the sale of 2,000 shares of sugar stock. The note from Hopkins, who handled all of the senator's stock transactions, is dated December 11, 1894, but does not provide the date on which the stock was sold.

13.   *New York World*, January 26, 1891, PC, XIX, 354; Peck, *Twenty Years*, p. 363; Merrill,

Cleveland, p. 189; Nathaniel W. Stephenson, *Nelson W. Aldrich: A Leader in American Politics* (New York: Charles Scribner's Sons, 1930), p. 120.

14.   Senate Report No. 606, 53rd Cong., 2nd sess.; Leach, "Twenty Years with Quay," July 3, 1904.

15.   Daniel H. Hastings to MSQ, January 20 and November 12, 1894, MSQ Papers; McClure, *Old Time Notes*, II, 586.

16.   McClure, *Old Time Notes*, II, 592; Davenport, *Power and Glory*, pp. 106-07.

17.   Davenport, *Power and Glory*, p. 109.

18.   Josh Nobie to MSQ, March 31, 1895, and A. K. McClure to MSQ, January 12, 1895, both in MSQ Papers.

19.   A. K. McClure to MSQ, February 4, 1895, MSQ Papers.

20.   McClure, *Old Time Notes*, II, 594; Dunn, *From Harrison to Harding*, I, 121.

21.   Leach, "Twenty Years with Quay," November 6, 1904.

22.   Frank Reeder to MSQ, April 4, 1895, Josh Nobie to MSQ, March 31, 1895, and Boies Penrose to MSQ, April 4, 1895 (2 letters), all in MSQ Papers.

23.   Boies Penrose to MSQ, April 4, 1895 (2 letters), MSQ Papers.

24.   Boies Penrose to MSQ (telegram), May 8, 1895, MSQ Papers; *Burlington Free Press* (Iowa), August 29, 1895, and *Pittsburgh Commercial Gazette*, August 29, 1895, PC, LII, 214 and 229.

25.   *New York Press*, August 29, 1895, PC, LII, 144.

26.   James M. Swank to Edward McPherson, July 30 and August 2, 1895, McPherson Papers.

27.   J. W. Gates to W. M. Douglas, August 29, 1895 (copy), MSQ Papers.

28.   *Utica Observer*, August 29, 1895, and *Pittsburgh Post*, August 31, 1895, PC, LII, 273 and 410.

29.   Samuel B. Dick to MSQ, July 1, 1895, Harry S. Levan and J. Albert Reber to MSQ, July 3, 1895, E. R. W. Searle to MSQ, July 31, 1895, all in MSQ Papers.

30.   "Senator Quay as a Reformer," p. 910.

31.   McClure, *Old Time Notes*, II, 588-89.

32.   *Cleveland Plain-Dealer*, August 29, 1895, PC, LII, 280; *Wilkes-Barre Record-Times*, September 2, 1895, PC, LIII, 44; Leach, "Twenty Years with Quay," November 27, 1904.

33.   John P. Persch to MSQ, May 2, 1895, MSQ Papers; MSQ to William McKinley, May 15, 1895, McKinley Papers; *New York Evening Post*, August 30, 1895, PC, LII, 294.

34.   *Huntingdon News* (Pennsylvania), August 29, 1895, PC, LII, 208.

35.   *Nashville Banner*, August 28, 1895, and *Cleveland Plain-Dealer*, August 29, 1895, PC, LII, 91 and 280.

36.   Stackpole, *Behind the Scenes*, p. 98.

37.   Joseph G. Cannon to MSQ, August 29, 1895, MSQ Papers; *Detroit Tribune*, September 3, 1895, PC, LIII, 64.

38.   *Kansas City Star*, August 29, 1895, PC, LII, 185. Arthur P. Gorman and Calvin S. Brice were Democratic leaders from Maryland and Ohio, respectively.

39.   Andrew Carnegie to MSQ, December 14, 1895, MSQ Papers; Andrew Carnegie to James M. Swank, quoted in Joseph Frazier Wall, *Andrew Carnegie* (New York: Oxford Univeristy Press, 1970), p. 449.

40.   *New York Evening Post*, August 28, 1895, and *Philadelphia Times*, August 29, 1895, PC, LII, 81 and 274.

41.   *Philadelphia Inquirer*, September 4, 1895, PC, LIII, 87.

42.   J. Howard Smiley to MSQ, June 27, 1895, Elisha W. Smith to MSQ, June 27, 1895, and C. C. Kauffman to MSQ, January 4, 1896, all in MSQ Papers.

43. *Wilkes-Barre Record-Times* and *Detroit Journal*, both September 3, 1895, PC, LIII, 43 and 49.

44. *New Haven Register*, August 29, 1895, and *Syracuse News*, August 30, 1895, PC, LII, 266 and 309; *Louisville Times*, September 3, 1895, PC, LIII, 47.

45. Charles C. Scaife to Stephen B. Elkins, August 31, 1895, Elkins Papers; Theodore Roosevelt to Henry C. Lodge, December 20, 1895, *Selections from the Correspondence of Theodore Roosevelt and Henry Cabot Lodge, 1884-1918*, 2 vols. (New York: Charles Scribner's Sons, 1925), I, 202.

46. Bascom N. Timmons, in the foreword to Charles G. Dawes, *A Journal of the McKinley Years* (Chicago: R. R. Donnelley, 1950), p. ix; Leon B. Richardson, *William Chandler, Republican* (New York: Dodd, Mead & Co., 1940), p. 512; Gosnell, *Boss Platt*, p. 114.

47. Olcott, *McKinley*, I, 305; Felt, "The Rise of Mark Hanna," pp. 282-85; Williams, *Years of Decision*, p. 101.

48. Hamilton Disston to MSQ, April 1, 1895, MSQ Papers; James M. Swank to MSQ, March 24, 1896, Chandler Papers.

49. Russell A. Alger to MSQ, May 8 and June 8, 1895, MSQ Papers.

50. Kohlsaat, *McKinley to Harding*, p. 30; Croly, *Hanna*, p. 178; Leech, *Days of McKinley*, pp. 69-70. Marcus, *Grand Old Party*, p. 203, feels that Kohlsaat and Croly were relying wholly on recollections, which Margaret Leech repeated, and that the evidence is not sufficiently conclusive to state that Hanna made such a trip to Pennsylvania and New York.

51. Croly, *Hanna*, pp. 178-79; Leech, *Days of McKinley*, p. 71; Cullom, *Fifty Years*, p. 163.

52. George DeVany to MSQ, February 24, 1896, MSQ Papers; *Erie Daily Times*, February 25, 1896, clipping in MSQ Papers; James S. Clarkson to S. M. Clark, January 24, 1900 (copy), Clarkson Papers; Robert M. McElroy, *Levi Parsons Morton: Banker, Diplomat and Statesman* (New York: G. P. Putnam's Sons, 1930), pp. 290, 296.

53. Livy S. Richard to MSQ, February 13, 1896, MSQ Papers.

54. Alfred C. Harmer to MSQ, February 19, 1896, and MSQ to Alfred C. Harmer (draft), February 20, 1896, MSQ Papers; Stone, *Tale of a Plain Man*, p. 166.

55. Resolution of the Erie County Convention (copy), February 25, 1896, MSQ Papers.

56. *St. Louis Republican*, September 5, 1895, PC, LIII, 151; Andrew James to MSQ, February 18, 1896, and Felix W. Newman to MSQ, February 25, 1896, both in MSQ Papers.

57. *Philadelphia Times*, April 24, 1896, clipping in MSQ Papers.

58. Quay telegram to the 64 delegates dated May 9, 1896 (copy written in his own hand), MSQ Papers. According to the *Official Proceedings of the Eleventh Republican National Convention . . . , June 16, 17, and 18, 1896* (Minneapolis: Harrison and Smith Co., Printers, 1896), p. 123, the telegram tally was accurate since Pennsylvania cast 58 votes for Quay and 6 for McKinley on the first and only ballot. All 61 replies are in the MSQ Papers.

59. Russell A. Alger to William McKinley, April 17, 1896, and Joseph Medill to Russell A. Alger, May 7, 1896, both in Alger Papers; Thomas C. Platt to MSQ, July 6, 1896, MSQ Papers; Platt, *Autobiography*, p. 312; Morgan, *McKinley and His America*, p. 201.

60. William McKinley to MSQ, June 4, 1896, McKinley Papers; Thomas C. Platt to MSQ, July 6, 1896, MSQ Papers; Leech, *Days of McKinley*, p. 74.

61. Beer, *Hanna*, pp. 141-42; John M. Blum, *The Republican Roosevelt* (Cambridge, Mass.: Harvard University Press, 1954), p. 47; McClure, *Old Time Notes*, II, 600-01.

62. *Official Proceedings of the Eleventh Republican National Convention*, pp. 120-22; Beer, *Hanna*, pp. 146-47.

63. *Official Proceedings of the Eleventh Republican National Convention*, p. 123; Festus P. Summers, *William L. Wilson and Tariff Reform* (New Brunswick, N. J.: Rutgers University Press, 1953), p. 243.

64. William McKinley to MSQ, June 23, 1896, MSQ Papers.

65. Mark Hanna to MSQ, July 2, 3, and 6, 1896, MSQ Papers; Martin, *Bosses*, pp. 84–85.

66. William McKinley to MSQ (dated June 7, 1896, but most likely the correct date was July 7, 1896), MSQ Papers.

67. DeSantis, *Republicans Face the Southern Question*, p. 255.

68. MSQ to William McKinley, October 20, 1896, McKinley Papers.

69. In one respect the 51 percent was a major achievement: not since 1872 had any party received a majority of the total popular vote cast in a presidential election.

12. Exercises in Defensive Power: 1897-1900

1. MSQ to Richard R. Quay, December 31, 1897, MSQ Papers.

2. Cullom, *Fifty Years*, p. 281.

3. *Cong. Rec.*, 55th Cong., 1st sess., XXX, pt. 2, 2041.

4. Leach, *Partial Portrait*, p. 13; Bloom, "Philadelphia North American," pp. 473–74.

5. Leach, "Twenty Years with Quay," July 3, 1904.

6. Stackpole, *Behind the Scenes*, pp. 263–67.

7. John Wanamaker to MSQ, January 2 and 27, 1896, and Henry C. Frick to MSQ, October 2, 1896, both in MSQ Papers; McClure, *Old Time Notes*, II, 596–97.

8. McClure, *Old Time Notes*, II, 597–98.

9. Stackpole, *Behind the Scenes*, pp. 267–68; Davenport, *Power and Glory*, pp. 111–12.

10. Stackpole, *Behind the Scenes*, p. 268.

11. MSQ to A. K. McClure, September 15, 1897, Autograph Collection of Simon Gratz, Historical Society of Pennsylvania; *"Commercialism in Politics": An Account of the Proceedings in the Case of the Commonwealth vs. Van Valkenberg* (pamphlet, 1898), pp. 4–5, 9–10, 52.

12. John Wanamaker to Levi F. Cook, June 24, 1897, McKinley Papers; *The Speeches of Hon. John Wanamaker on Domination in Pennsylvania Politics* (Philadelphia: Business Men's League of the State of Pennsylvania, c. 1898), pp. 3–5.

13. *Speeches on Quayism*, p. 7; Appel, *Wanamaker*, p. 318; Stone, *A Plain Man*, p. 170.

14. Stone, *A Plain Man*, p. 173; McClure, *Old Time Notes*, II, 601–02; "The Pennsylvania Campaign," p. 437.

15. *Matthew Stanley Quay: A Man of the People* (pamphlet), p. 5; Disbrow, "Herbert Welsh," pp. 67–68.

16. "Pennsylvania Campaign," p. 437.

17. Disbrow, "Herbert Welsh," p. 69.

18. "The Week," pp. 341, 419–20.

19. Bloom, "Philadelphia *North American*," p. 486; "Senator Quay and the Republican Machine," *Outlook*, 62 (1899), 15–16.

20. Davenport, *Power and Glory*, p. 58; Leach, "Twenty Years with Quay," June 4, 1905.

21. *Philadelphia Inquirer*, April 22, 1899; Blankenburg, "Forty Years," p. 236.

22. John S. Hopkins to MSQ, June 20, 1893, MSQ Papers.

23. Petition of MSQ to the Judges of the Supreme Court of Pennsylvania (copy), November 21, 1898, MSQ Papers.

24. *Philadelphia Inquirer*, April 22, 1899.

25. Ibid.

26. *San Francisco Bulletin*, April 30, 1899; Croly, *Hanna*, p. 283.

27. Leach, "Twenty Years with Quay," July 3, 1904.

28. A. S. L. Shields to MSQ, October 25, 1900, and J. Clayton Erb to MSQ, November 1, 1900, both in MSQ Papers; Blankenburg, "Forty Years," p. 237.

29. J. Clayton Erb to MSQ, November 1, 1900, MSQ Papers; *Philadelphia Inquirer*, April 22, 1899.

30. *San Francisco Bulletin*, April 30, 1899.

31. *Philadelphia Inquirer*, April 22, 1899.

32. George W. Bartch to MSQ, April 21, 1899, with clipping from the *Salt Lake City Tribune* attached, MSQ Papers; William H. Lyons to MSQ, April 23, 1899, MSQ Papers; McClure, *Old Time Notes*, II, 606.

33. Jacob S. Kimball to MSQ, April 23, 1899, Robert B. Robinson to MSQ, April 23, 1899, Robert Walthorn to MSQ, April 24, 1899, and Charles E. W. Fisher to MSQ, May 4, 1899, all in MSQ Papers.

34. *Philadelphia Inquirer*, April 22, 1899; J. J. Snodgrass to MSQ, April 29, 1899, with clipping from the *New York Journal*, MSQ Papers.

35. P. A. Johns to MSQ, April 21, 1899, William B. McIlhenny to MSQ, April 24, 1899, Harry Woodruff to MSQ, April 22, 1899, all in MSQ Papers.

36. *Cong. Rec.*, 56th Cong., 1st sess., XXXIII, pt. 1, 1; George Wharton Pepper, *Philadelphia Lawyer: An Autobiography* (Philadelphia: Lippincott, 1944), pp. 78–79; *Philadelphia Inquirer*, April 22, 1899; "Quay and the Constitution," p. 328.

37. *Cong. Rec.*, 56th Cong., 1st sess., XXXIII, pt. 3, 2467–68; Pepper, *Autobiography*, p. 79; Thomas F. Dawson, *Life and Character of Edward Oliver Wolcott; Late a Senator of the United States from the State of Colorado*, 2 vols. (Knickerbacher Press, 1911), II, 88.

38. *Cong. Rec.*, 56th Cong., 1st sess., XXXIII, pt. 3, 2310, 2233, 2467–68.

39. Ibid., pt. 2, 1051; Dawson, *Wolcott*, II, 88–89.

40. *Cong. Rec.*, 56th Cong., 1st sess., XXXIII, pt. 1, 646; Boies Penrose to William E. Chandler, March 1, 1900, Chandler Papers; Boies Penrose to Stephen B. Elkins, March 9, 1900, Elkins Papers; Leon B. Richardson, *William Chandler, Republican* (New York: Dodd, Mead & Co., 1940), p. 590.

41. Walter T. Burns to MSQ, February 14, 1900, and Texas Senate Resolution to Senators Horace Chilton and Charles A. Culberson, February 14, 1900 (copy), both in MSQ Papers.

42. Mark Hanna to MSQ, April 21, 1899, and George H. Stone to MSQ, April 23, 1899, both in MSQ Papers; Coolidge, *Old-Fashioned Senator*, p. 416; Croly, *Hanna*, pp. 284–85.

43. Gibbons, *Wanamaker*, I, 363; McClure, *Old Time Notes*, II, 610.

44. *Cong. Rec.*, 56th Cong., 1st sess., XXXIII, pt. 1, 646.

45. William D. Orcutt, *Burrows of Michigan and the Republican Party: A Biography and a History*, 2 vols. (Longmans, Green and Co., 1917), II, 127–28.

46. William Wilhelm to MSQ, April 27, 1900, MSQ Papers; Francis T. Tobin to MSQ, April 24, 1900, Samuel W. Pennypacker to MSQ, April 25, 1900, Frank A. Hower to MSQ, April 27, 1900, all in MSQ Papers; Davenport, *Power and Glory*, p. 149; Martin, *Bosses*, p. 96.

47. Stealey, *Twenty Years in the Press Gallery*, pp. 155, 454; McClure, *Old Time Notes*, II, 610.

48. Orcutt, *Burrows*, II, 135.

49. Unidentified newspaper clipping, MSQ Papers.

50. George G. Vest to MSQ, April 24, 1899, MSQ Papers. The date shown is incorrect and perhaps reflects Vest's emotional state at the time of writing; all indications are that the letter was written on April 25, 1900.

51. Orcutt, *Burrows*, II, 128–29, 135.

13. Leader of the Anti-Hanna Forces: 1900-1904

1. Davenport, *Power and Glory*, p. 149; Martin, *Bosses*, p. 96.

2. Clark, *My Quarter Century*, I, 465; William Allen White, *Autobiography* (New York: Macmillan, 1946), p. 329.

3. MSQ to William McKinley, May 21, 1900, McKinley Papers.

4. Francis T. Tobin to MSQ, April 24, 1900; Samuel W. Pennypacker to MSQ, April 25, 1900; Frank A. Hower to MSQ, April 27, 1900, all in MSQ Papers.

5. Platt, *Autobiography*, p. 386; Olcott, *McKinley*, II, 266, 269.

6. *Proceedings of the Twelfth Republican Convention*, pp. 95–97; Woodburn, *Political Parties*, p. 162; Gosnell, *Boss Platt*, pp. 121–22; Henry F. Pringle, *Theodore Roosevelt: A Biography* (New York: Harcourt, Brace and Co., 1931), p. 222.

7. Clark, *My Quarter Century*, I, 465; Pringle, *Roosevelt*, pp. 222–23.

8. Platt, *Autobiography*, pp. 387–88; Kohlsaat, *McKinley to Harding*, p. 88.

9. Gosnell, *Boss Platt*, p. 120; Stoddard, *As I Knew Them*, p. 248; Beer, *Hanna*, p. 225.

10. Merrill and Merrill, *Republican Command*, p. 76; Martin, *Bosses*, p. 100.

11. Thomas R. Ross, *Jonathan Prentiss Dolliver: A Study in Political Integrity and Independence* (Iowa City: State Historical Society of Iowa, 1958), p. 161; Kohlsaat, *McKinley to Harding*, p. 88; Watson, *Memoirs*, p. 58.

12. Platt, *Autobiography*, p. 212; White, *Autobiography*, p. 329; "Behold How These Brethren Love One Another," p. 4.

13. Quay, *Pennsylvania Politics*, p. 181.

14. Ibid., pp. 9, 11, 79; Leach, "Twenty Years with Quay," December 18, 1904.

15. Quay, *Pennsylvania Politics*, p. 28.

16. Ibid., pp. 30–31, 52, 58, 82, 171–72.

17. Members of various labor associations (3 pages of signatures) to MSQ, October 1900, MSQ Papers.

18. Quay, *Pennsylvania Politics*, pp. 37, 174–75, 176–78.

19. Ibid., pp. 21, 30, 121, 129–30, 150–51, 158.

20. Ibid., pp. 21, 179–80; John T. Rice to MSQ, January 17, 1901, MSQ Papers.

21. Quay, *Pennsylvania Politics*, pp. 11, 122; Leach, "Twenty Years with Quay," July 3, 1904.

22. B. W. Green to MSQ and Frederick Haas to MSQ, both October 15, 1900, MSQ Papers.

23. MSQ to Fred H. Cope, November 12, 1900, MSQ Papers. This is a copy of the letter sent to all Republican legislators.

24. Thomas Davis to MSQ, December 18, 1900, and Charles Miller to William A. Stone, January 2, 1901, both in MSQ Papers.

25. *Philadelphia Inquirer*, January 17, 1901; Davenport, *Power and Glory*, p. 150; Certificate of Election, MSQ Papers; Blankenburg, "Quay," p. 210.

26. Benson Herrold to MSQ, January 16, 1901, MSQ Papers; Davenport, *Power and Glory*, p. 151.

27. *Philadelphia Inquirer*, January 17, 1901; Leach, "Twenty Years with Quay," July 3, 1904.

28. Clipping from the *Boston Herald*, January 18, 1901, with an attached note; unidentified newspaper clipping; both in MSQ Papers.

29. Stone, *Plain Man*, pp. 176, 178; Cullom, *Fifty Years*, p. 235.

30. Quay, *Pennsylvania Politics*, p. 188.

31. Roosevelt, *Autobiography*, p. 155; John M. Blum, *The Republican Roosevelt* (Cambridge, Mass.: Harvard University Press, 1954), p. 38.

32. Brownlow, *Passion for Politics*, p. 350; Blum, *Republican Roosevelt*, p. 38.

33. Frederic Bancroft, ed., *Speeches, Correspondence and Political Papers of Carl Schurz*, 6 vols. (New York: G. P. Putnam's Sons, 1913), VI, 380–81; Blum, *Republican Roosevelt*, p. 47.

34. Theodore Roosevelt to MSQ, June 7, 1902, MSQ Papers; *Pittsburgh Press*, June 11, 1902.

35. Theodore Roosevelt to MSQ, September 27, 1902, Letter Books, VI, 257–58, Roosevelt Papers.

36. MSQ to Theodore Roosevelt, October 6, 1902, Roosevelt Papers; Theodore Roosevelt to MSQ, October 14, 1902, Letter Books, VI, 397, Roosevelt Papers.

37. Foulke, *Fighting the Spoilsmen*, p. 188.

38. MSQ to Theodore Roosevelt, February 17, 1904, Roosevelt Papers; Theodore Roosevelt to MSQ, February 19, 1904, MSQ Papers; Foulke, *Fighting the Spoilsmen*, p. 188.

39. Roosevelt, *Autobiography*, pp. 474–75; Sullivan, *Our Times*, I, 437.

40. Roosevelt, *Autobiography*, p. 475.

41. MSQ to Theodore Roosevelt, October 26, 1902; Theodore Roosevelt to MSQ, October 31, 1902, Letter Books, VII, 108; both in Roosevelt Papers.

42. "M. Quay, Reformer," p. 165; Stackpole, *Behind the Scenes*, pp. 82, 104.

43. *Pittsburgh Press*, June 8, 1902; McClure, *Old Time Notes*, II, 624.

44. Bancroft, *Speeches of Carl Schurz*, VI, 380–81.

45. Theodore Roosevelt to MSQ, August 26 and 27, September 1 and 4, October 7, 1903, MSQ Papers.

46. Theodore Roosevelt to Owen Wister, November 19, 1904, Letter Books, XXII, 20–21, Roosevelt Papers.

47. Theodore Roosevelt to George H. Putnam, November 5, 1904, Letter Books, XXII, 445–46, Roosevelt Papers.

14. The Senator's Career Faces West: 1902-1904

1. Bowers, *Beveridge*, p. 194.

2. *Cong. Rec.*, 57th Cong., 1st sess., XXXV, pt. 7, 7198–99; Bowers, *Beveridge*, pp. 182, 194.

3. Bowers, *Beveridge*, pp. 182–83, 194.

4. *Cong. Rec.*, 57th Cong., 1st sess., XXXV, pt. 7, 7198–7200.

5. Ibid., pp. 7200, 7356–57.

6. Bowers, *Beveridge*, p. 197.

7. Ibid., pp. 197–99.

8. Ibid., pp. 200–01.

9. Elting E. Morison, ed., *The Letters of Theodore Roosevelt*, 6 vols. (Cambridge, Mass.: Harvard University Press, 1951–52), V, 649n1, 739n1.

10. Ibid., V, 739n1.

11. Robert M. LaFollette, *Autobiography: A Personal Narrative of Political Experiences*, 7th ed. (Madison, Wis.: Robert M. LaFollette Company, 1913), p. 58.

12. Roosevelt, *Autobiography*, p. 156.

13. Resolution of the Seneca Nation, March 21, 1903, MSQ Papers.

14. Oliver, "Quay," p. 8.

15. MSQ to Theodore Roosevelt (telegram), June 28, 1903, Roosevelt Papers; "Career and Character of Quay," p. 14.

16. Steffens, *Autobiography*, pp. 419–20; Roosevelt, *Autobiography*, pp. 156–57.

17. Steffens, *Autobiography*, p. 420; Roosevelt, *Autobiography*, p. 157.

18. "Address of Mr. Penrose, of Pennsylvania" and "Address of Mr. Foraker, of Ohio," *Matthew Stanley Quay: Memorial Addresses Delivered in the Senate and House of Representatives* (Washington, D.C.: U.S. Government Printing Office, 1905), pp. 45, 80.

19. MSQ to William Flinn, May 10, 1904, MSQ Papers; James S. Clarkson to Samuel Fessenden (copy), May 26, 1904, box 2, Clarkson Papers; Theodore Roosevelt to Agnes B. Quay (telegram), May 28, 1904, MSQ Papers.

20. *Philadelphia Record*, June 1, 1904.

21. *Pittsburgh Dispatch*, May 30, 1904.

22. Ibid.

23. Bowers, *Beveridge*, p. 207.

Bibliography

I N a two-party system the party boss, either as an arbiter or as an enforcer, must demand compromise from his constituent factions, candidates, and officeholders. He always prefers to be the arbiter, but not every decision can be finessed. Regardless of which role is required, he must maneuver to keep his methods and intrigues as secret as possible. That way he can obscure his own heavy-handedness and preserve the dignity of those from whom he extracted the necessary compromise, whether by friendly word or hidden bludgeon.

Matt Quay, Tom Platt, Mark Hanna, the Camerons, as well as many other state and local leaders, were most comfortable when maneuvering clandestinely behind the scenes. Although they possessed the talent to move directly to the crux of almost any issue, their course of action was generally circuitous in order to bewilder the public and mislead the opposition. This obfuscation has also complicated the task of researchers attempting to explain why newspaper editorials, dogmatic pronouncements by local politicians, platform declarations, and public opinion might point in one direction, but the nineteenth-century boss was able to redirect the party in contradiction of all of these indicators.

The reconstruction of Matt Quay's impact on society is particularly difficult because of his daughter's feeling that she had to protect his reputation. Coral Quay had witnessed the devastating attacks against him during his lifetime and was determined that they would not be perpetuated after his death. In her opinion the revelations in the *New York World*, written by William Shaw Bowen in 1890 with funds supplied by Quay's enemies, were a national embarrassment that lingered for more than a year, partly because the press insisted on rehashing the details. On the state level, John Wanamaker's published speeches on *Quayism and Boss Domination in Pennsylvania Politics* (c. 1898) cast another dark shadow over Quay's professional reputation. Coral agonized over these exposés, as well as over the constant filing of charges, publishing of defaming pamphlets, and delivering of vitriolic attacks on the senator's conduct by Republican rivals and independent reformers.

In 1904, the same year that Senator Quay died, Coral was shocked by a different kind of revelation. Another determined young woman, Ida Tarbell, with equal vehemence for her cause, published her *History of the Standard Oil Company* assailing the great name of Rockefeller. To aspiring American families at the turn of the century—proud of their accomplishments (as Coral

281

was of her father's carreer) and desirous of being favorably remembered in the pages of history—the Rockefellers were a model to be emulated. If the pen of a muckraker could place the Rockefeller name under a social cloud, how much more vulnerable were the less secure families before the new breed of reformers who were delving into so many of society's institutions?

Coral Quay was frightened by the possibilities in the Tarbell exposé, but at the same time she felt a filial responsibility to preserve the most favorable image of her father's career. This was a natural and logical reaction, one that was shared by similarly situated families, particularly thsoe with financially independent, intelligent, and unmarried daughters who could dwell on a father's career. For more than fifty years, in the belief that her action protected his reputation, Coral steadfastly refused to have his papers studied objectively. They were never catalogued, and at her death they were found cached in ladies' hat and suit boxes that had been stored in vacant corners of her home anywhere from the basement to the attic especially the bedroom closets. Fortunately the third generation did not continue Coral's defensive attitude. With her passing, Stanley Quay, the boss's grandson, generously entrusted the boxes containing the senator's papers to this author.

The Quay material can be divided into three categories: correspondence, newspaper clippings, and a miscellany of pamphlets, documents, and published volumes. The correspondence, identified in the notes as the Matthew Stanley Quay Papers (MSQ Papers), is extensive (approximately five thousand items), scattered in time, and hopelessly incomplete. The greatest disappointment is the correspondence from other national leaders; the few existing letters from Benjamin Harrison, James S. Clarkson, Tom Platt, Mark Hanna, William McKinley, and Theodore Roosevelt are not particularly significant. As might be expected, the coverage of state politics, although uneven, is the richest. There are 800 items on the contest for Republican state chairman in 1895, and 250 items on control of the party's state convention in1896; another 2,200 to 2,500 letters pertaining to state politics 1866–1904 represent the bulk of the MSQ Papers.

In contrast, the newspaper clippings are exceptionally abundant because Senator Quay was among the first subscribers to a clipping service (Henry S. Romeike of New York). The fifty three bound volumes of Press Comments (PC) contain approximately 29,400 entries and cover only 1878 and 1888–1895; there are almost 3,000 items on the 1888 campaign alone. Both pro- and anti-Quay opinions are represented; the only common denominator among the entries is the mention of Quay's name. The clippings have been assembled from newspapers in all states. The coverage represents rural and urban areas, along with Republican, Democratic, and independent points of view.

The only repositories with even modest Quay holdings are the Library of Congress (LC) and the University of Pittsburgh. The LC collection of approximately one hundred fifty pieces is designated as the Matthew S. Quay Papers and covers the period 1876–1927. Many of these items are typed copies or photostats of original documents found in the Pennsylvania Historical Society, the Hayes Memorial Library, or in other LC collections such as the papers of James Garfield, John Sherman, and Theodore Roosevelt. The three boxes of Quay Family Papers, 1836–1927, in the Archives of Industrial Society at the University of Pittsburgh, contain correspondence and newspaper clippings that were once a part of the collection in my possession. The university acquired these materials from the late John W. Oliver, who in the 1920's began the task of writing a Quay biography. He was forced to abandon the project, however, because Coral Quay would not make the bulk of her father's papers available to him.

In addition to newspaper coverage, Quay's exploits were reported widely in contemporary magazines and pamphlets. The *Nation* was his most persistent critic throughout the last two decades of the nineteenth century, but the single most caustic article appeared in *Arena* the year after his death. Written by Rudolph Blankenburg, a long-time opponent, "Forty Years in the Wilderness" is an eighty-four-page, six-installment attack detailing Quay's "misrule" in the

Commonwealth. Although they devoted less space to him, both *Harper's Weekly* and the *Atlantic Monthly* were more analytical. The latter, particularly in "The Ills of Pennsylvania," discussed the roots of political corruption in the state and demonstrated how the political machine constantly compromised and outmanuevered the reformers. In 1902 Evan Holben lamented in his *Stories and Reminiscences* that the state's Democrats met the same fate.

When contemporary criticism was most vicious, the Quay forces generally countered with a pamphlet. The public was mollified with such biased items as *M. S. Quay and the Soldiers* (n.d.), *How Quay's Clever Move Saved the McKinley Bill* (c. 1892), *The Great Conspiracy of Four Years Ago: An Inside Story of the Republican Campaign in Which Harrison Defeated Cleveland (1892)*, *Hon. M. S. Quay and the Great Campaign of 1888: What His Colleagues of the Republican National Committee Think of Him* (1891), *Matthew Stanley Quay: A Man of the People* (c. 1898). His opponents within the Republican party had their own pamphleteers who produced such works as *Republicansim vs. Quayism* (1892) and *Pennsylvania's Representatives in the U.S. Senate* (1892).

A more positive, partially documented, yet apocryphal account of the senator's character was cited many times during his career by partisans and recorded in detail in an address by Joseph C. Sibley in *Matthew Stanley Quay: Memorial Addresses Delivered in the Senate and House of Representatives* (Washington, D.C. : U.S. Government Printing Office, 1905). It intertwined the senator's career with that of Rudyard Kipling, who was purportedly commissioned by an unidentified London magazine to write a feature story on the typical American boss. After accepting the assignment Kipling, according to Republican lore, learned that Quay was an appropriate subject for study and arranged for an interview at his Beaver home. He was ushered into the senator's library, which made an immediate and startling impression on him. Not expecting to encounter such an extensive book collection in a backcountry community, he at once focused his attention on the rare and scholarly volumes neatly shelved in the paneled bookcases. The books provided a natural basis for an introductory exchange that developed into hours of literary discussion. Kipling returned to his lodging for the night without a word on the character of bossism being uttered. Quay invited him to return the next day, with an understanding that the interview would continue. He reappeared at the appointed hour, and the literary conversation resumed where it had been broken off the night before. A third session followed the pattern of the first two. Kipling, partly embarrassed and partly awed, cabled the London magazine: "I have been unable to locate the political boss, but if you desire an article upon America's foremost literary critic, I can furnish you with the copy."

Although the details of this encounter cannot be fully substantiated, Kipling's visit to Beaver cannot be doubted. The best evidence suggests, however, that Kipling was not attracted by such a mundane topic as bossism, but by the charms of a woman, one who had played a major role in his career in India. She was Edmonia Hill, whose husband, S. A. Hill, had been a government meteorologist and professor of science at Muir College. In a foreign land, with hours of idle time each day, Edmonia, an intelligent American girl from Beaver, became interested in Kipling and his work. He, in turn, grew to respect her opinions and accepted her as a valued critic and confidant. The Hills left India before Kipling. They went to Beaver, where Edmonia's father, Professor R. T. Taylor, a minister and president of Beaver College, lived with his wife and younger daughter, Caroline. Returning to London by way of the Pacific and California, Kipling accepted an invitation to visit them in 1889. He spent nearly two months in Beaver, and during that visit probably met the community's few prominent citizens. If Quay was at home, the two surely met, but at no point, not even in his *American Notes*, did Kipling record the fact. To have found a literary scholar in the political ranks should certainly have astonished him since he harbored a lifelong distrust of politicians. There is reason, therefore, to keep the Kipling evaluation of Quay among the lore.

Understandably there was no analytical account of the senator's career at the time of his death.

He was active in politics until the end, and the record was still incomplete. Isaac Pennypacker quickly sensed that the career of a man who had served all Republican presidents since the founding of the party should be preserved and analyzed for posterity. He was the first to propose the idea of a biography to the Quay family. In doing so, he stated his determination to be both thorough and objective. Indicating his intention to collect oral and written statements from the senator's surviving colleagues, he requested that the family send letters to specific individuals soliciting their cooperation. He even announced his plan to ask the aged Don Cameron for a frank statement about the treasury scandal of 1880. When John A. Glenn, a deputy in the office of Pennsylvania's auditor general, also announced in 1905 his intention to publish an account of the senator's career, Pennypacker asked Coral Quay to confirm that his proposal had the "official" family sanction. Although the impact of this threatened rivalry is not known, neither carried out his project. The challenge was not seriously taken up again until the 1920s when Professor Oliver attempted to reconstruct the senator's career. Nothing has appeared since.

One of the major difficulties in assessing Quay's character and diverse political talents, as perhaps Pennypacker and Glenn discovered, is that he himself wrote very little for publication. He contributed an article, "The Man or the Platform" to the *North American Review*. Other limited insights may be drawn from the editorial columns of the *Beaver Radical*, the weekly newspaper that he edited from December 11, 1869, to December 20, 1872, and from his widely circulated volume of published speeches entitled *Pennsylvania Politics: The Campaign of 1900* (Philadelphia: William J. Campbell, 1901).

Memoirs of Quay's Contemporaries

With few of Quay's own writings available, it is necessary to turn to the correspondence, autobiographies, and reminiscences of his contemporaries in order to understand the sources and extent of his state and national power. At the state level the two most graphic accounts of this type are McClure's *Old Time Notes of Pennsylvania*, and Frank Willing Leach's "Twenty Years with Quay," a scrapbook of forty-two detailed newspaper articles that Leach first published in the Sunday editions of the *Philadelphia North American* between July 3, 1904, and June 25, 1905. Although highly descriptive and extensive in coverage, both must at times be checked against other sources for accuracy. Leach's work is particularly good for its thumbnail biographies of many lesser state politicians. These sources, supplemented by the autobiographies of Leach, Pennypacker, and Stone, survey the state setting for Quay's career. His national involvement intersected the lives of a much larger group. The list of state and national contemporaries who interpreted or commented upon one or more aspects of his career is as follows.

Brownlow, Louis. *A Passion for Politics: An Autobiography of Louis Brownlow, First Half.* Chicago: University of Chicago Press, 1955.

Clark, Champ. *My Quarter Century of American Politics.* 2 vols. New York: Harper & Brothers, 1920.

Cullom, Shelby M. *Fifty Years of Public Service: Personal Recollections.* Chicago: A. C. McClurg & Co., 1911.

Dawes, Charles G. *A Journal of the McKinley Years.* Chicago: R. R. Donnelley & Sons, 1950.

Depew, Chauncey M. *My Memories of Eighty Years.* New York: Charles Scribner's Sons, 1924.

Foraker, Joseph B. *Notes of a Busy Life.* 2 vols. Cincinnati: Stewart & Kidd, 1917.

Foulke, William D. *Fighting the Spoilsmen: Reminiscences of the Civil Service Reform Movement.* New York: G. P. Putnam's Sons, 1919.

Hoar, George F. *Autobiography of Seventy Years.* 2 vols. New York: Charles Scribner's Sons, 1903.

Leach, Frank Willing. *A Partial Portrait by Himself, 1855-1943.* Lancaster, Pa.: Wickersham Press, 1943.

————. "Twenty Years with Quay." *Philadelphia North American*, July 3, 1904–June 25, 1905.
McClure, Alexander K. *Old Time Notes of Pennsylvania*. 2 vols. Philadelphia: John C. Winston Co., 1905.
Peck, Harry T. *Twenty Years of the Republic, 1885–1905*. New York: Dodd, Mead & Co., 1907.
Pennypacker, Samuel W. *The Autobiography of a Pennsylvanian*. Philadelphia: John C. Winston Co., 1918.
Platt, Thomas C. *Autobiography*. Edited by Louis J. Lang. New York: B. W. Dodge and Co., 1910.
Roosevelt, Theodore. *Autobiography*. New York: Charles Scribner's Sons, 1925.
Stone, William A. *The Tale of a Plain Man*. N.p.: William A. Stone, 1917.
Watson, James E. *As I Knew Them: Memoirs of James E. Watson, Former United States Senator from Indiana*. Indianapolis: Bobbs-Merrill, 1936.

Archives

The most useful archival collections were the following:

Russell A. Alger Papers, William L. Clements Library, University of Michigan
Wharton Barker Papers, Manuscripts Division, Library of Congress
James Addams Beaver Manuscripts, Pennsylvania Historical Collections, Pennsylvania State University Library
Correspondence and Papers of Simon Cameron, 1824–1892 (microfilm, esp. reel no. 10), Pennsylvania Historical and Museum Commission, Harrisburg
James Sullivan Clarkson Papers, Manuscripts Division, Library of Congress
Walter Quintin Gresham Papers, Manuscripts Division, Library of Congress
Benjamin Harrison Papers, 1848–1901, Manuscripts Division, Library of Congress
Rutherford B. Hayes Papers, Rutherford B. Hayes Library, Fremont, Ohio
William McKinley Papers, 1847–1902, 86 vols., Manuscripts Division, Library of Congress
Theodore Roosevelt Papers, Manuscripts Division, Library of Congress
John Sherman Papers, Manuscripts Division, Library of Congress
James M. Swank Papers, Historical Society of Pennsylvania

Other collections not so directly related to Quay, but valuable for their contribution to the politics of the general period are: William E. Chandler Papers (esp. 102 and 129) in the Library of Congress; A. L. Conger Collection in the Rutherford B. Hayes Library; Stephen B. Elkins Papers, West Virginia Collection, West Virginia University Library; Papers of James A. Garfield (esp. 54 and 55) in the Library of Congress; Papers of Edward McPherson (esp. 38 and 40), Library of Congress; and Louis T. Michener Papers, Library of Congress.

Political History Monographs

The third of a century (1870–1904) during which Quay asserted his greatest influence has been widely covered in historical literature. Heading the list are six recently published interpretations of these years: Morton Keller, *Affairs of State*, Robert D. Marcus, *Grand Old Party*, H. Wayne Morgan, *From Hayes to McKinley*, and R. Hal Williams, *Years of Decision*, plus two volumes by Paul Kleppner, *The Cross of Culture* and *The Third Electoral System*.

Bernardo, C. Joseph. "The Presidential Election of 1888." Diss. Georgetown, 1949.
Bloom, Robert L. "The Philadelphia *North American*, 1839–1925: A History." Diss. Columbia, 1952.
Bradley, Erwin Stanley. *The Triumph of Militant Republicanism: A Study of Pennsylvania and Presidential Politics, 1860–1872*. Philadelphia: University of Pennsylvania Press, 1964.

Bryce, James. *The American Commonwealth*, 2 vols. New York: Macmillan, 1891.

DeSantis, Vincent P. *Republicans Face the Southern Question: The New Departure Years, 1877-1897*. Baltimore: The Johns Hopkins Press, 1959.

Dobson, John M. *Politics in the Gilded Age: A New Perspective on Reform*. New York: Praeger, 1972.

Dunn, Arthur Wallace. *From Harrison to Harding: A Personal Narrative Covering a Third of a Century, 1888-1921*. 2 vols. New York: G. P. Putnam's Sons, 1922.

Garrity, John A. *The New Commonwealth*. New York: Harper & Row, 1968.

Ginger, Ray. *Age of Excess: The United States from 1877 to 1914*. New York: Macmillan, 1965.

Hirshson, Stanley P. *Farewell to the Bloody Shirt: Northern Republicans & the Southern Negro, 1877-1893*. Bloomington: Indiana University Press, 1962.

Jaher, Frederic Cople. *Doubters and Dissenters: Cataclysmic Thought in America, 1885-1918*. New York: Free Press of Glencoe, 1964.

Josephson, Matthew. *The Robber Barons: The Great American Capitalists, 1861-1901*. New York: Harcourt, Brace and Co., 1934.

Keller, Morton. *Affairs of State: Public Life in Late Nineteenth Century America*. Cambridge, Mass.: Belknap Press, 1977.

Kleppner, Paul. *The Cross of Culture: A Social Analysis of Midwestern Politics, 1850-1900*. New York: The Free Press, 1970.

_____. *The Third Electoral System, 1853-1892: Parties, Voters, and Political Cultures*. Chapel Hill: University of North Carolina Press, 1979.

Knoles, George Harmon. *The Presidential Campaign and Election of 1892*. Palo Alto: Stanford University Press, 1942.

Leech, Margaret. *In the Days of McKinley*. New York: Harper & Brothers, 1959.

Marcus, Robert D. *Grand Old Party: Political Structure in the Gilded Age, 1880-1896*. New York: Oxford University Press, 1971.

Merrill, Horace S., and Merrill, Marion G. *The Republican Command, 1897-1913*. Lexington: The University Press of Kentucky, 1971.

Morgan, H. Wayne. *From Hayes to McKinley: National Party Politics, 1877-1896*. Syracuse: Syracuse University Press, 1969.

_____. *William McKinley and His America*. Syracuse: Syracuse University Press, 1963.

Thayer, George. *Who Shakes the Money Tree? American Campaign Financing Practices from 1789 to the Present*. New York: Simon and Schuster, 1973.

Thomas, Harrison Cook. *The Return of the Democratic Party to Power in 1884*. New York: Columbia University, 1919.

Williams, R. Hal. *Years of Decision: American Politics in the 1890s*. New York: John Wiley & Sons, 1978.

Woodburn, James A. *Political Parties and Party Problems in the United States*. New York: G. P. Putnam's Sons, 1906.

Reflections of Political Journalists

Kohlsaat, Herman. *From McKinley to Harding: Personal Recollections of Our Presidents*. New York: Charles Scribner's Sons, 1923.

Stackpole, Edward J. *Behind the Scenes with a Newspaperman: Fifty Years in the Life of an Editor*. Philadelphia: Lippincott, 1927.

Stealey, Orlando Oscar. *Twenty Years in the Press Gallery: A Concise History of Important Legislation from the 48th to the 58th Congress*. New York: Orlando O. Stealey, 1906.

Steffens, Lincoln. *The Autobiography of Lincoln Steffens.* New York: Harcourt, Brace and Co., 1931.

———. *The Shame of the Cities.* New York: Peter Smith, 1948.

Stoddard, Henry L. *As I Knew Them: Presidents and Politics from Grant to Coolidge.* New York: Harper and Brothers, 1927.

———. *It Costs to Be President.* New York: Harper and Brothers, 1938.

Sullivan, Mark. *Our Times: The United States, 1900-1925.* 6 vols. New York: Charles Scribner's Sons, 1926-1927.

Bossism in the Late Nineteenth Century

Dorsett, Lyle W. *Bosses and Machines in Urban America.* St. Charles: Forum Press, 1974.

Gosnell, Harold F. *Boss Platt and His New York Machine: A Study of the Political Leadership of Thomas C. Platt, Theodore Roosevelt and Others.* Chicago: University of Chicago Press, 1924.

Haeger, John, and Weber, Michael, eds. *The Bosses.* St. Charles: Forum Press, 1974.

Holben, Evan. *Stories and Reminiscences.* N.p.: E. F. Ochs & Bro., 1902.

Josephson, Matthew. *The Politicos, 1865-1896.* New York: Harcourt, Brace, 1938.

Loth, David G. *Public Plunder: A History of Graft in America.* New York: Carrick & Evans, Inc., 1938.

Macy, Jesse. *Party Organization and Machinery.* New York: The Century Co., 1904.

Martin, Ralph G. *The Bosses.* New York: G. P. Putnam's Sons, 1964.

Riordan, William L., ed. *Plunkitt of Tammany Hall.* New York: Knopf, 1948.

Rothman, David J. *Politics and Power: The United States Senate, 1869-1901.* Cambridge, Mass.: Harvard University Press, 1966.

Tarr, Joel Arthur. *A Study in Boss Politics: William Lorimer of Chicago.* Urbana: University of Illinois Press, 1971.

Yearley, Clifton K. *The Money Machines: The Breakdown and Reform of Governmental and Party Finance in the North, 1860-1920.* Albany: State University of New York Press, 1970.

Zink, Harold. *City Bosses in the United States: A Study of Twenty Municipal Bosses.* Durham: Duke University Press, 1930.

Political Biographies

Adams, Henry. *The Education of Henry Adams: An Autobiography.* New York: Heritage Press, 1942.

Appel, Joseph H. *The Business Biography of John Wanamaker: Founder and Builder.* New York: Macmillan, 1930.

Beer, Thomas. *Hanna.* New York: Knopf, 1929.

Bowers, Claude G. *Beveridge and the Progressive Era.* New York: Literary Guild, 1932.

Bradley, Edward Sculley. *Henry Charles Lea: A Biography.* Philadelphia: University of Pennsylvania Press, 1931.

Chidsay, Donald B. *Gentleman from New York: A Life of Roscoe Conkling.* New Haven: Yale University Press, 1935.

Coolidge, Louis A. *An Old-Fashioned Senator, Orville H. Platt of Connecticut: The Story of a Life Unselfishly Devoted to the Public Service.* New York: G. P. Putnam's Sons, 1910.

Croly, Herbert. *Marcus Alonzo Hanna: His Life and Work.* New York: Macmillan, 1923.

Davenport, Walter. *Power and Glory: The Life of Boies Penrose.* New York: G. P. Putnam's Sons, 1931.

Felt, Thomas E. "The Rise of Mark Hanna." Diss. Michigan State, 1960.

Gibbons, Herbert Adams. *John Wanamaker*. 2 vols. New York: Harper & Brothers, 1926.

Gresham, Matilda. *Life of Walter Quintin Gresham, 1832-1895*. 2 vols. Chicago: Rand McNally & Co., 1919.

Lambert, John R. *Arthur Pue Gorman*. Baton Rouge: Louisiana State University Press, 1953.

Lambert, Oscar Doane. *Stephen Benton Elkins*. Pittsburgh: University of Pittsburgh Press, 1955.

Leech, Margaret, and Brown, Harry J. *The Garfield Orbit*. New York: Harper & Row, 1978.

Merrill, Horace Samuel. *Bourbon Leader: Grover Cleveland and the Democratic Party*. Boston: Little, Brown and Co., 1957.

Muzzey, David Saville. *James G. Blaine: A Political Idol of Other Days*. New York: Dodd, Mead & Co., 1934.

Nevins, Allan. *Grover Cleveland: A Study in Courage*. New York: Dodd, Mead & Co., 1948.

Olcott, Charles S. *The Life of William McKinley*. 2 vols. Boston: Houghton Mifflin, 1916.

Peskin, Allan. *Garfield: A Biography*. Kent, Ohio: Kent State University Press, 1978.

Sievers, Harry J. *Benjamin Harrison, Hoosier Statesman: From the Civil War to the White House, 1865-1888*. New York: University Publishers, Inc., 1959.

———. *Benjamin Harrison, Hoosier President: The White House and After*. Indianapolis: Bobbs-Merrill Company, Inc., 1968.

Welch, Richard E., Jr. *George Frisbie Hoar and the Half Breed Republicans*. Cambridge, Mass.: Harvard University Press, 1971.

Magazine Articles

"Behold How These Brethren Love One Another." *Review of Reviews*, 22 (1900), 4-5.

Blankenburg, Rudolph. "Forty Years in the Wilderness; or Masters and Rulers of 'The Freemen' of Pennsylvania." *Arena*, 33 (1905), 1-10, 113-27, 225-39, 345-60, 457-74, and 569-83.

———. "Quay." *Independent*, 53 (1901), 209-11.

"Career and Character of Quay." *Current Literature*, 37 (1904), 13-14.

"Costly Bosses." *Nation*, 66 (1898), 455-56.

Disbrow, Donald W. "Herbert Welsh, Editor of City and State, 1895-1904." *Pennsylvania Magazine of History and Biography*, 94 (1970), 62-74.

Dozer, Donald M. "Benjamin Harrison and the Presidential Campaign of 1892." *American Historical Review*, 54 (1948), 49-77.

Evans, Frank B. "Wharton Barker and the Republican National Convention of 1880." *Pennsylvania History*, 27 (1960), 28-43.

"The Fundamental Fallacy." *Nation*, 52 (1891), 4-5.

Hinckley, T. C. "George Osgoodby and the Murchison Letter." *Pacific Historical Review*, 27 (1958), 359-70.

Hirshson, Stanley P. "James S. Clarkson Versus Benjamin Harrison, 1891-1893: A Political Saga." *Iowa Journal of History*, 58 (1960), 219-27.

"The Ills of Pennsylvania." *Atlantic Monthly*, 88 (1901), 558-66.

Kehl, James A. "The Unmaking of a President: 1889-1892." *Pennsylvania History*, 39 (1972), 469-84.

Kelley, Brooks M. "Simon Cameron and the Senatorial Nomination of 1867." *Pennsylvania Magazine of History and Biography*, 87 (1963), 375-92.

"King George; King Matthew." *Nation*, 66 (1898), 218-19.

"The Latest Exposure of Quay." *Nation*, 67 (1898), 271-72.

"M. Quay, Reformer." *Nation*, 76 (1903), 165-66.

Marcosson, Isaac F. "The Fall of the House of Quay." *World's Work*, 11 (1906), 7119-24.

"The New Senators." *Harper's Weekly*, 31 (1887), 63.

Oliver, John W. "Matthew Stanley Quay." *Western Pennsylvania Historical Magazine*, 17 (1934), 1-12.

"The Origin of the Boss System." *Nation*, 35 (1882), 194.

"Pennsylvania Again." *Nation*, 64 (1897), 376-77.

"The Pennsylvania Campaign." *Nation*, 66 (1898), 437-38.

"Pennsylvania Republicans." *Nation*, 45 (1887), 148-49.

Pennypacker, Isaac. "Quay of Pennsylvania." *American Mercury*, 9 (1926), 357-64.

Quay, Matthew S. "The Man or the Platform." *North American Review*, 154 (1892), 514.

"Quay and the Constitution." *Nation*, 68 (1899), 327-28.

"Quayism in Pennsylvania." *Nation*, 53 (1891), 250.

"Republican Tactics in Pennsylvania." *Nation*, 53 (1891), 154-55.

"The Strategy of National Campaigns." *McClure's Magazine*, 15 (1900), 483-94.

"Representative Kennedy's Speech." *Public Opinion*, 9 (1890), 519-22.

"The Republican Independents in Pennsylvania." *Nation*, 34 (1882), 456-57.

"Senator Quay and the Republican Machine." *Outlook*, 62 (1899), 13-16.

"Senator Quay as a Reformer." *Harper's Weekly*, 41 (1897), 910.

Stewart, John D., II. "The Deal for Philadelphia: Simon Cameron and the Genesis of a Political Machine, 1867-1872." *Journal of the Lancaster County Historical Society*, 77 (1973), 41-56.

"The Week." *Nation*, 67 (1898), 341, 419-20.

Welch, Richard E., Jr. "The Federal Elections Bill of 1890: Postscripts and Prelude." *Journal of American History*, 52 (1965), 511-26.

Index